THE OFFICIAL
Formula 1™
SEASON REVIEW 2004

This edition published in 2005 by Motorbooks International, an imprint of MBI Publishing Company, Galtier Plaza, Suite 200, 380 Jackson Street, St. Paul, MN 55101-3885 USA

Editor Bruce Jones
Managing Editors Steve Rendle, Stewart Williams

Design Lee Parsons

Contributors Mark Hughes, Bruce Jones, Stephane Samson, Duncan Spires, Dom Taylor

Photographs All by LAT (Steven Tee, Lorenzo Bellanca, Charles Coates, Michael Cooper, Steve Etherington, Peter Spinney, Martyn Elford, Glenn Dunbar, Malcolm Griffiths) except for Ferrari Media images on pages 30-35, and Bruni pit fire image on page 194 courtesy of John Jopp/LAT

Illustrations Patricia Soler

Editorial Director Matt Bishop
Publishing Directors Karl Penn, Mark Hughes

ISBN 0-7603-2174-4

Printed in the UK

THE OFFICIAL
Formula 1™
SEASON REVIEW 2004
FOREWORD BY BERNIE ECCLESTONE

حلبة البحرين الدولية
Bahrain International Circuit

Bahrain's diverse culture can be traced back over 4,000 years to an ancient civilisation known as Dilmun. Strategically positioned between the first cities of Mesopotamia, the Indus Valley and China, the need to travel encouraged the building of Dhows and positioned Bahrain as the centre of an influential trading network. Based on a rich sea trade, Bahrain prospered in metals, pearls and incense and, together with foreign influences, developed a cosmopolitan culture that today sees traditional handicrafts, falconry and a lively souk rub shoulders with one of the world's most advanced motor racing facilities.

The Bahrain International Circuit at Sakhir is acknowledged as the most advanced racing venue in the World and combines state-of-the-art digital data systems with a modern interpretation of Arabic architecture to create a truly unique venue in the heart of the Gulf. Now, as the venue gears up for the next race, a wealth of partnership opportunities and activities are being structured to encourage local, regional and international businesses to come and share the facilities and experience the full spectrum of benefits motor racing has to offer.

If you would like to know how the Bahrain International Circuit could provide a centre for your business, a platform for corporate hospitality, or if you just wish to reserve your place at the 2005 Bahrain Grand Prix, or other events, please contact us and find out more about the Bahrain International Circuit.

Commercial Department
Tel: +973 1745 0000
Fax: +973 1745 1111

Visit our website: www.bahraingp.com

THE HOME OF MOTORSPORT IN THE MIDDLE EAST

1st in the Middle East

CONTENTS

FOREWORD

For me, the most significant thing was that Formula One continued to push the boundaries in 2004. We had new events at Bahrain and China, each having built magnificent new venues for their races. It's good for them, as it gives them something that ranks alongside the Olympics in terms of the prestige and business it attracts, but they can have it every year instead of every four years. It's very good for us, as it gives the sport yet more to offer sponsors, which in the long term can only be good news. The benefits of being involved in the emerging Chinese market are very obvious. I think this is the future.

The TV audiences have been up at most places this year, even though Michael Schumacher pretty much dominated the season. On balance, I'm pretty pleased with the season. For sure, it would have been closer without the 'Michael effect' – the guy is just on a higher level – but on the other hand we were watching history being made. It's the sort of thing people will tell their grandkids about. Besides, even with Michael and Ferrari around, there were still some extremely close races.

This sport has always gone in cycles, and one day the Ferrari/Schumacher cycle will be over and there will be someone else emerging as the king. That in itself will be a fascinating thing to see. The other cycle is that of the manufacturers. They've invested a lot over the years because F1 has been a very attractive place for them to be in terms of image and marketing. But they cannot all win, and so we saw an element of survival of the fittest this year. I think that can only be for the good. The real racers will invariably win out and that's how F1 has always been. It's a tough place to be, a very demanding place. That's as it should be at the top of the tree.

We've got changes coming – F1 is always changing, as it adapts to the world around it – but it will always be the ultimate. That part will be unchanging.

BERNIE ECCLESTONE

Formula One not only attracts huge TV viewing audiences, but also celebrity fans. Here, Bernie Ecclestone fills in film star George Clooney on the latest news

MICHAEL SCHUMACHER

At his imperious best, Michael swept all before him en route to claiming his seventh F1 title, and now he wants more...

The opening race always shows how the teams really compare with each other. No wonder, then, that Michael looks so ecstatic after his dominant win in Australia. He was to claim a dozen more

MICHAEL, THE 2004 SEASON IS NOW OVER AND IT HAS BEEN AMAZINGLY SUCCESSFUL FOR YOU. HOW WOULD YOU DESCRIBE IT?

MICHAEL SCHUMACHER: Even if the 2004 season seems now long behind us, I'm still at a loss for words when I have to talk about it. I guess I still can't believe how fantastic it has been. Maybe it's because I am somebody who is always more focused on the things to come, rather than looking back. My mind is more on the next race or next season, than on the championship title or things from the past. All I can do is shake my head in disbelief when I think of everything Ferrari has accomplished this season.

COULD YOU IMAGINE SUCH A SITUATION WHEN YOU JOINED FERRARI, NINE YEARS AGO?

MICHAEL SCHUMACHER: In 1996, none of us would have dared to imagine that our tireless efforts would lead to this. We really had to work hard to achieve all these wins. We put in long and tiresome hours and had to cope with some heavy set-backs, so everyone at Ferrari can be really proud now. When we celebrated winning both championships in Maranello with all 800 members of the Gestione Sportiva, I found that to be more than appropriate. People often tend to forget how incredibly important the dedication of every single person working at the factory is.

WHAT GOES ON AT THE RACE TRACK IS JUST THE TIP OF THE ICEBERG, BUT THE FOUNDATION FOR ALL OF THIS IS SET IN MARANELLO. RIGHT?

MICHAEL SCHUMACHER: Yes. All the people there are putting so much passion, effort and foresight into their work... It's not a coincidence that Ferrari hasn't had any technical problems in more than 50 races now. It shows the heart and soul that this team puts into its job. I'm a part of Ferrari, and I love it. I love being a part of this big family. These victories belong to all of us.

TELL US ABOUT YOUR CAR, THE F2004...

MICHAEL SCHUMACHER: I've been able to use a fantastic car this year, surely the best I've ever driven. Ferrari was not so dominant in 2003, but the way we reacted over the winter showed how strong we are. Every car has its limits of course, and when you're driving close to the limit it's always difficult to drive. There are problems such as understeering and oversteering. The only thing that changes is that the limits are pushed further year after year. The F2004 pushed them very, very far indeed. From the very beginning, I could see that we had made a big step forward with this car. We didn't expect to be so strong in Melbourne. I think the opposition was surprised. So were we!

BUT YOU CERTAINLY KNEW THAT THE CAR WAS GOOD?

MICHAEL SCHUMACHER: I had seen the data from the wind tunnel and saw some of the parts during the winter, but when I saw the new car for the first time, I just thought: "Wow. It's beautiful. It's for sure one of the most beautiful Ferraris of all time." I would never have thought the team would be able to build an F1 car with such a low centre of gravity, so small and tight. Our guys did a great job, really. Despite the one engine per weekend rule, we didn't break a single V10 on the track. Also, the aerodynamic guys have taken quite an aggressive approach to the whole thing: although the F2004 looked pretty similar to last year's car, it was much more efficient.

DID YOU HAVE TO DEVELOP THE CAR AS MUCH AS IN 2003?

MICHAEL SCHUMACHER: Last year was a big battle for the championship, so we were trying to develop the car very hard and hit maximum performance for every race. This year, of course, it's been a little bit easier in that respect – we've still made quite a lot of improvements, but they've been more structured rather than having to react to every race. The result was typical Ferrari.

IN WHICH WAY?

MICHAEL SCHUMACHER: That's one thing Rory Byrne, our Chief Designer, believes in: he won't put anything on the car unless it actually has a performance improvement, no matter what it looks like. It still needs careful consideration to put a successful F1 car together. It's not easy. There are lots of teams with very good facilities in F1, but they haven't quite found the performance yet. Ferrari think a car must evolve step by step. In my view, they are right. I feel that every car I have driven has been an improvement on the last one.

DID YOU BACK OFF AND CRUISE IN SOME RACES?

MICHAEL SCHUMACHER: I think it's fair to say that we've not pushed the car all the time for the whole race this year. In the closing stages of the race, if we were in a comfortable position, we were looking after the car. Obviously, there was no point in just screaming around and risking a failure. But in the early stages, the mid-stages of the race, certainly until after the last pit stop, we've been pushing it pretty hard. It never let us down. I think the car's strength is that there are no real weak areas. It was good in all departments: just well engineered, easy to set up and fairly easy to work with and so on. That's the secret – there's no magic involved, that's for sure.

HAVING A GOOD CAR IS ONE THING. THEN YOU HAVE TO MAKE IT WORK!

MICHAEL SCHUMACHER: Exactly. F1 is a demanding sport, and the car is just a tool. The team has to get the best out of it: mechanics, engineers, drivers. We all have to be disciplined, to discuss things in precise detail and never lose sight of the main reason why we're all here racing. That's the basis of a healthy, productive working relationship. The most important thing as far as I'm concerned is that the information passing between us is very exact.

IS IT TRUE THAT ANY FERRARI TEAM MEMBER WHO COMES TO A TECHNICAL BRIEFING LATE IS FINED?

MICHAEL SCHUMACHER: It is true: the penalty is 10 euros for every minute you're late. I've paid the fine myself sometimes, but I'm not the biggest contributor to the scheme... To me, precision is extremely important. Every part of an F1 car has to be perfect, and to achieve that level of excellence, it's first things first, like being on time. On the rigour side, 2004 has also been a very good year. Working with this team has been, once again, tremendously satisfying. I think we've proved that we can respond to a challenge, and we'll continue to do that in the future.

WHAT IS YOUR BEST MEMORY FROM 2004?

MICHAEL SCHUMACHER: It's almost impossible to choose... Ferrari got the constructors' title in Budapest. Spa-Francorchamps, where I clinched my seventh crown, was also special. In Monza, we were able to celebrate our success at home: great. What a race it was! And what a podium! Standing up there was incredible. Yes, I came in second this time and Rubens won, but he absolutely deserved to win that day. I'm glad that we were able to make the tifosi happy in this way – to be perfectly honest, I hadn't expected this to be possible after the first lap. My car spun, and Rubens had to make an early pit stop because of the tyres: "We'll be lucky if we can score a few points," I thought. But then it happened differently, as we all know now.

HOW WAS THE PARTY AFTERWARDS?

MICHAEL SCHUMACHER: Splendid. The 150 guests, consisting of the whole Ferrari F1 team, including sponsors and friends, were in great spirits. It seemed as if the state of amazement, which had taken hold of everyone on the track – and especially me – after winning the championship, had dissolved into no-holds-barred joy.

ANY MORE GOOD MEMORIES?

MICHAEL SCHUMACHER: There are so many! I think I'll never forget the Japanese Grand Prix podium. Standing up there with Ralf is always really tremendous for me. He drove a great race. I was really happy for him for having such a successful comeback after that long break. My worst day this year? I guess the death of Umberto Agnelli was a sad day for the whole team.

DO YOU SEE YOURSELF AS A MEGASTAR?

MICHAEL SCHUMACHER: Not really. I feel I'm an ordinary guy who just happens to maybe drive faster than others. Normally, if someone says hello to me I go and shake their hand. But when you're in a crowd, it's hard to satisfy everyone's expectations. The best thing to do in such conditions is to keep your head down and make your way through – at least this is my experience from the past couple of years. Fans might not understand that, which I do understand on the other hand, but still it is a shame…That said, I'll never complain about my situation. I'm lucky enough to make a living doing what I love most. F1 isn't like being on the assembly line. My mechanics deserve more respect than I do. They often have to work awful hours and see their loved ones even less often than I do, so I try to be as close to them as possible.

IS IT DIFFICULT TO BE A FATHER AND AN F1 DRIVER?

MICHAEL SCHUMACHER: Sometimes, but F1 has had to fit in with my family life. I'm very happy to be doing what I'm doing now. However, if it turned into a 40-race season tomorrow, or I had to test every day, I'd definitely have more of a problem. I think I'd hang up my gloves. My family comes first, and I'll never compromise on that.

SO, WHAT NOW?

MICHAEL SCHUMACHER: Some people think seven titles are enough, but I'm still hungry. I'm still in love with F1, you see. I have a brilliant time on the track. The competition is tough at the moment, and that makes things even more exciting. I achieved my goal when I won my first title with Ferrari back in 2000. Everything that has come since is a bonus. I just love racing. I still get goose bumps every time I pull my visor down. Yes, I'll be 35 next year. So what?

SO YOU HAVEN'T FINISHED YET?

MICHAEL SCHUMACHER: I still think of myself as 25. I play football with Fernando Alonso and Giancarlo Fisichella. I'm in good shape physically. But no, to tell you the truth, I don't feel my age. I'll still be fighting hard in 2005. I'm already thinking of the new season and about how the new rules will change the approach – I had a small insight into what we can expect at my last test this year at Jerez. It was a case of coping with it, although it seemed so slow at first. It will be different, but it will be interesting. I'll want my eighth championship as if it was the first one.

Clockwise from above. Winning at Hockenheim was one of many special moments for Michael in 2004. Success at the Nürburgring restored him to winning ways after the disappointment of Monaco. Michael's relationship with Ross Brawn and Jean Todt is still special. Never let it be said that Michael has lost his desire to win...

Twenty drivers from 10 teams lined up for the end-of-term photograph, but who impressed Jordan?

DRIVER RANKING

Eddie Jordan is bashful about being a talent scout, but he was, don't forget, the man who brought Michael Schumacher into Formula One – so we asked him to assess each of this year's F1 drivers

"The man who made Michael Schumacher?" I'd love to say "yes", but only one man made Michael Schumacher. That's Michael himself.

At Jordan, we did give Schuey his first break in Formula One. It was at a crucial time, when his career had reached a crossroads and not many doors were being opened to him in the F1 paddock. We also gave Ayrton Senna his first drive in F3, and it's been a privilege to have been involved with the careers of two all-time greats, as it has with so many other young talents.

I'm probably best-known for my work with youngsters. I don't want to knock it, but at the same time I wouldn't want it to say 'talent scout' on the top of my epitaph – it sounds a bit 'Hicksville'!

There's one thing that drives me mad about F1, though. Some of the big teams – and they know precisely who I'm talking about – invest fortunes in technology: the tyres, the engines and the wind tunnels. Then they won't spend time with the drivers.

There are only two things directly in touch with the car during a Grand Prix: the tyres on the ground and the driver at the steering wheel. It doesn't make sense to neglect the driver when all of your investment is being translated through one item!

Some people will say it's blarney but, possibly because the Irish are people's people, we've always had a knack at Jordan of making young drivers believe in themselves. I used to say, "Look me in the eyes, tell me you are fast enough, that you can do it, that you will do anything to achieve it." Maybe I used to frighten the crap out of people? Whatever, they found another gear.

We gave Ayrton his first ever drive in F3 at Silverstone in 1982. The previous weekend we had been on pole position with James Weaver. I gave Ayrton the same settings and he was three-tenths faster than pole time had been. There was no doubt he was a genius. The speed was just as staggering as that of Michael Schumacher, nine years later.

Trevor Foster rang me from Schuey's first F1 test and said, "Jesus, I don't know. Maybe it's a quick day…" In F3 you used to get really quick days because of track conditions, but quick days don't happen in F1! Then we thought maybe the cones had been removed at the back of the club circuit on which he was running. They hadn't. He really was just that fast.

These days, the mind-boggling complexity of F1 cars means that the manufacturer teams can't always invest time and effort in young hopefuls. That's a huge shame.

People sometimes ask me what driver combination I would run in a perfect world where money was not a factor – young or experienced? They don't get much joy from me. I tell them Michael in one car and Michael in the other. And Michael in the spare…

MICHAEL SCHUMACHER

NATIONALITY German
DATE OF BIRTH 3/1/69
PLACE OF BIRTH Kerpen, Germany
GRANDS PRIX 213
WINS 83
POLES 63
FASTEST LAPS 65
POINTS 1186
HONOURS F1 World Champion 1994, 1995, 2000, 2001, 2002, 2003, 2004, German F3 Champion 1990

The greatest driver ever to walk the planet. When you get to your mid-thirties, most people become slightly more guarded, but we saw this year that age has not affected him. If anything, Michael has become quicker, more professional and even more calculated.

People say he's destroying the championship. That's not his fault. He pushes himself beyond what anyone else aspires to and drives those around him to similar heights. That's why he's now got a car that doesn't break.

At the rate he's going, his only problem is to know when to go. Great people have done unbelievable things, but ruined it by staying just that bit too long. Michael cannot go defeated: he has got to go out as a champion. This time last year I said I think he should consider retirement. Now he's had the greatest year of his life. I'll shut the hell up now!

RUBENS BARRICHELLO

NATIONALITY Brazilian
DATE OF BIRTH 23/5/72
PLACE OF BIRTH São Paulo, Brazil
GRANDS PRIX 198
WINS 9
POLES 13
FASTEST LAPS 15
POINTS 451
HONOURS British F3 Champion 1991, European Formula Opel Champion 1990

Rubens spent four years with us at Jordan and, make no mistake, has developed into a great driver in his own right. I don't know of any other driver who could play that supporting role as well as he does.

Eddie Irvine said being Michael Schumacher's partner was like being hit over the head with a cricket bat. I don't see it like that. Ask yourself where else would Rubens have won two races this year? For sure he will never win a championship with Michael there but, right at this moment, who else is going to win a title? He gives Michael maximum support and Michael is not above repaying some of that when the time is right.

F1's worst job? Rubens is earning a good salary and having a fabulous time winning races. There's no need to feel sorry for him – I think he's the one having the last laugh.

JENSON BUTTON

NATIONALITY British
DATE OF BIRTH 19/1/80
PLACE OF BIRTH Frome, England
GRANDS PRIX 84
WINS 0
POLES 1
FASTEST LAPS 0
POINTS 130
HONOURS Formula Ford Festival winner 1998, European Super A Kart Champion 1997

The revelation of the season, and the face of British motorsport for years to come. One big question mark, though. The German GP was, prior to China, perhaps the race of his life. Then, just two days later, he announces he wants to go elsewhere, join another team! What level of complaint makes you do that? We've talked about the warmth and love that a young driver needs; something must have gone badly wrong.

What impressed me was that he fought on and showed, whether the CRB ruled that he went or stayed, that he could get on with things. He didn't just say "they're w*****s, I'm out of here" – he was totally professional and produced some great drives.

He had a good car, of course, and if Honda's horsepower figures are to be believed Jenson ought to have been right up there where he was, but he is good. Real good.

FERNANDO ALONSO

NATIONALITY Spanish
DATE OF BIRTH 29/7/81
PLACE OF BIRTH Oviedo, Spain
GRANDS PRIX 51
WINS 1
POLES 3
FASTEST LAPS 1
POINTS 114
HONOURS Formula Nissan Champion 1999, Italian & Spanish Kart Champion 1997, World Kart Champion 1996

This guy just knows that he is going to be World Champion one day and that, to me, is half of the battle.

The Renault was down on horsepower compared to the top runners, and with the cars now so reliable that meant that the drivers were never going to be able to compete. In that respect, this was always going to be a stand-still year for Alonso.

It is a sign of his class that his valuation in the marketplace remains as high as ever. We all know how brilliant he is. He's got natural talent, flair, style, that little Spanish swagger that [golfer Seve] Ballesteros had.

Journalists point out that he 'only' out-qualified Trulli eight-seven but Jarno is a great qualifier. Besides, unless you know what fuel levels and tyres drivers are on, the qualifying records journos keep in their little books don't mean shit!

JUAN PABLO MONTOYA

NATIONALITY Colombian
DATE OF BIRTH 20/9/75
PLACE OF BIRTH Bogota, Colombia
GRANDS PRIX 68
WINS 4
POLES 11
FASTEST LAPS 11
POINTS 221
HONOURS Indy 500 winner 2000, Champ Car Champion 1999, Formula 3000 Champion 1998

He's enormously quick and a potential champion, but this season he didn't live up to the huge reputation that he has built up since coming into F1.

So much depends on having not only the right car, but also the right environment, and it was clear that he didn't believe Williams was going in the right direction. The connection between the two just wasn't there.

The bad chemistry with his team-mate can't have helped either, nor the destabilising effect of Ralf's accident. The shame of it is that he and Ralf are both really good racers who are sensible and fast – this should have been a recipe for the best fun and all-out performance.

You can't help but like Montoya. He is an opportunist who has big balls and proved again this season that he can overtake in places you wouldn't normally expect. Write this boy off at your peril.

JARNO TRULLI

NATIONALITY Italian
DATE OF BIRTH 13/7/74
PLACE OF BIRTH Pescara, Italy
GRANDS PRIX 130
WINS 1
POLES 2
FASTEST LAPS 0
POINTS 117
HONOURS German F3 Champion 1996, World Kart Champion 1994

I only had one bet all year. In Monaco I had a crazy feeling that Jarno would qualify on pole position, and therefore have a chance of winning. I got 20-to-1 for the race win and 14-to-1 to get pole!

Michael aside, I don't believe there was another driver in the paddock capable of doing what Jarno did there with such a horsepower deficit. Too often, though, he follows brilliant races with indifferent ones. The way he lost third place to Rubens [Barrichello] at the final corner in Magny-Cours was a big factor in Renault's decision to sack him.

Jarno needs to be loved. If the rumours of him feeling an outsider in the team were true, that would have been a killer blow. The Japanese GP at Suzuka, where he qualified sixth for Toyota, underlined that he is a world-class qualifier and can take his chance when he gets it.

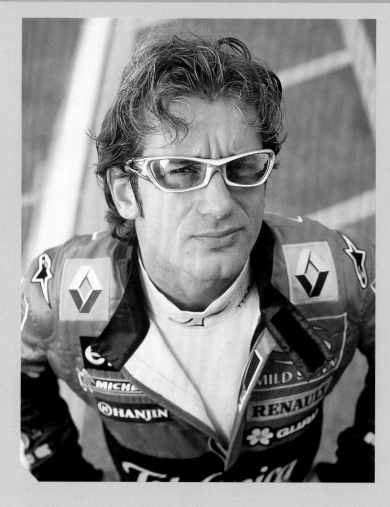

KIMI RAIKKÖNEN

NATIONALITY Finnish
DATE OF BIRTH 17/10/79
PLACE OF BIRTH Espoo, Finland
GRANDS PRIX 68
WINS 2
POLES 3
FASTEST LAPS 6
POINTS 169
HONOURS British Formula Renault Champion 2000, Finnish & Nordic Kart Champion 1998

One of a handful of pretenders to Michael Schumacher's throne. Kimi was frustrated by McLaren's problems in the first half of the season but, given the MP4-19B, was able to raise his game at the right time. Impressive in the British GP at Silverstone, he was brilliant at Spa and thoroughly deserved his win.

One of the things that gives me a belief in Kimi – something that hasn't always been backed up by what I've seen of him – is Ron Dennis's undying faith in him. The team cocoons him, much as it did Mika Häkkinen in the 1990s. It's hard to know Kimi well, but I have a lot of respect for Ron and it's clear that he would rather lose an arm than lose this guy.

Next year we could witness an epic battle at McLaren: the Ice Man up against the Colombian Hero. It will be absolutely fascinating to see who comes out on top.

TAKUMA SATO

NATIONALITY Japanese
DATE OF BIRTH 28/1/77
PLACE OF BIRTH Tokyo, Japan
GRANDS PRIX 36
WINS 0
POLES 0
FASTEST LAPS 0
POINTS 39
HONOURS British F3 Champion 2001

I'm completely biased on this one, because I think that Taku's year at Jordan really made him. He was being banished to a test driver role for 2003, was seen as a crasher, and would not have made it to BAR for this past season without Honda and Jordan.

I adore this guy. He's a breath of fresh air: sparky, intelligent, a great fighter and a driver who can overtake.

Taku didn't start racing until very late and it's incredible what he's achieved in seven years. He's hard on equipment sometimes, but that doesn't make you a bad driver. I'd have him back any time!

At the US GP at Indianapolis this year, Taku made it on to the podium but there's still more to come. In time, if he can build confidence, get the team around him and learn from having a quick team-mate, I promise you that he will be the first Japanese driver to win a Grand Prix.

RALF SCHUMACHER

NATIONALITY German
DATE OF BIRTH 30/6/75
PLACE OF BIRTH Kerpen, Germany
GRANDS PRIX 128
WINS 6
POLES 5
FASTEST LAPS 7
POINTS 259
HONOURS Formula Nippon Champion 1996, Macau F3 GP winner 1995

People will ask if it is mad for Ralf to be moving from Williams to Toyota? I believe that time will prove it to be a shrewd decision – Toyota will make its way to the top.

Why does Toyota want him? Because he's one of the hardcore of six drivers who are potential race winners and championship contenders.

He didn't really showcase those qualities this season, and the fact that he was moving clearly had a negative effect. He did take the team's only pole, in Canada, but his campaign was overshadowed by that gigantic accident at Indianapolis. He was very lucky to survive.

Ralf's a fighter, and that showed in a gutsy comeback, but there was an element of fortune in that second place at Suzuka. It is a specialist circuit, and with only limited running available he had a big advantage from his time racing in Japan.

DAVID COULTHARD

NATIONALITY British
DATE OF BIRTH 27/3/71
PLACE OF BIRTH Twynholm, Scotland
GRANDS PRIX 175
WINS 13
POLES 12
FASTEST LAPS 18
POINTS 475
HONOURS Macau F3 winner 1991, British Junior Formula Ford Champion 1989, Scottish Kart Champion 1988

DC is very hard to judge: as soon as you begin to think, "I'm not sure about him", he puts in a blinder of a race and you wonder how you ever arrived at such a stupid decision.

With his personality, he would have made a perfect World Champion but, after this season, I fear it's now over for him.

Kimi [Räikkönen] is very much a latter-day Mika [Häkkinen] figure at McLaren and that must have affected DC. Nobody likes to know they are being replaced, but DC is a great professional, and you've never heard one bad word from him.

Should he be out of F1? I would say no. He can still do a job. If he ever got stuck and wanted to buy a team, he could come and talk to me – I could make him a very young team principal! He could drive for himself if he wants, but I don't know how he's going to negotiate the money.

GIANCARLO FISICHELLA

What Fizzy achieved at Sauber was one of the highlights of this past season. He has always had spectacular speed, but I also think that he's improved his driving a lot. You saw this year that he was good enough to make some unconventional pit-stop strategies pay off. I truly believe that he is a guy who, given the right circumstances and the right equipment, could still be World Champion.

NATIONALITY Italian
DATE OF BIRTH 14/1/73
PLACE OF BIRTH Rome, Italy
GRANDS PRIX 142
WINS 1
POLES 1
FASTEST LAPS 1
POINTS 116
HONOURS Italian F3 Champion & Monaco F3 GP winner 1994

FELIPE MASSA

Comprehensively punished by Giancarlo [Fisichella] this season, you have to remember that he has just returned from a year away from racing as a test driver, and is still a novice who lacks his team-mate's experience. Felipe had a reputation as a crasher, but most drivers are absolutely desperado in their first year, and he looked a lot calmer this time round. Next season is the acid test.

NATIONALITY Brazilian
DATE OF BIRTH 25/4/81
PLACE OF BIRTH São Paulo, Brazil
GRANDS PRIX 34
WINS 0
POLES 0
FASTEST LAPS 0
POINTS 16
HONOURS Euro F3000 Champion 2001, European Formula Renault Champion 2000

MARK WEBBER

Bloody fast, with his feet on the ground, Mark is a great driver who understands the car and has the respect of other drivers. He's hard, and takes no prisoners, but is fair. Williams are gonna love him. This season underlined his speed, particularly with those eye-catching qualifying performances in Malaysia and Japan. Even with a Williams drive secured, he still fought hard.

NATIONALITY Australian
DATE OF BIRTH 27/8/76
PLACE OF BIRTH Queanbeyan, Australia
GRANDS PRIX 50
WINS 0
POLES 0
FASTEST LAPS 0
POINTS 26
HONOURS Formula Ford Festival winner 1996

OLIVIER PANIS

Olivier has decided to retire before he was retired by the team, and that was the right decision. He knew there would be changes in the team for 2005, and staying on as a test driver is the perfect situation for him. Toyota needs two drivers to kick ass and demand changes if the team is going to progress to the top rung, and Olivier was too friendly a guy to do that.

NATIONALITY French
DATE OF BIRTH 2/9/66
PLACE OF BIRTH Lyon, France
GRANDS PRIX 158
WINS 1
POLES 0
FASTEST LAPS 0
POINTS 76
HONOURS Formula 3000 Champion 1993, French Formula Renault Champion 1989

ANTONIO PIZZONIA

Three seventh places from four Grands Prix wasn't a bad return from a man thrown in at the deep end by Williams. There's no doubting that Antonio is quick and he could one day come back and make a big show. The pressure on young drivers is enormous these days as they have a very small timescale in which to make a big impact.

NATIONALITY Brazilian
DATE OF BIRTH 11/9/80
PLACE OF BIRTH Manaus, Brazil
GRANDS PRIX 15
WINS 0
POLES 0
FASTEST LAPS 0
POINTS 6
HONOURS British F3 Champion 2000, British Formula Renault Champion 1999

CHRISTIAN KLIEN

The Austrians were so desperate to get a driver into Formula One that the kid was fast-tracked into the top flight far too early in his career. He needed the kind of grounding that Mark Webber had enjoyed. Whether Jaguar was able to do the same job for Christian as it was for Mark, I don't know, but he was always going to struggle.

NATIONALITY Austrian
DATE OF BIRTH 7/2/83
PLACE OF BIRTH Hohenems, Austria
GRANDS PRIX 18
WINS 0
POLES 0
FASTEST LAPS 0
POINTS 3
HONOURS Marlboro Masters winner 2003, German Formula Renault Champion 2002

CRISTIANO DA MATTA

I think he's a quick driver, and a nice kid, but it just never happened for him this year. He did an amazing job for Toyota in Champ Car in the United States, deserved his chance in F1, and looked to be doing a decent job last season. However, the Toyota team went through quite an upheaval this year, and he never shone.

NATIONALITY Brazilian
DATE OF BIRTH 19/1/73
PLACE OF BIRTH Belo Horizonte, Brazil
GRANDS PRIX 28
WINS 0
POLES 0
FASTEST LAPS 0
POINTS 13
HONOURS Champ Car Champion 2002, Brazilian F3 Champion 1994

NICK HEIDFELD

Nick had some good races and some that weren't good enough, and he'd be the first to admit that. The fuss surrounding the Williams test mid-season led to a drop-off in form, but he bounced back in Japan, where he was great. He's always up for the fight, however bad things are. He could, given the right car, spring a big surprise.

NATIONALITY German
DATE OF BIRTH 10/5/77
PLACE OF BIRTH Monchengladbach, Germany
GRANDS PRIX 85
WINS 0
POLES 0
FASTEST LAPS 0
POINTS 28
HONOURS Formula 3000 Champion 1999, German F3 Champion 1997

TIMO GLOCK

Timo joined the select bend to have scored points in their first Grand Prix on his debut for us in Canada. He's solid, brings the car home and takes criticism well, which is important for a young driver. He thrives on fair and honest feedback and doesn't get all huffy if you say, "Come on Timo, that was crap and you can do better"!

NATIONALITY German
DATE OF BIRTH 18/3/82
PLACE OF BIRTH Lindenfels, Germany
GRANDS PRIX 4
WINS 0
POLES 0
FASTEST LAPS 0
POINTS 2
HONOURS German Formula BMW Champion 2001

ZSOLT BAUMGARTNER

I know from his spell at Jordan that Zsolt is a sensationally nice person, and he is a national hero after Indianapolis when he became the first Hungarian driver to score a World Championship point. The big question mark is his outright speed, and it's hard to see how he can find the serious level of improvement he needs to make it into a top team.

NATIONALITY Hungarian
DATE OF BIRTH 1/1/81
PLACE OF BIRTH Budapest, Hungary
GRANDS PRIX 20
WINS 0
POLES 0
FASTEST LAPS 0
POINTS 1
HONOURS None

RICARDO ZONTA

Ricardo is a very good test driver who gives good feedback, and I thought that he was okay when he came in for da Matta. However, he's too nice for his own good. You need someone to make a big start, battle in the first corner and fight like a terrier; you don't need to be telling a driver "push" – he should be able to inspire himself.

NATIONALITY Brazilian
DATE OF BIRTH 23/3/76
PLACE OF BIRTH Curitiba, Brazil
GRANDS PRIX 37
WINS 0
POLES 0
FASTEST LAPS 0
POINTS 3
HONOURS FIA GT Champion 1998, F3000 Champion 1997, Brazilian F3 Champion 1995

JACQUES VILLENEUVE

Jacques was on a hiding to nothing at Renault. Having not driven for some time, he was never going to blow off Alonso. He is a big-team kind of performer, and would slot in well at Ferrari, for instance, but the Sauber move for 2005 is a strange one. Don't underestimate him, though – the fact that he came back at all speaks volumes for him.

NATIONALITY Canadian
DATE OF BIRTH 9/4/71
PLACE OF BIRTH St Jean Sur Richelieu, Canada
GRANDS PRIX 134
WINS 11
POLES 13
FASTEST LAPS 9
POINTS 219
HONOURS World Champion 1997, Champ Car Champion & Indy 500 winner 1995

MARC GENÉ

A brilliant tester and a bloody quick driver, but two races wasn't a long enough run to see what Marc could really do. The whole situation at Williams mid-season was somewhat confused, and that must rub off on the drivers. With no continuity, the drivers must always have been looking over their shoulders, so it can't have been easy.

NATIONALITY Spanish
DATE OF BIRTH 29/3/74
PLACE OF BIRTH Sabadell, Spain
GRANDS PRIX 36
WINS 0
POLES 0
FASTEST LAPS 0
POINTS 5
HONOURS Formula Nissan Champion 1998, Superformula Champion 1996

GIORGIO PANTANO

There's no doubting Giorgio's speed, and he definitely has a role to play in Formula One. There were times when his team-mate [Nick Heidfeld] brought the car home but Giorgio didn't, and we expected a bit more from him, but he had every right to expect a bit more from us too. On balance, for a first year, I can have no complaints.

NATIONALITY Italian
DATE OF BIRTH 4/2/79
PLACE OF BIRTH Conselve, Italy
GRANDS PRIX 14
WINS 0
POLES 0
FASTEST LAPS 0
POINTS 0
HONOURS Formula 3000 Champion 2003, German & Swiss F3 Champion 2000

GIANMARIA BRUNI

Formula One was financial suicide for a lot of teams this season, and it's hard to assess youngsters when the machinery plays such an important role. All you can ask is for the driver to keep his cool, keep plugging away and beat his team-mate. Gianmaria comprehensively out-qualified his team-mate [Baumgartner], but the jury remains out.

NATIONALITY Italian
DATE OF BIRTH 30/5/81
PLACE OF BIRTH Rome, Italy
GRANDS PRIX 18
WINS 0
POLES 0
FASTEST LAPS 0
POINTS 0
HONOURS Euro Formula Renault Champion 1999, Italian Formula Campus 1998

JOHN McQUILLIAM
JORDAN

SAM MICHAEL
WILLIAMS

BOB BELL
RENAULT

MIKE GASCOYNE
TOYOTA

MARK GILLAM
JAGUAR

CAR OF THE YEAR

With Ferrari winning 15 of the 18 Grands Prix, their F2004 chassis was the car to beat. But which was next best? We asked the Technical Directors of all 10 teams to rank the chassis.

A glance at the results shows that the Ferrari F2004 must have been the car of the year. However, the order of merit behind is not so clear. In order to see the other 11 cars' merits - including the revised cars from McLaren and Toyota – through the eyes of those who really appreciate what goes into making a car go fast, with consideration for the budgets available, we asked the Technical Directors of all 10 teams to rank the cars. These are their findings, which might not be the order that you had in mind. Then again, they have the advantage of being able to get up close to the cars, appreciate the tweaks and changes introduced, and keep an ear open for the inside stories.

CAR RANKING

Car	Rank
Ferrari F2004	1
Renault R24	2
BAR 006	3
McLaren MP4-19B	4
Williams FW26	5
Sauber C23	6
Jaguar R5	7
Toyota TF104B	8
McLaren MP4-19	9
Toyota TF104	10
Minardi PS04	11
Jordan EJ14	12

GABRIELE TREDOZI
MINARDI

GEOFF WILLIS
BAR

ADRIAN NEWEY
McLAREN

WILLY RAMPF
SAUBER

ROSS BRAWN
FERRARI

FERRARI F2004

Ferrari just squeezed home in front in 2003 and, with Williams and McLaren both apparently gaining momentum, it seemed that the goalposts might move this season. That impression was bolstered when the F2004 was launched, as the first new Ferrari in three seasons that was scheduled to make its debut at the first race. Significantly, its wheelbase was 5cm shorter, and the weight distribution was moved forward. But observers immediately noted that it didn't look too different from its predecessor; Ferrari hadn't worked hard enough in the winter, was the consensus. Of course, they were wrong. The launch car didn't show all its bells and whistles, and in early testing its potential was disguised by the intense Bridgestone test programme. That saw compounds, constructions and shapes evaluated separately before a definitive tyre spec – in essence wider and squarer-shouldered – was readied just before the season. Ross Brawn, Rory Byrne, Aldo Costa and the rest had got their sums right: from Melbourne on, the car was unbeatable. Reliability was as good as ever, and the 053 engine, developed by Paolo Martinelli and Gilles Simon, never missed a beat. Much emphasis was placed on the ever-closer relationship with Bridgestone, and the fruits were seen in Hungary where the embarrassing defeat of a year earlier was turned into a crushing victory. The downside was that the Bridgestone didn't perform at its best on its first lap, which proved a handicap in qualifying and at the start of races. The team worked around that, and took advantage of its consistency over longer runs.

RENAULT R24

Renault finished 2003 on a high, and the team was full of confidence that the R24 would continue the good work of its predecessor. The biggest hurdle to overcome was a switch from the troublesome wide-angle engine design to a more traditional narrower V10, which inevitably meant a compromise in terms of a higher centre of gravity. Renault was familiar with the narrower vee from its glory days, but the engine team was given an unexpected Anglo flavour when Rob White was headhunted from Cosworth to head up the programme. The R23 had been kind to its tyres, and after winter testing the team claimed that the R24 was even better. It also proved to be more reliable, and it had Renault's joker up its sleeve: an ability to get off the line that all but guaranteed a gain of two or three positions.

Alonso started the season with a strong third in Australia, but it was soon apparent that the car was difficult when pushed to the limits, and didn't inspire confidence in the drivers. Trulli took pole and scored a brilliantly judged win in Monaco, but as the season went on his team-mate got the upper hand. The Italian struggled in the middle of the year with a car that he could no longer come to terms with, and his surprise late season replacement, Jacques Villeneuve, fared no better. However, Alonso boosted his reputation with a series of strong drives into the points, showing an apparent ability to drive around the problems.

BAR 006

Without doubt, BAR made the most spectacular improvement over the winter, under the leadership of Technical Director Geoff Willis. The 006 impressed from its first test outings and, while rivals were sceptical, the proof came when the season started in earnest. A switch to Michelin tyres played a major role, and the team confounded the theory that it takes time to gel with a new supplier. Button reported that the 006 was a vast improvement on the 005; it was more stable under braking, and changed direction better. It was very forgiving, and competitive on almost every type of track. Honda helped by raising its game after years of treading water: the new V10 was shorter, smaller and had a lower centre of gravity. It was just what Willis had ordered. However, there were to be numerous engine failures in the first half of the year that, for reasons no-one was able to explain, afflicted only Takuma Sato. Historically, BAR had struggled with reliability, but engine apart, that was put right in 2004. The testing promise was more than fulfilled, and when Button picked up his first podium in Malaysia, not even he could have predicted how often he would climb the steps, thanks to the car's consistent pace and his own canny driving. However, at times he was critical of an apparent lack of development – France was a low point – and he also often lost places at starts, although that issue was addressed by the end of the season.

McLAREN MP4-19B

4

As Räikkönen and Coulthard struggled with the MP4-19 it became apparent that McLaren faced a wasted season unless something radical was done. Ron Dennis and Martin Whitmarsh made the bold decision to start again by preparing a completely revised car for the middle of the season, and not to waste time by making small changes to the original package. Bearing in mind the failure of the MP4-18, it was a risk. However, it paid off. The new car was in fact more different from the MP4-19 than that had been from the MP4-18, suggesting that McLaren had got a little out of synch on its type numbering. It had a new, higher chassis, plus very different sidepods and diffuser among a host of other changes. After good initial tests, the MP4-19B appeared as early as Magny-Cours in July, and the drivers

immediately reported that it was better, and in particular was much more stable under braking. It was easier to drive in general, and kinder to its tyres, although the weight distribution was still not ideal. A revised engine solved earlier oil-system problems and gave 20bhp more than its immediate predecessor, but it was higher than was ideal. At least the car was quick, though. It showed promise in France, was a genuine contender in Britain and Germany (where a wing failure caused Räikkönen to crash heavily). Finally, at Spa, the Finn scored a superb win on a stop-start day blighted by safety cars. It remains to be seen whether the MP4-20 will put the team back on top.

WILLIAMS FW26

5

The long-held theory that all modern F1 cars would look identical if painted the same colour was blown into the weeds by the Williams FW26, thanks to its unique 'walrus' nose. The distinctive front of the car was a result of the switch to a twin-keel chassis, but from the start the team insisted that its novel shape was not hugely significant. The FW26 was designed by Gavin Fisher, with the key aero input from Antonia Terzi. Patrick Head had long been taking a back seat in the design process, which was emphasised when Sam Michael was promoted to the role of Technical Director before the Spanish GP, as the veteran Head took a further step out of the limelight. Early tests suggested that the FW26 was going to be fast, but the PR did not match the reality. 'When we first went out with the 26

we realised that it was almost pretty equal in speed to the 25,' noted Ralf Schumacher late in the season. And that wasn't fast enough to make a serious impression on Ferrari. Montoya looked good in Malaysia, but elsewhere form was patchy, and the drivers weren't shy in bemoaning the lack of development. By Hungary, pride had been swallowed, and a more traditional nose appeared on the car – it hadn't even been track tested before the race. The temporary absence of Schumacher made it hard to gauge form, but on his return the German put in an impressive run to second at Suzuka.

SAUBER C23

6

Not much was expected of Sauber in 2004, but the team achieved a solid overall performance, and Giancarlo Fisichella and Felipe Massa were regular visitors to the lower reaches of the points. The C23 caused consternation when it broke cover, due to its uncanny resemblance to the 2003 Ferrari. It did of course use the gearbox from that car, but externally the biggest clue that the team had at least paid attention to the F2003-GA was the ditching after three years of the twin-keel layout. Benefits to stiffness and weight distribution were cited by Technical Director Willy Rampf and his design team, but otherwise they claimed it was a conservative car. Preparations were disrupted by a crash in testing for Massa caused by a suspension failure, but that was soon resolved. However, the Brazilian

suffered another failure in Canada, and was very lucky to escape unscathed. Budget restrictions meant that Sauber never took advantage of the opportunity to run a third car on Fridays, but when their much-publicised new wind tunnel came on line in the middle of the season, the benefits were obvious. A new aero package for Silverstone included a more efficient engine cover, and provided an immediate boost. The team often used imaginative strategies to get the C23 into the points, stopping either significantly later or earlier than its rivals. Fisichella was just the right man to take advantage, and the Italian earned himself a seat at Renault despite having a year left on his Sauber deal.

JAGUAR R5

Despite much hype, the Jaguar R5 proved little better than its predecessors, and the team achieved few hard results in its final season with works support from the Ford Motor Company. Jaguar doesn't have a Technical Director, with the R5 the result of a team effort that included Engineering Director Ian Pocock, Head of Vehicle Design Robert Taylor, and aero boss Ben Agathangelou. Like previous Jaguars, the R5 was blighted with a lack of reliability in pre-season testing, and the car continued to prove hard on its tyres, a characteristic displayed in 2003 that at least made it a good one-lap special. Cosworth appeared to drop the ball in terms of performance, and the loss of Rob White to Renault before the start of the season – plus the later departure of veteran Nick Hayes – indicated

that there was much going on behind the scenes. Overall, money was tight and there was little scope for chassis development. Mark Webber did his best with the equipment he had, and performed miracles to get onto the front row in Malaysia, only for electronic problems to see him bog down at the start. A series of breakages confirmed that the R5 was, along with the McLaren, the least reliable package at the start of the year, but things did improve. Webber also qualified well at the other end of the season in Japan, but in between most points earned were the result of humble seventh and eighth places. Rookie Christian Klien could do little to help move things along.

7

TOYOTA TF104B

Much like McLaren, Toyota opted to dig itself out of its problems not by making small and frequent changes, but by introducing a new car, a feat it managed by Hockenheim – some two races after the new McLaren was revealed. Its gestation was overseen by Mike Gascoyne, who repeated the process of upgrading and refining design systems that he'd already used at Jordan and Benetton. The TF104B featured a new chassis that was 6kg lighter and had a lower centre of gravity than its predecessor, and which entailed a new crash test. An engine upgrade was worth 17bhp. The car didn't run as a complete entity until the German GP, and by any standards was a disappointment. In the fallout in the days after the race, Cristiano da Matta was sacked and replaced by Zonta, presumably because he hadn't been happy with

the changes. As the year went on, there was no dramatic improvement in form, although new boy Jarno Trulli did a solid job in qualifying on his debut in Japan. Gascoyne was unconcerned by the lack of a miracle cure. In his eyes the key thing was to prove that the work could be done on time and as planned: 'We produced the car, and on our first run, having had no time to test it, from the data we immediately got the aero improvement that we'd expected. They hadn't been able to do that before. They'd always done updates, and they never worked. So really it was a case of that methodology.'

8

McLAREN MP4-19

McLaren had a bizarre season in 2003. The MP4-17D was developed as an interim measure, and yet it was raced all the way to the end of the season, with consistent results keeping Kimi Räikkönen in championship contention. That wasn't the original plan, but problems with MP4-18 meant that the much-vaunted car never raced, despite an extensive test programme. The team was determined to put things right this year, and Adrian Newey called the MP4-19 a 'reliable and raceable' version of the model that never appeared in public. There was great optimism after Kimi gave the car its first test at Jerez in early January, but that soon evaporated in a cloud of problems that covered everything from cockpit comfort to poor engine performance. The weight distribution was biased towards the

rear, as the team still had a bigger fuel tank than it needed, while the opposition had shrunk theirs. That hurt the rear tyres, especially as temperatures went up. And endless engine dramas meant that testing miles were reduced and it was hard to solve the chassis problems. At the end of the day, it was simply not quick enough and, by the time Melbourne rolled around, everyone knew the true situation. The car was also hopelessly unreliable, and poor Räikkönen struggled even to score a point in the early races, although at least by the North American events the reliability issue had been addressed, and some useful points were gathered. However, the car was not seen again after the US GP.

9

TOYOTA TF104

Much was expected of Toyota's third pukka F1 car, especially after the team's strong end to the 2003 season. However, the TF104 was largely disappointing. The design team was led by Gustav Brunner and, having arrived only in December, new Technical Director Mike Gascoyne had no influence on its initial incarnation. It looked quite different from the TF103, with a narrower rear and very different sidepods. The main aim was to address the inconsistency that had been a Toyota trait, as Brunner explained: 'Last year's car was very quick, but not always. Sometimes it was very quick in the morning, but not in the afternoon. Most of it is down to the stability of the aerodynamics, so we concentrated a lot on this.' The car also featured a compact titanium gearbox, with all its

internals built in-house, which had the advantage of being both light and stiff. Unfortunately, the inconsistency remained and, once the season started, Olivier Panis and Cristiano da Matta continued to struggle to find the 'sweet spot' of the car, and a disastrous first outing in Australia proved to be a real wake-up call. Ricardo Zonta's role as third driver on Fridays helped with the set-up work. Gascoyne concentrated on sussing out the overall state of the team and trying to get the right pieces in place. Only later did he get involved in overseeing the development of the car, a process that resulted in the TF104B. Its introduction meant that the original wasn't seen after Silverstone.

10

MINARDI PS04

The indefatigable Paul Stoddart soldiered into 2004 with yet another mild upgrade of what had gone before. Buying the 2002 Arrows equipment proved to be a blind alley, and of little use when this year's package was put together. The main advantage of the bullet-proof existing equipment was its relatively long life, a major plus when the pennies are being counted. The upgraded PS04 was overseen as usual by Technical Director Gabriele Tredozi, with former Lotus and Benetton man Andy Tilley heading the engineering side. The Cosworth CR-3L engines were showing their age, and left the team with little to fight for but the back of the grid. Very often, reliability was guaranteed by a change before the race that earned the black cars a penalty demotion from the back of the grid… to the back. Gianmaria

Bruni was no Mark Webber or Justin Wilson, but he came with a good pedigree. However, he achieved little as the year went on, and was sometimes overshadowed by the steady Zsolt Baumgartner, of whom little was expected. Indeed the Hungarian was very good at bringing the car home, and earned a point in a race of high attrition at Indianapolis. The team suffered a setback at Monza when Zsolt's chassis was written off after an assault from Giorgio Pantano in practice. The underrated Bas Leinders drove the third car throughout the year, but often had to make do with tired engines and brakes, getting little return for his investment. He was occasionally given new parts to assess.

11

JORDAN EJ14

Jordan went into the winter in a parlous financial state, despite Giancarlo Fisichella's opportunistic win in the 2003 Brazilian GP. However, Eddie Jordan did his usual wheeling and dealing while his boys got on with the job of building a car. When the EJ14 emerged, it carried the jokey branding of 'Lazarus,' suggesting that rumours of the team's imminent demise were premature. With Gary Anderson and Henri Durand both gone, the car was the work of a team led by John McQuilliam, one of the survivors of the 'Class of 1999,' who took Jordan to third in that year's championship. A much-improved chassis was allied to aerodynamic developments under the eye of Nicola Petrucci. The car featured a return to a single-keel concept that helped weight distribution. The team also tidied up the

ancillaries around the Cosworth engine, and claimed to have a neater package than rivals Jaguar. Jordan was supposed to have a V10 spec that matched that of Jag, but from the start of the year the team complained that it wasn't getting the performance it had been promised. Inevitably, the overstretched budget meant that there was little chance to develop the package, and it was rarely fast enough to do anything except run ahead of Minardi. Nick Heidfeld's talents largely went to waste, apart from a solid seventh in Monaco, while multiple disqualifications handed the team three more points in Canada. Designer Mark Smith was due to return to the team at the end of the season, following a successful spell at Renault.

12

FERRARI
F2004
SCARLET PASSION

The F2004 was the pick of the crop, so it's no surprise that the technical directors voted for it as the car of 2004. Outwardly, it broke little new ground, but it was styled to near perfection, with every single part maximising its function. The 053 V10 was a gem too, proving both powerful and reliable. Then, of course, Michael Schumacher and Rubens Barrichello did the rest.

These studio shots, taken at the time of the car's launch, make the Ferrari F2004 look like a piece of art, at any point from nose to tail, with suspension (2), flick-ups (3) and sidepod chimney cowlings (4) all making their purpose clear

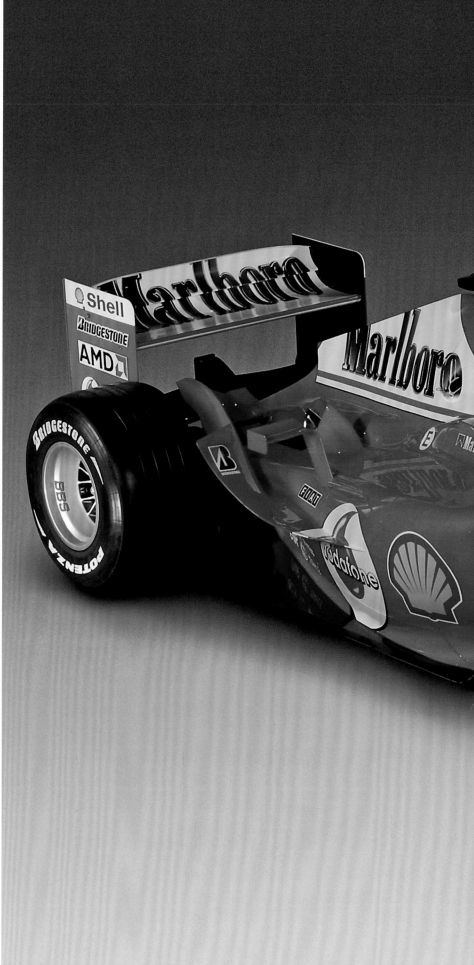

This elevated view from the front (1) emphasises Rory Byrne's aerodynamic thinking, showing clearly how he and his design team wanted the air to flow over the front wing and down the length of the F2004 to the rear wing. One of the car's greatest assets was the skill of the team's engineers and mechanics (2). Ferrari's prancing horse (3) remains the most evocative of all emblems. The painstaking detail of design put into just one of the many front wing formats (4) used by the F2004 through the season is clear for all to see

This pair of shots from the side (1) and above (2) give further evidence of how aerodynamic parts such as the front wing, barge boards, flick-ups and rear bodywork are shaped to channel air flow to maximum effect, moving it away from the main obstructions: the wheels. Numerous parts such as this sidepod chimney exhaust (3) and flick-up wing (4) were introduced during the year. To many, the speed of the F2004 was a blur (5)

TEAM STATISTICS

All the facts and stats for the 10 teams, listing their leading personnel plus the ingredients that make their cars go fast

FERRARI

TECHNICAL SPECIFICATIONS

ENGINE

MAKE/MODEL Ferrari 053
CONFIGURATION 2997cc V10 (90deg)
SPARK PLUGS NGK
ECU Magneti Marelli
FUEL Shell
OIL Shell
BATTERY Magneti Marelli

TRANSMISSION

GEARBOX Ferrari
FORWARD GEARS seven
DRIVESHAFTS undisclosed
CLUTCH undisclosed

CHASSIS

CHASSIS MODEL Ferrari F2004
FRONT SUSPENSION LAYOUT independent pushrod-activated torsion springs
REAR SUSPENSION LAYOUT independent pushrod-activated torsion springs
DAMPERS Sachs
TYRES Bridgestone
WHEELS BBS
BRAKE DISCS Brembo
BRAKE PADS Brembo
BRAKE CALLIPERS Brembo
RADIATORS undisclosed
FUEL TANK ATL
FUEL TANK CAPACITY undisclosed
INSTRUMENTS Magneti Marelli

DIMENSIONS

LENGTH 4545mm
WIDTH 1796mm
HEIGHT 959mm
WHEELBASE 3050mm
TRACK front 1470mm **rear** 1405mm
WEIGHT 605kg (including driver)

PERSONNEL

PRESIDENT Luca di Montezemolo
GENERAL DIRECTOR Jean Todt (pictured)
TECHNICAL DIRECTOR Ross Brawn
ENGINE DIRECTOR Paolo Martinelli
DIRECTOR OF FORMULA 1 RACING ACTIVITIES Stefano Domenicali
CHIEF DESIGNER Rory Byrne
SENIOR AERODYNAMICIST John Iley
RACE TECHNICAL MANAGER Nigel Stepney
RACE ENGINE MANAGER Mattia Binotto
DRIVERS Rubens Barrichello, Michael Schumacher
CHIEF RACE ENGINEER Luca Baldisserri
RACE ENGINEER (Schumacher) Chris Dyer
RACE ENGINEER (Barrichello) Gabriele Delli Colli
FRIDAY TEST DRIVER n/a
TEST DRIVER Luca Badoer
CHIEF MECHANICS Francesco Barletta, Alessandro Palermo
TOTAL NUMBER OF EMPLOYEES 800
NUMBER IN RACE TEAM 90
TEAM BASE Maranello, Italy
TELEPHONE +39 0536 949450 **WEBSITE** www.ferrari.com

TEAM STATS

IN F1 SINCE 1950
FIRST GRAND PRIX Britain 1950
STARTS 704
WINS 182
POLE POSITIONS 178
FASTEST LAPS 178
PODIUMS 553
POINTS 3344.5
CONSTRUCTORS' TITLES 14
DRIVERS' TITLES 14

SPONSORS

Marlboro, Vodafone, Bridgestone, FIAT, Shell, AMD, Olympus

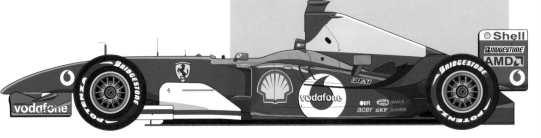

Deutsche Post 🐴 **World Net**
MAIL EXPRESS LOGISTICS FINANCE

See you next season.

DHL's first season as Official Logistics Partner of Formula One™ has come to an end. With flexibility, reliability, and speed, we delivered goods and documents to the circuits in 16 countries around the world from March to October. All year round and in over 220 countries to you: **www.dhl.com**

WILLIAMS

TECHNICAL SPECIFICATIONS

ENGINE

MAKE/MODEL BMW P84
CONFIGURATION 2998cc V10 (90deg)
SPARK PLUGS Champion
ECU BMW
FUEL Petrobras
OIL Castrol
BATTERY RS

TRANSMISSION

GEARBOX Williams F1
FORWARD GEARS seven
DRIVESHAFT Williams / Pankl
CLUTCH AP Racing

CHASSIS

CHASSIS MODEL Williams F1 BMW FW26
FRONT SUSPENSION LAYOUT Williams F1 torsion bar
REAR SUSPENSION LAYOUT Williams F1 torsion bar
DAMPERS Williams F1
TYRES Michelin
WHEELS OZ Racing
BRAKE DISCS Carbone Industrie
BRAKE PADS Carbone Industrie
BRAKE CALLIPERS AP Racing
RADIATORS Marston
FUEL TANK ATL
FUEL TANK CAPACITY 135 litres (101.3kg)
INSTRUMENTS Williams

DIMENSIONS

LENGTH 4500mm
WIDTH 1800mm
HEIGHT 950mm
WHEELBASE 3100mm
TRACK front 1470mm **rear** 1420mm
WEIGHT 600kg (including driver)

PERSONNEL

TEAM PRINCIPAL Frank Williams (pictured)
DIRECTOR OF ENGINEERING Patrick Head
TECHNICAL DIRECTOR Sam Michael
DIRECTOR (BMW MOTORSPORT) Mario Theissen
HEAD OF ENGINE DEVELOPMENT Heinz Paschen
CHIEF DESIGNER Gavin Fisher
CHIEF AERODYNAMICIST Antonia Terzi
RACE TEAM MANAGER Dickie Stanford
DRIVERS Marc Gené, Juan Pablo Montoya, Antonio Pizzonia, Ralf Schumacher
RACE ENGINEER (Montoya) Tony Ross
RACE ENGINEER (Schumacher/Gené/Pizzonia) Gordon Day
FRIDAY TEST DRIVER n/a
TEST DRIVERS Marc Gené, Antonio Pizzonia
RACE TEAM CHIEF MECHANIC Carl Gaden
TOTAL NUMBER OF EMPLOYEES 500
NUMBER IN RACE TEAM 70
TEAM BASE Grove, England
TELEPHONE +44 (0)1235 777700, **WEBSITE** www.bmw.williamsf1.com

TEAM STATS

IN F1 SINCE 1973
FIRST GRAND PRIX Argentina 1973
STARTS 496
WINS 113
POLE POSITIONS 124
FASTEST LAPS 128
PODIUMS 289
POINTS 2435.5
CONSTRUCTORS' TITLES 9
DRIVERS' TITLES 7

SPONSORS

HP, Allianz, Budweiser, FedEx,
Niquitin CQ, Accenture, Reuters,
Castrol, Michelin, Petrobras, Hamleys

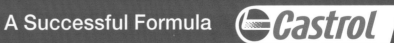

McLAREN

TECHNICAL SPECIFICATIONS

ENGINE

MAKE/MODEL Mercedes-Ilmor FO 110Q
CONFIGURATION 3000cc V10 (90deg)
SPARK PLUGS undisclosed
ECU TAG Electronic Systems
FUEL Mobil
OIL Mobil 1
BATTERY GS

TRANSMISSION

GEARBOX McLaren
FORWARD GEARS seven
DRIVESHAFTS McLaren
CLUTCH McLaren

CHASSIS

CHASSIS MODEL McLaren MP4-19/MP4-19B
FRONT SUSPENSION LAYOUT Inboard torsion bar/
damper system operated by pushrod and bellcrank, with a
double wishbone arrangement
REAR SUSPENSION LAYOUT Inboard torsion bar/
damper system operated by pushrod and bellcrank, with a
double wishbone arrangement
DAMPERS Penske/McLaren
TYRES Michelin
WHEELS Enkei
BRAKE DISCS Hitco
BRAKE PADS AP Racing
BRAKE CALLIPERS AP Racing
RADIATORS undisclosed
FUEL TANK ATL
FUEL TANK CAPACITY undisclosed
INSTRUMENTS TAG Electronic Systems

DIMENSIONS

LENGTH undisclosed
WIDTH 1800mm
HEIGHT 950mm
WHEELBASE undisclosed
TRACK front undisclosed **rear** undisclosed
WEIGHT 600kg (including driver)

PERSONNEL

TEAM PRINCIPAL, CHAIRMAN AND GROUP CEO Ron Dennis (pictured)
VICE PRESIDENT MERCEDES-BENZ MOTORSPORT Norbert Haug
CEO FORMULA ONE Martin Whitmarsh
MANAGING DIRECTOR Jonathan Neale
TECHNICAL DIRECTOR Adrian Newey
TECHNICAL DIRECTOR (MERCEDES-ILMOR) Mario Illien
EXECUTIVE DIRECTOR OF ENGINEERING Neil Oatley
CHIEF DESIGNER Mike Coughlan
HEAD OF AERODYNAMICS Peter Prodromou
TEAM MANAGER Dave Ryan
DRIVERS David Coulthard, Kimi Räikkönen
HEAD OF RACE ENGINEERING Steve Hallam
RACE ENGINEER (Coulthard) Phil Prew
RACE ENGINEER (Räikkönen) Mark Slade
FRIDAY TEST DRIVER n/a
TEST DRIVERS Pedro de la Rosa, Alex Wurz
CHIEF MECHANIC Stephen Giles
TOTAL NUMBER OF EMPLOYEES undisclosed
NUMBER IN RACE TEAM undisclosed
TEAM BASE Woking, England
TELEPHONE +44 (0)1483 261000 **WEBSITE** www.mclaren.com

TEAM STATS

IN F1 SINCE 1966
FIRST GRAND PRIX Monaco 1966
STARTS 577
WINS 138
POLE POSITIONS 115
FASTEST LAPS 114
PODIUMS 367
POINTS 2858.5
CONSTRUCTORS' TITLES 8
DRIVERS' TITLES 11

SPONSORS

West, SAP, Warsteiner, Hugo Boss,
Schüco, Mobil 1

RENAULT

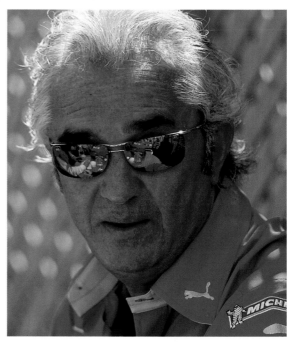

PERSONNEL

CHAIRMAN AND CEO Patrick Faure
MANAGING DIRECTOR Flavio Briatore (pictured)
DEPUTY MANAGING DIRECTOR Bernard Dudot
TECHNICAL DIRECTOR (CHASSIS) Bob Bell
TECHNICAL DIRECTOR (ENGINE) Rob White
EXECUTIVE DIRECTOR OF ENGINEERING Pat Symonds
HEAD OF ENGINE OPERATIONS Denis Chevrier
CHIEF DESIGNERS Mark Smith/Tim Densham
HEAD OF AERODYNAMICS Dino Toso
SPORTING MANAGER Steve Nielsen
DRIVERS Fernando Alonso, Jarno Trulli, Jacques Villeneuve
RACE ENGINEERS (Alonso) Paul Monaghan, Rod Nelson, Rémi Taffin
RACE ENGINEERS (Trulli/Villeneuve) Alan Permane, Nick Chester, Fabrice Lom
FRIDAY TEST DRIVER n/a
TEST/THIRD DRIVER Franck Montagny
CHIEF MECHANIC Jonathan Wheatley
TOTAL NUMBER OF EMPLOYEES 800
NUMBER IN RACE TEAM 60-70
TEAM BASE Enstone, England
TELEPHONE +44 (0)1608 678000 **WEBSITE** www.renaultf1.com

TEAM STATS

IN F1 SINCE 2002
FIRST GRAND PRIX Australia 2002
STARTS 174
WINS 17
POLE POSITIONS 36
FASTEST LAPS 19
PODIUMS 52
POINTS 528
CONSTRUCTORS' TITLES 0
DRIVERS' TITLES 0

These statistics include those of Renault's original F1 team that ran 1977-1985 and not those of the Toleman/Benetton team from which it metamorphosed for the 2002 season

SPONSORS

Mild Seven, Elf, Michelin, Hanjin, i-mode, Guru, Telefonica

TECHNICAL SPECIFICATIONS

ENGINE

MAKE/MODEL Renault RS24
CONFIGURATION 3000cc V10 (72deg)
SPARK PLUGS Champion
ECU Magneti Marelli
FUEL Elf
OIL Elf
BATTERY Renault F1

TRANSMISSION

GEARBOX Renault F1
FORWARD GEARS six
DRIVESHAFTS Renault F1
CLUTCH AP Racing

CHASSIS

CHASSIS MODEL Renault R24
FRONT SUSPENSION LAYOUT carbon-fibre wishbones, with pushrods operating inboard titanium rocker, torsion bar and dampers
REAR SUSPENSION LAYOUT carbon-fibre wishbones, with pushrods operating vertically mounted torsion bars and horizontally mounted dampers mounted on gearbox casing
DAMPERS Penske
TYRES Michelin
WHEELS OZ Racing
BRAKE DISCS Hitco
BRAKE PADS Hitco
BRAKE CALLIPERS AP Racing
RADIATORS Marston
FUEL TANK ATL
FUEL TANK CAPACITY undisclosed
INSTRUMENTS Renault

DIMENSIONS

LENGTH 4600mm
WIDTH 1800mm
HEIGHT 950mm
WHEELBASE 3100mm
TRACK front 1450mm **rear** 1400mm
WEIGHT 605kg (including driver)

CRÉATEUR D'AUTOMOBILES

Clio RENAULTSPORT

You may mistake the new Clio Renaultsport 182 for a regular, just popping down to the shops Clio. But then you may not know it shares an engine with the Formula Renault racing car. Yes, the very same Formula Renault racing car that's being driven by the next generation of Formula One drivers at tracks across Europe. For more information call 0800 52 51 50 or visit www.renault.co.uk. Or to follow all the Formula Renault and Clio Cup racing, speed over to www.renaultsport.co.uk.

The new Clio Renaultsport 182.
Sure, it looks like a normal Clio.

BAR

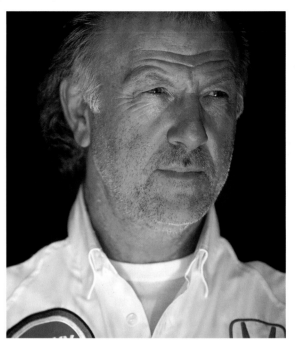

PERSONNEL

TEAM PRINCIPAL David Richards (pictured)
F1 PROJECT LEADER (HONDA) Takeo Kiuchi
MANAGING DIRECTOR Nick Fry
TECHNICAL DIRECTOR Geoff Willis
CHIEF DESIGNER (MECHANICAL) Joerg Zander
CHIEF DESIGNER (COMPOSITES) Kevin Taylor
ENGINE DIRECTOR (HONDA RACING DEVELOPMENT) Shuhei Nakamoto
SENIOR AERODYNAMICISTS Simon Lacey, Mariano Alperin-Bruvera, Willem Toet
RACE TEAM MANAGER Ron Meadows
DRIVERS Jenson Button, Takuma Sato
CHIEF RACE ENGINEER Craig Wilson
SENIOR RACE ENGINEER (Button) Andrew Shovlin
SENIOR RACE ENGINEER (Sato) Jock Clear
FRIDAY/TEST DRIVER Anthony Davidson
TEST DRIVER Enrique Bernoldi
CHIEF MECHANIC Alastair Gibson
TOTAL NUMBER OF EMPLOYEES 440
NUMBER IN RACE TEAM 60
TEAM BASE Brackley, England
TELEPHONE +44 (0)1280 844000 **WEBSITE** www.barf1.com

TEAM STATS

IN F1 SINCE 1999
FIRST GRAND PRIX Australia 1999
STARTS 101
WINS 0
POLE POSITIONS 1
FASTEST LAPS 0
PODIUMS 13
POINTS 182
CONSTRUCTORS' TITLES 0
DRIVERS' TITLES 0

SPONSORS

Lucky Strike/555, Honda, Michelin,
Intercond, Brunotti, Ray Ban, Alpinestars,
Mac-Tools

TECHNICAL SPECIFICATIONS

ENGINE

MAKE/MODEL Honda RA004E
CONFIGURATION 3000cc V10 (90deg)
SPARK PLUGS NRG
ECU Honda Athena
FUEL Elf
OIL Nisseki
BATTERY Yuasa

TRANSMISSION

GEARBOX BAR/Honda/XTrac
FORWARD GEARS seven
DRIVESHAFTS Pankl
CLUTCH AP Racing

CHASSIS

CHASSIS MODEL BAR Honda 006
FRONT SUSPENSION LAYOUT wishbones, with pushrod-activated torsion springs and rockers, mechanical anti-roll bar
REAR SUSPENSION LAYOUT wishbones, with pushrod-activated torsion springs and rockers, mechanical anti-roll bar
DAMPERS Koni
TYRES Michelin
WHEELS BBS
BRAKE DISCS Brembo
BRAKE PADS Brembo
BRAKE CALLIPERS Alcon
RADIATORS IMI Marston/Showa
FUEL TANK ATL
FUEL TANK CAPACITY 140 litres (105kg)
INSTRUMENTS BAR

DIMENSIONS

LENGTH 4465mm
WIDTH 1800mm
HEIGHT 950mm
WHEELBASE 3140mm
TRACK front 1460mm **rear** 1420mm
WEIGHT 600kg (including driver)

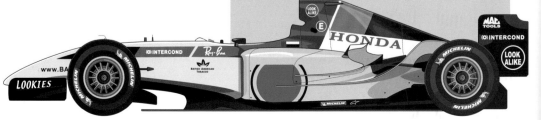

B·A·R HONDA 2004
an amazing performance!

KONI are proud to be their team supplier

KONI & Motor Racing. It's a story that goes back a long time. 50 years ago we made our motorsport debut, and we've been present on the Formula One™ grid for 46 years.

You may never be a Formula One™ driver,
but we can make you feel like one.

SAUBER

PERSONNEL

TEAM PRINCIPAL AND CEO Peter Sauber (pictured)
TECHNICAL DIRECTOR Willy Rampf
HEAD OF POWER-TRAIN Osamu Goto
HEAD OF VEHICLE ENGINEERING Jacky Eeckelaert
SENIOR AERODYNAMICIST Seamus Mullarkey
TEAM MANAGER Beat Zehnder
DRIVERS Giancarlo Fisichella, Felipe Massa
RACE ENGINEER (Fisichella) Giampaolo Dall'Ara
RACE ENGINEER (Massa) Mike Krack
FRIDAY TEST DRIVER n/a
TEST DRIVER Neel Jani
CHIEF MECHANIC Urs Kuratle
TOTAL NUMBER OF EMPLOYEES 290
NUMBER IN RACE TEAM 55
TEAM BASE Hinwil, Switzerland
TELEPHONE +41 (0)1937 9000 **WEBSITE** www.sauber.ch

TEAM STATS

IN F1 SINCE 1993
FIRST GRAND PRIX South Africa 1993
STARTS 198
WINS 0
POLE POSITIONS 0
FASTEST LAPS 0
PODIUMS 6
POINTS 176
CONSTRUCTORS' TITLES 0
DRIVERS' TITLES 0

SPONSORS

Petronas, Credit Suisse, Red Bull

TECHNICAL SPECIFICATIONS

ENGINE

MAKE/MODEL Ferrari 053 (badged Petronas 04A/B)
CONFIGURATION 2997cc V10 (90deg)
SPARK PLUGS NGK
ECU Magneti Marelli
FUEL Petronas Primax
OIL Petronas Syntium
BATTERY Sauber

TRANSMISSION

GEARBOX Ferrari
FORWARD GEARS seven
DRIVESHAFTS Sauber spec
CLUTCH AP Racing

CHASSIS

CHASSIS MODEL Sauber C23
FRONT SUSPENSION LAYOUT upper and lower wishbones, inboard springs and dampers, actuated by pushrods
REAR SUSPENSION LAYOUT upper and lower wishbones, inboard springs and dampers, actuated by pushrods
DAMPERS Sachs
TYRES Bridgestone
WHEELS OZ Racing
BRAKE DISCS Brembo
BRAKE PADS Brembo
BRAKE CALLIPERS Brembo
RADIATORS Calsonic
FUEL TANK ATL
FUEL TANK CAPACITY undisclosed
INSTRUMENTS Sauber electronics

DIMENSIONS

LENGTH 4600mm
WIDTH 1800mm
HEIGHT 1000mm
WHEELBASE 3120mm
TRACK front 1470mm **rear** 1410mm
WEIGHT 600kg (including driver)

JAGUAR

PERSONNEL

GROUP VICE-PRESIDENT (FORD) Richard Parry-Jones
CEO, PREMIER PERFORMANCE DIVISION Tony Purnell (pictured)
MANAGING DIRECTOR David Pitchforth
DIRECTOR OF ENGINEERING Ian Pocock
HEAD AERODYNAMICIST Ben Agathangelou
HEAD OF VEHICLE PERFORMANCE Mark Gillan
HEAD OF VEHICLE DESIGN Robert Taylor
HEAD OF VEHICLE SCIENCE Chris Hammond
MANAGING DIRECTOR, ENGINEERING (COSWORTH) Nick Hayes
TEAM MANAGER David Stubbs
DRIVERS Christian Klien, Mark Webber
RACE ENGINEER (Klien) Stefano Sordo
RACE ENGINEER (Webber) Peter Harrison
FRIDAY/TEST DRIVER Bjorn Wirdheim
CHIEF MECHANIC Darren Nichols
TOTAL NUMBER OF EMPLOYEES 350
NUMBER IN RACE TEAM 80
TEAM BASE Milton Keynes, England
TELEPHONE +44 (0)1908 279700 **WEBSITE** www.jaguar-racing.com

TEAM STATS

IN F1 SINCE 1997*
FIRST GRAND PRIX Australia 1997*
* As Stewart Grand Prix
STARTS 134
WINS 1
POLE POSITIONS 1
FASTEST LAPS 0
PODIUMS 5
POINTS 88
CONSTRUCTORS' TITLES 0
DRIVERS' TITLES 0

SPONSORS

HSBC, Red Bull, UGS, DuPont, AT&T,
Pioneer, Michelin, Beck's, Amik Italia Spa

TECHNICAL SPECIFICATIONS

ENGINE

MAKE/MODEL Cosworth CR-6
CONFIGURATION 2998cc V10 (90deg)
SPARK PLUGS Champion
ECU Pi Systems
FUEL Castrol
OIL Castrol
BATTERY Jaguar Racing

TRANSMISSION

GEARBOX Jaguar
FORWARD GEARS seven
DRIVESHAFTS Jaguar
CLUTCH AP Racing

CHASSIS

CHASSIS MODEL Jaguar R5
FRONT SUSPENSION LAYOUT Cast titanium uprights,
upper and lower carbon wishbones and pushrods, torsion bar
springing and anti-roll bar
REAR SUSPENSION LAYOUT Cast titanium uprights,
upper and lower carbon links and pushrods, coil springs and
torsion anti-roll bar
DAMPERS Koni
TYRES Michelin
WHEELS OZ Racing
BRAKE DISCS Carbone Industrie or Brembo
BRAKE PADS Carbone Industrie or Brembo
BRAKE CALLIPERS AP Racing
RADIATORS Marston
FUEL TANK AVL
FUEL TANK CAPACITY 126.6 litres (95kg)
INSTRUMENTS Pi Systems, Jaguar Racing

DIMENSIONS

LENGTH undisclosed
WIDTH 1800mm
HEIGHT 950mm
WHEELBASE undisclosed
TRACK front undisclosed **rear** undisclosed
WEIGHT 600kg (including driver)

TOYOTA

PERSONNEL

CHAIRMAN AND TEAM PRINCIPAL Tsutomu Tomita
PRESIDENT John Howett (pictured)
VICE-PRESIDENT Toshiro Kurusu
TECHNICAL DIRECTOR (CHASSIS) Mike Gascoyne
TECHNICAL DIRECTOR (ENGINE) Luca Marmorini
DIRECTOR TECHNICAL CO-ORDINATION Keizo Takahashi
CHIEF DESIGNER Gustav Brunner
TEAM MANAGER Richard Cregan
DRIVERS Cristiano da Matta, Olivier Panis, Jarno Trulli, Ricardo Zonta
CHIEF RACE ENGINEER Dieter Gass
RACE ENGINEER (Panis, Australia to Germany) Humphrey Corbett
RACE ENGINEER (Panis, Hungary to Japan) Remi Decorzent
RACE ENGINEER (Da Matta, Australia to Germany) Remi Decorzent
RACE ENGINEER (Zonta, Hungary to China) Ossi Oikarinen
RACE ENGINEER (Zonta, Brazil only) Remi Decorzent
RACE ENGINEER (Trulli, Japan and Brazil) Ossi Oikarinen
FRIDAY/TEST DRIVERS Ryan Briscoe, Ricardo Zonta
TOTAL NUMBER OF EMPLOYEES 600
NUMBER IN RACE TEAM 80
TEAM BASE Cologne, Germany
TELEPHONE +49 (0) 223 4182 3444 **WEBSITE** www.toyota-f1.com

TEAM STATS

IN F1 SINCE 2002
FIRST GRAND PRIX Australia 2002
STARTS 51
WINS 0
POLE POSITIONS 0
FASTEST LAPS 0
PODIUMS 0
POINTS 27
CONSTRUCTORS' TITLES 0
DRIVERS' TITLES 0

SPONSORS

Panasonic, Avex, Denso, Ebbon-Dacs, ESPN Star
Sports, Intel, Kärcher, KDDI, Time Inc., Esso

TECHNICAL SPECIFICATIONS

ENGINE

MAKE/MODEL Toyota RVX-04
CONFIGURATION 3000cc V10 (90deg)
SPARK PLUGS Denso
ECU Toyota/Magneti Marelli
FUEL Esso
OIL Esso
BATTERY Panasonic

TRANSMISSION

GEARBOX Toyota
FORWARD GEARS seven
DRIVESHAFTS Toyota
CLUTCH Sachs/AP Racing

CHASSIS

CHASSIS MODEL Toyota TF104/TF104-B
FRONT SUSPENSION LAYOUT pushrod with torsion bar
REAR SUSPENSION LAYOUT pushrod with torsion bar
DAMPERS Sachs/Toyota
TYRES Michelin
WHEELS BBS
BRAKE DISCS Brembo
BRAKE PADS Brembo
BRAKE CALLIPERS Brembo
RADIATORS Nippon-Denso
FUEL TANK ATL
FUEL TANK CAPACITY undisclosed
INSTRUMENTS Toyota

DIMENSIONS

LENGTH 4627mm
WIDTH 1800mm
HEIGHT 950mm
WHEELBASE 3090mm
TRACK front 1425mm **rear** 1411mm
WEIGHT 600kg (including driver)

JORDAN

PERSONNEL

CHIEF EXECUTIVE Eddie Jordan (pictured)
COMMERCIAL DIRECTOR Ian Phillips
HEAD OF RACE AND TEST ENGINEERING James Robinson
HEAD OF DESIGN John McQuilliam
HEAD OF AERODYNAMICS Nicolo Petrucci
TEAM MANAGER Tim Edwards
DRIVERS Timo Glock, Nick Heidfeld, Giorgio Pantano
RACE ENGINEER (Heidfeld) Gerry Hughes
RACE ENGINEER (Pantano/Glock) Dominic Harlow
FRIDAY/TEST DRIVERS Timo Glock, Robert Doornbos
CHIEF MECHANIC Andrew Stevenson
TOTAL NUMBER OF EMPLOYEES 201
NUMBER IN RACE TEAM 50
TEAM BASE Silverstone, England
TELEPHONE +44 (0)1327 850800 **WEBSITE** www.f1jordan.com

TEAM STATS

IN F1 SINCE 1991
FIRST GRAND PRIX USA 1991
STARTS 231
WINS 4
POLE POSITIONS 2
FASTEST LAPS 2
PODIUMS 18
POINTS 275
CONSTRUCTORS' TITLES 0
DRIVERS' TITLES 0

SPONSORS

Benson & Hedges, Puma, RE/MAX
Europe, Phard, TB, Trust, Kingdom of
Bahrain

TECHNICAL SPECIFICATIONS

ENGINE

MAKE/MODEL Ford-Cosworth RS2
CONFIGURATION 2998cc V10 (90deg)
SPARK PLUGS Champion
ECU Pi Systems
FUEL Elf
OIL Elf
BATTERY Panasonic

TRANSMISSION

GEARBOX Jordan
FORWARD GEARS seven
DRIVESHAFTS Pankl
CLUTCH Jordan/AP Racing

CHASSIS

CHASSIS MODEL Jordan EJ14
FRONT SUSPENSION LAYOUT pushrods activating
chassis-mounted dampers and torsion bars, unequal length
wishbones, front anti-roll bar and cast uprights
REAR SUSPENSION LAYOUT pushrods activating
gearbox-mounted dampers and torsion bars, unequal length
wishbones, front anti-roll bar and cast uprights
DAMPERS Jordan/Penske
TYRES Bridgestone
WHEELS BBS
BRAKE DISCS Brembo/Carbone Industrie
BRAKE PADS Brembo/Carbon Industrie
BRAKE CALLIPERS AP Racing
RADIATORS Marston/Secan
FUEL TANK ATL
FUEL TANK CAPACITY over 126 litres (over 95kg)
INSTRUMENTS Jordan/TAG/Pi

DIMENSIONS

LENGTH 4670mm
WIDTH 1800mm
HEIGHT 950mm
WHEELBASE more than 3000mm
TRACK front 1480mm **rear** 1418mm
WEIGHT 600kg (including driver)

MINARDI

PERSONNEL

TEAM PRINCIPAL Paul Stoddart (pictured)
DIRECTOR YOUNG DRIVER DEVELOPMENT Gian Carlo Minardi
TECHNICAL DIRECTOR Gabriele Tredozi
SPORTING DIRECTOR John Walton (deceased)
TEAM MANAGER Massimo Rivola
SENIOR ENGINEER Andy Tilley
SENIOR AERODYNAMICIST Loic Bigois
DRIVERS Zsolt Baumgartner, Gianmaria Bruni
RACE ENGINEER (Baumgartner) Laurent Mekies
RACE ENGINEER (Bruni) Riccardo Adami
FRIDAY/TEST DRIVER Bas Leinders
TEST DRIVER Tiago Monteiro
CHIEF MECHANIC Paolo Piancastelli
TOTAL NUMBER OF EMPLOYEES 112
NUMBER IN RACE TEAM 61
TEAM BASE Faenza, Italy
TELEPHONE +39 0546 696 111 **WEBSITE** www.minardi.it

TEAM STATS

IN F1 SINCE 1985
FIRST GRAND PRIX Brazil 1985
STARTS 322
WINS 0
POLE POSITIONS 0
FASTEST LAPS 0
PODIUMS 0
POINTS 31
CONSTRUCTORS' TITLES 0
DRIVERS' TITLES 0

SPONSORS

Superfund, Tosinvest, CIB Lizing, Uniqa,
Standox, Santogal, Fondmetal, Golden
Palace, Allegrini, X-Drinks, Wilux

TECHNICAL SPECIFICATIONS

ENGINE

MAKE/MODEL Cosworth CR-3
CONFIGURATION 2998cc V10 (72deg)
SPARK PLUGS Champion
ECU Magneti Marelli
FUEL Elf
OIL Elf
BATTERY Fiamm

TRANSMISSION

GEARBOX Minardi
FORWARD GEARS six
DRIVESHAFTS Minardi
CLUTCH AP Racing

CHASSIS

CHASSIS MODEL Minardi PS04B
FRONT SUSPENSION LAYOUT Upper/lower carbon-wrapped steel wishbones, pushrod-activated torsion springs/rockers, mechanical anti-roll bars
REAR SUSPENSION LAYOUT Upper/lower carbon-wrapped steel wishbones, pushrod-activated torsion springs/rockers, mechanical anti-roll bars
DAMPERS Sachs (to Minardi specification)
TYRES Bridgestone
WHEELS OZ Racing
BRAKE DISCS Hitco/Brembo
BRAKE PADS Hitco/Brembo
BRAKE CALLIPERS Brembo
RADIATORS Minardi/Secan
FUEL TANK ATL
FUEL TANK CAPACITY undisclosed
INSTRUMENTS Magneti Marelli

DIMENSIONS

LENGTH 4548mm
WIDTH 1800mm
HEIGHT 950mm
WHEELBASE 3097mm
TRACK front 1480mm **rear** 1410mm
WEIGHT 600kg (including driver)

Inner strength:
AMG 5.5-liter V8 supercharged engine
with 350 kW (476 hp) and 700 Nm

Love at first sight becomes obsession
after the first date

The fascination of form:
the CLS 55 AMG

Smooth and composed: AMG sports suspension
and AMG high-performance brake system

Mercedes-Benz

JENSON BUTTON

This was Jenson's watershed year
when his big opportunity arrived.
No victories came, but the BAR
driver was seldom off the podium

I couldn't wait for Melbourne. All winter we had been setting really strong testing times, but the world at large seemed suspicious. They thought we were showboating, doing low-fuel runs all the time to try and bag a couple of extra sponsors. But I knew we were in good shape. With the BAR Honda 006, designed by Geoff Willis and his team, and the switch to Michelin rubber, I knew how much better the package was than what we'd had in 2003.

Even when I qualified fourth in Melbourne, half a second behind the Ferraris but equalling Montoya's time, there were still people who expected to see me in the pits after about five laps but, when I came in on lap 11, the same time as Barrichello's front-row Ferrari, it started to dawn on people that we'd done a very good job over the winter. I should have finished fourth, but we lost out with a fuel-rig problem at the second stop, and our tyre choice wasn't suited to the cooler race conditions so I had to be content with sixth

Perhaps I should say here and now, in light of what was to come, that as early as pre-Christmas 2003, there were journalists asking my advisors about the chances of me going back to Williams in 2005. It's not a question of disloyalty, it's a case of knowing the market place and knowing your options.

Anyway, back to the track. We now knew what Ferrari's level was, but were convinced we had the potential to be 'best of the rest'. We didn't quite manage it at Sepang, but I did finish third, taking a first podium for both myself and the team. It felt great, especially because I'd been robbed at the 11th hour in Malaysia before, when Michael nicked a podium from me on the last lap. He seemed very much aware of that and was genuinely chuffed for me, which was nice.

Afterwards, I received a big hug from my dad. It was a defining moment. All those late nights prepping kart engines, driving to far-flung parts of the country, those early starts and now this. The kind of moments that stay with you for life.

In Bahrain we did it again: third. This time there were only the Ferraris ahead. We had a revised rear suspension that we'd tested at Ricard and the car felt strong but, as in Malaysia, I didn't feel that we'd got the best one-lap performance out of it. My fastest lap in free practice, for example, was 0.6s quicker than Michael's pole time. We were still learning about the Michelins, of course, and given that there was also an engine update due, everyone had good cause for optimism.

We also thought the 006 would go particularly well at Imola. Honda had made great strides, the car braked well and was especially good over the kerbs. My first pole position was a fantastic start. I was a quarter of a second quicker than Michael. He'd made a mistake but, even so, he reckoned it would have been very close.

I had a good start from the front row of the grid and drove a great first lap. I was almost 3s in front at the end of it, partly due to Michael and Juan Pablo having a bit of a moment at Tosa. As well as that, there was the opening-lap performance of the Michelin compared with the Bridgestone, but Michael's general speed was all too obvious. He hauled me back in pretty damn quickly.

I was kind of hoping that a good pit stop and a strong 'out'-lap on fresh Michelins would give me half a chance of maintaining my lead. But Michael soon put a stop to that! I came in on lap 9, Michael stopped two laps later, and when he came out I could barely see him! It was mind-boggling. On pure pace, Ferrari was around a second a lap quicker than us. Michael was just gone.

It's funny how your perceptions change. There I was finishing second, driving a

Jenson shares his delight at achieving his first podium finish with his father, John, at the Malaysian Grand Prix at Sepang, where he finished third. More were to follow, a great many more...

strong race, and still feeling a tinge of disappointment. Don't get me wrong, I was delighted to be second, and so was the team, but Ferrari was 20s up the road. We were a bit disappointed about that when, just a few short weeks earlier, we'd have been delighted about blowing Williams away. It's a tough business and you always need to feel you're going forward.

This was also a time when all sorts of people were writing about the 'new' Jenson Button. Well, sorry, but I was the same Jenson Button I'd always been. You don't just suddenly make a dramatic improvement. It never ceases to amaze me how few people seem to realise that F1 is driven by car performance.

If there's one thing that success does do, it's focus the team. The realisation that you can fight at the front of every race heightens everyone's anticipation. Motivation suddenly grows and you can almost feel the buzz.

The Spanish Grand Prix brought us down to earth with a bit of a bump. Barcelona was the scene of so many of our strong winter testing laps, and I was really confident. But when I made a mistake on my qualifying lap by running wide over a kerb, and lined up 14th, I was furious. From where I was, it was purely damage limitation, and I had to make do with a point for eighth. One to forget.

Monaco got us back on track again, with another second place, and I also kept up my record of scoring points in every race. Unfortunately, so did Jarno Trulli, and it was my old team-mate who beat me across the line by half a second. It was the first time this year that Michael and Ferrari failed to take the 10 points, and so it was a bit frustrating to miss out on the opportunity to score my first win. I went home still third in the drivers' championship, but Jarno was just a point behind.

By now, we were right into the meat of F1's hectic 2004 schedule, and Nürburgring followed just a week later. I was confident that we could challenge the Ferraris for a front row slot here and I was right, just not in the way that I thought. It was Taku who put a BAR on the front row, while I struggled with grip and had to make do with fifth. In the race, though, I managed to finish on the podium again – my fifth in seven races – due to Taku's misfortune, but Jarno kept the pressure on by finishing fourth. In the constructors' championship, Alonso's results meant that Renault had a 15-point margin over us.

After two races in a week, we then had a fortnight's gap before more back-to-back races in Canada and the USA. In Montréal, qualifying was promising, and I lined up second despite locking a wheel at the hairpin. It wasn't a surprise to find Schumacher on pole. It was a surprise when it was Ralf in a Williams! In the race, I found myself with too much oversteer and could do nothing about either of the Ferraris, or Ralf. Fourth place became third after the event, when both Williams entries were excluded for a brake-duct infringement.

I then had the opportunity to spend a few days in New York with Louise – what a mega place! – before heading to Indy, which always seems to be so massive. Unfortunately, we lost our 100% point-scoring record when I had a gearbox problem, but Taku scored with a fine third – his first podium.

Back to Europe again and Magny-Cours where, despite being just 0.3s off the pole, I lined up fourth and finished fifth. It could have been another podium, but the anti-stall chimed in at my third stop and I lost a crucial few seconds. Jarno was now back to within two points of me in the drivers' championship.

The British Grand Prix, my home race, was frustrating. We hoped that a new aero package would put us right in the thick of it, but we didn't get the required

result, so opted to revert to the standard aero package and, despite driving my heart out, fourth was all I could manage. On reflection, McLaren's new MP4-19B was obviously a big step and so Kimi Räikkönen came back into the picture. When a team like McLaren is down, it doesn't stay down, and so I guess it was just a dose of reality. Even so, I wasn't in party mood, so was pleased to leave the star performance on stage to Louise, with her singing, on Sunday night at the GP party!

The German Grand Prix started with trouble and finished as the greatest race of my life. I had an engine let go on Friday, which put me back to 13th on the grid. Then our FTT (Front Torque Transfer) system was banned and we had to remove it before Saturday practice. I did a long first stint and was up to fifth after the stops, then Juan Pablo ran wide and I passed DC in the pits at the second stops. That left Fernando, who I almost got at the last stop but not quite. So I finally overtook him on the circuit to grab second after we'd had a good race against each other. To cap it all, I had to hold my helmet on because a securing strap had come loose and air was getting under the lid and trying to lift it off my head. All in all, a busy and memorable afternoon!

Then, of course, all hell broke loose. There I was, having a few days break on DC's boat in the Med, when news of my intended move to Williams broke. There were underlying issues at BAR that I don't want to go into, but my decision was solely driven by the view that BMW Williams will ultimately afford me the best opportunity to win the World Championship.

Given the nature of the situation, it always looked as if it would go to the Contract Recognition Board – that's all I'll say – and so the best approach was to say nothing. When it came out, of course, I was put in a difficult position, as were all of the parties. I have had more comfortable weekends than Hungary, but I have to say that the guys in the race team were professional and understanding. We all just got on with the job.

I was as determined as ever to give my all for the team until the end of the year, and a double points score in Hungary was great for us, but quickly reversed by a double retirement at Spa. Monza, though, was key. We were strong and, again, I looked as though I could give Ferrari a hard time on home territory. Especially after Michael spun on lap 1, and Rubens chose intermediates at the start. But their recovery pace was just stunning. Still, a podium from me and fourth from Takuma meant that we finally overhauled Renault and moved into

Clockwise from below. Posing with David Richards, father John and his third place trophy at Sepang; leading away from pole at Imola; being congratulated by champion Schumacher

Concentrating on racing and working with his engineers to develop his chassis, while his destiny for 2005 was sorted, paid dividends for Jenson, as he was fastest of all but the Ferrari duo

second place in the constructors' championship. Still it was not over yet. We had not secured second place and there were three more races to go.

I was really looking forward to racing in China, and the circuit lived up to our expectations. The new facilities and track lay-out were exceptional. The race was very exciting, and it was fantastic to finish on the podium in the first-ever Chinese Grand Prix and to achieve my fourth second place finish of the season. My result combined with Taku's sixth place meant that the team moved nine points ahead of Renault in the constructors' championship, with two races remaining.

Heading to Japan next, BAR celebrated its 100th Grand Prix which was pretty special. It was an unusual weekend to say the least. With a typhoon threatening the area, qualifying was cancelled on Saturday and rescheduled for Sunday morning. Having a day off over a race weekend was strange. Although having qualy and the race on the same day proved exciting, I prefer to have them on separate days. Achieving another podium by finishing third, with Taku finishing fourth, was a fantastic result for the team.

With even more points scored over Renault in Japan, the only likelihood now of them beating us in the constructors' championship was if they finished in first and third place at the Brazilian Grand Prix and neither Taku nor I finished the race. Unfortunately, I was disappointed to retire from the final race of the year with an engine problem, although Taku went on to finish sixth. BAR ended the year second in the championship – an incredible achievement for the entire team; including the test team and everyone at the factory. Third place in the drivers' championship with 10 podiums is also a pretty special way for me to end the season.

JUAN PABLO MONTOYA

The season was quite a
struggle for the Colombian,
but it ended in style with a
wonderful victory in Brazil

I think it would be fair to say that 2004 didn't live up to my expectations, or those of the BMW WilliamsF1 Team. In 2003, I was in contention for the World Championship, and Ferrari looked beatable. In fact, if it hadn't been for the stewards' decision to penalise me for tangling with Rubens at Indy, I might have been coming into 2004 as World Champion. Anyway, it's all ancient history now. It's a pity my final season with WilliamsF1 didn't give us both more, but I was delighted to give the team a farewell present with victory in Brazil.

The new car certainly looked different, and when I first saw it I was kind of excited. You've got to assume that the aero people believed that they had found something to do that weird-looking nose, and I was hoping that maybe we'd taken the jump on the others and that it might take them some time to catch up.

I first tried the car at the launch in Jerez and we quickly got the thing dialled in. It felt pretty good, it had a good balance and the times seemed very competitive. The problem was, as always in winter testing, that you don't really know where you stand. Most importantly, Ferrari tended not to test at the same places and same times as the rest of us. Also, you don't know who's running light. We certainly noticed the very fast times BAR were doing at Barcelona, but we weren't sure if that was genuine or running a bit light. Looking back, they were probably running about the same weight as us but simply going faster.

It all came out in the open at Melbourne. In qualifying, I think we had a bit of a tyre advantage. I had a bit of a moment pushing really hard trying to make up the difference, but got a bit out of shape through the fast chicane. If it hadn't been for that I could probably have got onto the front row, maybe a couple of tenths off Michael. I started third, but the race showed the true picture. Even though I lost time at the first corner by going over the grass trying to defend my position from Alonso, our pace showed where we really were. I had a bit of a fight with Ralf [Schumacher] and would have finished fourth but for a couple of problems at the pit stops. But even without the problems, we would have been half a minute off.

Melbourne is always a Ferrari track though, and we were hoping that we'd turn it around at Sepang, which has been a good track for us. We closed the gap, but they still beat us. Actually, this was the closest I got to a win until my victory in Brazil. The early laps were damp and I had more grip than Michael and Rubens [Barrichello]. It took a few laps to find a way by Rubens, then I was right on Michael's gearbox. There was an opportunity to pass, but it was marginal so I left it, thinking I'd soon get another chance. But then it began to dry out and the chance never came. I was able to stay with him, but I think we were flattered by our tyres.

From there, we just sort of levelled off. I was running third – a very distant third behind the two red things – when I lost my hydraulics late in the race in Bahrain. I finished a very distant third in Imola where we were around 1s per lap slower than Ferrari. In Spain, we were a bit optimistic with our brake ducts trying to make up the performance difference. I got onto the front row, but we overheated our brakes, forcing me to retire. At Monaco, where I'd won in 2003, I was running only seventh when there was the incident in the tunnel with Michael. At the Nürburgring, Panis ran over my nose at the first corner. In Canada, I was fighting with Button for fourth. At Indy, I was black-flagged for the start, but only after running for over an hour – and so it went on.

At Magny-Cours, we had a revised car. The rear bodywork was altered quite a lot as they changed the aerodynamics. The first thing I did was crash it! It had begun to rain, and was just really, really slippery. I stood on the brakes and just nothing happened, then all of a sudden I was going backwards, still going very fast. I thought "oh, I'm going to hit the barrier" and then, bam, I hit it. I thought it had stopped, and I opened my eyes, but the car was rolling over so I closed my eyes again. Actually, the first set of body spares for the new body was just arriving from England in the truck as I was having the accident. So that was pretty neat!

That aside, there were moments during the weekend where the car seemed quite competitive. In qualifying, it was quite close with [pole man] Alonso in the first couple of sectors, but then I just went a bit too deep into the fast chicane and I had to get out off the gas. But, as was often the case, you didn't get to see the real picture in qualifying because of the way our tyres worked compared with Ferrari's. In the race, we weren't any closer to the pace than before really. We'd brought the car to the race without having had the chance to test it, so I was sort of hoping that we'd find more from it when we tested, but we didn't really.

To be honest, the revised car didn't feel all that different from the old one really. A few races later, at Hungary, we had more changes as we went back to a conventional nose, and kept it for the rest of the year. But that didn't make a big difference either. Basically, we were lacking downforce. That was the top and bottom of it. There were side issues – a bit of instability on corner entries and stuff – but generally they came from that first problem.

It seemed that whatever changes were made didn't really make up for the aero shortfall. There were some tracks, like Imola, where the balance of the car was fantastic. But then you look at the times and you're 1s off. The power was okay, the balance was great. It was just downforce, and then the side issues feed off that. Like, we were often really hard on our rear tyres, because we didn't have

enough rear-end grip, so the tyres would slide and go off. That was a problem at some races, like Hockenheim for example. It meant that while you were, say, 1s off when everything was working, by the time you'd degraded the tyres, there could be stages when you were 2–2.5s off. It doesn't matter what you do with strategy, or how well you drive, when that's your basic deficit in pace.

There were still plenty of moments I really enjoyed. I particularly enjoyed passing Michael around the outside of the Bus Stop at Spa. I don't think he was expecting that! It's always nice to be able to put some pressure on Michael.

Then we came to Brazil. It's one of those tracks where the set-up you use brings the car into a much better part of its aero profile. We qualified second to Rubens, but the guy we were worried about more was Räikkönen just behind us, because we heard he was two-stopping. But then it began to rain just before the start, and that played into our hands. Like most of the field, we started on wets, but it dried pretty quick and we were in to change them on lap 5, same as Kimi. That put everyone onto a three-stop, and so now it was a straight fight with Kimi. It was kind of neat going down pitlane with him side by side. He had the line to get the place coming out of there, but I was able to position myself so that I got a better exit onto the backstraight, and was able to pass him into Turn 4. From there, it was a case of pushing but not making any mistakes. It was great to win, especially as it was here that I was robbed of a win in my third race back in 2001.

I was asked a lot about the atmosphere in the team, because it had been announced before the season started that I was going to McLaren for 2005. But the atmosphere was okay: I still enjoyed the company of the guys on my car, I just wish that we could have given them more to cheer about. My relationship with Frank [Williams] remained good, and I take away a lot of good memories from my four years with the team that gave me my start in F1. I wish them well for the future.

Above: The original FW26 lacked downforce. Below: Juan Pablo enjoyed putting one over Michael Schumacher at Spa after the FW26 had been given a conventional nose

FERNANDO ALONSO

The Spaniard was excited as
Renault introduced a brand
new engine and were still
able to rank third overall

For me, 2004 was a year that showed how well our team works. The aim was to finish in the top three, and we did that – but it says a lot about the character of Renault that in the end it was disappointing not to finish second in the World Championship. We achieved our objectives but still wanted more…

The season started with a brand new engine. We had some difficulties with the car early in the season, and there were some reliability problems in the middle of the year. But each time we met the challenge, solved the problems and came out stronger. It was a year in which we learned a lot of things and continued to mature. We built up our level of competitiveness at the race weekends and always concentrated on the race rather than on stealing headlines. Sometimes we surprised ourselves by performing very strongly at circuits where we didn't expect to be competitive, but at the start of the year everybody was predicting Renault would trip up after a lot of changes internally. I think those people got used to looking for us at the front of the field by the end of the year… We went to every race thinking we could fight for the podium. It didn't always happen that way, but that conviction says a lot about how the team has developed.

So, what about the season? Well, the first thing was the car and engine. Renault was the only team to start the year with a 100% new engine and it was reliable straight away. That was the main target in 2004, to score points from the start of the season and try to out-score our opponents. Using the new engine was the right thing to do, no question: it was more powerful, we developed it all the way to the end of the year and never compromised reliability. As for the car, it was harder to drive than the 2003 car, but it was also a big step forward. Give a racing driver the choice between a difficult, quick car and an easier, slower one and you know what the answer will be… For me, it's a question of character. The R202 had its own personality, just like the R23. This season, the R24 had its individual characteristics, but the lap times were competitive. A bad car doesn't win races, and the R24 was one of only four cars to do that this year. Without a doubt, it was the most competitive Renault I've ever driven.

After a few races it was clear Ferrari were in a league of their own, but we were right there behind them. For me, though, it was a slightly crazy season. I didn't have much luck in the first part. We got a strong podium in Australia, but then I seemed to be coming from the back of the grid each time, like in Malaysia and Bahrain. The Spanish Grand Prix was a difficult race, I crashed in Monaco, had a problem at the Nurburgring, then retired in Canada and the USA through no fault of my own and, maddeningly, each time we had a problem it was a podium finish that we lost. Things were better in the second half of the year, with second place at Magny-Cours chasing Michael, then podiums at Hockenheim and in Hungary. However, we definitely missed opportunities to really put our mark on the season. Jarno won in Monaco, and we could have had a one-two, but the Belgian Grand Prix really stands out as a race that we should have won. I was leading, pulling away, then a tiny part on the engine failed.

People look at a season and only see the numbers: third in the constructors' championship and fourth in the drivers' standings for me. Those are good numbers, but they don't tell the true story. The performance was there, but we didn't have the luck or the consistency to make the most of it at each race. However, when you look to the future, what do you want to be: consistent and slower, or fast and slightly inconsistent? We know our car will get better for 2005 and we will improve that consistency. In 2004, we weren't ready to take advantage of all the opportunities that came our way. That will definitely change next year.

Somehow, though, it doesn't seem fair to have a driver summing up a team's season, because we're just the most visible part of a huge effort. Other drivers talk about their team being like a family but, after three years with Renault, I understand what they mean. Take Flavio. In the last three years, all the drivers have been to his place in Kenya in the winter break to train and get to know each other. That's when you see his human side. At the races we're all working, all under pressure, but when you know the real person beneath, that improves the relationship. My father comes to the races with me and gives me his perspective, keeps my feet on the ground. There are my engineers, my mechanics: guys who know how to translate my feelings into making our car go quicker. All around, human relationships are very important. F1 is not just about technology and science, as there is a human side that makes everything happen.

I was supported by a lot of people this year. The thousands of people from Renault in the grandstands at Magny-Cours cheering for us are a fantastic memory. Then of course there are the Spanish fans, willing me on 100%. It's amazing when you think that two years ago the races weren't even on the television – now we have millions of people watching. For me, it's a strange feeling, because I don't think my personality has changed in the past three years, I am the same Fernando with the same friends. But now, so many people are interested in what you say, how you act, what you're doing, and they become very demanding when it comes to getting results! Fame, though, brings a responsibility: you have to set a good example and be a good model for others. I'm always proud to wear the Spanish flag when I race, to represent our country to the world.

It's a great feeling to succeed on behalf of Spain when we do well, and also to help F1 succeed in Spain. But it goes beyond the paddock too. Just before Malaysia this year, Madrid suffered from a terrible terrorist attack, and I was moved to express my solidarity with the victims and my sympathy for them. F1 is a small world, and it is important to be able to see beyond the paddock gates.

That's my approach to F1 as well. I was never pre-destined to be an F1 driver. It was my dream, but if I had not made it, that would have been okay too, as there have been many talented people who didn't succeed. That's not a casual attitude, or arrogance, but it allows me to value what I have and fight even harder to keep it. I have achieved the first part of my dream. The next one is to be World Champion. So when will it happen? It is impossible to say, maybe in two years or maybe later. There are no miracles in F1 though and no superheroes. You need to build a team, progress together, grow up together and then put all those parts together into a season with almost no mistakes. Everything needs to be at its peak. The team has been working on the R25 for a long time now and the same is true for the engine. Like with every new car, it looks promising and we have high hopes. So, if all the pieces come together, then maybe we can fight for a title. I hope the opportunity will come soon and with Renault. When it does, we will be there and ready to seize it.

Top: The R24 couldn't match the Ferraris, but it was the best Renault Fernando has driven to date. Right: Fernando signs an autograph for a fan, loving all of their ardent support

KIMI RÄIKKÖNEN

Runner-up in 2003, Kimi had a
difficult time in '04, but the
signs are that he'll be back out
at the front for McLaren in '05

For me, most of this year was a question of waiting. We knew quite early on that the MP4-19 wasn't fully competitive, and it was always a question of waiting for the revised car – the MP4-19B – before we could really compete. On the one hand, the first half of the year was quite frustrating but, on the other, you know that with McLaren and Mercedes on your side things aren't going to be bad forever. Sure enough, as soon as we got the 19B out on the track, our season turned around.

Our victory at Spa was very, very satisfying. I'd like to talk about that more than the other races! It was great for us drivers coming back to Spa after it had been missing from the calendar in 2003. It's a fantastic challenge, and you feel you can really make a difference there. The more you put in, the more you get back. But for us, we were looking forward to it even more because the 19B was coming good.

We'd brought it out mid-season, in France. There it was, immediately a big improvement on the 19. Basically, it had a much more stable rear end that allowed you to brake with more confidence and allowed you to take more speed into the high-speed corners. I immediately felt very at home with it. At Magny-Cours, we were quite quick in the practices – top-four sort of pace – but I made a mistake in qualifying that left me down in ninth, and that decided my race really, so we didn't get to see the car's potential there.

But at the next race at Silverstone it was more clear. There I qualified on pole. I don't think we were kidding ourselves that this meant we were now faster than Ferrari – because their tyre situation disguised their pace in qualifying, and also we were fairly sure Michael was on a two-stop strategy, whereas we were on a three – but for sure we had closed a lot of the gap. I'd first tested the 19B at Silverstone a few weeks before this race and it really did feel very good round there. Through the fast corners in particular it worked very well. In the race we knew we had to get as much time over Michael as possible because of our extra stop, and it was fantastic to be able to just wring the car's neck on the first lap and have a big lead. Starting from pole means you can do this and not be slowed by what everyone else is doing. It sounds obvious, but it really makes a huge difference.

Anyway, we led until our first pit stop, and I think we had Rubens handled, but we were only 7.4s ahead of Michael and he still had a few more low-fuel laps to do. On my out-lap I lost time getting by Sato and then, more seriously, by the two Minardis who were fighting each other and didn't seem to see me. The combination of those things meant Michael got ahead of us at that point.

We followed Michael for most of the race, and it was just getting to the time when we were starting to think about our final fuel stop when there was a safety car period for Trulli's accident. This was good news for us, because it meant we got to pit under the safety car and not lose any time. Unfortunately, there were two backmarkers between Michael and me in the queue behind the safety car. We knew that Michael would be at his weakest immediately after the safety car came in, because of how much quicker our tyres were at that point, and so we needed to be right behind him to take advantage. By the time I got past the other two guys Michael had had time to get his tyres up to speed and there was nothing I could do.

Then we went to Hockenheim and our pace was even stronger. I overtook Alonso on the first lap to go second right behind Michael. This time we were on the same strategy, so it was a straight fight and I was looking forward to it very much. We made up some time on him at around the first stops and I was just 1s behind

and with more fuel on board. I was able to press him. He went faster, and I was able to go with him and we left the rest far behind. I was very confident at this point. I knew that we could go longer, we had similar pace, and therefore I thought we would be able to get ahead at the next stops. But we never got to do the second stop because the rear wing failed and put me into the tyre barriers.

The Hungarian Grand Prix was a disaster because we chose the wrong compound of tyres. We were tricked in the Friday practices by the way the track conditions changed. It made it seem like the harder compound was faster, when in fact it wasn't, and this was made even worse by the cool temperatures in qualifying. In the end, it didn't matter anyway because there was a software problem with the engine in the race and I had to retire.

But that brought us to the Belgian Grand Prix, and you can appreciate how we felt: there was a momentum building as we came into it, with Hungary just an interruption. The conditions for qualifying were crazy, with rain, then drying, then rain again. We weren't as lucky with our slot as Renault, but I thought we were going to be the fastest of the wet-tyre users. Then, near the end of the lap, the braking area for the Bus Stop chicane was more slippery than the rest of the track, and I ran straight on and sort of half-spun. It meant I was only 10th on the grid. I wasn't thinking of victory as we sat on the grid, but Spa is a funny place where lots can happen, so it was just a question of staying out of trouble into the first corner, then pushing as hard as possible and seeing where we were.

I decided to stay outside for the first turn and not get mixed up with the craziness. So I couldn't believe it when I got hit by a Sauber [Massa], even though I was on the outside. Anyway, I got round the corner, people were driving into each other on the inside and I just sort of drove around them all. I came out in fifth, but I wasn't sure if the car was damaged. I radioed the team that I might be coming in because it felt a bit funny as I went down the hill and through Eau Rouge. Actually, the diffuser was damaged from the hit. Once I'd satisfied myself that it wasn't a tyre or broken suspension I decided to stay out.

Even before the first lap was over there was a safety car, and so I lined up right behind Michael. This was good news. This was the situation I'd been hoping for at Silverstone. We knew he would be struggling in the early laps after the safety car because of the way his tyres behave differently to ours. So, as soon as the safety car came in, I attacked. Actually, it was very straightforward. I got better traction out of the hairpin and passed him down the hill quite easily.

Now I was up to fourth, with my team-mate David Coulthard ahead of me. But I had a problem. I was having trouble with the gearshift, probably also from the hit at the first corner. The car was pushing forward and the gears weren't going in. For a couple of laps it was very tricky and I almost spun off. Then it was working again.

I got a run on DC through Eau Rouge and was able to pass him into Les Combes, and that left just the two Renaults in front of me. But then I began to get trouble with the gearshift again. I almost spun a few times because it locked the rear end completely. I was changing switches on the steering wheel, trying to get some sort of idea how I could push again. We have different settings for engine braking, so one of them was working but it was an extreme one, almost locking the rear wheels. I was using it at the hairpin and the chicane because otherwise I couldn't stop the car. Then I would change the position for the other corners.

One of the Renaults pitted and the other spun off, and suddenly I was leading. I built up a good lead over Michael, but then it was all taken off me when just after my second stop the safety car came out again and allowed Michael to get his stop for free. That wiped out the 12s I had built up over him. I knew that I would be quicker over the lap after the safety car came in, but we also knew that we had to protect ourselves down the hill and up to Les Combes the first time. I had to make sure that I came out of the hairpin well in front of him so he couldn't slipstream me. I was able to do this and then pull away from him for a few laps.

Then, just a few laps from the end, there was yet another safety car period. This allowed Michael to get on my tail again but, as before, I was able to sprint away from him when the safety car came in. The car felt really good at this time, on low fuel, and I was really enjoying the circuit. That's how I set the race's fastest lap just one from the end. When I saw the flag it was a big, big relief after the season we had had. I knew for sure that we were back, that this was more like the Team McLaren Mercedes everyone expected, and that we were back in the fight.

Above right: Kimi's season all came together when he won the Belgian GP, but he had had his scares in the race. Right: The MP4-19B was a major step forward from the MP4-19

GLOBAL CHALLENGERS

Formula One is on the move, with 2004 heralding the arrival of Bahrain and China into the World Championship. Although very different in character from each other, both made an enormous impression on their debuts

BAHRAIN

That the FIA Formula One World Championship is heading for new regions is no surprise. The complications of impending European Union tobacco bans has been one aspect and the presence of dollar-laden government-supported circuit plans another compelling argument.

Bernie Ecclestone's mantra has always been that as a world championship, F1 should play on a world stage and so a presence in the Middle East and Asia was logical. But the first of the Brave New World ventures, Bahrain, was, at first glance, less so.

China can boast 200 times the population of Bahrain, which has a head count of less than 700,000. Originally, the Bahrainis had been planning to build a national venue, with the blessing of the King, Shaikh Hamad bin Isa Al Khalifa, himself a keen motorsport fan. Ecclestone put them in touch with circuit guru Hermann Tilke, who was responsible for Sepang in Malaysia as well as the redesign at Hockenheim and the Chinese project. It wasn't long before the plan had metamorphosed into a full-blown Grand Prix facility.

As well as the new circuit forming the central hub of all proposed motorsport development in Bahrain, there was also considerable prestige involved in winning the race to bring F1 to the Middle East. Many assumed that it would be a contest inevitably won by Dubai, which is rapidly evolving as a business, holiday and sporting destination. However, although Bahrain itself, as opposed to its rulers, is not hugely wealthy, it's linked by a causeway to Saudi Arabia, with an extremely rich population almost half the size of the United Kingdom, many of whom spend their R&R time in Bahrain.

The deal that would put Bahrain on the F1 calendar was signed off with Ecclestone in September 2002, and the circuit and infrastructure were built in record time. Originally, the plan was to have the race towards the back end of the 2004 season, but it was then brought forward by six months.

As December 2003 became January 2004, there were rumours that the project was running behind schedule and couldn't possibly sustain a race with its landmark 04-04-04 date, around which ticket sales were marketed. Ecclestone despatched organisational trouble-shooter Philippe Gurdjian, who had experience of Grands Prix at Paul Ricard, Magny-Cours, Barcelona and Sepang. In the end, the Bahrainis brought it in a day early – March 6 as against the targeted March 7…

On arrival, the F1 circus was spellbound. The facilities were expansive and first-rate, and the circuit itself drew praise. It had been no easy task. The climate and the land-base had been issues during construction, which had demanded a series of controlled explosions to the sand/rock surface. Fears that wind and sand would cause problems when the cars were out on the track were addressed by using high-grip asphalt.

In terms of lay-out, the need for overtaking had been carefully borne in mind, to the extent of a couple of revisions made to the original plans. The 3.36-mile 14-turn circuit followed Sepang principles in having a long straight into a tight hairpin, with the avoidance of a quick corner on to the straight. The thinking was that the cars' front-end aerodynamics must not be key to the corner on to the main straight as that would prevent a driver from following closely enough to launch an overtaking bid at the end of it. In simple terms, it had to be more "new Hockenheim" than Barcelona.

The downhill direction changes through the sweeping Turns 5/6/7 provided a dramatic viewing spot and the entry to Turn 10 was tricky, the camber falling away and demanding precision.

Williams test driver Marc Gené was the first man to drive the new circuit, thereby stoking, of course, F1 paddock paranoia about Williams and Michelin stealing a march in obtaining meaningful tyre data. This, some said, evened up the suspicion about Shell, contracted to Ferrari of course, being involved in laying the surface…

"Overall the lay-out is good," Gené said. "It's not a really challenging track as there's no real high-speed stuff, but the most important thing is that we should see a race – it should be good for overtaking."

The dominance of Michael Schumacher and Ferrari in the Grand Prix meant that Gené's expectations were slightly optimistic, but he was right about the overtaking. The opportunities at Turn 2 were enough to goad Ralf Schumacher into collecting the first reprimand under F1's new penalty system when he collided with Takuma Sato, who later showed how it should be done, successfully pulling the same move on David Coulthard.

Fears over the sand and track surface proved unfounded and the only slight hiccough, addressed instantly, was a sharp-edged manhole cover causing a couple of punctures. It had been a superb logistical effort to pull the race off and any gaps in the grandstands on race day were more likely down to the fact that in Bahrain weekends fall on Thursday/Friday not Saturday/Sunday.

Sand, stone, an oasis,
ultra-modern facilities
and a culture new to F1
made the first visit to
Bahrain extra exciting

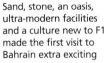

CIRCUIT MODIFICATIONS

Ultra-modern venues such as Bahrain and China represent state-of-the-art thinking, both in terms of layout and safety facilities.

At Sakhir, for example, an attempt was made to keep the track surface clean by compacting sand, water and cement together to form hard areas next to the kerbs. It was labelled "stabilised concrete" by circuit guru Hermann Tilke, but actually turned out to be a little unstable... There was concern about the amount of debris kicked up whenever anyone left the circuit and a different surface, similar to the Astroturf material seen at other tracks, will be adopted next year.

Updating existing circuits was an ongoing process. Barcelona had a new Turn 10 hairpin, which shortened the back straight, allowing a greater run-off area. "The new corner turned left about 60m earlier," confirmed FIA race director Charlie Whiting, "and that enabled us to get in a little bit of asphalt run-off area, which we are very much in favour of." It was also hoped it would create a more realistic overtaking opportunity, but the speed of the previous corner, the 125mph Campsa, militated against that.

For years, not only has Monte Carlo afforded no room for manoeuvre for drivers, but team personnel have always endured cramped working conditions too. This year, finally, there was relief, as the new permanent Monaco pits were available for the first time. Entering the pits was also now slightly different. Instead of the cramped temporary pits on the driver's right, the much more capacious garages were on the left.

One of Formula One's other great classical venues, Spa-Francorchamps, also underwent change for 2004, with a reworking of the Bus Stop chicane. "That was done because the first part of the chicane, the left and right elements, are so close together that the drivers were all straight-lining it," Whiting explained. "Whatever we did with kerbs or bollards never seemed to work properly. What we wanted to do was introduce a nice flowing left and right sequence which, I think, worked. The drivers at first said that they didn't think overtaking would be possible there, but it was. We basically wanted to get away from all those discussions about did so-and-so cut the chicane too much, or did he not?"

Whiting was also deeply satisfied with Astroturf kerb boundaries. "Although it doesn't come under the heading of track modifications as such," he says, "It works absolutely brilliantly. It solved all the problems at Hungary, the Hockenheim first corner, Nürburgring's fourth corner, the Acque Minerali chicane at Imola, and basically all the places where we had problems on the exit of corners. Two metres of it and the whole problem just disappears, and not just for F1 either. At Hockenheim, for example, where every car swept over the kerbs with impunity, even the Porsches didn't do it. There is just no grip on it and they all want to keep away from it. On top of that, it's zero maintenance and it continues to look green. It's been a major success."

SHANGHAI

Labelled as commercially the most important race in F1 history, the Chinese Grand Prix, at the futuristic Shanghai International Circuit, was a stunning event.

The race had been long-discussed and a long while in the planning stages. There were serious counter-proposals from Zhuhai and Beijing and, in the end, it was Formula One Management that approved the choice of Shanghai.

China wanted F1 and the Shanghai International Circuit president, Mao Xiaohan, was given an open cheque book by the three government-owned bodies that funded the deal. Not only did the circuit and infrastructure cost upwards of £250 million to build, but the Chinese also agreed a franchise fee of around £17.5 million per annum to host the race until 2010.

From being given the green light, the circuit construction took only around 18 months with as many as 7000 workers active on the project at the most intensive phase, working day and night on a shift basis. It was built on what had previously been a 300-metre deep swamp, but both Tilke and his Chinese construction experts were confident enough that it wouldn't sink thanks to the circuit being built on a foundation of polystyrene blocks.

The circuit lay-out is based on the shape of the Chinese world "Shang" – which means "above".

As Tilke explains, it happened more by accident than design: "We drew the first plan and went to Shanghai. One of the Chinese suddenly became very agitated and said: 'This circuit forms a Shang!' We had no idea what a Shang looked like, but of course we immediately took up the concept and went from there. Being the first part of the name of the city made the whole deal even cooler. I think the Chinese are trying to get the track into the *Guinness Book of Records* as the biggest Chinese sign."

The circuit structure contains two incredible wing-shaped elements that span the track. One contains the Paddock Club/restaurant area, with the other occupied by the media centre. As day becomes night and you leave the circuit in the evening, the whole place is picked out in blue neon lights. It resembles a James Bond set, springing from the bowels of what would otherwise be a barren and featureless stretch of land.

The drivers gave Shanghai a unanimous thumbs-up. The 15-turn track had the Tilke trademark long straight into a tight hairpin, with Ralf Schumacher involved again, this time taken out by an optimistic lunge from David Coulthard. But, as Michael Schumacher pointed out, SIC had a character very much its own.

"It's simply different, which is not what has been said about some of the Tilke-designed tracks," reckoned the seven-times champion. "The corner combinations, like Turn 1 and Turn 13, we don't have elsewhere, and the banking is interesting. Then you get into the tight business of Turn 3 and it's challenging because you can make mistakes there and also make up a lot of time. I like it."

Olivier Panis was gobsmacked by the whole place: "I mean. It's just massive," he said, "it's not like anything else we've got at all. If you're not careful, you can get lost in the paddock!"

He was right. The team debrief/admin/PR offices, all first-class air-conditioned facilities, were in 26 special stilted buildings astride a lake at the back of the

paddock. They were apparently modelled on Shanghai's 400-year-old Yu Yuan Gardens, although this seemed to escape most of F1's culture vultures, who were more concerned with finding the right door before they missed their debrief!

For first-time visitors, getting to SIC was an experience in itself. Foreigners are not permitted to drive in China and the road discipline is, er, interesting. The Williams marketing department were among those were involved in a sizeable shunt and one can see why the Chinese government imposes restrictions on car purchase. Presently, you must first purchase a registration number, sold at auctions in the large cities. They go for as much as £3000, which is around half the price of the smallest car. With vehicle numbers set to snowball, things can only get, er, more interesting…

The scale and grandeur of the new circuits contrasted hugely with some of the more classic F1 venues and caused everyone to appreciate that private enterprise can't compete with government funding on such a massive scale. Ecclestone was probably only being mildly tongue-in-cheek when he said: "In 10 years, Europe will be a third-world economy. Asia and America will rule the world…"

The F1 teams and drivers loved the spectacular Shanghai circuit, while every visitor was wowed by the cosmopolitan city

1 Formula One is a blaze of colour wherever it goes, but nowhere more than in the public areas where the tifosi unfurl their flags. **2** It's hard to believe, but 10 years have passed since Ayrton Senna's death at Imola. **3** Foster's and grid girls are a welcome constant at every Grand Prix... **4** ...As are photographers looking for that special shot, as here at Indianapolis where they shoot the line of bricks by the start/finish line

5 Monaco remains the most spectacular venue of all, standing firm as the cars flash by. **6** The sort of pit board that Michael liked to see in 2004, with team-mate Barrichello in his wake and Button best of the rest. **7** Not only was BAR the most improved team of the year, but its livery one of the most striking

1 The stunning new Shanghai International Circuit took every visitor's breath away. Jenson Button is shown crossing the bridge to BAR's team centre. 2 The expansion of F1 around the globe has attracted a whole raft of new fans. 3 F1 sponsors like to show off F1's prettiest face

4 Nowhere other than Italy do the fans go to such obvious extremes to catch a view of their heroes. **5** The Tifosi certainly aren't shy about letting it be known which team they support. **6** "Alright Mr F1 driver, we've got your every move covered"

TAGHeuer

WHAT ARE YOU MADE OF ?

TAGHeuer FORMULA 1

SWISS AVANT-GARDE SINCE 1860

ROUND **1**

AUSTRALIA
2004 FORMULA 1™
FOSTER'S AUSTRALIAN
GRAND PRIX
Melbourne

ROUND **2**

MALAYSIA
2004 FORMULA 1™
PETRONAS MALAYSIAN
GRAND PRIX
Kuala Lumpur

ROUND **3**

BAHRAIN
2004 FORMULA 1™
GULF AIR BAHRAIN
GRAND PRIX
Bahrain

ROUND **4**

SAN MARINO
FORMULA 1™ GRAN
PREMIO FOSTER'S DI
SAN MARINO 2004
Imola

ROUND **5**

SPAIN
FORMULA 1™ GRAN
PREMIO MARLBORO
DE ESPAÑA 2004
Catalunya

ROUND **6**

MONACO
FORMULA 1™
GRAND PRIX DE
MONACO 2004
Monte Carlo

ROUND **7**

EUROPE
2004 FORMULA 1™
ALLIANZ GRAND PRIX
OF EUROPE
Nürburgring

ROUND **8**

CANADA
FORMULA 1™
GRAND PRIX DU
CANADA 2004
Montréal

ROUND **9**

USA
2004 FORMULA 1™
UNITED STATES
GRAND PRIX
Indianapolis

RACE REPORTS

The season ran from Australia to Brazil, this time via Bahrain and China, but still no-one could topple Michael Schumacher

FERRARI SHOCK

The dominance of Ferrari at the opening round of the 2004 World Championship set people asking just what had gone so badly wrong at Williams and McLaren

"Let's just see where we are at Malaysia," countered Michael Schumacher, almost apologetically after Ferrari had destroyed the opposition in the opening race of the new season.

"This track always suits our car very well," continued the champ, "whereas Malaysia is traditionally much tougher for us. We won't know the true picture until then." The picture of this race was of two red cars running away and hiding from the others, without even appearing to try, Rubens Barrichello staying right with his team-mate until the final stint when brake concerns forced him to ease off. Fernando Alonso's Renault was comfortably the best of the rest in third but even he was half a minute behind the victor at the end.

There were a few 'what ifs' – how would Juan Pablo Montoya's Williams have fared had he not clattered over the Turn 1 grass seconds after the start, and how much pace did the cooler-than-predicted conditions cost the Michelin runners? – but they were details. They might have affected the way the race played out, but not the final result. At Melbourne at least, Ferrari appeared to have an advantage of around a second per lap over the opposition.

If this was to be a repeat of Ferrari's 2002 dominance, the sport would be relying heavily on Barrichello to at least make Schumacher work. At Melbourne he did so for three of the four stints, but doing this in his team-mate's slipstream ultimately overheated his brakes.

ROUND **1**

AUSTRALIA
2004 FORMULA 1™
FOSTER'S AUSTRALIAN
GRAND PRIX
Melbourne

That Ferrari's Michael
Schumacher won came
as no surprise. That he
did so at a canter really
rocked the opposition

LAP BY LAP
ACTION

58 laps / 191 miles

Montoya runs wide at the first bend as Alonso chases the Ferraris

Start to Lap 4

Michael Schumacher and Barrichello both get away well at the start, while Alonso jumps ahead of Button. Barrichello lets Schumacher lead into the first corner with Alonso third as Montoya runs wide onto the grass, dropping behind Button, Trulli (up from ninth on the grid) and Ralf Schumacher. By the end of the first lap, Schumacher is 1s clear of Barrichello. On lap 2, Montoya passes Ralf Schumacher to grab sixth place back. As the two Ferraris draw away on lap 3, there's a battle for fifth place as Trulli tries to hold off the Williams duo. On lap 4, Schumacher's lead over Barrichello is nearly 2s with the gap back to Alonso 2.8s.

Laps 5 to 12

The gap between the Ferraris is the same by lap 8, but they're now 5s ahead of Alonso. There's a gap back of more than 15s to Button, Trulli, Montoya, Ralf Schumacher and Webber, with Sato busy holding off the McLarens for ninth. On lap 10, Montoya heads for pit lane to begin the major pit stops. Kimi Räikkönen retires with a water pump failure, ending a disappointing day for the McLaren team. Barrichello, Alonso and Button head for pit lane on lap 11. The stops continue on lap 12 with Michael Schumacher, Trulli, Ralf Schumacher, Sato and da Matta all coming in. When Michael rejoins, he's only 1.5s ahead of Barrichello, with Alonso 6s behind the Brazilian.

Montoya dives past Ralf Schumacher to claim sixth place

Laps 13 to 26

On lap 13, Webber, running briefly in third place, pits for the first time. Sato has a big off on lap 16 but manages to hold on to his position. On lap 18, Michael Schumacher has trouble with traffic and the gap to Barrichello drops to less than 1s, but Alonso is still dropping back. Massa has a high-speed spin on lap 19, but continues in 11th. The order is still the same on lap 24, but Schumacher has extended his lead again to 2.9s. Alonso comes in for his second pit stop and drops behind Button. Further back, Montoya passes Trulli for sixth place. Third-placed Button pits on lap 26, but he's delayed because of a fuel nozzle problem. Montoya also pits and falls from sixth place to eighth.

Kimi Räikkönen endures a curtailed start to his campaign

Laps 27 to 35

The stops continue, with Ralf Schumacher and Trulli stopping on lap 28. Ralf rejoins ahead of Button to take fourth place. Trulli re-emerges behind Button and Montoya. Barrichello pits on lap 29, but when he rejoins in second place his car has a brake problem and he soon loses ground to Michael Schumacher who stops on lap 30 and rejoins in the lead, more than 5s clear of Barrichello. On lap 32, the race order is clear, with Schumacher pulling away from Barrichello and Alonso more than 20s behind. The Spaniard is followed by Ralf Schumacher, Button, Montoya, Trulli and Coulthard. Everyone else has been lapped. On lap 33, Fisichella forces his way past Heidfeld to grab 12th after a lengthy battle.

Jenson Button's pit crew races to get him back out onto the track

Laps 36 to 44

On lap 36, Michael Schumacher's lead has gone out to 9s, while Alonso's Renault continues to drop back from Barrichello. Montoya overtakes Button on lap 39 to promote himself to fifth place. The final round of pit stops begin on lap 40 with Alonso the first to call in. He rejoins well ahead of fourth-placed Ralf Schumacher. On lap 41, Trulli makes his pit stop, but he remains in seventh place when he rejoins. Sixth-placed Button stops on lap 42 and holds his position, albeit emerging a lap behind leader Michael Schumacher. On lap 44, Barrichello and Montoya make their final stops, both maintaining their positions.

Jordan and Sauber were left to fight over the minor positions

Lap 45 to the finish

The two Schumacher brothers both pit on lap 45, but they retain their positions for the run to the chequered flag. On lap 51 Schumacher backs off. Button unlaps himself on lap 54 as Schumacher eases off further, allowing Barrichello to close the gap between them. However, he has matters under control and, on lap 58, Michael Schumacher claims his 71st Grand Prix victory with Barrichello finishing in second place and Alonso third. The remaining points go to Ralf Schumacher, Montoya, Button, Trulli and Coulthard for claiming fourth through to eighth places respectively. Jaguar's Christian Klien is top rookie, in 11th.

Michael Schumacher acknowledges another victory

INSIDE LINE
MICHAEL SCHUMACHER

I was thinking even as we tested in the days leading up to the first race that the new car was a potential pole car for Melbourne. I knew that we would be very, very competitive because, having seen the last test at Imola, knowing the characteristics of the circuit, knowing the development we have done with the car, with the guys, I knew we would be very strong. As strong as we were? No, I didn't anticipate that.

I took pole and I won the race but in both these achievements I was pushed hard by my team-mate Rubens [Barrichello]. The gap between us in qualifying was almost nothing and you saw in the race we were really together until he faced his problems, so it's whoever can make his car work a little bit better than the other.

I had no particular problems at the start of the race but, despite going over to manual starts, it was clear that Renault still had a better getaway system than us. We had dedicated a certain amount of time in every test for that, but it still was not enough. It was something we needed more work on.

The race was tough from the beginning, right through the first half of the race before Rubens had some problems. He was pushing very, very hard and it was really a close fight. I couldn't allow any mistakes. One mistake and he could have had the advantage.

After Rubens had his problems and dropped back, obviously we had a big margin on the rest of the field and so we were able to slow down a little towards the end. But you can never take this race as a forecast for the rest of the year. This circuit suits us well and you would have seen a similar performance here in 2003 if that race had been straightforward, plus the cooler temperatures might have helped us a little too.

Q THE BIG QUESTION

Where had Ferrari's staggering superiority come from?

Winter testing had not generally pointed in this direction – not until just 11 days before the first race, at least. While Ferrari had pounded around their Fiorano test track and the nearby Mugello, the rest of the F1 circus put in their test miles at the Spanish venues of Barcelona, Jerez and Valencia.

BAR, Renault and Williams appeared quite closely matched in Spain, and each had cause for real optimism. There were some ominous signs that McLaren's new MP4/19 was not the force the team were hoping for, however.

Ferrari, when they did appear at Barcelona, did so with the 2003 car and were quick, but generally no quicker than the rest. The new F2004 was reported to have knocked 0.3s off the Fiorano lap record on its second day of running, but that news was greeted with suspicion. Only Ferrari were there to verify it, after all.

But then came the Imola test. Renault had been there the week before and had been delighted to have all but equalled the best ever time there, recorded by Schumacher's Ferrari. However, this time Schumacher knocked a huge 0.8s off that benchmark with the F2004. Significantly, Bridgestone were particularly delighted. All through the winter the Japanese company – which had been on the receiving end of some criticism of its wares in 2003 – had worked on a new range of compounds and constructions. Each of these programmes had run in parallel and it was only at the Imola test that the new compound and new construction ranges were brought together. They now had their answer – one that reverberated through the F1 community.

Ferrari led from the start, with Renault and BAR the best of the rest, McLaren out of the frame

PAT SYMONDS
RENAULT CHIEF OF ENGINEERING

We came away from this race confirming where we thought we were in winter testing. We were not that happy with the R24 as we came into this race. Both our drivers were telling us it was more difficult to drive than the R23 and we knew our engine was nowhere near where it would be later.

Tyre selection was the key to our third place. We knew the pit lane speed limit increase took 2.8s off a pit stop and that there had been a change to the pit lane that would save further time, but we couldn't get enough detail about that before we got there to be able to model it. It was clear, though, that it was going to be a three-stop race and therefore we felt we didn't need a safe back-up tyre. So we took a choice of two quite close compounds, one for hot weather, one for cool. The track temperatures were only in the mid-20s on race day and so our W-compound proved spot-on. It wasn't a tyre that anyone else had opted to bring to Melbourne.

Fernando [Alonso] qualified fifth and Jarno [Trulli] ninth. I had told them not to risk much in first qualifying. Jarno took this more to heart than Fernando and in the second session Jarno still hadn't really got a feel for the car because he'd been too cautious before. That also meant he was out too early in the running order of second qualifying, so hurting him even more.

Fernando got a great start, beat Montoya into the first corner and from there he had quite a lonely race, not on a pace with the Ferrari but comfortably clear of the rest. Jarno got hit from behind by Sato into the first turn and that damaged his diffuser. It meant the car lost around 2% of its aero performance – and that was enough to spoil his race. He did a good job in defending from Montoya for a long time but didn't have the pace to hold him off at the second stops and he finished seventh.

Immediately after the race we were quite bullish, despite Fernando finishing a long way behind the two Ferraris. Melbourne is a track where we expected them to go particularly well. But then when I sat down the week after and did a proper post-race analysis, I suddenly got an awful feeling that Ferrari hadn't in fact been going as fast as they might have. When you looked at the critical stages of the race and you saw what Michael [Schumacher] could pull out, it looked a bit ominous.

Tyre choice was the key to Alonso's third place, but he could do nothing about the Ferraris' pace

TAKEO KIUCHI
HONDA F1 PROJECT LEADER

If you look at the lap time data, you can see that we were around a second per lap slower in the race than the Renault, whereas in qualifying we had been slightly quicker. So, although Jenson [Button] was able to qualify equal third fastest, in the race he was only sixth fastest.

There were three basic reasons for this. Firstly, we didn't yet know enough about how to run the Michelin tyres. Secondly, we didn't have the correct rear suspension geometry to go with the Michelins. Thirdly, we were a little conservative with our engines in the race. Running reduced revs and one or two other things accounted for about an extra 0.5s per lap. We had run successful race distances in testing, but testing is never quite the same as a race meeting. The sequences and heat cycles are very different and so we wanted at least one race weekend to establish this data.

All three of our drivers [including our test driver Anthony Davidson] had some problems in the practices with a gearbox potentiometer failure. We changed to a different type after this race. This hurt Takuma [Sato] quite badly as he lost a lot of Saturday track time. Even so, he did well to go seventh fastest. Aside from the problem with the potentiometer, we were pleased with the performance of our new gearbox. This has internal gears designed and built by Honda in a BAR carbon-fibre casing.

In the race, it was maybe too cool for our tyres because of the way we had set the car up and Jenson found it was not consistent. If you look at the data, his first stint average lap time was around 1m 26.3s, his second 1m 26.9s, his third 1m 27.6s. The team tried changing the balance of the car at the stops but basically we were out of our temperature range. The two Williams cars were able to pass Jenson in the third stint.

Takuma damaged his front wing at the first corner. It was structurally alright, but the aerodynamics were compromised. The team prepared a replacement wing and fitted it at Takuma's second pit stop. You can see how much that improved the car as his average in the stint before that had been 1m 28.2s and this improved to 1m 27.0s, and he was able to catch and pass Felipe Massa's Sauber to finish the race in ninth place, just out of the points.

	Qualifying	Race	Stint 1	Stint 2	Stint 3	Stint 4
Button (BAR)	1m 24.998s		1m 26.049s	1m 26.058s	1m 25.991s	1m 26.314s
Alonso (Renault)	1m 25.699s		1m 25.088s	1m 25.439s	1m 25.258s	1m 26.630s

Button had the pace to qualify third, but his race pace was a second off that of Alonso's Renault

RACE RESULTS
AUSTRALIA
MELBOURNE

© [2004] Formula One Administration Ltd,
6 Princes Gate, London, SW7 1QJ.
No reproduction without permission.
All copyright and Database rights reserved

FIA Formula 1
WORLD CHAMPIONSHIP

RACE DATE March 7th
CIRCUIT LENGTH 3.295 miles
NO. OF LAPS 58
RACE DISTANCE 191.123 miles
WEATHER dry and cloudy, 19°C
TRACK TEMP 24°C
RACE ATTENDANCE 121,500
LAP RECORD Michael Schumacher,
1m 24.125s, 141.010mph, 2004

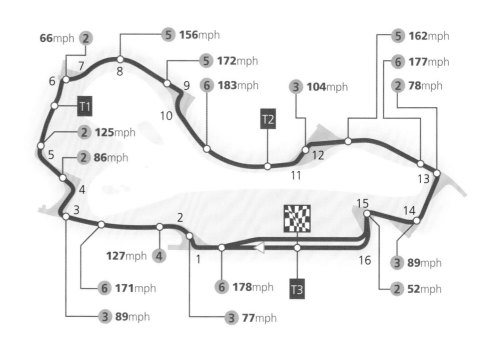

	PRACTICE 1		
	Driver	**Time**	**Laps**
1	M Schumacher	1m25.127s	4
2	R Barrichello	1m25.361s	9
3	J Trulli	1m27.025s	10
4	D Coulthard	1m27.264s	5
5	F Alonso	1m27.359s	14
6	JP Montoya	1m27.462s	12
7	R Schumacher	1m27.675s	11
8	J Button	1m27.867s	7
9	A Davidson	1m27.921s	25
10	M Webber	1m28.089s	6
11	R Zonta	1m28.118s	17
12	K Räikkönen	1m28.233s	5
13	T Sato	1m28.874s	6
14	C da Matta	1m28.955s	11
15	G Fisichella	1m29.120s	6
16	O Panis	1m29.169s	12
17	N Heidfeld	1m29.826s	11
18	B Wirdheim	1m30.033s	23
19	C Klien	1m30.046s	7
20	G Pantano	1m30.100s	18
21	T Glock	1m30.618s	11
22	Z Baumgartner	1m32.886s	14
23	G Bruni	1m33.236s	8
24	F Massa	no time	0
(Bas Leinders unable to get super licence in time)			

	PRACTICE 2		
	Driver	**Time**	**Laps**
1	M Schumacher	1m24.718s	14
2	R Barrichello	1m24.826s	21
3	J Trulli	1m25.757s	22
4	J Button	1m25.786s	15
5	F Alonso	1m25.853s	22
6	R Schumacher	1m25.882s	26
7	JP Montoya	1m26.206s	18
8	D Coulthard	1m26.215s	16
9	M Webber	1m26.312s	17
10	K Räikkönen	1m26.579s	18
11	G Fisichella	1m26.601s	27
12	T Sato	1m26.967s	13
13	F Massa	1m26.969s	24
14	R Zonta	1m27.155s	24
15	A Davidson	1m27.516s	11
16	C da Matta	1m27.710s	11
17	C Klien	1m27.724s	18
18	O Panis	1m27.807s	16
19	N Heidfeld	1m27.826s	14
20	B Wirdheim	1m28.781s	29
21	G Bruni	1m28.991s	18
22	Z Baumgartner	1m29.708s	9
23	G Pantano	1m30.061s	17
24	T Glock	1m30.291s	4

	PRACTICE 3		
	Driver	**Time**	**Laps**
1	M Schumacher	1m25.786s	13
2	R Barrichello	1m26.159s	8
3	JP Montoya	1m26.195s	13
4	R Schumacher	1m26.390s	11
5	D Coulthard	1m26.428s	5
6	F Alonso	1m26.610s	7
7	K Räikkönen	1m26.725s	6
8	M Webber	1m26.804s	5
9	J Trulli	1m26.817s	14
10	J Button	1m26.995s	11
11	O Panis	1m27.107s	16
12	C da Matta	1m27.717s	14
13	G Fisichella	1m27.744s	9
14	F Massa	1m28.341s	15
15	T Sato	1m28.438s	12
16	C Klien	1m28.572s	7
17	G Pantano	1m30.057s	13
18	N Heidfeld	1m30.233s	13
19	G Bruni	1m31.310s	12
20	Z Baumgartner	1m32.295s	14

	PRACTICE 4		
	Driver	**Time**	**Laps**
1	M Schumacher	1m25.093s	13
2	JP Montoya	1m25.255s	9
3	R Schumacher	1m25.628s	9
4	R Barrichello	1m25.649s	12
5	F Alonso	1m25.908s	11
6	O Panis	1m25.916s	14
7	J Trulli	1m25.927s	9
8	M Webber	1m26.066s	11
9	K Räikkönen	1m26.127s	8
10	D Coulthard	1m26.133s	11
11	J Button	1m26.403s	14
12	C da Matta	1m26.597s	17
13	C Klien	1m27.088s	14
14	F Massa	1m27.172s	13
15	G Fisichella	1m27.195s	12
16	T Sato	1m27.592s	9
17	N Heidfeld	1m27.755s	14
18	G Pantano	1m28.825s	12
19	G Bruni	1m30.496s	16
20	Z Baumgartner	1m31.763s	13

Best sectors – Qualifying			Speed trap – Qualifying		
Sector 1	M Schumacher	28.168s	1	G Fisichella	198.040mph
Sector 2	M Schumacher	22.519s	2	R Barrichello	197.543mph
Sector 3	R Barrichello	33.554s	3	M Schumacher	196.984mph

Michael Schumacher
"A perfect race but a tough one in the early stages, when Rubens was pushing me hard. I knew we would be competitive but I didn't expect this performance."

Juan Pablo Montoya
"I didn't take advantage of my third place on the grid. I went off track at Turn 1 trying to defend my position from Alonso and lost four places. Overtaking wasn't easy."

Kimi Räikkönen
"I stalled at the start and lost places but managed to regain most of them during the first couple of corners. Unfortunately I retired early with an engine failure."

Fernando Alonso
"I made a great start despite Montoya forcing me onto the grass. I found myself third after he outbraked himself and from then on it was a pretty easy race."

Jenson Button
"My start wasn't great and a refuelling delay meant Ralf passed me in the pits. Then Juan got by on track. But it was good to finish in the points in the first race."

Rubens Barrichello
"I was happy with my start and tried to pass Michael into Turn 1, but it was too risky. I pushed him hard but then I started having brake problems so I backed off."

Ralf Schumacher
"I wasn't happy with the result even though I made up four places from my grid position. The team did an excellent job in the pits but we were a second off Ferrari."

David Coulthard
"The one point we achieved was little consolation after a very unsatisfying weekend for us. I gained places at the start but eighth was all we could manage."

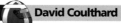

Jarno Trulli
"Overall, it was a disappointing race from my perspective. I got a very good start but Sato hit me and damaged the diffuser and the car then lacked grip. It was tough."

Takuma Sato
"It was quite a busy race. The start was good but I was squeezed into Turn 1 and hit Trulli's Renault, damaging my nose cone. We changed it at the second stop."

POSITIONS LAP BY LAP

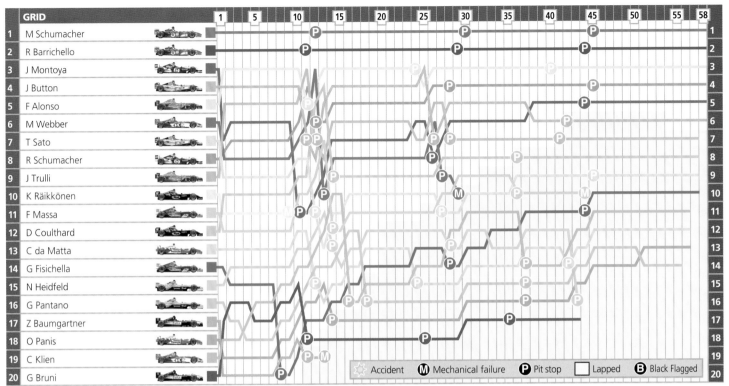

GRID				1	5	10	15	20	25	30	35	40	45	50	55	58	
1	M Schumacher																1
2	R Barrichello																2
3	J Montoya																3
4	J Button																4
5	F Alonso																5
6	M Webber																6
7	T Sato																7
8	R Schumacher																8
9	J Trulli																9
10	K Räikkönen																10
11	F Massa																11
12	D Coulthard																12
13	C da Matta																13
14	G Fisichella																14
15	N Heidfeld																15
16	G Pantano																16
17	Z Baumgartner																17
18	O Panis																18
19	C Klien																19
20	G Bruni																20

Accident ⓜ Mechanical failure ⓟ Pit stop ☐ Lapped Ⓑ Black Flagged

QUALIFYING

	Driver	Pre-qual time	Pos	Time
1	M Schumacher	1m25.301s	2	1m24.408s
2	R Barrichello	1m25.992s	8	1m24.482s
3	JP Montoya	1m25.226s	1	1m24.998s
4	J Button	1m25.898s	6	1m24.998s
5	F Alonso	1m25.928s	7	1m25.699s
6	M Webber	1m26.232s	9	1m25.805s
7	T Sato	1m26.737s	11	1m25.851s
8	R Schumacher	1m25.445s	3	1m25.925s
9	J Trulli	1m27.357s	15	1m26.290s
10	K Räikkönen	1m25.592s	4	1m26.297s
11	F Massa	1m26.833s	12	1m27.065s
12	D Coulthard	1m25.652s	5	1m27.294s
13	C da Matta	1m28.274s	17	1m27.823s
14	G Fisichella	1m26.286s	10	1m27.845s
15	N Heidfeld	1m27.469s	16	1m28.178s
16	G Pantano	1m29.156s	18	1m30.140s
17	Z Baumgartner	1m32.606s	20	1m30.681s
18	O Panis	1m27.253s	13	no time
19	C Klien	1m27.258s	14	no time
20	G Bruni	1m30.912s	19	no time

RACE

	Driver	Car	Laps	Time	Fastest	Avg. mph	Stops
1	M Schumacher	Ferrari F2004	58	1h24m15.757s	1m24.125s	136.093	3
2	R Barrichello	Ferrari F2004	58	1h24m29.362s	1m24.179s	135.728	3
3	F Alonso	Renault R24	58	1h24m50.430s	1m25.086s	135.166	3
4	R Schumacher	Williams-BMW FW26	58	1h25m16.180s	1m25.824s	134.486	3
5	JP Montoya	Williams-BMW FW26	58	1h25m24.293s	1m25.286s	134.273	3
6	J Button	BAR-Honda 006	58	1h25m26.355s	1m25.982s	134.219	3
7	J Trulli	Renault R24	57	1h24m16.785s	1m26.275s	133.720	3
8	D Coulthard	McLaren-Mercedes MP4-19	57	1h24m21.176s	1m26.328s	132.603	2
9	T Sato	BAR-Honda 006	57	1h24m44.971s	1m26.077s	132.978	3
10	G Fisichella	Sauber-Petronas C23	57	1h25m22.074s	1m26.282s	132.015	3
11	C Klien	Jaguar-Cosworth R5	56	1h24m34.124s	1m27.840s	130.925	2
12	C da Matta	Toyota TF104	56	1h24m41.762s	1m27.820s	130.728	3
13	O Panis	Toyota TF104	56	1h25m22.928s	1m27.807s	129.677	2
14	G Pantano	Jordan-Ford EJ14	55	1h24m16.656s	1m28.523s	129.031	2
R	F Massa	Sauber-Petronas C23	44	Engine	1m26.846s		2
R	N Heidfeld	Jordan-Ford EJ14	43	Clutch	1m27.503s		3
NC	G Bruni	Minardi-Cosworth PS04	43	1h25m15.517s	1m30.161s		3
R	M Webber	Jaguar-Cosworth R5	29	Gearbox	1m25.952s		2
R	Z Baumgartner	Minardi-Cosworth PS04	13	Engine	1m30.621s		1
R	K Räikkönen	McLaren-Mercedes MP4-19	9	Engine	1m27.936s		0

CHAMPIONSHIP

	Driver	Pts
1	M Schumacher	10
2	R Barrichello	8
3	F Alonso	6
4	R Schumacher	5
5	JP Montoya	4
6	J Button	3
7	J Trulli	2
8	D Coulthard	1

	Constructor	Pts
1	Ferrari	18
2	Williams-BMW	9
3	Renault	8
4	BAR-Honda	3
5	McLaren-Mercedes	1

Fastest Lap
M Schumacher 1m24.125s,
on lap 29 (141.010mph)
New lap record

Fastest through speed trap
F Massa 201.261mph
Slowest through speed trap
G Pantano 192.870mph

Fastest pit stop
F Alonso 20.294s
Slowest pit stop
G Bruni 17m36.035s

Giancarlo Fisichella
"I lost a lot of time early in the race behind Heidfeld who was driving very defensively and I knew I was much quicker. Once I got by I was immediately able to prove this."

Mark Webber
"Disappointing not to finish my home race but these things happen. I lost sixth and seventh gears and had to retire. Before then we were competitive behind Montoya."

Olivier Panis
"It was a disappointing start to the season for us. After our pre-season testing I really expected us to be in a better position. We were far away from the top teams."

Nick Heidfeld
"We noticed something wrong with the clutch and at the pit stop it didn't work at all – the car just kept pushing and I hit two mechanics. I retired thanks to the clutch."

Gianmaria Bruni
"I made a good start, passing Zsolt, Panis and Klien on the first lap but then around lap 20 the engine started to misfire, so I stopped for repairs until the final 10 laps."

Felipe Massa
"I had a great fight early in the race with Kimi and managed to overtake him. I then spun on lap 19 after picking up understeer and later retired with an engine problem."

Christian Klien
"To finish my first Grand Prix in 11th place was fantastic. My start was slightly slower than I had hoped, but I managed to stay out of trouble and then overtook Panis."

Cristiano da Matta
"It was a difficult race for us. The car's performance was not good at all, but at least it meant we were under no illusions from then on and the car was reliable."

Giorgio Pantano
"Finishing the race was the target for this, my first Grand Prix, and I did it. We kept ourselves relatively close to the field and finished just two laps down on Michael."

Zsolt Baumgartner
"Things went well until lap 8 when I started struggling with engine problems. The guys tried to fix it and I went back out but it stopped altogether on lap 16."

MADE TO FIGHT

Ferrari's dominance in the opening round wasn't repeated in Malaysia as Montoya made his Williams fly as he fought hard to topple Schumacher

Win number 72 wasn't as easy for Michael Schumacher as 71 had been; there had at least been someone in his mirrors from time to time. And when that someone was Juan Pablo Montoya, Michael knew it was best not to offer him even half a chance. But it appeared to be a delicate balance that Michael was treading; he certainly had the necessary pace and drove for much of the distance with something in hand. But if push came to shove and he had to battle it out, did his tyres have the consistency? That was an unknown on what is historically a Bridgestone bogey circuit and so the World Champion spent almost all of the race monitoring the progress of his Williams rival and setting his pace accordingly, keeping himself tantalisingly just out of reach.

It might have been different. A brief shower of rain just before the start tilted things very much in Michelin's favour for the first three laps or so and, in hindsight, that was Montoya's only real window of opportunity. The Colombian was unable to capitalise because he'd been held up during the first lap by Schumacher's team-mate Rubens Barrichello, who was struggling even more than Michael in the wet on account of running a harder compound of Bridgestone tyre. Afterwards, Montoya was irate at what he saw as Ferrari team tactics late in the race, but actually the Brazilian had unintentionally done his best work for the reigning World Champion on that opening lap, protecting him from Montoya in the one brief window when the Williams was a true danger.

Michael Schumacher was made to work for his 72nd win, which is why he's so happy as he and Montoya spray Button

ROUND **2**

MALAYSIA
2004 FORMULA 1™
PETRONAS MALAYSIAN
GRAND PRIX
Kuala Lumpur

LAP BY LAP
ACTION

56 laps / 193 miles

Michael Schumacher and Barrichello lead Montoya on lap 1

Start and first lap

Räikkönen is caught out by the damp track and spins on the parade lap, but he's able to retake his grid position. At the start, Mark Webber gets away very slowly from the outside of the front row, and at the first corner, it's a Ferrari 1–2 with Michael Schumacher heading Barrichello. Montoya slips into third position, with Räikkönen fourth and Button and Trulli disputing fifth. At the end of the first lap, Michael Schumacher leads Barrichello by 2s, Webber crosses the line in eighth place. Alonso has advanced from the back of the grid to ninth place.

Coulthard, Ralf Schumacher and Webber fight for position on lap 2

Laps 2 to 4

On lap 2, with half the track dry and the other half damp, Barrichello runs wide allowing Montoya and Räikkönen to move up to second and third. Montoya closes quickly to within a second of Schumacher. The Trulli–Button battle continues with Jenson getting ahead. Further back Ralf Schumacher re-passes Webber while Sato has a spin and drops to 15th. As the track dries on lap 3, Michael Schumacher pulls away, increasing his lead to 1.6s. Montoya pulls away from Räikkönen while Barrichello drops back, followed by Button with Trulli on his tail and Coulthard chasing. Ralf Schumacher is passed by Webber and Alonso. On lap 4, Michael Schumacher sets the fastest lap, increasing his lead. Alonso gets ahead of Webber.

Ralf Schumacher's race was run with a blown engine after 27 laps

Laps 5 to 10

By lap 5, Schumacher has increased his lead to 3.2s. Webber suffers a puncture, and drives slowly to the pits, promoting Ralf Schumacher to ninth. Michael Schumacher pits on lap 9 and Montoya leads with Räikkönen second, Barrichello third and then the Button–Trulli duo in fourth and fifth. Also pitting are Coulthard, Alonso, Massa, Christian Klien and Bruni. On lap 10, Montoya stays in the lead and with Räikkönen, Barrichello and Trulli all pitting, Button moves up to second with Ralf Schumacher third and Michael fourth. Trulli rejoins ahead of Barrichello. Webber pits for a drive-through penalty for speeding in pitlane.

Jenson Button and Kimi Räikkönen tussled for much of the Grand Prix

Laps 11 to 20

Ralf Schumacher pits on lap 11, rejoining in 11th place, behind Alonso. Montoya and Button both pit on lap 12, leaving Michael Schumacher in the lead again. Montoya rejoins behind Räikkönen but then passes him to retake second. Trulli gets ahead of Räikkönen to grab fourth with Button fifth and Barrichello down to sixth. On lap 14, Montoya closes the fluctuating gap to 4.6s, Schumacher losing time passing Webber.

Räikkönen clambers out after his McLaren also suffers engine failure

Laps 21 to 30

Alonso passes Coulthard on lap 24 to grab sixth place, but both men pit at the end of the lap. Alonso takes on a lot of fuel and drops behind Coulthard, Massa and Sato. Webber spins off into retirement. On lap 25, the second round of pit stops continues with Räikkönen pitting, this allowing Barrichello to move to fourth and Ralf Schumacher to fifth. Kimi rejoins in sixth. The top three all pit on lap 26. Barrichello thus leads, with Michael rejoining second ahead of Montoya, Ralf Schumacher and Trulli. Räikkönen is sixth. On lap 28, after leading for two laps Barrichello pits and leads again. Ralf Schumacher retires with a blown engine, promoting Button to fourth and Räikkönen to fifth. Trulli is sixth. Montoya again begins closing on Schumacher.

Michael Schumacher is greeted by his exultant pit crew at the finish

Laps 31 to 40

By lap 32, Montoya is 5s behind Schumacher. Further back, Heidfeld hits gear-change trouble and retires on lap 34. Montoya fades again on lap 39 and heads for pitlane. He rejoins in fifth place behind Button, Räikkönen and Barrichello. Schumacher, Button and Räikkönen all stop on lap 40. Michael comes out in the lead but Montoya is stuck behind Barrichello.

Lap 41 to the finish

Räikkönen retires on lap 41 with a blown engine, promoting Trulli to fifth with Coulthard sixth. On lap 44, Barrichello pits but by then Montoya is more than 9s behind Schumacher and settles for second. Barrichello rejoins fourth. Panis drives straight through the pits on lap 45 and rejoins. He's later given a drive-through penalty for speeding in pitlane. On lap 53, Sato retires with engine failure. At the end of lap 56, Michael Schumacher takes his 72nd win, with Montoya second and Jenson Button third, delighted with his first F1 podium finish.

INSIDE LINE
JUAN PABLO MONTOYA

This went pretty well for us generally, but we just weren't quite at Ferrari's level. There were a couple of things that hurt us – one at the beginning of the race and one near the end – that had they not happened might have allowed me to beat Michael, but we'll never know.

I think we had a tyre advantage with Michelin, even though it mightn't have looked it. We had good race pace throughout a stint and I think Ferrari just had enough of a car advantage that Michael was able to go fast enough to stay ahead. However, I'd say we were more consistent and I think that was down to the tyres.

My start to the race was much better than in Australia. The car moved off the line very quickly but I then had to swerve because Webber had bogged down and when you swerve you lose momentum. Had it not been for that I think I could probably have beaten Rubens into the first corner and the way the damp surface was playing into our hands with the Michelins, I'm sure I could have attacked Michael and got past. Basically, I had three or four laps when conditions favoured us in which to get past. As it was, I had

to spend the first lap getting by Rubens and I arrived on Michael's tail maybe one lap too late. Actually, I thought there was an opportunity to pass him on the third lap but it was a bit marginal and so I left it, thinking I'd get a better chance. However, as it turned out, I never did because the track began to dry and then there wasn't very much between us.

After our third and final stops I came out about 3.5s behind Michael, but then I was held up by Massa in the Sauber – the blue Ferrari! – and that was my lap on new tyres on which I would normally expect to make up around a second on the Bridgestone runners. The lap after that Ferrari used a bit of strategy by having Rubens hold me up. I went to pass him but straight away he blocked me. It was into Turn 4, and he just closed the door and backed off his pace, then the lap before he came in he pushed again. So I lost a bit of time and there were only 12 laps to go, so I just backed off and cruised to the flag. Without that, I think the end of the race could've been very interesting because our tyres were just getting better and better.

Q THE BIG QUESTION

Did Ferrari use team tactics by having Rubens Barrichello prevent Michael being attacked by Montoya in the final stint?

Montoya believed so. "I don't think it's good for racing what they did there," fumed Montoya afterwards. "They spoilt what could have been a very exciting finish."

Montoya had just made his third and final stop and then on his first flying lap on new rubber – the lap on which the relative characteristics of his Michelins and Schumacher's Bridgestones might have been expected to give the Colombian driver a big advantage – he was held up by Felipe Massa in one of the Ferrari-powered Saubers. A lap after that, he encountered Barrichello, running in a temporary second place on account of not having made his final pit stop yet. After having rebuffed the Williams into Turn 4, Barrichello's next two laps were around 1.4s slower than those immediately preceding them. "The first of them I was delayed lapping Fisichella," explained Barrichello, "and then there was a misunderstanding as we came to lap Baumgartner as he didn't move the way I was anticipating. It's bullshit to say I was deliberately holding Juan back. Obviously I didn't want to let him past, but the only reason I was slow on those two laps was because of lapping."

"I'm sure Rubens didn't do it deliberately," said Williams' Sam Michael, "and no I cannot see that it cost us victory. It's one thing catching Michael, quite another getting past. At the point where Juan was, I'm sure he was really wound up in the fight and it was just a bit of emotion coming out."

Barrichello held off Montoya late in the race, dropping his pace before his final pit stop

Montoya was able to fly
in the laps immediately
after his pit stops, then
Schumacher came good

SAM MICHAEL
WILLIAMS
TECHNICAL
DIRECTOR

If you look at our pace with Juan compared to Michael Schumacher after the first two pit stops you can see we were running quicker than them for a while. In the six laps after the first stops Juan got a 6.4s gap down to 3.3s. But then Ferrari just seemed to up their pace and we couldn't go with them. It was the same after the second stops when Juan got the gap down to 3.7s from around 8s, but Michael still had enough in hand to make sure he was in front at the final stop.

It could be to do with the respective compound choices of our Michelins and their Bridgestones, and maybe they had a compound that was a little too soft for them and which therefore had a bit of degradation in the first few laps. But it's difficult to read in stuff like that, as there are so many possible explanations and you have only half the data – your own – to work out what is driving the patterns you're seeing. For example, the point on lap 19 when Michael suddenly began going around 0.5s faster than he had been doing might simply have been a reflection that he had been playing with us, looking after his tyres while keeping

just out of our reach and when we got a bit too close he responded.

Certainly, after the second stops, you saw that gap see-saw a little more. We had the traditional first lap performance advantage from our Michelins and that was reflected in Juan's first flying lap of 1m 34.2s, the fastest of the race and a full 0.6s faster than Michael's fastest. Juan is particularly good on cold tyres and that was a superb lap. It ate up some of the advantage Michael had built up at the end of the previous stint, but after that it appeared as if Michael was just using Juan's pace as a guide to his own and when we got near the final stops he suddenly upped his pace by 0.5s – and again we couldn't respond.

My guess is that they were a little marginal on tyre degradation and wanted to go no faster than they had to and our pace determined theirs. However, ultimately our pace wasn't quite good enough to take them into their tyre degradation window.

After first pit stops		
Lap	Schumacher (Ferrari)	Montoya (Williams)
14	1m 36.4s	1m 34.6s
15	1m 36.7s	1m 36.3s
16	1m 36.4s	1m 35.9s
17	1m 36.0s	1m 35.8s
18	1m 36.2s	1m 36.0s
Gap had come down from 6.4s to 3.3s. Now Ferrari ups pace		
19	1m 35.6s	1m 36.2s
20	1m 36.2s	1m 36.0s
21	1m 35.9s	1m 36.7s
22	1m 35.4s	1m 36.3s
23	1m 35.0s	1m 36.1s
24	1m 35.1s	1m 35.9s
As each makes his in-lap, the gap is up to 8.2s		

DAVID PITCHFORTH
JAGUAR MANAGING DIRECTOR

Mark Webber's exertions in qualifying second were for naught as he fumbled his getaway

To have qualified Mark Webber on the front row with our budget, against cars that cost twice as much to build, stands as a great achievement for Jaguar Racing. Unfortunately, we had a starting problem that caught us out under the full glare of publicity of that front row, and that too comes down to the depth of expertise and facilities that a full budget buys you.

The perception is that our car was quick in Malaysia but afterwards lost performance. Actually, we maintained our level of performance but other teams improved theirs. The reason for that is the way we decided to launch R5. We did the car early and developed it as much as we could before Melbourne and that sort of broke the mould of how it's usually done. Once we got back to Europe, as everyone who had come up with their cars later put their developments on, so we got leapfrogged. This left us out of phase with them in our development and that benefitted us when we arrived in Malaysia.

The background to the start problem, where both our cars were very slow away, goes back to the rule change banning launch control for 2004. In previous years, we had a really good launch control system and it's now obvious that we didn't fully understand what that had been doing for us. What launch control does for you is to learn all about the characteristics, say, of the clutch and it's all in there and learnt. When we went to manual starts and having the driver do the clutch bite point, it took some time to understand all that. The launch control had been covering up some sins we didn't know we had. If there's enough money to test extensively you find that out before one of your cars is sitting on the front row of the grid.

Mark did a superb job for us, and not only here. There are two things about him. One is how leading and motivating a team is hard-wired into him. The other is his performance in the car and he's particularly brilliant at one-lap qualifying.

RACE RESULTS
MALAYSIA
KUALA LUMPUR

RACE DATE March 21st
CIRCUIT LENGTH 3.444 miles
NO. OF LAPS 56
RACE DISTANCE 192.879 miles
WEATHER hot, humid, overcast, 35°C
TRACK TEMP 45°C
RACE ATTENDANCE 90,000
LAP RECORD Juan Pablo Montoya,
1m 34.223s, 131.595mph, 2004

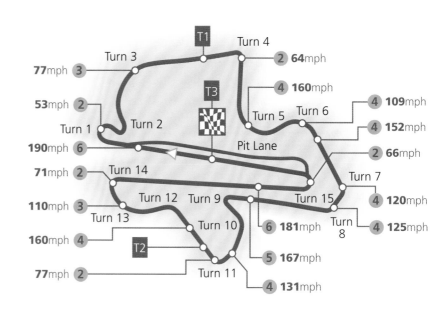

PRACTICE 1			
	Driver	**Time**	**Laps**
1	M Schumacher	1m34.437s	11
2	R Barrichello	1m35.380s	8
3	A Davidson	1m35.970s	21
4	R Zonta	1m36.147s	21
5	R Schumacher	1m36.229s	11
6	K Räikkönen	1m36.314s	5
7	M Webber	1m36.478s	6
8	JP Montoya	1m36.606s	9
9	J Button	1m37.018s	5
10	F Alonso	1m37.119s	13
11	D Coulthard	1m37.438s	4
12	O Panis	1m37.590s	12
13	J Trulli	1m37.816s	10
14	G Fisichella	1m37.995s	5
15	T Sato	1m38.023s	6
16	B Wirdheim	1m38.086s	18
17	C Klien	1m38.554s	11
18	C da Matta	1m38.734s	11
19	T Glock	1m38.788s	18
20	N Heidfeld	1m38.831s	8
21	G Pantano	1m39.860s	14
22	G Bruni	1m41.149s	6
23	Z Baumgartner	1m42.556s	15
24	F Massa	1m42.718s	5
25	B Leinders	1m43.424s	15

PRACTICE 2			
	Driver	**Time**	**Laps**
1	K Räikkönen	1m34.395s	17
2	R Schumacher	1m34.693s	24
3	M Webber	1m35.054s	20
4	M Schumacher	1m35.094s	22
5	JP Montoya	1m35.100s	23
6	J Trulli	1m35.115s	20
7	F Massa	1m35.288s	21
8	F Alonso	1m35.300s	20
9	D Coulthard	1m35.301s	13
10	R Barrichello	1m35.373s	19
11	J Button	1m35.407s	19
12	O Panis	1m35.524s	19
13	R Zonta	1m35.850s	27
14	C Klien	1m35.996s	19
15	T Sato	1m36.292s	6
16	G Fisichella	1m36.353s	28
17	A Davidson	1m36.708s	5
18	B Wirdheim	1m36.883s	21
19	C da Matta	1m36.907s	7
20	N Heidfeld	1m37.725s	19
21	G Bruni	1m37.818s	19
22	Z Baumgartner	1m38.588s	10
23	T Glock	1m38.796s	27
24	G Pantano	1m39.324s	16
25	B Leinders	1m41.485s	23

PRACTICE 3			
	Driver	**Time**	**Laps**
1	M Schumacher	1m33.391s	7
2	F Alonso	1m34.175s	12
3	R Schumacher	1m34.239s	8
4	R Barrichello	1m34.362s	9
5	D Coulthard	1m34.415s	9
6	J Trulli	1m34.482s	14
7	JP Montoya	1m34.547s	12
8	M Webber	1m34.770s	5
9	J Button	1m34.839s	11
10	G Fisichella	1m35.516s	9
11	C da Matta	1m35.678s	4
12	T Sato	1m35.697s	16
13	O Panis	1m35.697s	10
14	F Massa	1m35.813s	10
15	C Klien	1m36.106s	8
16	N Heidfeld	1m37.194s	9
17	G Pantano	1m38.302s	11
18	Z Baumgartner	1m39.013s	13
19	G Bruni	1m39.209s	11
20	K Räikkönen	no time	4

PRACTICE 4			
	Driver	**Time**	**Laps**
1	M Schumacher	1m33.526s	11
2	JP Montoya	1m33.563s	8
3	R Schumacher	1m33.973s	8
4	J Trulli	1m34.041s	12
5	R Barrichello	1m34.061s	9
6	J Button	1m34.128s	13
7	K Räikkönen	1m34.163s	10
8	D Coulthard	1m34.181s	10
9	F Alonso	1m34.194s	10
10	M Webber	1m34.381s	12
11	O Panis	1m34.929s	16
12	F Massa	1m34.943s	5
13	C Klien	1m34.953s	16
14	G Fisichella	1m35.036s	10
15	T Sato	1m35.144s	13
16	C da Matta	1m35.441s	15
17	N Heidfeld	1m36.607s	11
18	G Pantano	1m38.059s	12
19	G Bruni	1m38.554s	13
20	Z Baumgartner	1m39.893s	13

Best sectors – Qualifying			Speed trap – Qualifying	
Sector 1	M Schumacher	24.064s	1 M Schumacher	192.572mph
Sector 2	M Schumacher	30.607s	2 R Barrichello	192.510mph
Sector 3	K Räikkönen	38.400s	3 R Schumacher	192.075mph

Michael Schumacher
"Tough fight all the way to the end, but I was quick enough when I needed to be at the start and end of each stint. It was pressure all the way from Montoya."

Juan Pablo Montoya
"I had a good first few laps and got in front of Rubens. Then I had quite a smooth race. Towards the end I was trying to catch Michael, my car feeling better and better."

Kimi Räikkönen
"It's never nice not to finish a race. We were close to a podium until we struggled with a fuel nozzle in my second stop. A few laps later my transmission broke."

Fernando Alonso
"I was pleased to score two points after I had spun in qualifying. The car was competitive but tricky to drive: the balance wasn't particularly good in the race."

Jenson Button
"There are no words to describe the feeling of your first podium. This one had been a long time coming. It was a tough race but so enjoyable being competitive."

Rubens Barrichello
"I pushed hard all race long, doing as much as I could. I ran a harder tyre than Michael and it didn't pay off. I lost a few places as they came up to temperature."

Ralf Schumacher
"I got trapped in traffic and fell to ninth at the start. I tried to overtake Webber on lap 3 but he didn't give me enough space. My front wing was damaged in the contact."

David Coulthard
"I made a good start, gained a few places and got involved in some quite exciting battles. I found it difficult to hold the car in the fast corners and very nearly lost it."

Jarno Trulli
"Finishing fifth was satisfying given that I started eighth. I got a good start but touched Jenson in Turn 1. I battled with him and Rubens until my tyres started to grain."

Takuma Sato
"An engine failure three laps from the end was very disappointing. The car was strong and we had good race pace. It was great to be racing with Alonso at the end."

POSITIONS LAP BY LAP

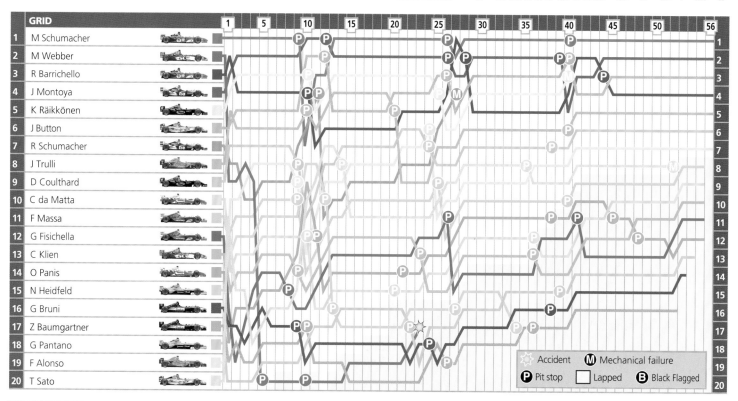

	GRID	
1	M Schumacher	
2	M Webber	
3	R Barrichello	
4	J Montoya	
5	K Räikkönen	
6	J Button	
7	R Schumacher	
8	J Trulli	
9	D Coulthard	
10	C da Matta	
11	F Massa	
12	G Fisichella	
13	C Klien	
14	O Panis	
15	N Heidfeld	
16	G Bruni	
17	Z Baumgartner	
18	G Pantano	
19	F Alonso	
20	T Sato	

Legend: ☼ Accident   Ⓜ Mechanical failure   Ⓟ Pit stop   ☐ Lapped   Ⓑ Black Flagged

QUALIFYING

	Driver	Pre-qual time	Pos	Time
1	M Schumacher	1m33.865s	4	1m33.074s
2	M Webber	1m34.016s	5	1m33.715s
3	R Barrichello	1m34.132s	6	1m33.756s
4	JP Montoya	1m34.941s	11	1m34.054s
5	K Räikkönen	1m33.452s	3	1m34.164s
6	J Button	1m34.528s	8	1m34.221s
7	R Schumacher	1m34.777s	9	1m34.235s
8	J Trulli	1m33.264s	2	1m34.413s
9	D Coulthard	1m34.321s	7	1m34.602s
10	C da Matta	1m35.684s	16	1m34.917s
11	F Massa	1m35.132s	13	1m35.039s
12	G Fisichella	1m34.877s	10	1m35.061s
13	C Klien	1m35.618s	15	1m35.158s
14	O Panis	1m35.247s	14	1m35.617s
15	N Heidfeld	1m36.769s	17	1m36.569s
16	G Bruni	1m38.729s	18	1m38.577s
17	Z Baumgartner	1m39.805s	19	1m39.272s
18	G Pantano	no time	20	1m39.902s
19	F Alonso	1m33.193s	1	no time
20	T Sato	1m34.971s	12	no time

RACE

	Driver	Car	Laps	Time	Fastest	Avg. mph	Stops
1	M Schumacher	Ferrari F2004	56	1h31m07.490s	1m34.819s	126.998	3
2	JP Montoya	Williams-BMW FW26	56	1h31m12.512s	1m34.223s	126.882	3
3	J Button	BAR-Honda 006	56	1h31m19.058s	1m34.967s	126.730	3
4	R Barrichello	Ferrari F2004	56	1h31m21.106s	1m35.350s	126.683	3
5	J Trulli	Renault R24	56	1h31m44.850s	1m35.039s	126.136	3
6	D Coulthard	McLaren-Mercedes MP4-19	56	1h32m00.588s	1m35.852s	125.777	3
7	F Alonso	Renault R24	56	1h32m15.367s	1m35.888s	125.411	2
8	F Massa	Sauber-Petronas C23	55	1h31m27.195s	1m36.570s	124.282	3
9	C da Matta	Toyota TF104	55	1h31m33.594s	1m36.544s	124.138	3
10	C Klien	Jaguar-Cosworth R5	55	1h32m07.028s	1m37.031s	123.387	3
11	G Fisichella	Sauber-Petronas C23	55	1h32m24.626s	1m36.675s	122.995	3
12	O Panis	Toyota TF104	55	1h32m38.018s	1m35.951s	122.698	5
13	G Pantano	Jordan-Ford EJ14	54	1h32m23.137s	1m39.527s	120.791	2
14	G Bruni	Minardi-Cosworth PS04	53	1h31m29.590s	1m39.911s	119.711	3
15	T Sato	BAR-Honda 006	52	Engine	1m35.679s	125.094	2
16	Z Baumgartner	Minardi-Cosworth PS04	52	1h31m11.143s	1m40.123s	117.848	3
R	K Räikkönen	McLaren-Mercedes MP4-19	40	Engine	1m35.156s		3
R	N Heidfeld	Jordan-Ford EJ14	34	Gearbox	1m37.433s		4
R	R Schumacher	Williams-BMW FW26	27	Engine	1m35.607s		1
R	M Webber	Jaguar-Cosworth R5	23	Spun	1m36.922s		2

CHAMPIONSHIP

	Driver	Pts
1	M Schumacher	20
2	R Barrichello	13
3	JP Montoya	12
4	J Button	9
5	F Alonso	8
6	J Trulli	6
7	R Schumacher	5
8	D Coulthard	4
9	F Massa	1

	Constructor	Pts
1	Ferrari	33
2	Williams-BMW	17
3	Renault	14
4	BAR-Honda	9
5	McLaren-Mercedes	4
6	Sauber-Petronas	1

Fastest Lap
JP Montoya 1m34.223s,
on lap 28 (131.595mph)
New lap record

Fastest through speed trap
R Schumacher   199.397mph
Slowest through speed trap
G Bruni   190.884mph

Fastest pit stop
J Trulli   24.763s
Slowest pit stop
G Fisichella   1m03.895s

 Giancarlo Fisichella

"I had moments in the first two corners and lost places, so we changed our strategy. The engine stalled in my second and third stops so I lost more time."

 **Mark Webber**

"I had a bad start and things didn't get much better. After overtaking Ralf twice he hit me from behind. I got a puncture, then a drive-through penalty and finally spun."

Olivier Panis

"My start was good but then someone pushed me and I spun. I was running strongly in 10th until a radio problem led to an unscheduled pit stop – a real pity."

Nick Heidfeld

"I had to retire after I got stuck in fifth gear. Realistically the race was over for me after no fuel went into the car in my first pit stop. Still, our pace was quite good."

 **Gianmaria Bruni**

"It was a tough race, particularly as I had to drive the last 30 laps without power steering but the balance was okay. It was my first 'full distance' Grand Prix finish."

Felipe Massa

"It was very difficult on new tyres on out-laps. That's why I had a moment in Turn 13 around lap 42 – I just couldn't hold the steering wheel! Michael just missed me."

Christian Klien

"My start wasn't good but I did actually enjoy the race. The rain made the first few laps difficult and I was pleased to stay on track. A sticking fuel cap cost me places."

Cristiano da Matta

"It was quite a difficult race. I suffered a lot of understeer and the adjustments we made during pit stops didn't help. I lost places running wide at Turn 4 at the start."

Giorgio Pantano

"A difficult weekend for me began with a problem in qualifying so I started from the pit lane. My drinks bottle failed in the race so it was quite exhausting by the finish."

Zsolt Baumgartner

"I struggled with a chassis imbalance – the front end was quite good but the rear was unstable. I passed Gimmi at the start but made a mistake and he got me back."

DESERT STORM

BAR looked to have the upper hand on Formula One's first visit to Bahrain, but Ferrari found their feet and came good for their second 1–2 finish of the year

It may have looked effortless as Ferrari cruised to a 1–2 in the very first Bahrain Grand Prix, with Michael Schumacher maintaining his 100% record for the season, but beneath the still waters was some frantic paddling.

Ferrari had been forced into a very uncharacteristic panic on Friday evening as their brake wear was revealed as far higher than their simulations had predicted, higher than they could hope to complete a race distance on. New bigger brake ducts were built up overnight but, even then, things were a little marginal. The aerodynamic penalty they brought meant that pole position wasn't a given for the Italian team. The respective performance cycles of Bridgestone and Michelin meant that Ferrari could be in real trouble in the race if they failed to secure pole. And all the while Jenson Button's BAR-Honda was putting in some scarily fast times. It took a very special effort from Schumacher to secure pole, despite a major brake-locking moment that would surely have ruined the lap had it been anyone other than Michael at the wheel.

Only then were Ferrari back in their usual comfort zone, able to control their own destiny. Michael duly dominated the race, going only as fast as needed while taking care to be easy on the brakes and not to let his tyres blister. Team-mate Rubens Barrichello stayed vaguely with him until a problem with a cross-threaded wheel nut at a pit stop. It didn't lose him a place, only a few seconds of margin.

It took until the final stint of the race for Button to retrieve the Ferrari-matching speed of his BAR, but he was half a minute behind the red cars by then. Nonetheless, he was mightily pleased with his second consecutive podium, even if it had come only after Juan Pablo Montoya's Williams suffered a late lack of hydraulic pressure.

Formula One as you've never seen it before: Michael Schumacher races through the desert

ROUND **3**

BAHRAIN
2004 FORMULA 1™
GULF AIR BAHRAIN
GRAND PRIX
Bahrain

LAP BY LAP
ACTION

57 laps / 191 miles

The Ferraris of Schumacher and Barrichello lead into the first turn

Start and lap 1

Heidfeld, Baumgartner and Räikkönen start from the back of the grid due to engine changes. Bruni is pushed into pitlane on the parade lap. Then, as the race starts, Michael Schumacher leads with Barrichello second and Montoya resisting a challenge from a fast-starting Trulli to slot into third. Sato and Ralf Schumacher pass the Renault. Button, da Matta, Coulthard, Panis and a fast-starting Webber are next up. But da Matta goes off and is passed by Webber, while Coulthard loses out to Panis. At the end of lap 1, Michael Schumacher is 1.5s clear of Barrichello, with Montoya a further 0.8s behind. Sato is now fourth ahead of Ralf Schumacher, Trulli, Button and Panis. Alonso pits with a damaged front wing.

Up you go... Takuma Sato tips Ralf Schumacher up on two wheels

Laps 2 to 8

On lap 2, Webber passes Coulthard to climb to ninth. Schumacher's lead is up to 4.1s by lap 6, with Barrichello now 6s clear of Montoya. Ralf Schumacher tries to pass Sato on lap 7, but Sato doesn't back off and the cars collide, pitching Schumacher into a spin and letting Trulli pass Sato. Ralf pits for repairs. On lap 8, Räikkönen retires with flames billowing from the back of his car.

Laps 9 to 12

Michael Schumacher, Webber, Coulthard and Massa pit on lap 9. Barrichello assumes the lead while Coulthard and Webber exit the pit lane side-by-side, Webber having to cede to the McLaren. On lap 10, Barrichello, Montoya and Trulli pit, leaving Sato in front with Button second. Montoya's stop confirms that the Williams cars are running less fuel than the Ferraris. Sato pits at the end of lap 11, leaving Button in the lead. On lap 12, Button pits and Michael Schumacher leads again, from Barrichello and Montoya. There's then a big gap back to Trulli, Sato, Button, Heidfeld, Coulthard and Webber.

Fernando Alonso found it almost impossible to pass Mark Webber

Laps 13 to 26

Heidfeld pits on lap 13, promoting Coulthard to seventh and Webber to eighth. On lap 17, Sato damages his front wing on a kerb and is passed for fifth by Button. Sato pits for a new nose and rejoins 14th. Coulthard and Webber pit on lap 23. Coulthard rejoins the race more quickly, ahead of Massa and Sato, but Webber is caught behind them. On lap 24, Michael Schumacher pits and Barrichello leads. Also pitting is Ralf Schumacher, who drops from eighth to 14th. Trulli pits on lap 25 and falls back behind Button. Montoya, Button, Fisichella and Alonso all pit on lap 26.

Takuma Sato and David Coulthard fight over sixth at mid-distance

Laps 27 to 44

Barrichello pits on lap 27 and Michael Schumacher is in the lead once more. Barrichello rejoins second, 12s behind, with Montoya third, Trulli fourth and Button fifth. Coulthard and Sato follow, while Webber and Alonso fight over eighth place. Alonso forces his way through on lap 31 when Webber makes a mistake. Further back, Ralf Schumacher punts Fisichella into a spin and moves ahead, along with da Matta. Sato passes Coulthard to take sixth on lap 33. Then, on lap 37, Sato and Panis make their final stops. Trulli, Coulthard and Webber all pit on lap 38, with Montoya calling in a lap later. Button pits on lap 40, rejoining ahead of Trulli to grab fourth place. Alonso stops and drops from eighth to 10th. Michael Schumacher stops on lap 41, allowing Barrichello back into the lead. Two laps later, Barrichello stops, and Schumacher goes back into the lead. Barrichello rejoins 10s ahead of Montoya, who is 3s ahead of Button.

Coulthard parks at the exit of the pitlane after ineffective repairs

Lap 45 to the finish

Sixth-placed Ralf Schumacher makes his final stop on lap 45, dropping him behind Sato, Alonso and Coulthard. Montoya slows with gearbox trouble on lap 47. Two laps later, Button passes Montoya for third place. Montoya falls behind Trulli on lap 50, while Sato is under pressure from Alonso for sixth. Coulthard pits and, after the team works on the car, the McLaren stops at the end of the pit lane, promoting Ralf Schumacher to eighth. Over the next three laps, Montoya is overtaken by Sato, Alonso, Ralf Schumacher, Webber and Panis, relegating him to 10th place. At the end of lap 57, Michael Schumacher records his third consecutive win. Barrichello finishes second and Button third. The remaining points go to Trulli, Sato, Alonso, Ralf Schumacher and Webber.

Michael Schumacher makes it three wins from three starts

INSIDE LINE
FERNANDO ALONSO

This was a very challenging race for me and although I took a lot of satisfaction in finishing sixth from almost a minute behind at the end of the first lap, I was very surprised by some of the dangerous driving of some of my competitors.

In qualifying, I had a big problem with the brake bias. I lost a lot of time at the first turn as the rear wheels locked up and so I wound more bias to the front. But even then as the lap went on I was still having problems with locking rears and I was putting more front bias on all the time. Then into the final turn I had a big lock-up and I was off the circuit a long way. I managed to get back on, but it ruined my lap. The team later traced the problem, but it all left me two rows off the back of the grid.

I was hoping to use our car's starting advantage to make up a lot of places off the grid, but as I came to pass Christian Klien he squeezed me hard towards the pit wall and I had to back off. Later in the lap I got down inside of him into Turn 4 but he just chopped across me even though I was already there. That damaged my front wing and I had to pit for a new wing at the end of the lap. At the same time, the team fuelled me up and changed me from a three-stop strategy to a two-stop. When I rejoined I was over half a minute behind the tail of the field and had a very heavy fuel load.

I pushed hard and once everyone had made their first stops I was ready to start passing people. The problem was that the car was fast over a lap but slow on the straights, so that made overtaking difficult. It took a few goes to get by Felipe Massa and my next target was Mark Webber. He did a couple of things that surprised me and made me have to take avoiding action, one time chopping across on me as I was already alongside, but in the end I managed to pass him. I quickly caught up to Takuma Sato – I'd made 25s on him since the first stops – but his car was too quick down the straights for me. I spent the last 14 laps trying to pass him, but it didn't work. I was satisfied to have set the race's second fastest lap, just a few tenths slower than Schumacher.

David Coulthard had every reason to look disgruntled with the speed of his MP4-19

Q THE BIG QUESTION

What is wrong at McLaren?

For the third race in succession, the McLaren MP4-19s suffered horrendous races. Kimi Räikkönen retired with his engine spurting out flames after just six of the 57 laps, this after an engine failure in practice had given him the regulation 10-place penalty on the grid. David Coulthard suffered a brake disc failure in practice, qualified 10th, 1.6s off the pace, and then retired from the race with a lack of pneumatic pressure.

A lack of engine reliability meant that lapping in practice also had to be limited, so reducing the team's chances of unlocking some speed from the car. The new Mercedes engine was believed to be well down on horsepower too after a difficult gestation. However, it was about more than just the engine.

Technical Director Adrian Newey later explained the problems with the chassis. "The car tested quite well in the winter," he related, "but as temperatures came up its characteristics changed. The temperatures altered the way the tyres worked and that caught us out."

The latest generation of front Michelins had found grip as the ambient temperature got higher, but the rears were unable to keep up. The car's weight distribution – with too much on the rear – was believed to be at fault and the reasons for that went back to the MP4-19's development from the unraced MP4-18 of 2003, a car that had been devised before race-fuel qualifying was sprung upon a surprised F1 community at the beginning of '03.

The rear suspension geometry exacerbated the problem of rear instability and made the car difficult under braking unless set up so stiffly at the front that there was then an issue of power understeer.

ROSS BRAWN
FERRARI
TECHNICAL
DIRECTOR

I was a little surprised at the ease of this one, I must say. I wouldn't have bet on us getting a 1–2 if you'd asked me on the Friday. At that point, I thought we were going to be in for a very tough time. Our cars were quite consistent, but the BAR was going very quickly indeed. Furthermore, we had a concern with the brakes and that was potentially a major worry.

This being a brand new circuit, we had to prepare based solely on our simulations, including brake wear. You do Turn 4, 6, 8 and 10 and the brakes don't cool but just get hotter and hotter, and by the time you get out of Turn 10 they're really hot. That's actually a thing our predictions didn't show us well. They didn't accumulate the temperature in that period and that has a major impact on wear rates.

It meant that we had to create

some new bigger brake ducts, giving us an all-nighter on Friday. That's an unusual situation for us and there were a few bleary eyes on Saturday. Even with the new ducts there was still a slight concern with Michael. Compared with Rubens, he was running a softer brake material, that gave better, more consistent braking, but wasn't as durable. He tried the harder material in Saturday practice but didn't like it, so we decided we would just have to monitor and manage the situation in the race itself.

Bigger ducts extract quite an aerodynamic performance penalty and really Michael's lap to get pole position was an extraordinary effort. He can still surprise us with some moments of magic that you can't quite believe and this was one of those occasions. His lap forced Montoya into an error trying to beat it and that allowed Rubens to stay on the front row. That really made things a lot easier for us.

It allowed us to control things from the front, meaning that we didn't get caught behind a Michelin car with a very different performance cycle, meaning we could look after our brakes and our tyres, all of which Michael did perfectly. But you can see looking at Button's third stint times, he would have been a big threat had he been able to do that earlier in the race and had he been able to qualify well.

Michael Schumacher and Rubens Barrichello were surprised to turn around Friday's problem

GEOFF WILLIS
BAR TECHNICAL DIRECTOR

During the two practices on Saturday morning we were comfortably quickest with Jenson [Button], and his 1m 29.5s lap in the second of those sessions was by far the fastest anyone managed all weekend. Yet, thereafter, we came nowhere near that.

A few things were driving that anomaly. People might assume that we were simply running light in the Saturday practice but, in fact, we were carrying a very sensible fuel load. The fact that Jenson was so quick led us to think "oh, the others must be running heavier" and so we put more fuel in for qualifying and qualified sixth. Then, come the first stops of the race, we stopped many laps later than the others and we thought "damn, we should've stayed where we were".

Another point is that we hadn't at that stage got a full understanding of how to get the best out of Michelins, specifically on what you do with the set up when the temperature changes – and it did drop a lot between Saturday morning and qualifying in the afternoon. With the qualifying rules as they are, there's not much you can do between qualifying and race and what we learned to do was set the car up for the race and then distort whatever changes you are allowed to do. We didn't really have that knowledge then and you have to remember that all our testing on these tyres had been done in the winter in very cool conditions. The climate out here made things very different.

There was another thing that we didn't pick up on at the time. We were out very early in the first session and late in the second one, with a very big gap in between, and Jenson, I think, was trying to keep focussed throughout. We've since found that it works far better if we treat them as entirely separate entities: do Q1 then relax, don't watch the timing screens and come back refreshed for Q2.

It was interesting to see Takuma [Sato] was quickest in sector two – where all the quick corners are – during qualifying. There's no shortage of bravery or talent there, but it's fairly typical of a new driver that he should be quick there. Experienced drivers all come to realise that the bits you need to focus your attention on are the slow corners. You spend more time in them here in Bahrain and there's more lap time to be found there.

	Sat practice 1	Sat practice 2	Qualifying
Button	1m 30.062s (1st)	1m 29.552s (1st)	1m 30.856s (6th)
M.Schumacher	1m 30.545s (3rd)	1m 30.407s (5th)	1m 30.139s (1st)
Qualifying	**Sector two**	**Overall**	
Sato	38.676s (1st)	1m 30.827s (5th)	
M.Schumacher	38.715s (3rd)	1m 30.139s (1st)	

Takuma Sato was fastest in the first sector, but off the pace in the more prevalent slower corners

RACE RESULTS
BAHRAIN

RACE DATE April 4th
CIRCUIT LENGTH 3.367 miles
NO. OF LAPS 57
RACE DISTANCE 191.793 miles
WEATHER warm, overcast, dry, 31°C
TRACK TEMP 32°C
RACE ATTENDANCE 40,000
LAP RECORD Michael Schumacher,
1m 30.252s, 134.262mph, 2004

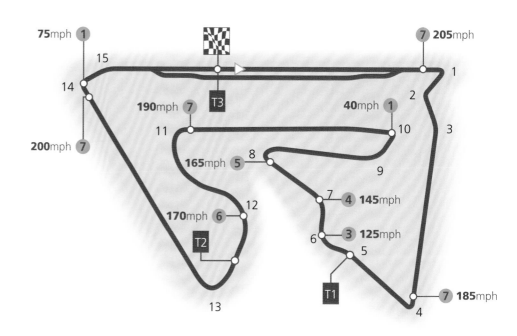

PRACTICE 1

	Driver	Time	Laps
1	M Schumacher	1m32.158s	13
2	R Barrichello	1m32.651s	13
3	A Davidson	1m32.958s	19
4	JP Montoya	1m33.027s	14
5	J Button	1m33.898s	13
6	D Coulthard	1m34.023s	10
7	R Zonta	1m34.289s	21
8	F Massa	1m34.488s	12
9	K Räikkönen	1m34.603s	10
10	T Sato	1m34.610s	12
11	R Schumacher	1m34.619s	13
12	J Trulli	1m34.796s	6
13	F Alonso	1m34.810s	10
14	N Heidfeld	1m34.872s	11
15	G Pantano	1m34.967s	17
16	G Fisichella	1m35.388s	8
17	T Glock	1m35.760s	16
18	M Webber	1m35.905s	11
19	O Panis	1m35.981s	14
20	C da Matta	1m36.359s	16
21	C Klien	1m36.645s	12
22	Z Baumgartner	1m37.049s	12
23	G Bruni	1m37.347s	12
24	B Wirdheim	1m37.443s	12
25	B Leinders	1m37.792s	18

PRACTICE 2

	Driver	Time	Laps
1	R Barrichello	1m31.450s	19
2	JP Montoya	1m31.451s	21
3	A Davidson	1m31.488s	29
4	M Schumacher	1m31.732s	22
5	C Klien	1m31.789s	20
6	R Schumacher	1m31.842s	25
7	J Button	1m31.879s	22
8	M Webber	1m32.041s	24
9	F Alonso	1m32.234s	23
10	R Zonta	1m32.335s	27
11	D Coulthard	1m32.495s	17
12	T Sato	1m32.680s	16
13	G Pantano	1m32.708s	18
14	C da Matta	1m32.761s	21
15	F Massa	1m33.031s	23
16	O Panis	1m33.049s	18
17	G Fisichella	1m33.061s	23
18	J Trulli	1m33.437s	12
19	T Glock	1m33.695s	27
20	Z Baumgartner	1m34.054s	14
21	B Wirdheim	1m34.317s	25
22	G Bruni	1m34.791s	16
23	B Leinders	1m36.248s	25
24	N Heidfeld	1m40.573s	5
25	K Räikkönen	no time	1

PRACTICE 3

	Driver	Time	Laps
1	J Button	1m30.062s	11
2	JP Montoya	1m30.121s	9
3	M Schumacher	1m30.545s	10
4	R Barrichello	1m30.616s	10
5	R Schumacher	1m30.651s	13
6	K Räikkönen	1m31.003s	14
7	T Sato	1m31.090s	10
8	D Coulthard	1m31.341s	9
9	F Alonso	1m31.485s	9
10	J Trulli	1m31.644s	17
11	C Klien	1m31.692s	4
12	O Panis	1m31.962s	16
13	C da Matta	1m32.183s	10
14	G Fisichella	1m32.210s	10
15	M Webber	1m32.276s	9
16	N Heidfeld	1m33.404s	10
17	G Pantano	1m33.474s	11
18	G Bruni	1m33.863s	11
19	Z Baumgartner	1m35.696s	9
20	F Massa	no time	1

PRACTICE 4

	Driver	Time	Laps
1	J Button	1m29.552s	14
2	R Schumacher	1m29.690s	9
3	JP Montoya	1m29.696s	13
4	T Sato	1m30.239s	19
5	M Schumacher	1m30.407s	11
6	J Trulli	1m30.472s	10
7	C da Matta	1m30.499s	12
8	R Barrichello	1m30.513s	11
9	F Alonso	1m30.774s	12
10	O Panis	1m30.934s	13
11	K Räikkönen	1m31.320s	9
12	C Klien	1m31.331s	12
13	M Webber	1m31.384s	12
14	G Fisichella	1m32.433s	11
15	F Massa	1m32.557s	12
16	N Heidfeld	1m32.816s	12
17	G Pantano	1m33.342s	7
18	G Bruni	1m34.590s	11
19	Z Baumgartner	1m35.901s	7
20	D Coulthard	no time	4

Best sectors – Qualifying		Speed trap – Qualifying		
Sector 1	JP Montoya	29.387s	1	JP Montoya	201.147mph
Sector 2	T Sato	38.676s	2	R Schumacher	200.526mph
Sector 3	M Schumacher	21.919s	3	M Schumacher	200.402mph

Michael Schumacher
"We looked good on Friday, struggled a bit on Saturday then took the front row and finished one-two. It was the dream result at the end of a superb weekend."

Juan Pablo Montoya
"Maybe I went for the wrong tyres as they didn't prove as quick in the race as I was expecting. I'd have come third but for gearbox problems with 10 laps to go."

Kimi Räikkönen
"I started last but made a good start and gained a few places during the first couple of laps. I was battling with a Jag for 11th when I lost power and my engine went."

Fernando Alonso
"In reality I started this race half a minute behind everybody else. After my first stop I just pushed all the way and the balance was perfect. Three points was good."

Jenson Button
"It was fantastic to be on the podium again so soon after my first in Malaysia. I dropped back to eighth at the start but after my first stop the car ran really well."

Rubens Barrichello
"I think the few drops of rain at the start worked against me, my brakes taking time to warm up. Michael outbraked me at the first corner and I could do nothing."

Ralf Schumacher
"I would define my final position as limitation of damages. The collision with Sato was an unfortunate race incident but I do think he was being a bit optimistic."

David Coulthard
"A points finish would have been possible but at the end I lost air in the pneumatic system of the engine. A disappointing outcome after an unsatisfying weekend."

Jarno Trulli
"I was very pleased to be fourth but we were capable of getting on the podium this afternoon. After my final stop the car became harder to drive as I lost grip."

Takuma Sato
"I was on the pace and could have achieved a stronger position than fifth. The tangle with Ralf was disappointing – he just closed the door on me and turned in."

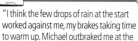

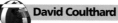

POSITIONS LAP BY LAP

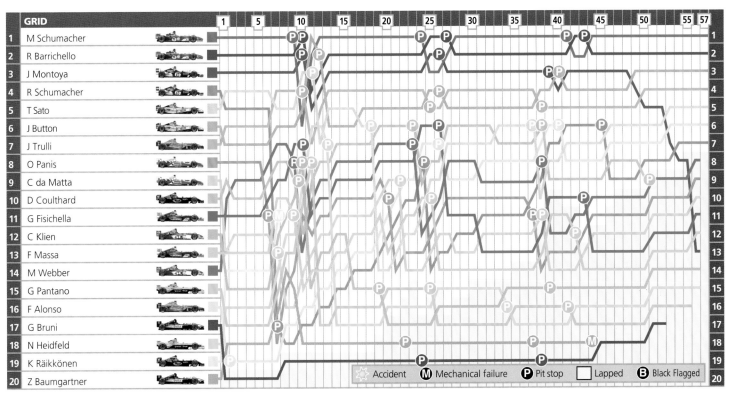

GRID			
1	M Schumacher		
2	R Barrichello		
3	J Montoya		
4	R Schumacher		
5	T Sato		
6	J Button		
7	J Trulli		
8	O Panis		
9	C da Matta		
10	D Coulthard		
11	G Fisichella		
12	C Klien		
13	F Massa		
14	M Webber		
15	G Pantano		
16	F Alonso		
17	G Bruni		
18	N Heidfeld		
19	K Räikkönen		
20	Z Baumgartner		

☀ Accident   Ⓜ Mechanical failure   Ⓟ Pit stop   ☐ Lapped   Ⓑ Black Flagged

QUALIFYING

	Driver	Pre-qual time	Pos	Time
1	M Schumacher	1m30.751s	4	1m30.139s
2	R Barrichello	1m31.283s	11	1m30.530s
3	JP Montoya	1m30.247s	2	1m30.581s
4	R Schumacher	1m29.968s	1	1m30.633s
5	T Sato	1m31.135s	9	1m30.827s
6	J Button	1m31.131s	8	1m30.856s
7	J Trulli	1m31.103s	7	1m30.971s
8	O Panis	1m31.001s	5	1m31.686s
9	C da Matta	1m31.329s	12	1m31.717s
10	D Coulthard	1m31.364s	13	1m31.719s
11	G Fisichella	1m31.203s	10	1m31.731s
12	C Klien	1m31.868s	14	1m32.332s
13	F Massa	1m32.152s	16	1m32.536s
14	M Webber	1m31.945s	15	1m32.625s
15	N Heidfeld	1m32.640s	17	1m33.506s
16	G Pantano	1m33.598s	18	1m34.105s
17	F Alonso	1m31.040s	6	1m34.130s
18	G Bruni	1m34.879s	19	1m34.584s
19	Z Baumgartner	1m35.632s	20	1m35.787s
20	K Räikkönen	1m30.353s	3	no time

RACE

	Driver	Car	Laps	Time	Fastest	Ave mph	Stops
1	M Schumacher	Ferrari F2004	57	1h28m34.875s	1m30.025s	129.858	3
2	R Barrichello	Ferrari F2004	57	1h28m36.242s	1m30.876s	129.824	3
3	J Button	BAR-Honda 006	57	1h29m01.562s	1m30.960s	129.209	3
4	J Trulli	Renault R24	57	1h29m07.089s	1m31.421s	129.075	3
5	T Sato	BAR-Honda 006	57	1h29m27.335s	1m31.101s	128.588	3
6	F Alonso	Renault R24	57	1h29m28.031s	1m30.654s	128.571	3
7	R Schumacher	Williams-BMW FW26	57	1h29m33.030s	1m30.781s	128.452	3
8	M Webber	Jaguar-Cosworth R5	56	1h28m39.255s	1m32.277s	127.473	3
9	O Panis	Toyota TF104	56	1h28m41.250s	1m32.401s	127.425	3
10	C da Matta	Toyota TF104	56	1h28m53.515s	1m32.319s	127.132	3
11	G Fisichella	Sauber-Petronas C23	56	1h28m54.515s	1m32.329s	127.108	3
12	F Massa	Sauber-Petronas C23	56	1h28m59.164s	1m32.690s	126.997	3
13	JP Montoya	Williams-BMW FW26	56	1h29m09.333s	1m30.977s	126.756	3
14	C Klien	Jaguar-Cosworth R5	56	1h29m24.651s	1m32.533s	126.394	3
15	N Heidfeld	Jordan-Ford EJ14	56	1h29m45.382s	1m33.284s	125.907	2
16	G Pantano	Jordan-Ford EJ14	55	1h28m50.551s	1m34.032s	124.929	3
17	G Bruni	Minardi-Cosworth PS04	52	1h30m00.129s	1m35.130s	116.587	2
R	D Coulthard	McLaren-Mercedes MP4-19	50	Engine	1m31.861s	-	3
R	Z Baumgartner	Minardi-Cosworth PS04	44	Engine	1m34.555s	-	3
R	K Räikkönen	McLaren-Mercedes MP4-19	7	Engine	1m33.527s	-	0

CHAMPIONSHIP

	Driver	Pts
1	M Schumacher	30
2	R Barrichello	21
3	J Button	15
4	JP Montoya	12
5	F Alonso	11
6	J Trulli	11
7	R Schumacher	7
8	T Sato	4
9	D Coulthard	4
10	F Massa	1
11	M Webber	1

	Constructor	Pts
1	Ferrari	51
2	Renault	22
3	Williams-BMW	19
4	BAR-Honda	19
5	McLaren-Mercedes	4
6	Sauber-Petronas	1
7	Jaguar-Cosworth	1

Qualifying notes
Heidfeld   Back 10 places for engine change
Räikkönen   Back 10 places for engine change
Bruni   Started from pits

Fastest Lap
M Schumacher 1m30.252s,
on lap 7 (134.262mph)
New lap record

Fastest through speed trap
R Schumacher   206.310mph
Slowest through speed trap
G Bruni   197.470mph

Fastest pit stop
F Alonso   25.234s
Slowest pit stop
G Bruni   37.611s

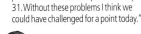

Giancarlo Fisichella

"I developed huge understeer and gear problems and then Ralf spun me on lap 31. Without these problems I think we could have challenged for a point today."

Mark Webber

"Great to get our first point. I started well and was up to tenth position on my first lap. I had a minor off on turn 13. It made no difference but I was lucky to catch it."

Olivier Panis

"A positive weekend for everyone at Toyota. We opted for an aggressive three-stop strategy, which I think was the best for us., but finishing ninth is frustrating."

Nick Heidfeld

"I was on a two-stop strategy and my first stop was so late that at one stage I was up to P6. I was happy to finish; that was the best thing about the weekend for me."

Gianmaria Bruni

"The mechanics did a fantastic job – my car wouldn't leave the grid but they got me going in the pits. The car was good in corners but down on power in straights."

Felipe Massa

"I lost a bit of ground in the first corner and I was really struggling for grip and had a big vibration early on. It was better on the last set but overall a very tough race."

Christian Klien

"At the start I had a slight coming together with Alonso on the third hairpin. I then raced with Kimi – the R5 felt good and I made the most of it, but I spun at turn 11."

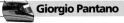

Cristiano da Matta

"It was a difficult race and disappointing after a strong weekend. I suffered a lack of grip throughout the race, which prevented me from making any significant gains."

Giorgio Pantano

"I did my best. We had a small problem with the braking and differential on the last 10 laps and during my second stint I had more understeer on the car."

Zsolt Baumgartner

"Straightaway I had electronics problems, like Gimmi, but I was able to reset the software in the cockpit. My pace was good and lap times not too far off the Jordans."

BAR TAKE THE LEAD

Jenson Button flirted with thoughts of a first victory for BAR at Imola, but it was that man Michael Schumacher who sent the tifosi home happy yet again

The momentum of Jenson Button's first ever F1 pole position carried his BAR-Honda to the front of the race until his first stop on lap nine. In the two laps that followed we got to see Michael Schumacher's true pace for the first time in the weekend – and it did for any hopes Button and the rest of the F1 contingent may have been carrying of taking the fight to Ferrari. Indeed, Schumacher's pace was of a different order and had been disguised in qualifying only by the usual difference in tyre characteristics between Bridgestone and Michelin. Before backing off late in the race, Schumacher had been 27s ahead of Button who, in turn, was 20s clear of anyone else.

We saw in this race that even if Schumacher did get stuck behind a faster-qualifying Michelin car he still had enough in hand in his free-air

laps to compensate and get into his own unbeatable rhythm. But what if he'd got stuck behind two of them? That would have been more than doubly difficult to overcome and this point was almost certainly on Schumacher's mind when he dealt ruthlessly with a challenge from Juan Pablo Montoya on the opening lap.

Button made brilliant use of Schumacher having to deal with the inconvenience of the combative Williams driver and made good an escape to the tune of 2.7s at the end of the opening lap. There was further hope when the length of Button's first pit stop gave rise to speculation that he might be on two stops to the three of Schumacher. However, it was all just a mirage, the delay coming through a BAR operational precaution against the possibility of stripping wheelnuts.

Jenson Button made the
early running for BAR,
but could do nothing as
the Ferraris came through

ROUND 4

SAN MARINO
FORMULA 1™ GRAN
PREMIO FOSTER'S DI
SAN MARINO 2004
Imola

Button leads the way at the start as the midfield bunches behind...

...leaving David Coulthard to rejoin from the first chicane's gravel trap

Start to lap 3

Button leads into the first corner, with Michael Schumacher slotting in to second place. Montoya is slower away, but Ralf Schumacher fails to pass. Bunching in the midfield results in Coulthard running into and going off, forcing him to head for the pits for repairs. At Tosa, Montoya tries to drive around the outside of Michael Schumacher. The Williams is squeezed off the track and loses momentum. Ralf Schumacher tries to sieze the moment by passing Montoya on the run towards Piratella but ends up on the grass, losing fourth place to Sato. At the end of lap 1, Button holds a large lead from Michael Schumacher, Montoya, Sato, Ralf Schumacher, Barrichello, Trulli, Webber, Alonso and da Matta. Coulthard rejoins a long way behind. Michael Schumacher begins to close on Button on lap 2, reducing the gap from 2.7s to 2.1s. Montoya is already a further 1.7s down in third place. Massa passes Panis for 11th place.

Laps 4 to 11

By lap 4 Michael Schumacher is on Button's tail, but can't find a way by. On lap 7 the pit stops begin with da Matta and Massa stopping. They drop from 10th and 11th to 15th and 14th as Massa makes a faster stop. Pantano goes off and retires. Montoya and Webber make their first stops on lap 8. Then, a lap later, Button stops from the lead and Schumacher immediately speeds up. Ralf Schumacher also stops, along with Panis and Klien. On lap 10, Michael Schumacher sets a very quick lap, while behind him Sato and Barrichello pit. Then, on lap 11, Michael Schumacher pits and emerges ahead of Button. Alonso also pits, leaving Trulli in second place.

Michael Schumacher got his head down and reeled in leader Button

Laps 12 to 25

Trulli is the last man to stop, coming in on lap 12, and so the new order sees Michael Schumacher ahead of Button, Montoya, Trulli, Ralf Schumacher, Barrichello, Alonso and Sato. On lap 16, Michael Schumacher's lead has extended to 10s. Towards the back of the field, Coulthard passes Klien for 16th. Heidfeld spins on lap 17, but stays in 15th. Massa passes Webber for 11th on lap 19, with Coulthard stopping as he's switched to a two-stop strategy. Fisichella stops the following lap, dropping from ninth to 14th. On lap 21, Räikkönen pits from ninth and rejoins 14th. Montoya makes his second stop on lap 25, falling from third to seventh, with Trulli advancing to fill third position.

Michael Schumacher's run of fast laps helped him emerge in the lead

Laps 26 to 37

Button stops on lap 26 but holds on to second place. Michael Schumacher stops a lap later, rejoining 18s ahead of Button. On lap 28, Ralf Schumacher and Barrichello stop again, and Ralf is released directly in front of Barrichello, fortunately without contact. Alonso is now running fourth. Sato stops, but remains eighth. Alonso stops on lap 30, moving Montoya and Ralf Schumacher up to fourth and fifth. Trulli pits on lap 31, and so Montoya is back to third ahead of Ralf, Trulli, Barrichello, Alonso and Sato. On lap 32, da Matta pits for a drive-through penalty for ignoring blue flags. He rejoins, but goes off almost immediately.

Near miss as Ralf Schumacher is flagged out in front of Barrichello

Laps 38 to 47

The Saubers both pit on lap 38. Coulthard pits on lap 40, but remains 14th. On lap 43, Montoya is the first frontrunner to make his final stop. This puts Ralf third. Button and Ralf both stop on lap 44. Button remains second, but Trulli moves to third with Alonso fourth and Montoya fifth, although the Renaults must stop again. Michael Schumacher and Trulli stop on lap 46. Schumacher stays in the lead, but Trulli falls behind Alonso, Montoya and Ralf.

Button congratulates Michael on his victory on Ferrari's home soil

Lap 48 to the finish

Alonso stops on lap 48, promoting Montoya to third with Ralf fourth. Alonso is ahead of Trulli and challenging Ralf. On lap 49, Nick Heidfeld retires with a mechanical failure. A lap later, Alonso tries to pass Ralf Schumacher on the inside. Ralf closes the gap, and the cars collide. Ralf spins and drops to eighth. Sato retires from seventh on lap 57 with a blown engine. This promotes Räikkönen to eighth but he is under pressure from Fisichella. On lap 62, Michael Schumacher takes the chequered flag to win with Button second. Montoya holds off Alonso for third. Behind them, Trulli holds off Barrichello for fifth and Räikkönen stays ahead of Fisichella as Panis and Coulthard fight for 11th all the way to the flag.

INSIDE LINE
JENSON BUTTON

It was fantastic to get my first F1 pole position. The car was really, really good here and I was enjoying pushing it and myself harder and harder. The key was in keeping the tyres from getting too hot in the final sector, so in the first couple of sectors you had to keep it smooth and try to keep the momentum up. Then you get to the final sector and it's all about those two chicanes – the Variante Alta and the final one on to the straight. At the first one, I just couldn't believe how much grip the car was giving me and through the weekend I just got faster and faster there – and it was interesting that this was where Michael [Schumacher] had his moment when he was trying to beat my time. But, even as I was enjoying the moment of the pole, I knew that Michael was going to be a much tougher challenge in the race.

It was a great feeling not having anyone in front of me as we lined up on the grid. That's just how I like it and it was the first time I'd experienced it in F1. I didn't really feel pressure. It felt like the pressure was on everyone else. I made a good start and I knew then that I had to go absolutely flat-out on the first lap because I felt that was when Michael was bound to try something. I just absolutely wrung the neck of my car and although I didn't see Michael's moment with Juan, all I was aware of was that the red car had fallen a long way back, which was very good news indeed.

Michael closed the gap after three or four laps, but still I was quite relaxed about that. There wasn't really anywhere where he could pass and it was just a question of who was able to go longer. Unfortunately, it was him. He was able to do two laps more and that's where he was able to leapfrog me, but I must say when he came out after his stop I was actually quite shocked by how much time he had made up.

The car wasn't quite so good on its second set of tyres and there was no question then of being able to challenge Michael for victory. After that, it was just a question of pushing hard on my own, because we in turn were well clear of anyone else. Ferrari were just a long way in front of anyone in race trim, just as they were all season.

Q THE BIG QUESTION

What happened between Montoya and Michael Schumacher at Tosa on the opening lap?

"He claims he didn't see me," ranted Montoya about this wheel-rubbing incident. "If so, he's either blind or stupid."

Montoya's anger was triggered by the way Schumacher pushed him out wide at Tosa on the first lap as the Williams driver attempted to drive around the Ferrari's outside. "He just put me on the grass. Last year, I get into a perfectly normal race incident with Rubens at Indy and I'm given a penalty that might have cost me the World Championship. Here, Michael does this and he gets away with it. I don't think it's fair."

Montoya knew that Schumacher was vulnerable on the opening lap on account of the Ferrari's Bridgestones taking longer to heat up than the Williams' Michelins. The Colombian had to make a move soon into the race and he duly attacked. After being rebuffed by the Ferrari at Villeneuve, Montoya was way quicker under braking into the following corner – Tosa – and, with Michael covering the inside line, he opted for the outside.

Did Michael have any comment to make? "No," he replied unemotionally, unwilling to get embroiled in an unnecessary slanging match.

In truth, it looked just like good old-fashioned hard racing to most observers. Mark Webber probably hit the nail on the head, saying: "There was definitely an issue of pride there. Juan had done an amazing job getting himself into a position where that move was going to work and from Michael's point of view that risked him looking pretty average, especially after Juan had succeeded in doing a similar thing to him at the Nürburgring last year."

"I think it's just what happens when those two get together," said Williams' Sam Michael. "It's always going to be like that. You've got two drivers who are aggressive anyway and will look to exert their authority on anyone who's around them. It was pretty close and Juan then nearly took Ralf out as he was defending after getting on the grass. That in turn put Ralf on the grass and that pretty much spoilt his race because it meant he was stuck behind Sato for the first stint. It's just the way the cookie crumbles. It's racing."

Montoya starts his move around the outside of Michael Schumacher into Tosa. It didn't work

ROSS BRAWN
FERRARI TECHNICAL DIRECTOR

Michael Schumacher's race pace was stunning, his best lap almost 0.8s better than Button's

We'd known right since the start of the year that we could be in trouble if we got stuck behind a Michelin car. Basically, the performance cycle of our Bridgestone tyres suggested that they didn't have the same instant one-lap performance as the Michelins – so hurting us in qualifying – but thereafter were much more consistent race tyres, allowing us to use our performance advantage. We'd got away with it in the first three Grands Prix, where Michael had been able to take pole and get away in front, and so run his own pace. However, Imola was the day of reckoning almost, where it was clear from Button's pace in the practices that we might not get pole, and we sort of planned our race around that.

We needed to ensure that Michael would get some critical laps in free air

in the race and we reckoned even if we got beaten away at the start, if we could get to the second round of pit stops ahead, we would be alright. So we fuelled Michael a little bit long, reckoning that would give him those crucial laps in free air.

As it happened, Michael was putting in a fantastic lap in qualifying and up until his moment at the Variante Alta pole looked on. If we extrapolated a lap by adding Michael's normal sector-three time with that much fuel on board to what he'd done in sectors one and two, he would have set a 1m 19.6s – which would have been pole by a tenth. As it was, the moment cost him 0.4s.

If you look at Michael's times on laps two and three – as he was catching Jenson and not being held back to their pace – and again on the two laps after Jenson pitted, you can see that he was around 0.8s faster, whereas it had been nip and tuck in qualifying and that's a pretty accurate measure of the difference in first-lap performance. Even so, I must say I was amazed at the laps Michael pulled out there, and to be so far in front after the first stops was a very big bonus and the foundation of the win. That's the thing with Michael: even when you're up against it, he can often pull something out of the bag to compensate.

Schumacher average lap when behind Button	1m 22.217s (Button 1m 22.083s)
Schumacher laps after Button pits	1m 21.239s
	1m 20.411s
Button in-lap	1m 22.368s
Schumacher in-lap	1m 20.534s
Best race lap (Schumacher)	1m 20.411s
Best race lap (Button)	1m 21.202s
= Schumacher faster by	0.791s
Qualifying	
Schumacher (actual)	1m 20.011s
Schumacher (extrapolated)	1m 19.600s
Button	1m 19.753s

Schumacher potentially faster than Button by 0.1s–0.15s in qualifying
Schumacher faster than Button in race by 0.791s
Therefore qualifying penalty of Bridgestone indexed to Michelin at Imola between 0.641s and 0.691s.

SAM MICHAEL

WILLIAMS TECHNICAL DIRECTOR

Before Michael Schumacher began slowing down, he was 47s ahead of Juan, with Jenson in between. That told the full story really – that Michael had around 1s per lap over us in race conditions. We'd known of this advantage since Melbourne, where the gap was very apparent. The amount of downforce we'd have needed to have found in the car to make up that much time would have been massive. Imola is a high-downforce circuit and our car simply didn't have the necessary downforce.

The gap to Ferrari was one thing, but here we were also a long way behind BAR, and I think that was reflective of the fact that in the early races we'd been carried along a little by our experience and their lack of experience on Michelin tyres. Yet, as they were building up their database so a different picture emerged.

Really, once Juan had his little moment with Michael on the first lap, there wasn't a lot to do for him strategically. We couldn't challenge Michael or Jenson and, at the same time, Sato in fourth was holding up a queue of cars behind him in the first stint, and that really ensured that Juan's place was well protected.

Strategically, we then had to find a way of helping Ralf. He'd got stuck behind Sato after Juan had put him on the grass after Tosa on the first lap, and although we were able to get by Sato at the stops quite easily, Trulli was able to run longer than us and so got past. At the next stops we had a good pit battle with Ferrari as Ralf and Rubens – who was right on his tail – pitted together. We kept him ahead and at the same time got back ahead of Trulli, putting Ralf fourth. But then Alonso, who had done his final stop late, came out just behind Ralf and tried to pass him into Tosa. They touched and Ralf spun, losing him three places.

It was a lacklustre race from us in terms of performance. We had no particular problems but weren't even in the fight. We salvaged a podium out of it, but really the gap to Michael of over 40s told its own story. We simply didn't have enough performance in the car.

Montoya simply couldn't live with the pace of the first two in the race, and so had to settle for third

RACE RESULTS
SAN MARINO
IMOLA

RACE DATE April 25th
CIRCUIT LENGTH 3.065 miles
NO. OF LAPS 62
RACE DISTANCE 189.897 miles
WEATHER warm and dry, 22°C
TRACK TEMP 32° C
RACE ATTENDANCE 82,000
LAP RECORD Michael Schumacher,
1m 20.411s, 137.259mph, 2004

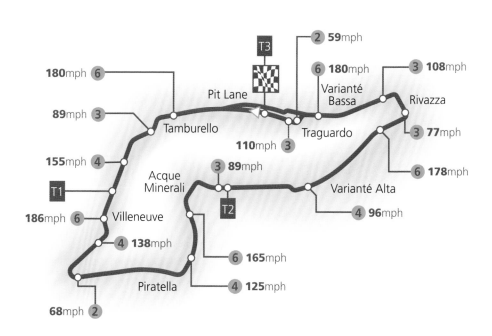

	PRACTICE 1		
	Driver	Time	Laps
1	M Schumacher	1m20.084s	11
2	R Barrichello	1m21.443s	12
3	R Schumacher	1m22.250s	13
4	A Davidson	1m22.398s	20
5	J Button	1m22.448s	10
6	JP Montoya	1m22.796s	11
7	J Trulli	1m22.927s	11
8	K Räikkönen	1m23.054s	4
9	F Alonso	1m23.083s	13
10	R Zonta	1m23.161s	20
11	D Coulthard	1m23.197s	8
12	M Webber	1m23.417s	11
13	G Fisichella	1m23.528s	9
14	F Massa	1m23.562s	13
15	O Panis	1m23.790s	13
16	T Sato	1m24.061s	11
17	B Wirdheim	1m24.152s	29
18	C da Matta	1m24.752s	12
19	N Heidfeld	1m24.955s	12
20	G Pantano	1m25.375s	12
21	C Klien	1m25.679s	9
22	T Glock	1m26.254s	14
23	G Bruni	1m27.933s	14
24	Z Baumgartner	1m29.312s	14
25	B Leinders	1m29.414s	19

	PRACTICE 2		
	Driver	Time	Laps
1	J Button	1m20.966s	25
2	T Sato	1m21.159s	25
3	M Schumacher	1m21.164s	23
4	K Räikkönen	1m21.586s	18
5	J Trulli	1m21.604s	25
6	A Davidson	1m21.643s	30
7	JP Montoya	1m21.661s	25
8	F Alonso	1m21.788s	25
9	D Coulthard	1m21.795s	17
10	R Schumacher	1m22.057s	24
11	R Barrichello	1m22.096s	20
12	M Webber	1m22.167s	28
13	O Panis	1m22.768s	22
14	C da Matta	1m22.780s	23
15	F Massa	1m23.043s	27
16	C Klien	1m23.211s	15
17	G Fisichella	1m23.335s	28
18	B Wirdheim	1m23.470s	25
19	R Zonta	1m23.500s	20
20	N Heidfeld	1m23.866s	15
21	G Pantano	1m24.091s	19
22	G Bruni	1m25.653s	16
23	Z Baumgartner	1m25.760s	10
24	B Leinders	1m27.025s	22
25	T Glock	no time	0

	PRACTICE 3		
	Driver	Time	Laps
1	M Schumacher	1m20.856s	13
2	J Button	1m21.165s	11
3	R Barrichello	1m21.583s	10
4	JP Montoya	1m21.764s	14
5	R Schumacher	1m21.864s	13
6	F Alonso	1m21.954s	13
7	T Sato	1m22.013s	11
8	D Coulthard	1m22.051s	6
9	K Räikkönen	1m22.164s	5
10	J Trulli	1m22.462s	13
11	M Webber	1m22.707s	10
12	O Panis	1m22.885s	14
13	G Fisichella	1m22.991s	6
14	F Massa	1m23.105s	10
15	C da Matta	1m23.482s	17
16	G Pantano	1m24.255s	13
17	N Heidfeld	1m24.907s	10
18	G Bruni	1m26.783s	11
19	Z Baumgartner	1m27.539s	13
20	C Klien	no time	2

	PRACTICE 4		
	Driver	Time	Laps
1	M Schumacher	1m20.125s	7
2	J Button	1m20.150s	15
3	F Alonso	1m20.844s	13
4	D Coulthard	1m20.844s	10
5	JP Montoya	1m20.975s	7
6	R Barrichello	1m20.996s	10
7	T Sato	1m21.159s	14
8	J Trulli	1m21.198s	12
9	K Räikkönen	1m21.199s	14
10	C da Matta	1m21.257s	13
11	R Schumacher	1m21.271s	10
12	O Panis	1m21.296s	12
13	M Webber	1m21.393s	16
14	G Fisichella	1m22.022s	10
15	F Massa	1m22.077s	8
16	C Klien	1m23.222s	8
17	N Heidfeld	1m23.551s	13
18	G Pantano	1m24.736s	7
19	G Bruni	1m26.199s	10
20	Z Baumgartner	1m27.451s	13

Best sectors – Qualifying			Speed trap – Qualifying	
Sector 1	M Schumacher	22.732s	1 R Barrichello	194.685mph
Sector 2	M Schumacher	26.649s	2 T Sato	194.063mph
Sector 3	J Button	30.137s	3 R Schumacher	192.883mph

 **Michael Schumacher**
" At the start, Jenson set a mind blowing pace: it was as though I was driving in the wet and he in the dry. As for my fight with Juan, I think it was just a racing incident."

 Juan Pablo Montoya
"Michael was slow out of the first few corners. I tried to pass but he closed the door twice, then hit me and pushed me on to the grass. This was not fair racing."

Kimi Räikkönen
"I was pleased to finish my first race of the season and get a point. I started from last so had to fight hard to make up positions. Imola is narrow so it's hard to overtake."

 **Fernando Alonso**
"Coulthard almost took me out at the first corner: some parts actually hit my helmet! As for the incident with Ralf, from where I was sitting he just closed the door on me."

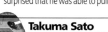 **Jenson Button**
"The first lap felt very good and I was able to pull away and lead the first stint. After Michael overtook me at the pitstop I was surprised that he was able to pull away."

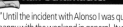 **Rubens Barrichello**
"My race was spoiled by traffic. I always had a slower car ahead of me, so was never able to push the car as hard as it could go. At least I scored three points."

Ralf Schumacher
"Until the incident with Alonso I was quite happy with the weekend in general. It was a shame. It was good to score points and we made the best of our package."

David Coulthard
"I took too much of a risk in the first corner and ended up damaging the nose of the car and going off track. The team replaced the nose but 12th was all we could do."

Jarno Trulli
"I was more than pleased with this result: starting ninth I made up four places at a circuit where it is hard to overtake, as well as keeping one of the Ferraris behind me."

Takuma Sato
"I had a very exciting start and there was a lot of fighting for position on the first lap. I then struggled for pace after gearbox problems, and then my engine gave up."

POSITIONS LAP BY LAP

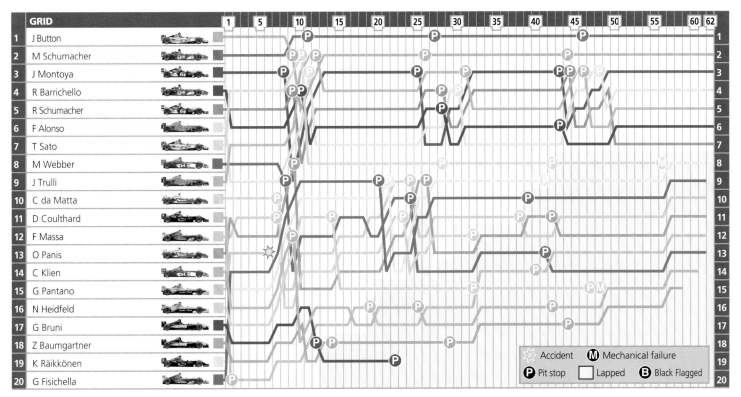

GRID			
1	J Button		
2	M Schumacher		
3	J Montoya		
4	R Barrichello		
5	R Schumacher		
6	F Alonso		
7	T Sato		
8	M Webber		
9	J Trulli		
10	C da Matta		
11	D Coulthard		
12	F Massa		
13	O Panis		
14	C Klien		
15	G Pantano		
16	N Heidfeld		
17	G Bruni		
18	Z Baumgartner		
19	K Räikkönen		
20	G Fisichella		

Key: ☆ Accident · Ⓜ Mechanical failure · Ⓟ Pit stop · ☐ Lapped · Ⓑ Black Flagged

QUALIFYING

	Driver	Pre-qual time	Pos	Time
1	J Button	1m20.632s	5	1m19.753s
2	M Schumacher	1m20.440s	3	1m20.011s
3	JP Montoya	1m19.805s	1	1m20.212s
4	R Barrichello	1m20.927s	7	1m20.451s
5	R Schumacher	1m20.423s	2	1m20.538s
6	F Alonso	1m21.799s	14	1m20.895s
7	T Sato	1m20.984s	8	1m20.913s
8	M Webber	1m21.458s	11	1m20.921s
9	J Trulli	1m21.669s	12	1m21.034s
10	C da Matta	1m21.737s	13	1m21.087s
11	D Coulthard	1m20.566s	4	1m21.091s
12	F Massa	1m22.154s	15	1m21.532s
13	O Panis	1m21.231s	10	1m21.558s
14	C Klien	1m22.246s	16	1m21.949s
15	G Pantano	1m24.643s	18	1m23.352s
16	N Heidfeld	1m23.055s	17	1m23.488s
17	G Bruni	1m26.463s	19	1m26.899s
18	Z Baumgartner	1m27.319s	20	1m46.299s
19	G Fisichella	1m20.716s	6	no time
20	K Räikkönen	1m21.181s	9	no time

RACE

	Driver	Car	Laps	Time	Fastest	Avg. mph	Stops
1	M Schumacher	Ferrari F2004	62	1h26m19.670s	1m20.411s	131.988	3
2	J Button	BAR-Honda 006	62	1h26m29.372s	1m21.201s	131.742	3
3	JP Montoya	Williams-BMW FW26	62	1h26m41.287s	1m21.870s	131.440	3
4	F Alonso	Renault R24	62	1h26m43.324s	1m21.650s	131.389	3
5	J Trulli	Renault R24	62	1h26m55.886s	1m21.666s	131.073	3
6	R Barrichello	Ferrari F2004	62	1h26m56.353s	1m21.873s	131.061	3
7	R Schumacher	Williams-BMW FW26	62	1h27m15.400s	1m21.689s	130.583	3
8	K Räikkönen	McLaren-Mercedes MP4-19	61	1h26m20.284s	1m22.500s	129.843	2
9	G Fisichella	Sauber-Petronas C23	61	1h26m21.263s	1m22.654s	129.819	2
10	F Massa	Sauber-Petronas C23	61	1h26m33.852s	1m22.895s	129.510	3
11	O Panis	Toyota TF104	61	1h26m58.490s	1m22.861s	128.892	3
12	D Coulthard	McLaren-Mercedes MP4-19	61	1h26m59.350s	1m22.951s	128.870	3
13	M Webber	Jaguar-Cosworth R5	61	1h27m08.421s	1m22.931s	128.647	3
14	C Klien	Jaguar-Cosworth R5	60	1h26m54.894s	1m23.647s	126.865	3
15	Z Baumgartner	Minardi-Cosworth PS04	58	1h26m40.096s	1m26.075s	122.982	3
16	T Sato	BAR-Honda 006	56	Engine	1m21.929s	129.980	1
R	N Heidfeld	Jordan-Ford EJ14	48	Transmission	1m23.381s	-	3
R	C da Matta	Jaguar-Cosworth R5	32	Spun off	1m23.108s	-	2
R	G Bruni	Minardi-Cosworth PS04	22	Brakes	1m26.857s	-	1
R	G Pantano	Jordan-Ford EJ14	6	Hydraulics	1m25.457s	-	0

CHAMPIONSHIP

	Driver	Pts
1	M Schumacher	40
2	R Barrichello	24
3	J Button	23
4	JP Montoya	18
5	F Alonso	16
6	J Trulli	15
7	R Schumacher	9
8	T Sato	4
9	D Coulthard	4
10	F Massa	1
11	M Webber	1
11	K Räikkönen	1

	Constructor	Pts
1	Ferrari	64
2	Renault	31
3=	BAR-Honda	27
3=	Williams-BMW	27
5	McLaren-Mercedes	5
6	Sauber-Petronas	1
8	Jaguar-Cosworth	1

Qualifying notes
Raikkonen	Back 10 places for engine change
Baumgartner	Back 10 places for engine change
Fisichella	1s added for yellow flag infringement

Fastest Lap
M Schumacher 1m20.411s, on lap 10 (137.259mph) New lap record

Fastest through speed trap
R Barrichello 199.010mph
Slowest through speed trap
G Bruni 186.520mph

Fastest pit stop
C da Matta 14.380s
Slowest pit stop
Z Baumgartner 35.378s

Giancarlo Fisichella
"We had good race pace, at times quicker than Kimi. Shame I lost the place to him. I got held up by a Minardi, Kimi got a run on me and overtook me on the straight."

Mark Webber
"I maintained my eighth position on the first few laps, my pit stop went to plan, but then I started to lose power owing to an intermittent electrical problem."

Olivier Panis
"Once again we proved the reliability of the TF104. I pushed very hard throughout the race and we did some good pit stops but we just didn't have enough pace."

Nick Heidfeld
"I had a high speed spin at Piratella but managed to get back on the circuit. There was no damage to the car. Overall the car was better than in the first three races."

Gianmaria Bruni
"It just wasn't our day. I felt a problem developing with the brake balance after my first stop and came into the pits. We decided to retire the car as a precaution."

Felipe Massa
"I made a good start and the car was very good in the first two stints. I don't know why, but it wasn't quite the same in the final one. I struggled to keep my rhythm."

Christian Klien
"I soon became boxed in at the back and it was difficult to make any headway. After my first stop I started to get blue-flagged, which always costs you a lot of time."

Cristiano da Matta
"I had a drive-through penalty, followed normal pit lane procedure but disabled the traction control. I was caught out by this at the first chicane and went off."

Giorgio Pantano
"I got a very good start and was in a good position so I wasn't happy about retiring, especially racing at home in Italy. I was really looking for a better result than this."

Zsolt Baumgartner
"I was happy to have finished and pleased that we had a reliable car. There were no problems and no mistakes. I thanked the team: they did a great job all weekend."

MICHAEL HITS FIVE

Michael Schumacher made it five wins from five starts, but he spent much of the Grand Prix convinced that his Ferrari was about to fail beneath him

Michael Schumacher made it a record-equalling five wins from the first five races of a season, but he wouldn't have bet on it early into the second stint of this race, even if the onlooking world would have done.

What the world outside Ferrari didn't know at this stage was that a primary exhaust had cracked. Not a major worry from a mechanical point of view, but such is the incredibly tightly packaged nature of a current F1 car's engine bay that it very often leads to heat-induced failures elsewhere. A mechanic noticed the problem at Schumacher's first stop and the telemetry readings confirmed it. Thoughts went back to Monaco 2000 when Schumacher had retired with rear suspension failure after an exhaust leak had weakened a carbon-fibre wishbone.

This time, temperature sensors told the team the suspension area wasn't in danger. But still there was the worry of a fire to the bodywork – deprived of airflow, it indeed briefly caught ablaze at the second pit stop but was quickly extinguished – or the melting of electrical circuitry. Every lap Schumacher wondered if it was about to stop.

But, of course, it didn't. This is Michael Schumacher and this is Ferrari. He had done enough on his first stop in-lap to jump the Renault of early leader Jarno Trulli, and had thereby broken the threat of his only true rival, team-mate Rubens Barrichello, whose two-stop strategy would have depended upon three-stopping Schumacher being held up perhaps one more stint than he was.

Jarno Trulli powers into the lead ahead of Michael Schumacher, but Ferrari's ace was to win

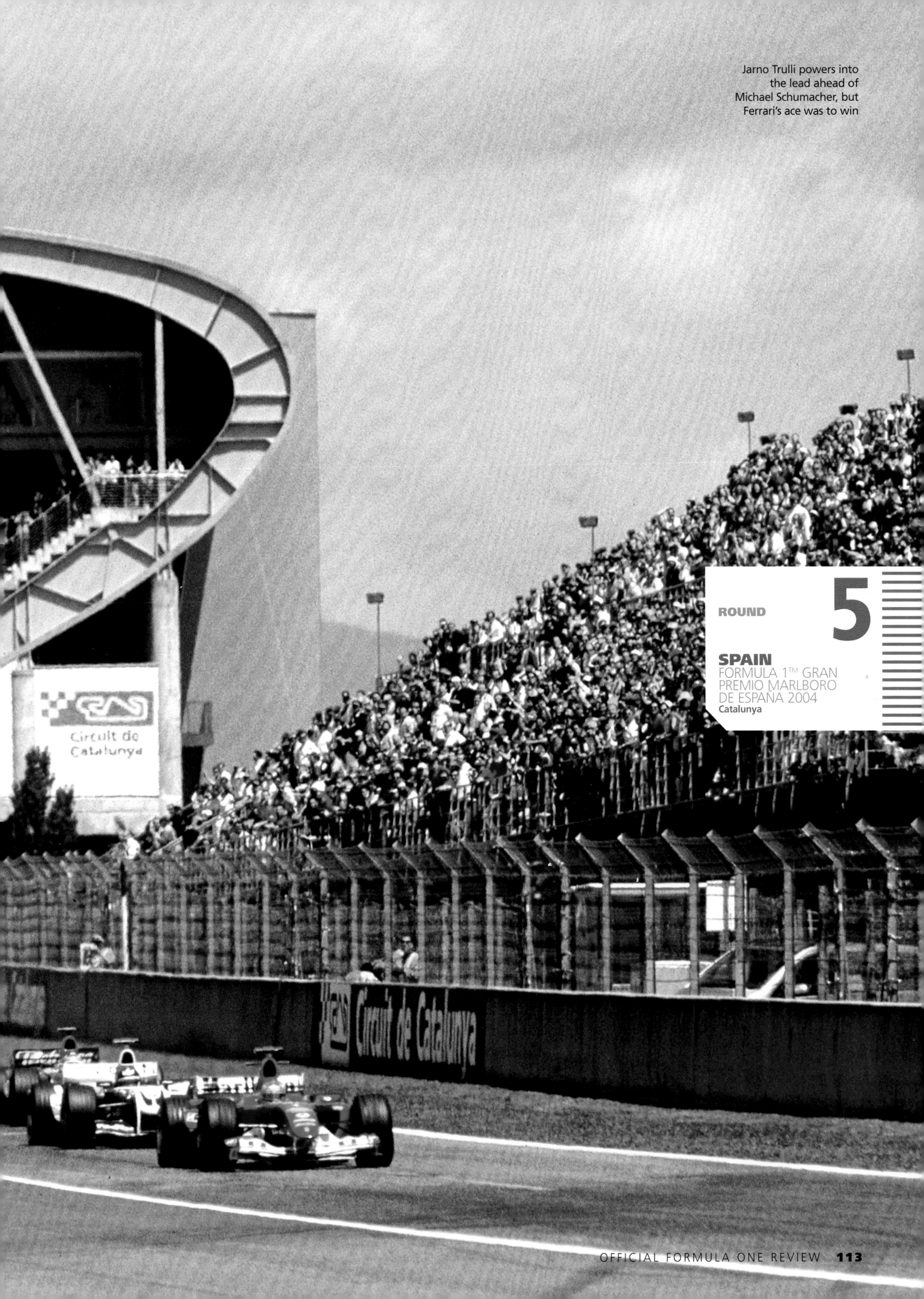
Circuit de Catalunya
Circuit de Catalunya

ROUND **5**

SPAIN
FORMULA 1™ GRAN PREMIO MARLBORO DE ESPAÑA 2004
Catalunya

LAP BY LAP ACTION

66 laps / 190 miles

Trulli heads Michael Schumacher and Sato through the first corner

Start to lap 7
Juan Pablo Montoya is slow away at the start, and Trulli gets off the line quickly, passing Michael Schumacher to lead. Sato squeezes ahead of Montoya for third. Barrichello holds on to his fifth place, while Alonso makes a great start to move to sixth at the end of the first lap, which also sees Ralf Schumacher dropping from sixth on the grid to ninth, and Webber falling to 15th but fighting back to end the lap in 12th. At the end of lap 1, Trulli is a full second ahead of Schumacher with Sato 1.2s behind the Ferrari. On lap 3, Button passes da Matta for 13th place.

Trulli locks up as he fights to keep Schumacher behind him early on

Laps 8 to 14
The pit stops begin on lap 8, with Alonso and Panis stopping from sixth and seventh, rejoining in 14th and 17th respectively. Trulli pits on lap 9, allowing Michael Schumacher to speed up. Montoya, Räikkönen, Webber, da Matta and Heidfeld all pit. Michael Schumacher pits a lap later and Sato leads with Barrichello chasing. Michael rejoins just ahead of Trulli. Coulthard, Ralf Schumacher and Button all stop. On lap 11, Sato pits and Barrichello goes into the lead. Michael Schumacher is 11s behind him with Trulli third, Fisichella fourth, Sato fifth and Massa sixth. Schumacher's Ferrari engine starts to sound a little rough on lap 13 but doesn't seem to affect his performance. Alonso passes Massa for sixth, and Ralf Schumacher passes Panis for 10th. On lap 14 Montoya passes Massa for seventh.

Schumacher emerges from his first pit stop ahead of Trulli. Job done!

Laps 15 to 26
On lap 15 Klien runs wide, allowing Ralf Schumacher to pass him for ninth. On lap 16 Klien stops. On lap 17 Barrichello stops and so Michael leads. He is 5.7s ahead of Trulli with Barrichello third, Sato fourth and Alonso fifth after Fisichella pits and rejoins ninth. Montoya is sixth. On lap 18 Massa stops, dropping from seventh to 15th. Baumgartner spins out of the race. By lap 23 Michael Schumacher's lead is more than 8s. Trulli pits and falls back to fifth behind Barrichello, Sato and Alonso. On lap 25 Schumacher stops for a second time but retains the lead. Alonso and Ralf Schumacher also stop. On lap 26 Sato, Montoya, Panis and Webber all pit.

Juan Pablo Montoya heads Massa, but he wasn't to reach the finish

Laps 27 to 40
On lap 27 the order re-emerges with Schumacher a couple of seconds clear of Barrichello, then Trulli third with Alonso now ahead of Sato. Fisichella is sixth ahead of Montoya and Räikkönen. Button stops on lap 28, falling from ninth to 12th. Räikkönen stops a lap later, falling to 12th. Panis pits for a drive-through penalty for speeding in pitlane. On lap 31, Button overtakes Klien for 10th. Bruni retires on lap 32. Heidfeld retires with an engine problem two laps after that. Fisichella stops on lap 40, falling from sixth to 10th.

Rubens Barrichello locks up as he presses on towards second place

Laps 41 to 45
The final stops begin on lap 41, with Trulli pitting for the third time. Massa also pits. Alonso moves to third, before pitting himself a lap later, promoting Sato back to third. Barrichello stops on lap 43, and Sato moves to second. Rubens rejoins in third, then Montoya stops, dropping from sixth to eighth. A lap down, Coulthard pits, dropping from 11th to 14th. On lap 44, Button stops, falling from seventh to 10th. Klien retires. Schumacher and Sato both pit on lap 45. Michael rejoins in the lead, but Sato falls to fifth behind Barrichello, Trulli and Alonso. Ralf Schumacher also stops and rejoins in sixth.

Gimme five! Michael Schumacher celebrates winning five on the trot

Lap 46 to the finish
On lap 46, Montoya comes into the pits and retires. Räikkönen pits, and rejoins in 12th. Ralf Schumacher passes Fisichella for sixth on lap 57. Then, on lap 50, Webber completes the pit stops, falling behind the two McLarens. Giorgio Pantano comes into the pits and retires on lap 51. Fifteen laps later, Michael Schumacher scores his 75th victory, this his fifth win in a row. Barrichello finishes second, with Trulli third, Alonso fourth, Sato fifth and Ralf Schumacher sixth. The final points are scored by Fisichella in seventh and Button in eighth. Massa, Coulthard, Räikkönen, Webber and da Matta complete the finishers.

INSIDE LINE
MICHAEL SCHUMACHER

It was early in the second stint of the Grand Prix that Ross [Brawn] told me about the exhaust problem. He didn't sound very optimistic as he was saying it and, knowing what an exhaust failure usually means, I wasn't too optimistic either. I really didn't think we were going to do it this time.

I had something to focus on the whole race because in the first stint Jarno [Trulli] was ahead of me. I thought I had a good start but I watched my mirrors and suddenly saw this blue car really flying. I still had the option to shut the door, but he was going so much faster that it wouldn't be very fair. I was hoping then that I'd be able to pass somehow and a couple of times due to the heavy headwind I got a good tow, but he was never really quite close enough so I had to wait for our pit-stop strategy to work.

Really, as long as he pitted one lap earlier or one lap later it was not too critical. I think either way would've worked. As it happened, I was able to jump him by staying out a lap longer, but my best lap time actually came on new tyres after a stop, so it could've worked either way.

Then Ross told me of the problem. There wasn't a lot they could do and I sort of had to do as much as I could in the way I drove. Actually, it meant I couldn't really slow down that much. There was a sort of correct window where I had to drive the engine, and to have slowed down would have hurt the situation. It was quite a mental strain, living with that the whole race. I was expecting the car to stop at any moment.

Luckily, it came through and that the car still made it to the finish even after having such a problem tells you the magnificent job the team has been doing. That's exceptional, really exceptional. These guys are so wonderful.

Q THE BIG QUESTION

Could Rubens have won the Spanish Grand Prix?
"Really, I needed Jarno to have held up Michael one more stint than he did," reported Rubens Barrichello on the feasibility of his two-stop strategy overcoming his team-mate's more conventional three-stop.

The combination of fuel consumption, lap-time sensitivity to weight, and high tyre degradation means that the Barcelona circuit is generally punishing to heavy fuel loads. However, Rubens reasoned that his only competition here was his team-mate Michael Schumacher and that he could still probably beat the leading Michelin runners, regardless of strategy, as Bridgestone seemed to have given Ferrari a particularly strong consistency advantage here. "I was very down about Imola," added Rubens, "where on the same strategy as everyone else I was stuck behind them all the race. I think I got two clear laps that whole race. With the car as good as it was, that was very frustrating. So to beat Michael I had to either try for pole or try doing something different. So this is what I did."

A pit stop costs around 21s at Barcelona. As long as Michael didn't make that much time over Rubens by his third stop, Barrichello would be looking good. In actual fact, Schumacher was 31s ahead as he made his final stop. Trulli had led the first stint, and analysis of the times suggests he was costing Schumacher around 1s per lap. Schumacher's second stint was for 15 laps. Coming out behind Trulli after the first stops instead of just a couple of car lengths ahead would potentially have cost Michael around 15s (although that might have been reduced by pitting early). Had Trulli's in- and out-laps been just a little better, things could have become very interesting for Barrichello.

Barrichello reckoned his two-stop strategy would have worked, with just a little help from others

PATRICK HEAD
WILLIAMS
TECHNICAL
DIRECTOR

It was a race in which Juan had very strong pace – he qualified on the front row – but ended in disappointment for us and him as he ran out of brakes. Basically, that was down to a misjudgement from us as to the size of brake duct we could use.

There's a very significant aerodynamic advantage to be had from smaller ducts, and the Barcelona circuit isn't especially hard on brakes but is very demanding aerodynamically.

Even so, our choice was quite a racy one, but based on the information of our Friday running, we felt it would be just the right side of marginal. Unfortunately, it wasn't. However, it was such a fine line that Ralf [Schumacher] was able to recognise the situation and adjust his driving accordingly and, by braking a little bit

earlier, managed to bring his car home in sixth place.

The difference in duct size we were choosing from gave an aero advantage of around 1%, which at Barcelona would equate to over 0.1s per lap. Over a race distance, that would translate to around 6s.

It may sound ridiculous that a team like Williams should make such a mistake, and it's true that it wasn't satisfactory, but the margins we're talking about are highly critical. Carbon-fibre brake disc wear goes exponential once it reaches a certain temperature and begins oxidising, and it can be that if your disc surface temperature is 840°C you're perfectly alright, but if it's 860° you're in deep trouble. It may have simply been that the difference in track grip between Friday and Sunday was enough to tip us over the edge by giving us more tyre grip and therefore more braking requirement.

Although Ralf coped with the problem and Juan didn't, I wouldn't necessarily say that was Juan's fault. We really should have been able to alert him to the problem sooner. By the time we alerted him, the situation had reached runaway proportions. Perhaps Ralf had experienced the problem before in his career and recognised the feeling.

Ralf finished sixth after adjusting his driving to cope with a brake problem

GEOFF WILLIS
BAR
TECHNICAL
DIRECTOR

Our chances were adversely affected by the moment that Jenson had in qualifying that left him 13th on the grid. So we were depending on Taku and he drove well, qualifying third and running in fourth place for the first couple of stints. He was being caught by [Fernando] Alonso's Renault as we approached the second stops.

They stopped one lap before us and their stop took 6.9s. We reckoned on going longer than that and didn't respond. We gave Taku a good stop at 8.1s. The difference in time should have equated to something like 10kg of fuel, which we reckoned should have given us an extra three laps, maybe four. In fact, we only got an extra two laps out of the tactic and Alonso got the place.

You might conclude from this that the Renault had better fuel consumption than us. You have to be careful because our only evidence is looking at the video and seeing how long their fuel rig was attached, and the errors are sufficient that you could get the calculation wrong by quite a lot. However, a pattern did seem to emerge through the season.

Better fuel consumption is a very significant advantage for two reasons. The length of your stop and the combination of lower fuel loads and new tyres can be very advantageous in track positioning. And, of course, you can qualify lighter for the same duration of stint.

Initially, I think Honda found it difficult to understand why we should focus on fuel consumption, but they have certainly taken it on board now.

The other critical point in Alonso passing Taku was that his out-lap was faster. Both our drivers found that the car was a bit twitchy on new tyres. I don't think there was any particular problem, but I think we still had something to learn about car set-up and tyre preparation in terms of pressures, temperatures and blankets.

Typical Barcelona fuel consumption: 2.68kg per lap
Regulation fuel flow 12 litres/second (approx 9kg/second depending on fuel density)
Typical fuel flow duration = stationary time minus 1s

	Alonso's lap 25 stop	Sato's lap 26 stop
Duration	6.9s	8.1s
Calculated stint duration	19 laps	23 laps
Actual stint duration	17 laps (2 less than calc)	19 laps (4 less than calc)

BAR's calculations on fuelling Sato longer than Alonso didn't prove correct and they lost position

RACE RESULTS
SPAIN
CATALUNYA

RACE DATE May 9th
CIRCUIT LENGTH 2.876 miles
NO. OF LAPS 66
RACE DISTANCE 189.777 miles
WEATHER warm and dry, 22°C
TRACK TEMP 37°C
RACE ATTENDANCE 108,300
LAP RECORD Michael Schumacher,
1m 17.450s, 133.667mph, 2004

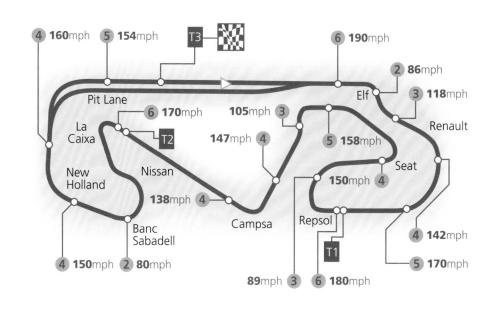

Circuit diagram with speeds:
4 160mph · 5 154mph · T3 · 6 190mph · 2 86mph · 3 118mph · Elf · Renault · Pit Lane · 6 170mph · 105mph · 3 · 5 158mph · La Caixa · T2 · 147mph 4 · Seat · New Holland · Nissan · 150mph 4 · Campsa · Repsol · 138mph 4 · Banc Sabadell · 4 150mph · 2 80mph · T1 · 4 142mph · 5 170mph · 89mph 3 · 6 180mph

PRACTICE 1

	Driver	Time	Laps
1	M Schumacher	1m15.658s	8
2	R Barrichello	1m16.033s	8
3	A Davidson	1m16.516s	26
4	R Zonta	1m16.688s	26
5	J Button	1m17.060s	6
6	R Schumacher	1m17.165s	12
7	F Alonso	1m17.429s	11
8	T Sato	1m17.481s	6
9	O Panis	1m17.489s	6
10	K Räikkönen	1m17.563s	5
11	JP Montoya	1m17.635s	10
12	M Webber	1m17.763s	11
13	D Coulthard	1m17.973s	7
14	J Trulli	1m18.341s	16
15	C da Matta	1m18.362s	12
16	B Wirdheim	1m18.603s	20
17	C Klien	1m18.615s	14
18	T Glock	1m18.658s	23
19	F Massa	1m18.760s	11
20	G Fisichella	1m18.886s	12
21	N Heidfeld	1m19.198s	16
22	G Pantano	1m19.925s	14
23	G Bruni	1m20.858s	16
24	B Leinders	1m21.058s	21
25	Z Baumgartner	1m21.535s	17

PRACTICE 2

	Driver	Time	Laps
1	J Button	1m15.935s	19
2	A Davidson	1m16.184s	34
3	R Zonta	1m16.864s	37
4	R Schumacher	1m16.433s	25
5	F Alonso	1m16.534s	20
6	R Barrichello	1m16.698s	28
7	M Schumacher	1m16.729s	25
8	J Trulli	1m16.734s	20
9	K Räikkönen	1m16.798s	17
10	C da Matta	1m16.833s	24
11	O Panis	1m16.925s	23
12	JP Montoya	1m17.067s	27
13	D Coulthard	1m17.069s	16
14	M Webber	1m17.178s	31
15	T Glock	1m17.568s	31
16	B Wirdheim	1m17.676s	21
17	F Massa	1m17.906s	22
18	T Sato	1m17.970s	4
19	G Fisichella	1m18.001s	24
20	N Heidfeld	1m18.117s	23
21	G Pantano	1m18.726s	21
22	G Bruni	1m19.149s	17
23	Z Baumgartner	1m20.313s	15
24	B Leinders	1m22.386s	31
25	C Klien	no time	2

PRACTICE 3

	Driver	Time	Laps
1	J Button	1m15.984s	10
2	J Trulli	1m16.015s	8
3	JP Montoya	1m16.048s	4
4	R Schumacher	1m16.233s	7
5	M Schumacher	1m16.519s	8
6	T Sato	1m16.685s	11
7	O Panis	1m16.721s	6
8	R Barrichello	1m16.795s	8
9	D Coulthard	1m17.106s	8
10	C da Matta	1m17.252s	8
11	G Fisichella	1m17.277s	6
12	F Alonso	1m17.294s	4
13	K Räikkönen	1m17.428s	8
14	F Massa	1m17.860s	7
15	N Heidfeld	1m18.643s	13
16	G Pantano	1m19.146s	10
17	C Klien	1m19.851s	18
18	Z Baumgartner	1m19.949s	12
19	G Bruni	no time	3
20	M Webber	no time	2

PRACTICE 4

	Driver	Time	Laps
1	T Sato	1m14.836s	13
2	M Schumacher	1m15.025s	11
3	JP Montoya	1m15.232s	13
4	J Trulli	1m15.457s	15
5	R Barrichello	1m15.540s	12
6	J Button	1m15.627s	11
7	D Coulthard	1m15.768s	13
8	F Alonso	1m15.874s	12
9	M Webber	1m15.895s	24
10	C da Matta	1m15.895s	18
11	K Räikkönen	1m15.983s	7
12	R Schumacher	1m16.308s	17
13	C Klien	1m16.648s	24
14	N Heidfeld	1m16.746s	12
15	G Fisichella	1m17.145s	12
16	F Massa	1m17.282s	6
17	G Pantano	1m17.665s	14
18	O Panis	1m18.392s	5
19	Z Baumgartner	1m20.449s	10
20	G Bruni	1m21.005s	5

Best sectors – Qualifying		Speed trap – Qualifying	
Sector 1 M Schumacher	21.789s	1 T Sato	202.328mph
Sector 2 M Schumacher	29.847s	2 J Button	201.396mph
Sector 3 M Schumacher	23.386s	3 M Schumacher	200.712mph

Michael Schumacher
"Five straight wins, 200 grands prix, 75 wins: so many nice numbers together! I waited for the pit stops to pass Trulli and then just let the strategy do the work."

Juan Pablo Montoya
"I started having brake problems in the very first part of the race, the pedal going very long. It seemed to get better, but then the brakes stopped working and I retired."

Kimi Räikkönen
"I made a good start from 13th and gained three places before the first corner, but it was quite clear that we weren't quick enough to do any better here."

Fernando Alonso
"Third and fourth was a great result for the team. I was stuck in the pack at the start and it took the first two stints to get clear. Everything went well from then on."

Jenson Button
"I was a little disappointed with the first stint because it just wasn't possible to overtake. Even so, considering where I started I was glad to salvage a point."

Rubens Barrichello
"I had a great race, after a difficult start. My two-stop strategy explained why I was happy to be fifth on the grid. We expected BAR to be quick, so the gamble paid off."

Ralf Schumacher
"I knew Barcelona was not among our favourite tracks but I expected more. I had to fight early on with brake problems so had to be very gentle on them to the end."

David Coulthard
"This was a very difficult race because obviously our performance was down. The positive things were that the car was reliable and our strategy was right."

Jarno Trulli
"I dedicated this podium to a very close friend of mine who was going through a very difficult time. As for the race, I made a dream start and pushed all the way."

Takuma Sato
"I made a good start and it was very exciting to be so close to the front of the grid. I was amazed by Trulli's start though – I just don't know how he did that!"

POSITIONS LAP BY LAP

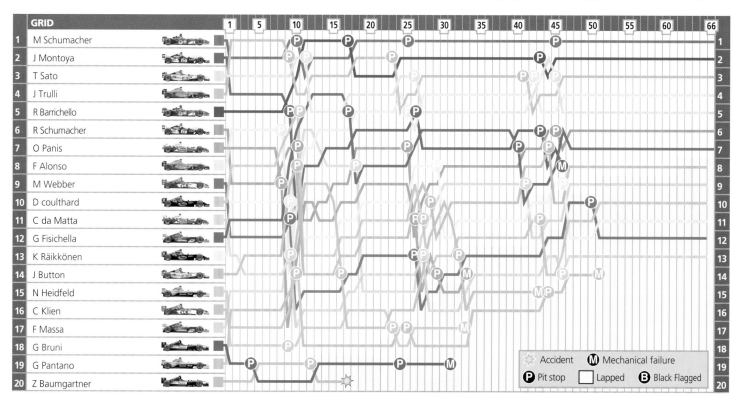

GRID			
1	M Schumacher		
2	J Montoya		
3	T Sato		
4	J Trulli		
5	R Barrichello		
6	R Schumacher		
7	O Panis		
8	F Alonso		
9	M Webber		
10	D coulthard		
11	C da Matta		
12	G Fisichella		
13	K Räikkönen		
14	J Button		
15	N Heidfeld		
16	C Klien		
17	F Massa		
18	G Bruni		
19	G Pantano		
20	Z Baumgartner		

☀ Accident Ⓜ Mechanical failure Ⓟ Pit stop ▢ Lapped Ⓑ Black Flagged

QUALIFYING

	Driver	Pre-qual time	Pos	Time
1	M Schumacher	1m16.320s	9	1m15.022s
2	JP Montoya	1m15.574s	1	1m15.639s
3	T Sato	1m16.434s	10	1m15.809s
4	J Trulli	1m16.156s	5	1m16.144s
5	R Barrichello	1m16.655s	13	1m16.272s
6	R Schumacher	1m16.040s	4	1m16.293s
7	O Panis	1m16.168s	6	1m16.313s
8	F Alonso	1m17.011s	15	1m16.422s
9	M Webber	1m16.212s	7	1m16.514s
10	D Coulthard	1m16.465s	12	1m16.636s
11	C da Matta	1m16.758s	14	1m17.038s
12	G Fisichella	1m15.746s	2	1m17.444s
13	K Räikkönen	1m16.240s	8	1m17.445s
14	J Button	1m16.462s	11	1m17.575s
15	N Heidfeld	1m17.043s	16	1m17.802s
16	C Klien	1m17.863s	17	1m17.812s
17	F Massa	1m15.771s	3	1m17.866s
18	G Bruni	1m20.372s	19	1m19.817s
19	G Pantano	1m17.965s	18	1m20.607s
20	Z Baumgartner	1m21.620s	20	1m21.470s

RACE

	Driver	Car	Laps	Time	Fastest	Avg. mph	Stops
1	M Schumacher	Ferrari F2004	66	1h27m32.841s	1m17.450s	130.000	3
2	R Barrichello	Ferrari F2004	66	1h27m46.131s	1m17.887s	129.672	2
3	J Trulli	Renault R24	66	1h28m05.135s	1m18.178s	129.205	3
4	F Alonso	Renault R24	66	1h28m05.793s	1m17.556s	129.189	3
5	T Sato	BAR-Honda 006	66	1h28m15.168s	1m17.678s	128.960	3
6	R Schumacher	Williams-BMW FW26	66	1h28m46.645s	1m18.548s	128.199	3
7	G Fisichella	Sauber-Petronas C23	66	1h28m49.949s	1m19.062s	128.119	2
8	J Button	BAR-Honda 006	65	1h27m40.536s	1m17.495s	127.842	3
9	F Massa	Sauber-Petronas C23	65	1h27m57.220s	1m18.819s	127.438	2
10	D Coulthard	McLaren-Mercedes MP4-19	65	1h28m14.419s	1m19.175s	127.024	3
11	K Räikkönen	McLaren-Mercedes MP4-19	65	1h28m17.262s	1m18.842s	126.956	3
12	M Webber	Jaguar-Cosworth R5	65	1h28m17.539s	1m18.617s	126.949	3
13	C da Matta	Toyota TF104	65	1h28m23.263s	1m19.112s	126.812	3
R	G Pantano	Jordan-Ford EJ14	51	Hydraulics	1m19.896s		3
R	JP Montoya	Williams-BMW FW26	46	Brakes	1m18.262s		3
R	C Klien	Jaguar-Cosworth R5	43	Throttle	1m19.142s		2
R	O Panis	Toyota TF104	33	Hydraulics	1m19.199s		3
R	N Heidfeld	Jordan-Ford EJ14	33	Gearbox	1m18.971s		2
R	G Bruni	Minardi-Cosworth PS04	31	Spun off	1m22.323s		2
R	Z Baumgartner	Minardi-Cosworth PS04	17	Spun off	1m23.390s		1

CHAMPIONSHIP

	Driver	Pts
1	M Schumacher	50
2	R Barrichello	32
3	J Button	24
4	F Alonso	21
	J Trulli	21
6	JP Montoya	18
7	R Schumacher	12
8	T Sato	8
9	D Coulthard	4
10	G Fisichella	2
11	F Massa	1
	M Webber	1
	K Räikkönen	1

	Constructor	Pts
1	Ferrari	82
2	Renault	42
3	BAR-Honda	32
4	Williams-BMW	30
5	McLaren-Mercedes	5
6	Sauber-Petronas	3
7	Jaguar-Cosworth	1

Fastest Lap
M Schumacher 1m17.450s, on lap 12 (133.667mph)
New lap record

Fastest through speed trap
J Button 207.599mph
Slowest through speed trap
Z Baumgartner 195.661mph

Fastest pit stop
J Trulli 20.997s
Slowest pit stop
K Räikkönen 31.696s

Giancarlo Fisichella
"When we were running together I was quicker than Montoya and kept ahead of him easily. My only problem was lapping traffic, which maybe cost me sixth place."

Mark Webber
"I suffered a slow start, so by the first corner I had already lost a few places. The pace of the R5 was good, but during my first stop we had a tyre-change problem."

Olivier Panis
"Coming in for my second pit stop I had a pit-limiter problem and got a drive-through penalty for speeding in pitlane. Later I stopped having lost hydraulic pressure."

Nick Heidfeld
"I lost hydraulic pressure, then the diff shut down, up and down shifts stopped working, and finally the gearbox went altogether. Naturally I was disappointed."

Gianmaria Bruni
"I had problems with brake locking. I adjusted the balance to try to improve things, but on the last lap the front wheels locked again and as a result I spun."

Felipe Massa
"I flat-spotted my front tyres in the first stint, giving me a lot of understeer. I could see Giancarlo. but he was pulling away. Still, it felt great to beat the McLarens."

Christian Klien
"I made up a few positions at the start, but made a small error at Turn 8 and lost a few too. I seemed to lose throttle control on lap 45 and was forced to stop the car."

Cristiano da Matta
"The car was slow in the first two stints so I wasn't really able to make any progress. It got better in the second half of the race but I lost valuable time being lapped."

Giorgio Pantano
"After we started pit stops a problem began with the hydraulics. Eventually it got so bad – and the car developed other hydraulic problems – so I just had to stop."

Zsolt Baumgartner
"It seemed like all the bad things that could happen did happen. I had to go on the dirty side of the track to let a Sauber past into Turn 9, lost grip and spun off."

A NEW WINNER

Michael Schumacher was toppled for the first time in 2004, as Renault's Jarno Trulli drove beautifully to score his maiden F1 win after seven years of trying

Michael Schumacher was very hacked off. It wasn't so much that he'd been beaten for the first time in 2004, nor that he'd failed to set a new record of victories in the first six races of a season. No, it was the manner in which he'd been denied a second bite at the win – by a rival, Juan Pablo Montoya, who was a whole lap down.

Could Schuey have made up 17s in as many laps over Jarno Trulli's Renault, enough to buy himself a late splash'n'dash? We will never know, but he was certainly up for trying until his tangle in the tunnel with the Williams as the safety car, deployed after Fernando Alonso's earlier accident in the tunnel, was preparing to come in.

Actually, it was easy to forget that Schumacher's was merely a story of what might have been. The real story – the one that actually unfolded – was a touching one of Trulli's maiden Grand Prix victory after seven years of trying. It could not have come at a more apposite place than Monte Carlo, where Trulli's skills have always meshed extremely well with the track's very specific demands. And even if Schumacher wasn't there at the end to make him fight for it, Jenson Button was instead, their late race duel bringing a great weekend to a perfect climax. For everyone, that is, except Ferrari and Michael Schumacher.

Trulli was in total control on the streets of Monte Carlo and he came away with his maiden victory

ROUND

6

MONACO
FORMULA 1™
GRAND PRIX DE
MONACO 2004
Monte Carlo

LAP BY LAP
ACTION

77 laps / 160 miles

Jarno Trulli gets his hammer down best and leads away from Alonso

Start to lap 3

The start of the race is aborted as Panis has a problem and is made to take the start from the back of the grid. He then fails to get away again on the parade lap, and so joins the race from pitlane. At the start, Trulli and Alonso get away well, with Alonso overtaking Button. Sato passes Michael Schumacher and Räikkönen to claim fourth place. Räikkönen slots in behind in fifth, with Michael Schumacher sixth, then Barrichello, Coulthard, Montoya and Webber. Klien touches Baumgartner and hits the wall. At the end of lap 1, Trulli is 0.8s clear of Alonso. By lap 3, the first three cars have pulled away from the field, which is bottled up behind Sato. However, his car is smoking with an engine problem, blowing up at Tabac. Sato pulls off, with Montoya and Webber passing through the smoke, but Coulthard slows and is hit from behind by Fisichella, who flies over the rear of the McLaren and lands inverted. The safety car is deployed. Fisichella is unhurt, but Coulthard pits to retire. Ralf Schumacher pits from 13th.

Fisichella climbs out of his inverted Sauber after flying over Coulthard

Laps 4 to 17

As the cars follow the safety car on lap 4, Heidfeld pits and rejoins without losing a position. The race restarts on lap 8, and Montoya passes Barrichello to take sixth. On lap 12, Trulli's lead over Alonso is out to 1.2s. Eighth-placed Webber retires and Ralf Schumacher passes Bruni for 13th. A lap later, Montoya pits, dropping from sixth to 10th. Pantano retires from 11th. By lap 16, Trulli's lead over Alonso has extended to 2.7s, with Button, Räikkönen, Michael Schumacher, Barrichello, da Matta, Massa, Heidfeld, Montoya, Panis, Ralf Schumacher and the Minardis following behind.

Alonso was caught out behind Ralf Schumacher, crashing in the tunnel

Laps 18 to 24

Button pits on lap 18, dropping from third to seventh. A lap after that, Räikkönen pits and rejoins still behind Button. Fourth-placed Barrichello pits on lap 20 as Michael Schumacher charges to make up lost ground. On lap 21, Massa pits, dropping from seventh to 10th. By lap 23 Trulli leads by 4.1s, with Alonso 4.4s ahead of third-placed Michael Schumacher. Da Matta pits and drops from fourth to seventh. Trulli pits on lap 24, and Alonso leads with Schumacher second. Trulli rejoins third.

Michael Schumacher limps back to the pits to retire

Laps 25 to 31

Alonso stops on lap 25 and Michael Schumacher takes the lead. Alonso rejoins third ahead of Button. On lap 26, Schumacher pits, rejoining behind Trulli and Alonso but ahead of Räikkönen and Button, followed by Barrichello, da Matta and Heidfeld. Räikkönen pits and retires with mechanical trouble on lap 28. Montoya passes Heidfeld a lap later at the Grand Hotel Hairpin. Then, on lap 31, Heidfeld pits, dropping to 10th place.

Trulli pushed hard to fend off a charging Button in the closing laps

Laps 32 to 46

On lap 32, Trulli builds his lead over Alonso, with Michael Schumacher third ahead of Button, Barrichello and da Matta. Ralf Schumacher pits from ninth on lap 37 and drops behind Heidfeld. Alonso tries to lap Ralf Schumacher in the tunnel on lap 42 but gets off line and crashes. The safety car comes out, triggering Button, da Matta, Montoya, Massa and Heidfeld to pit. Trulli pits a lap later and, behind the safety car, Michael Schumacher leads with Montoya immediately behind him on the track, albeit a lap down. The drivers prepare to restart on lap 46, as Michael Schumacher slows in the tunnel and is hit by Montoya, putting both into the barriers. The German drives around to the pits and retires.

Trulli and Button are radiant on the podium. Barrichello looks lost

Lap 47 to the finish

On lap 47, with the safety car withdrawn, Trulli drops Button and Barrichello. Montoya is fourth, da Matta fifth, Massa sixth and Heidfeld seventh. Ralf Schumacher and Panis are two laps down. On lap 52, da Matta pits for a drive-through penalty for ignoring blue flags, dropping him to sixth. Barrichello calls in on lap 55, remaining third nearly 40s behind Button. On lap 70, Ralf Schumacher retires with a mechanical problem. By lap 74, Button has closed to within 1s of Trulli, but can't pass. On lap 77, Trulli wins, with Button 0.497s behind. Barrichello is third, Montoya fourth, while Massa finishes 0.1s ahead of da Matta. Heidfeld is seventh with Panis and Baumgartner the only other finishers.

INSIDE LINE
JARNO TRULLI

I waited so long for this, and it came at the best place, Monaco. My first pole position and my first win. It couldn't have been more perfect. I drove a perfect race, leading from the beginning, and even with Michael on the track I would have won anyway. I was just managing the race, controlling it, looking after my tyres. I felt I could do anything and just respond when I needed to. I'd done that earlier in the race coming up to the first stops when Fernando [Alonso] was behind me. He was pushing me but, when I needed to, I responded. I knew I was quicker.

You always have to believe you can do it, and I knew that I had a good car. When things go wrong and you can't do much about it, it's tough, but you have to be strong, you have to be stubborn and you have to believe and trust in yourself. I have always been working well inside the team and I am working well with Fernando. Last year he got away with a victory and a pole position, and for me it was hard because things weren't coming around very well for me.

But I am the kind of person who never gives up. I knew that the team was growing up. In the beginning of the season, we had some handling problem and straight away the team reacted and focussed on this matter. We had some car improvement in the last two races before Monaco and obviously this makes you feel more confident. After that, I am very determined and stubborn. I always think that I can do it and, in the end, I do it. This was my weekend. Sometimes it is not, but this was my weekend, definitely. Really it hasn't changed anything. I will probably just be more confident but life doesn't change for me, it's just a little satisfaction.

I faced threats at different times from Fernando, Michael and Jenson, but I felt in control all the time. The second safety car for Fernando's accident changed things a bit with Michael, but still it was in my hands. At the end with Jenson, I knew he would put pressure on me but you can't overtake here and I just didn't want to take any risks.

It's all over for Michael Schumacher after his clash in the tunnel with Juan Pablo Montoya

Q THE BIG QUESTION

Who was the tinker in the tunnel?

Ever since the Austrian Grand Prix in 2003 when Michael Schumacher and Juan Pablo Montoya almost collided behind the safety car at the A1-Ring, there has been a niggle between them about this very point of etiquette. Montoya insists that Schumacher uses the safety car to make himself so dangerous and unpredictable that no challenger sitting in his wake dare try to take advantage on the restart.

Schumacher has always countered that as the race leader he's entitled to do whatever he sees fit if he's behind the safety car. However, back in Austria a year before, they were fighting for the lead. Here on the streets of Monte Carlo, Montoya was a lap down.

The kink in the tunnel may not be the most obviously safe place to suddenly brake hard, but it's actually the last decent stretch of fast running before the

racing lap begins on the start/finish straight. Schumacher was livid. "It's quite simple. I was the leading car and I was shoved out of the way by a lapped car."

"He was doing burn-outs, I was doing burn-outs," said Montoya. "I accelerated really hard and suddenly he braked really hard. I was going to run into the back of him. I tried to avoid him as much as I could. I put my car against the wall. Where else was I supposed to go – over the wall? His right rear touched my left front and that was it.

"It's not the first time something like this has happened with [Schumacher], it's just the first time that it has bitten him. I'm not blaming him for what happened. Like the stewards, I would put it down to a racing incident. I know he has a different view, but I don't care."

There are many incidents involving Montoya, someone said to Schumacher. "Yeah, come to think of it, that is true!" replied Michael. "You have a valid point."

Trulli sails majestically towards his first Grand Prix win, controlling the race from the front

PAT SYMONDS
RENAULT CHIEF OF ENGINEERING

I think Michael Schumacher could have finished no higher than second unless something had gone wrong with us. We couldn't lose the Grand Prix, as our strategy was to cover Michael and I second-guessed correctly what they might do because I was concerned about his pace towards the end of the stints. We had a quick enough car and we could afford to do long stints too, and that's how we covered him. With a quick car the strategy becomes considerably easier.

When they stayed out [during the second safety car period] I was surprised, but afterwards I thought why not? If they had shadowed us, there was no way they could have won. By staying out, they needed 17s in 17 laps, and there was just no way in the world they were 1s per lap quicker than us. That didn't worry me at all. They didn't have the pace necessary to make that work. The only time I was worried was when Jarno let Jenson Button get close. It didn't worry him, as he had it all under control and that was the way he preferred to control his race, but it felt a bit uncomfortable for me. All the time you were thinking it would only take one little slip, and when they came to lap the Minardi on the last lap my heart was in my mouth.

Fernando was absolutely on the same pace as Jarno. There was no reason as we approached the final stops to think that they might not have swapped positions. We weren't engineering anything; it would have been down to the drivers. Fernando is particularly good around pit stop time because not only is he very fast then but he's also very bright. At the first stops he wasn't able to do it because he wasn't as happy with his car, but was much more so after that.

As for his crash, his misunderstanding lapping Ralf [Schumacher] in the tunnel was very unfortunate. He said that Ralf allowed him alongside then accelerated. Maybe it wasn't deliberate, but as a backmarker being shown blue flags the onus is on you to facilitate the pass.

Over the years, I've seen so many drivers who when they score their first win they get that confidence. If Jarno had any fault, it was maybe that he didn't have the self-esteem that he should have had. I hope that the win proves to be the switch that he needs to really turn things around.

ROSS BRAWN
FERRARI TECHNICAL DIRECTOR

Well, first let's say that Jarno Trulli and Renault absolutely deserved their win. They were extremely quick all meeting, didn't make a single error and, had it not been for the second safety car, then we would definitely have been beaten anyway.

That said, I think that safety car definitely opened a window for us with Michael. People asked why we didn't come in. Well, it was because we weren't going to beat them that way. We still had fuel on board for another 17 laps, and we felt that we may as well give him a chance and see what he could do.

With Jarno coming in when the safety car was deployed, we reasoned Michael had about 15 laps less fuel than Jarno had which, around here, is worth about 0.6s. So he would've been 0.6s faster because he had less

fuel. At the end of his first stint he did a lap that was 0.4s faster than Jarno, so potentially the car was 0.4s faster, making a total of 1s per lap taking the lower fuel load into account. That makes 17s over 17 laps. The Monaco pit lane is 13s long. We would have had a very short fuel stop, as you'd

only need around 4s for the 14–15 laps we needed to the end – adding up to 17s. Which means we would still have had a chance of winning the race. It was a chance – a slim chance because everything would have had to go right – but if I was to put my money on anyone, Michael would be the guy.

	Best lap stint 1
Trulli	1m 14.870s (lap 22)
Schumacher	1m 14.439s (lap 23)
Difference	0.431s

	Calculated lap 46 fuel loads
	(racing resumption after s.car)
Trulli	64kg
Schumacher	34kg
Difference	30kg

Calculated Monaco lap time advantage of 30kg lower fuel load @ 0.025s/lap per 1kg = **0.75s**

17 laps @ advantage of 0.75s + 0.431s (1.181s/lap) = **20.077s**

Time penalty of Monaco pit stop = **13s + stationary time**
Calculated necessary stationary time for 15 laps of fuel to get to end of race (30kg @ 9kg/sec) = 3.33s. Plus 1s rig attach/detach = **4.33s**
Stop time + stationary time = **17.33s**

Theoretically, under perfect circumstances and assuming Trulli had nothing in hand, Schumacher could have exited his final stop 2.747s ahead of Trulli, in the lead.

Ross Brawn's calculations suggested that flat-out Schumacher could, just, have outrun Trulli to win

RACE RESULTS
MONACO
MONTE CARLO

RACE DATE May 23rd
CIRCUIT LENGTH 2.075 miles
NO. OF LAPS 77
RACE DISTANCE 159.812 miles
WEATHER Warm, dry, sunny, 23°C
TRACK TEMP 37°C
RACE ATTENDANCE 100,000
LAP RECORD Michael Schumacher,
1m 14.439s, 100.373mph, 2004

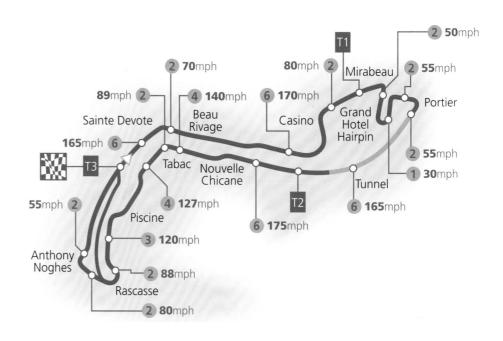

	PRACTICE 1		
	Driver	**Time**	**Laps**
1	M Schumacher	1m16.502s	14
2	T Sato	1m17.279s	24
3	J Button	1m17.339s	19
4	R Zonta	1m17.426s	28
5	D Coulthard	1m17.524s	16
6	F Alonso	1m17.686s	22
7	A Davidson	1m17.791s	36
8	J Trulli	1m17.856s	24
9	JP Montoya	1m17.937s	16
10	K Räikkönen	1m17.952s	18
11	G Fisichella	1m18.338s	16
12	R Barrichello	1m18.621s	14
13	C da Matta	1m18.889s	22
14	O Panis	1m19.218s	17
15	M Webber	1m19.261s	8
16	F Massa	1m19.335s	16
17	C Klien	1m19.487s	29
18	G Pantano	1m20.528s	18
19	T Glock	1m20.534s	15
20	B Wirdheim	1m20.680s	18
21	N Heidfeld	1m21.141s	17
22	G Bruni	1m21.201s	27
23	Z Baumgartner	1m22.203s	18
24	B Leinders	1m23.361s	12
25	R Schumacher	no time	3

	PRACTICE 2		
	Driver	**Time**	**Laps**
1	M Schumacher	1m14.741s	24
2	A Davidson	1m15.141s	32
3	R Barrichello	1m15.319s	27
4	J Trulli	1m15.472s	28
5	K Räikkönen	1m15.479s	14
6	J Button	1m15.520s	30
7	T Sato	1m15.664s	23
8	R Zonta	1m15.690s	34
9	F Alonso	1m15.701s	28
10	JP Montoya	1m16.097s	29
11	D Coulthard	1m16.229s	16
12	R Schumacher	1m16.556s	31
13	C da Matta	1m16.743s	31
14	G Fisichella	1m16.748s	30
15	O Panis	1m17.007s	24
16	G Pantano	1m17.309s	24
17	F Massa	1m17.422s	31
18	T Glock	1m17.756s	28
19	N Heidfeld	1m17.873s	18
20	C Klien	1m17.988s	15
21	G Bruni	1m18.822s	24
22	Z Baumgartner	1m18.829s	19
23	B Leinders	1m20.370s	25
24	B Wirdheim	no time	2
25	M Webber	no time	0

	PRACTICE 3		
	Driver	**Time**	**Laps**
1	M Schumacher	1m15.751s	9
2	R Barrichello	1m15.770s	9
3	M Webber	1m16.273s	19
4	J Button	1m16.358s	14
5	J Trulli	1m16.374s	8
6	F Alonso	1m16.386s	10
7	K Räikkönen	1m16.400s	15
8	T Sato	1m16.540s	15
9	JP Montoya	1m16.559s	13
10	D Coulthard	1m16.756s	13
11	R Schumacher	1m16.863s	9
12	G Fisichella	1m17.209s	11
13	C da Matta	1m17.409s	12
14	G Pantano	1m18.117s	13
15	O Panis	1m18.299s	11
16	C Klien	1m18.390s	21
17	N Heidfeld	1m19.221s	12
18	Z Baumgartner	1m23.963s	6
19	G Bruni	no time	3
20	F Massa	no time	2

	PRACTICE 4		
	Driver	**Time**	**Laps**
1	M Schumacher	1m14.014s	16
2	J Trulli	1m14.016s	19
3	T Sato	1m14.020s	22
4	F Alonso	1m14.138s	16
5	JP Montoya	1m14.212s	12
6	J Button	1m14.646s	15
7	D Coulthard	1m14.670s	13
8	R Schumacher	1m14.752s	15
9	K Räikkönen	1m15.034s	18
10	R Barrichello	1m15.174s	17
11	G Fisichella	1m15.709s	14
12	C da Matta	1m15.861s	25
13	C Klien	1m16.101s	22
14	F Massa	1m16.332s	19
15	N Heidfeld	1m16.385s	15
16	O Panis	1m16.431s	15
17	G Pantano	1m16.700s	19
18	M Webber	1m17.173s	4
19	Z Baumgartner	1m19.467s	12
20	G Bruni	no time	0

Best sectors – Qualifying			Speed trap – Qualifying		
Sector 1	T Sato	19.360s	1	M Schumacher	183.810mph
Sector 2	J Trulli	36.711s	2	F Massa	183.810mph
Sector 3	J Trulli	17.733s	3	R Schumacher	183.375mph

Michael Schumacher
"Jarno did a fantastic job. I don't think I could have challenged him. Nevertheless, when the accident in the tunnel with Juan happened I was leading the race."

Juan Pablo Montoya
"Start ninth in Monaco and you can't hope to finish fourth. With regards to the contact with Michael, he braked very hard, I moved to avoid him but we touched."

Kimi Räikkönen
"The engineers could see that there was a problem with the engine's pneumatic system and told me to come in and retire. We had been reasonably competitive."

Fernando Alonso
"Everything was going well and I was quite comfortable behind Jarno. I was lapping Ralf, he pushed me wide in the tunnel. There was no grip so I lost control."

Jenson Button
"It was a very tough but incredibly exciting race for me. I was getting frustrated stuck behind da Matta for three and a half laps. After I broke free I started catching Jarno."

Rubens Barrichello
"I think I was lucky to finish – third place was my birthday gift from God. It felt like something was broken in the suspension. I could only bring the car slowly home."

Ralf Schumacher
"After a few laps I lost fifth gear, then sixth and seventh. By the last few laps I had only fourth. I did the best I could, but I had to retire with just a few laps to go."

David Coulthard
"I couldn't see anything because of Sato's engine smoke. Fisichella flew over me and landed upside down. We were lucky it wasn't a more serious accident."

Jarno Trulli
"Taking my first win was a wonderful feeling. I believed in myself and the team. The car was perfect, the strategy correct and the pit stops just fantastic."

Takuma Sato
"I immediately felt a loss of engine power and saw some smoke, then my race was over. It was unfortunate that the smoke caused Coulthard and Fisichella to crash."

POSITIONS LAP BY LAP

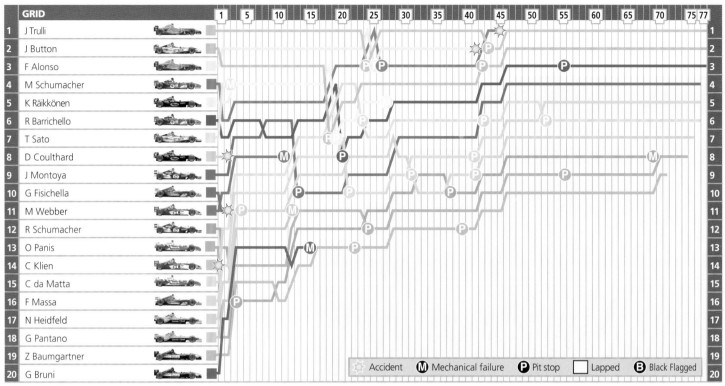

GRID			1	5	10	15	20	25	30	35	40	45	50	55	60	65	70	75 77	
1	J Trulli																		1
2	J Button																		2
3	F Alonso																		3
4	M Schumacher																		4
5	K Räikkönen																		5
6	R Barrichello																		6
7	T Sato																		7
8	D Coulthard																		8
9	J Montoya																		9
10	G Fisichella																		10
11	M Webber																		11
12	R Schumacher																		12
13	O Panis																		13
14	C Klien																		14
15	C da Matta																		15
16	F Massa																		16
17	N Heidfeld																		17
18	G Pantano																		18
19	Z Baumgartner																		19
20	G Bruni																		20

Accident Mechanical failure Pit stop Lapped Black Flagged

QUALIFYING

	Driver	Pre-qual time	Pos	Time
1	J Trulli	1m14.993s	8	1m13.985s
2	R Schumacher	1m14.483s	1	1m14.345s
3	J Button	1m14.799s	4	1m14.396s
4	F Alonso	1m14.816s	6	1m14.408s
5	M Schumacher	1m15.927s	14	1m14.516s
6	K Räikkönen	1m14.659s	2	1m14.592s
7	R Barrichello	1m15.329s	11	1m14.716s
8	T Sato	1m14.931s	7	1m14.827s
9	D Coulthard	1m14.728s	3	1m14.951s
10	JP Montoya	1m15.029s	9	1m15.039s
11	G Fisichella	1m14.814s	5	1m15.352s
12	M Webber	1m16.161s	15	1m15.725s
13	O Panis	1m15.125s	10	1m15.859s
14	C Klien	1m16.379s	16	1m15.919s
15	C da Matta	1m15.738s	13	1m16.169s
16	F Massa	1m15.436s	12	1m16.248s
17	N Heidfeld	1m16.914s	17	1m16.488s
18	G Pantano	1m17.674s	18	1m17.443s
19	Z Baumgartner	1m20.468s	19	1m20.060s
20	G Bruni	1m20.740s	20	1m20.115s

RACE

	Driver	Car	Laps	Time	Fastest	Avg. mph	Stops
1	J Trulli	Renault R24	77	1h45m46.601s	1m14.870s	90.650	2
2	J Button	BAR-Honda 006	77	1h45m47.098s	1m15.220s	90.643	2
3	R Barrichello	Ferrari F2004	77	1h47m02.367s	1m15.763s	89.580	2
4	JP Montoya	Williams-BMW FW26	76	1h46m10.808s	1m15.395s	89.133	2
5	F Massa	Sauber-Petronas C23	76	1h46m58.629s	1m17.151s	88.469	2
6	C da Matta	Toyota TF104	76	1h46m58.753s	1m16.232s	88.467	2
7	N Heidfeld	Jordan-Ford EJ14	75	1h46m58.271s	1m18.262s	87.310	2
8	O Panis	Toyota TF104	74	1h46m32.220s	1m16.494s	86.496	2
9	Z Baumgartner	Minardi-Cosworth PS04	71	1h45m51.401s	1m21.886s	83.523	3
10	R Schumacher	Williams-BMW FW26	69	Gearbox	1m17.588s	86.172	2
R	M Schumacher	Ferrari F2004	45	Accident	1m14.439s	-	1
R	F Alonso	Renault R24	41	Accident	1m15.226s	-	1
R	K Räikkönen	McLaren-Mercedes MP4-19	27	Engine	1m16.203s	-	1
R	G Bruni	Minardi-Cosworth PS04	15	Brakes	1m21.592s	-	2
R	G Pantano	Jordan-Ford EJ14	12	Hydraulics	1m19.415s	-	1
R	M Webber	Jaguar-Cosworth R5	11	Electronics	1m17.466s	-	0
R	T Sato	BAR-Honda 006	2	Engine	1m21.368s	-	0
R	D Coulthard	McLaren-Mercedes MP4-19	2	Accident	1m20.560s	-	0
R	G Fisichella	Sauber-Petronas C23	2	Accident	1m20.804s	-	0
R	C Klien	Jaguar-Cosworth R5	0	Accident	-	-	0

CHAMPIONSHIP

	Driver	Pts
1	M Schumacher	50
2	R Barrichello	38
3	J Button	32
4	J Trulli	31
5	JP Montoya	23
6	F Alonso	21
7	R Schumacher	12
8	T Sato	8
9	F Massa	5
10	D Coulthard	4
11	C da Matta	3
12	G Fisichella	2
	N Heidfeld	2
14	M Webber	1
	K Räikkönen	1

	Constructor	Pts
1	Ferrari	88
2	Renault	52
3	BAR-Honda	40
4	Williams-BMW	35
5	Sauber-Petronas	7
6	McLaren-Mercedes	5
7	Toyota	4
8	Jordan-Ford	2
9	Jaguar-Cosworth	1

Qualifying notes
R Schumacher Back 10 places for engine change
Baumgartner Started from pit lane

Fastest Lap
M Schumacher 1m14.439s,
on lap 23 (100.373mph)
New lap record

Fastest through speed trap
M Schumacher 188.275mph
Slowest through speed trap
G Bruni 172.057mph

Fastest pit stop
C da Matta 14.856s
Slowest pit stop
C da Matta 47.844s

Giancarlo Fisichella
"Sato's engine exploded, I had no vision at all. Suddenly there was a McLaren. The next thing I heard was the bang and I was upside down. I was okay but frustrated."

Mark Webber
"I was pleased with where we qualified, since I knew that our strategy would allow us to chase points, but on lap 11 I suffered a loss of drive and the car came to a stop."

Olivier Panis
"With all the problems we had at the start where the car stalled twice, to finish eighth was positive for the team. I did my best to make it to the finish with a brake problem."

Nick Heidfeld
"I was so happy to score not just one but two points. It meant so much for me and for the team. I think we employed the right strategy when the safety car came out."

Gianmaria Bruni
"I was able to keep up a reasonable pace, but then I lost first gear. It didn't cost me too much time, but I developed a glitch with third and second and had to stop."

Felipe Massa
"After Giancarlo's crash I found my second set of tyres was very good and I could concentrate on a good finish. Da Matta was behind so I was never able to relax."

Christian Klien
"I miscalculated the build-up of traffic at the Mirabeau corner, and as everyone pushed together I ran into Nick Heidfeld. I should have been up there in the points."

Cristiano da Matta
"This was probably the strongest pace we had had since the start of the season. We had a fourth place on our hands today but took sixth because of blue-flag problems."

Giorgio Pantano
"I had a gear problem – the down-shift function wasn't working, it was locking in fourth gear. I came in to see if we could fix it, but it was impossible and I had to stop."

Zsolt Baumgartner
"I had a gearbox problem just after the first corner. I reset the system and was able to get going again. It was a tough race physically and I was pleased to finish."

BACK ON TRACK

Michael Schumacher bounced back from the disappointment of Monaco to dominate at the Nürburgring, where Kimi Räikkönen hinted at a McLaren revival

Seven days after his Monaco disaster, here was Michael Schumacher getting back into the comfort zone of dominant victory, back at a conventional track that played to the strengths of his car. His margin of superiority was exaggerated here by Kimi Räikkönen spending all of the first stint holding up a queue of five of Michael's would-be pursuers because of tyre degradation borne of an optimistic compound choice. Not that it changed the outcome of

Schuey's victory: that was almost pre-destined.

Räikkönen fell by the wayside early into the second stint with the inevitable Mercedes engine failure, but what his slow pace should have done was guarantee that Rubens Barrichello's two-stop strategy worked to perfection. As in Spain, opting to stop one time less than the others in preference to taking on Michael on equal terms, Rubens was gifted an opportunity as the quick three-stopping BARs and Renaults had much of their strategy advantage over him nullified by being stuck behind the Finn's McLaren. It effectively did for the chances of the Renaults, but not for an inspired Takuma Sato.

The BAR driver came back hard at Barrichello going into his final stint, then made a move from such a long way back that the Ferrari driver discounted it happening. But it did, and they clashed, Barrichello getting away unscathed and coming home second, Sato sent pitward for a new nose – gifting team-mate Jenson Button with third – before suffering an engine failure.

It was back to winning ways for the Ferrari crew as Michael Schumacher took the chequered flag

ROUND **7**

EUROPE
2004 FORMULA 1™
ALLIANZ GRAND PRIX
OF EUROPE
Nürburgring

LAP BY LAP
ACTION

60 laps / 192 miles

Start and lap 1

Michael Schumacher gets away well and Trulli sticks with him before Sato makes a lunge under braking and emerges second. Then Sato and Trulli tangle as the cars head down the hill, letting Räikkönen through to second with Alonso and Sato in pursuit. Behind them, Montoya locks up at the first corner, veers left to avoid running into Barrichello, but tips Williams team-mate Ralf Schumacher into a spin, the German losing his front wing. Ralf is hit by da Matta and they both retire, with Montoya pitting for repairs. At the end of lap 1, Michael leads by 2.4s as Räikkönen is pressured by Alonso.

Ooops, Montoya clashes with his team-mate Ralf Schumacher...

Laps 2 to 10

Michael stretches his lead to 3.9s on lap 2, with a train of cars forming behind Räikkönen. By lap 7, it's 17s. Michael pits on lap 8, indicating that he was running light in qualifying. He rejoins in seventh. Räikkönen leads and continues to delay those behind. The Finn pits on lap 9, and Alonso takes the lead. Trulli pits as well, Alonso a lap later, leaving Sato in front with Barrichello second and Button third, as Räikkönen retires with a blown motor.

...then Ralf lands nose first in the Turn 1 gravel after clipping da Matta

Laps 11 to 18

Sato stays in the lead with Barrichello chasing him, but Michael moves to third on lap 11 as Button pits. This puts Coulthard up to fourth, with Klien fifth and Button rejoining in sixth. Sato pits on lap 12, and so Barrichello leads from Michael. Sato rejoins in third. On lap 13, Button passes Klien for fourth. Alonso makes a mistake on lap 14 and loses time. Barrichello stops on lap 15 and drops to third behind Michael and Sato. Coulthard is yet to stop and is delaying Button. Klien pits on lap 16, and Webber moves to sixth, but stops two laps later.

Räikkönen steps out after yet another Mercedes engine failure

Laps 19 to 25

Button passes Coulthard around the outside at Turn 1 on lap 19 to grab fourth. The Scot finally pits on lap 20 and falls into the midfield fight. Montoya has worked his way up to 10th by lap 22 by staying out after his first-lap stop. Panis has his second pit stop on lap 23, and falls from eighth to 10th. When he rejoins, he almost collides with Michael, the leader having to swerve in avoidance. Fisichella finally pits on lap 24, indicating that he is on a two-stop strategy. He falls from fifth to eighth, coming out behind Coulthard. Button comes into the pits for his second stop on lap 25, falling behind the two Renaults.

Button was helped to third when team-mate Sato hit trouble

Laps 26 to 41

Sato stops for the second time on lap 26, and Barrichello moves back to second. Coulthard, who is running seventh, goes out with a mechanical problem. Michael and Trulli pit on lap 28, by which time Michael is so far ahead that he rejoins in the lead, still 6s ahead of Barrichello. Montoya continues his progress by passing Klien for 10th. Alonso and Heidfeld pit on lap 30, and so Button moves to fourth again. Alonso rejoins in sixth. Button pits for the last time on lap 38, but comes out behind Sato who must pit again. By lap 40, Michael is 17s ahead of Sato. Barrichello, in third, has a full tank, but holds off Button with Trulli and Alonso fifth and sixth, and Fisichella, on a two-stop strategy, seventh.

After having a front wing fitted, Sato's engine gave up the ghost

Lap 42 to the finish

Alonso comes in for his last stop on lap 42 and falls behind Fisichella. Michael, Sato, Trulli and Fisichella all stop on lap 44 and, as Sato rejoins, Barrichello passes him. As Michael rejoins the race, he nearly hits Webber. Button has his final pit stop on lap 45 and stays fourth. Sato tries to pass Barrichello for second at Turn 1 on lap 46, and they collide. Sato loses part of his front wing and pits, dropping to fifth. Sato retires with engine failure on lap 48. The order is now set, with Michael comfortably ahead of Barrichello. Button is third and closing, but unlikely to catch Rubens. Trulli is fourth and Alonso fifth, while Fisichella is sixth and under attack from Webber. A lap down, Montoya is eighth, while Massa and Heidfeld dispute ninth all the way to the end. Michael scores a dominant win on lap 60, with Ferrari getting a 1–2, Barrichello staying ahead of Button.

Barrichello congratulates his race-winning team-mate, Schumacher

INSIDE LINE
TAKUMA SATO

This was a really strong weekend for me all the way through to the race. Obviously I was very disappointed not to finish, and there was also the accident with Rubens Barrichello when I was fighting for second place. Overall, my emotions from this race were very, very positive, as I qualified on the front row for the first time in my F1 career, and I was going to split the Ferraris in the race despite having been held up during the first stint.

In pre-qualifying we were fastest and, although we were quite light on fuel there, we did a very similar lap in second qualifying with a proper fuel load on board – more than Michael [Schumacher] as it turned out.

At the start, Jarno [Trulli] came past from the row behind, and with his car's fantastic starts that wasn't really a surprise, but I was able to hang on and then outbrake him into the first turn. That put us side-by-side and allowed Kimi [Räikkönen] to get among us, and then into Turn 4 Jarno hit me and that allowed Kimi and Fernando [Alonso] past. So I was fourth during that first stint and

really being held up by Kimi, who I think was having some problems.

I was thankful we had put a good fuel load in the car, because after Kimi pitted I was able to stay out for three more laps and push really hard, allowing me to get out behind just the two Ferraris and leave the others behind.

Michael was obviously out of reach, but Rubens [Barrichello], on a two-stop compared to my three, was the one I was really racing with. Coming up to my final stops I was going really fast, and if I could have done one more lap I was almost certain to come out of the pits ahead of Rubens, but it was too critical. We might have had just enough fuel to do it, but it would have been very tight. So we came out just behind Rubens, but I had a lot of grip on my new tyres and on the second lap I caught him up at the first corner. I had to make my move then before the new tyre grip went away, and I knew that I could outbrake him. But he just seemed not to see me and we hit. Then, later, I had an engine failure. I was disappointed, but happy too.

Q THE BIG QUESTION

Takuma Sato: loose cannon or demon racer?

"I thought what he did was a bit amateurish," said Rubens Barrichello of Takuma Sato's controversial passing attempt on him that resulted in a collision.

"He needs to calm down," said Jarno Trulli, who had been spectacularly outbraked by Sato into the same turn at the start, and then clashed with him three corners later.

Sato, typically, was unconcerned by such reactions. "I was totally in control. It was from quite a long way back, but I had to make my move on Rubens on that lap because after I would have lost my new tyre advantage. I was perfectly in control, my wheels were not locked up, I was going to make the apex. So how could I have been too late? It was more a question of why Rubens didn't seem to see me.

"I'm sure Rubens is saying 'oh what an idiot Sato is'," said his engineer Jock Clear, "but I'm equally sure he won't really be thinking that. He'll be thinking 'bloody hell, he's strong' and he won't turn in on him next time they're close together. For sure, there's an element of laying down territory when you're a new guy, and actually it reminds me a lot of Jacques [Villeneuve] in his early time in F1 in that respect. Show him half a door and he will take it.

"He may look back on this and think 'that was my chance to score my only podium', but I very much doubt that. I think at the end of his career, when he's won a championship and 25 Grands Prix, he'll look back and think 'I could've got an extra podium if I hadn't tried to pass Barrichello'."

Takuma Sato proved that he isn't a driver prepared to bow to the reputation of others

Being lapped meant being shown the blue flag and that cost Toyota and Panis dear

MIKE GASCOYNE
TOYOTA TECHNICAL DIRECTOR

This was quite a bleak result for us, with Olivier [Panis] finishing back in 11th and Cristiano [da Matta] being taken out in the first few seconds of the race. We were actually not as bad as that made us look, but it illustrates how the problems spiral when you don't have enough basic performance in the car.

We were just slow enough to start getting lapped, and that just fritters away such huge chunks of time. If you can be just a little bit quicker, so that you don't get lapped, suddenly you look twice as good. But when you get lapped you're going off line, getting your tyres dirty, getting blue-flagged – and it just compounds. Olivier was shown blue flags twice on what were critical positioning in- or out-laps when he was fighting for position. That actually lost us a place to [Nick] Heidfeld. We shouldn't really have been behind a Jordan and, had it just been a straight race between us, without the random blue flags, we wouldn't have been. It just happened to fall in a sequence that hurt us particularly badly. The guys asked me 'what can we do about the blue-flag situation?' and I said it's simple: let's design a car that's fast enough not to be shown them.

The trouble with our car is generally we qualify alright, because the engine is good, but it doesn't have enough downforce and its weight is too high up in the car. The net effect of that, aside from lack of performance, is high tyre degradation and at tracks that induce that anyway we really struggle. The Nürburgring is one of those circuits. We qualified half-respectably [Panis 10th, da Matta 11th] because over one lap the tyre grip could overcome some of our problems. But we knew that in the race we would just be going backwards because of the tyre degradation.

Any time the degradation is lower and we can run a two-stop strategy, like at Indianapolis, we do alright. And then, of course, we're not getting lapped. So the difference over a race distance between a good and a bad track for us might only be 20s in performance, but in actual time it can be more than double that.

Panis/M Schumacher Lap Comparison

Before Panis's second stop on lap 23, he has lost **63.359s** to Schumacher.
Panis lapped by Schumacher on lap 25
Average lap time deficit to Schumacher before Panis's second stop: **2.88s/lap**
By lap 29, after Schumacher's second stop, Panis is **86.48s** behind.
Average lap time deficit to Schumacher in seven laps since being lapped: **3.30s/lap**
Panis losing average of an extra **0.42s** per lap once he starts to be lapped
= extra **13s** over remaining race distance of 31 laps.

MARTIN WHITMARSH
McLAREN
MANAGING
DIRECTOR

Although Kimi [Räikkönen] qualified on the second row and ran in second place until his retirement, the overwhelming emotion in the team coming away from the Nürburgring was one of failure, not progress. After all, we had three engine failures during the weekend of one of our home Grands Prix.

There was no developmental reason why the car appeared more competitive here. Both Kimi and David [Coulthard] reported that the 19A's usual oversteer characteristics actually helped at a track like this where a lot of the corners are understeer-inducing, and that the track doesn't have many of the sort of high-speed corners where the messages the car gave didn't give them confidence. There were odd signs through the season that you could get some performance from the car – like when the track was cold or at a test when you had a lot of time to set it up. However, you've got to have a car that inspires confidence in the driver, and generally this car just didn't have that, although at the Nürburgring that particular problem wasn't as prevalent as usual.

David lost the chance of a good qualifying run when his engine failed on the pre-qualifying in-lap after he had set a very good time. Kimi was able to do a very good job in qualifying, and because F1 today is in large part about track positioning at the beginning of the race, he was able to be well up in the race too. He was then suffering with tyre degradation, as we had gone for a softer compound than most and the weather was hotter than forecast when the choice was made. Yet it all came to nothing with another engine failure.

The engine failures weren't related to one single component. The thing to be learned, though, was to make sure that all the principal players in the programme work in concert as a team. We had good people in both Brixworth and Stuttgart that were prepared to accept change, others who weren't. We were not being as process-driven as we needed, and the problems were coming from all sorts of directions. We were simply not a benchmark team in that area.

We weren't failing as a consequence of lack of resource, or lack of effort, or lack of quality engineers. We were failing because we weren't bringing that together with the appropriate team work and processes needed to get the job done.

Engine failures blighted McLaren's weekend. This is Coulthard getting out before his qualifying run

RACE RESULTS

EUROPE
NÜRBURGRING

RACE DATE May 30th
CIRCUIT LENGTH 3.199 miles
NO. OF LAPS 60
RACE DISTANCE 191.938 miles
WEATHER warm and dry, 21°C
TRACK TEMP 34°C
RACE ATTENDANCE 106,000
LAP RECORD Michael Schumacher,
1m 29.468s, 128.741mph, 2004

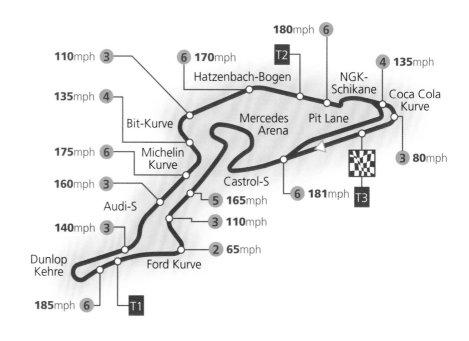

180mph 6
110mph 3
6 170mph
T2
Hatzenbach-Bogen
NGK-Schikane
4 135mph
135mph 4
Coca Cola Kurve
Bit-Kurve
Mercedes Arena
Pit Lane
175mph 6
Michelin Kurve
3 80mph
160mph 3
Castrol-S
140mph 3
Audi-S
5 165mph
6 181mph T3
3 110mph
Dunlop Kehre
Ford Kurve
2 65mph
185mph 6
T1

PRACTICE 1

	Driver	Time	Laps
1	A Davidson	1m29.447s	19
2	M Schumacher	1m29.631s	14
3	R Barrichello	1m29.865s	12
4	M Webber	1m31.448s	6
5	R Zonta	1m31.587s	23
6	K Räikkönen	1m31.643s	4
7	F Massa	1m31.673s	9
8	R Schumacher	1m31.680s	14
9	F Alonso	1m31.768s	16
10	J Button	1m31.770s	11
11	JP Montoya	1m31.782s	10
12	O Panis	1m31.910s	10
13	D Coulthard	1m32.301s	5
14	T Sato	1m32.500s	10
15	J Trulli	1m32.696s	15
16	C da Matta	1m32.915s	15
17	T Glock	1m33.925s	15
18	N Heidfeld	1m33.971s	10
19	C Klien	1m34.402s	11
20	G Pantano	1m34.488s	15
21	B Wirdheim	1m35.043s	9
22	Z Baumgartner	1m35.186s	13
23	G Bruni	1m35.455s	17
24	B Leinders	1m37.609s	15
25	G Fisichella	no time	2

PRACTICE 2

	Driver	Time	Laps
1	K Räikkönen	1m29.355s	18
2	J Button	1m29.618s	18
3	R Schumacher	1m29.677s	28
4	D Coulthard	1m29.700s	17
5	J Trulli	1m29.919s	23
6	R Barrichello	1m29.943s	24
7	A Davidson	1m30.028s	32
8	F Alonso	1m30.163s	22
9	M Schumacher	1m30.227s	9
10	T Sato	1m30.283s	17
11	JP Montoya	1m30.337s	20
12	M Webber	1m30.466s	29
13	O Panis	1m30.497s	24
14	C da Matta	1m30.531s	25
15	R Zonta	1m30.949s	33
16	G Fisichella	1m30.974s	26
17	B Wirdheim	1m31.760s	26
18	T Glock	1m32.080s	29
19	C Klien	1m32.217s	15
20	F Massa	1m32.310s	12
21	G Bruni	1m32.643s	19
22	Z Baumgartner	1m32.986s	18
23	N Heidfeld	1m33.175s	20
24	G Pantano	1m33.393s	17
25	B Leinders	1m34.538s	19

PRACTICE 3

	Driver	Time	Laps
1	J Button	1m29.485s	11
2	R Schumacher	1m30.192s	7
3	T Sato	1m30.261s	7
4	JP Montoya	1m30.369s	11
5	M Schumacher	1m30.418s	10
6	K Räikkönen	1m30.532s	5
7	J Trulli	1m30.551s	5
8	F Alonso	1m30.600s	5
9	R Barrichello	1m30.681s	5
10	O Panis	1m31.248s	11
11	C da Matta	1m31.814s	11
12	G Fisichella	1m31.816s	9
13	F Massa	1m32.206s	10
14	M Webber	1m32.206s	5
15	N Heidfeld	1m32.690s	13
16	Z Baumgartner	1m32.898s	14
17	G Pantano	1m33.226s	12
18	G Bruni	1m33.499s	9
19	C Klien	1m33.917s	16
20	D Coulthard	no time	2

PRACTICE 4

	Driver	Time	Laps
1	J Button	1m28.827s	13
2	M Schumacher	1m29.064s	15
3	T Sato	1m29.127s	15
4	K Räikkönen	1m29.354s	12
5	R Barrichello	1m29.545s	13
6	F Alonso	1m29.555s	13
7	D Coulthard	1m29.955s	14
8	R Schumacher	1m30.176s	9
9	O Panis	1m30.277s	14
10	C da Matta	1m30.316s	16
11	G Fisichella	1m30.519s	13
12	M Webber	1m30.867s	18
13	J Trulli	1m30.986s	11
14	C Klien	1m31.061s	15
15	F Massa	1m31.504s	11
16	N Heidfeld	1m31.956s	12
17	Z Baumgartner	1m32.753s	15
18	G Bruni	1m32.894s	15
19	G Pantano	1m33.383s	13
20	JP Montoya	no time	10

Best sectors – Qualifying			Speed trap – Qualifying	
Sector 1	M Schumacher	28.940s	1 M Schumacher	193.680mph
Sector 2	M Schumacher	36.795s	2 T Sato	193.442mph
Sector 3	K Räikkönen	22.610s	3 R Barrichello	192.634mph

Michael Schumacher
"I dedicated this result to the memory of Umberto Agnelli who was a great supporter of our team. I was able to build up a good lead as Kimi held up the field."

Juan Pablo Montoya
"At the first corner Rubens, who was in front of me, braked quite early and both Ralf and I locked tyres. Panis hit my front tyre which threw me straight into Ralf."

Kimi Räikkönen
"I was obviously extremely frustrated and disappointed. I was at the front after getting past Sato and Trulli on lap 1. There was no doubt things were looking good."

Fernando Alonso
"Raikkonen held me up a lot during the first stint, which meant that after I pitted I came out among traffic. The steering later became vague but I protected my place."

Jenson Button
"Considering the problem I had with grip throughout the weekend, third was a great result. This podium was luckier than the previous four, but a podium nonetheless."

Rubens Barrichello
"Running two stops almost worked, as I went from seventh to second, but I had to push in traffic. Sato's move was amateurish. Luckily I saw his nose and moved over."

Ralf Schumacher
"What happened was obviously a shame. I am 100% sure Juan didn't do it on purpose. Shame I hit Cristiano da Matta too, but I was a passenger by that time."

David Coulthard
"The race was going well. I had a good start from the back of the grid, making the most of other people getting into trouble on lap 1, and went from 20th to ninth."

Jarno Trulli
"The race was nearly over at the first corner – if I hadn't opened the door, Sato would have taken me out. In the confusion I pressed the pit-lane speed limiter."

Takuma Sato
"I was extremely disappointed, ending up with engine failure. After my last pit stop I had a lot of grip and was confident I could take Rubens. Unfortunately we touched."

POSITIONS LAP BY LAP

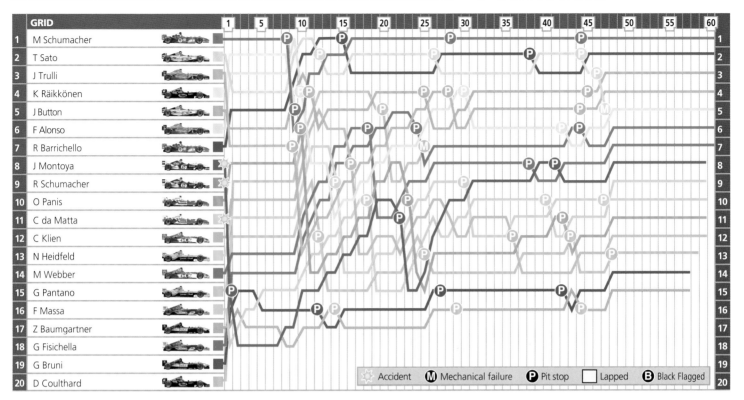

	GRID		1	5	10	15	20	25	30	35	40	45	50	55	60	
1	M Schumacher															1
2	T Sato															2
3	J Trulli															3
4	K Räikkönen															4
5	J Button															5
6	F Alonso															6
7	R Barrichello															7
8	J Montoya															8
9	R Schumacher															9
10	O Panis															10
11	C da Matta															11
12	C Klien															12
13	N Heidfeld															13
14	M Webber															14
15	G Pantano															15
16	F Massa															16
17	Z Baumgartner															17
18	G Fisichella															18
19	G Bruni															19
20	D Coulthard															20

Accident   **M** Mechanical failure   **P** Pit stop   Lapped   **B** Black Flagged

QUALIFYING

	Driver	Pre-qual time	Pos	Time
1	M Schumacher	1m28.278s	2	1m28.351s
2	T Sato	1m27.691s	1	1m28.986s
3	J Trulli	1m29.905s	13	1m29.135s
4	K Räikkönen	1m28.897s	6	1m29.137s
5	J Button	1m28.816s	5	1m29.245s
6	F Alonso	1m29.069s	8	1m29.313s
7	R Barrichello	1m29.014s	7	1m29.353s
8	JP Montoya	1m29.092s	9	1m29.354s
9	R Schumacher	1m28.655s	3	1m29.459s
10	O Panis	1m29.243s	10	1m29.697s
11	C da Matta	1m29.272s	11	1m29.706s
12	C Klien	1m30.933s	15	1m31.431s
13	N Heidfeld	1m32.216s	18	1m31.604s
14	M Webber	1m30.579s	14	1m31.797s
15	G Pantano	1m31.928s	17	1m31.979s
16	F Massa	1m31.879s	16	1m31.982s
17	Z Baumgartner	1m33.061s	19	1m34.398s
18	G Bruni	1m33.077s	20	deleted
19	G Fisichella	1m29.327s	12	no time
20	D Coulthard	1m28.717s	4	no time

RACE

	Driver	Car	Laps	Time	Fastest	Avg. mph	Stops
1	M Schumacher	Ferrari F2004	60	1h32m35.101s	1m29.468s	124.379	3
2	R Barrichello	Ferrari F2004	60	1h32m53.090s	1m30.101s	123.977	2
3	J Button	BAR-Honda 006	60	1h32m57.634s	1m30.457s	123.876	3
4	J Trulli	Renault R24	60	1h33m28.774s	1m31.131s	123.189	3
5	F Alonso	Renault R24	60	1h33m36.088s	1m31.065s	122.966	3
6	G Fisichella	Sauber-Petronas C23	60	1h33m48.549s	1m31.413s	122.756	2
7	M Webber	Jaguar-Cosworth R5	60	1h33m51.307s	1m31.893s	122.695	2
8	JP Montoya	Williams-BMW FW26	59	1h32m46.774s	1m31.424s	122.049	3
9	F Massa	Sauber-Petronas C23	59	1h33m16.843s	1m32.729s	121.394	2
10	N Heidfeld	Jordan-Ford EJ14	59	1h33m17.176s	1m32.121s	121.386	3
11	O Panis	Toyota TF104	59	1h33m43.733s	1m32.506s	120.813	3
12	C Klien	Jaguar-Cosworth R5	59	1h33m51.086s	1m32.804s	119.655	2
13	G Pantano	Jordan-Ford J14	58	1h33m06.003s	1m32.772s	119.567	4
14	G Bruni	Minardi-Cosworth PS04	57	1h33m28.380s	1m35.555s	117.037	3
15	Z Baumgartner	Minardi-Cosworth PS04	57	1h33m50.760s	1m34.666s	116.572	2
R	T Sato	BAR-Honda 006	47	Engine	1m30.004s	-	4
R	D Coulthard	McLaren-Mercedes MP4-19	25	Engine	1m32.337s	-	1
R	K Räikkönen	McLaren-Mercedes MP4-19	9	Engine	1m31.670s	-	1
R	R Schumacher	Williams-BMW FW26	0	Accident	-	-	0
R	C da Matta	Toyota TF104	0	Accident	-	-	0

CHAMPIONSHIP

	Driver	Pts
1	M Schumacher	60
2	R Barrichello	46
3	J Button	38
4	J Trulli	36
5	F Alonso	25
6	JP Montoya	24
7	R Schumacher	12
8	T Sato	8
9	F Massa	5
	G Fisichella	5
11	D Coulthard	4
12	C da Matta	3
	M Webber	3
14	N Heidfeld	2
15	K Räikkönen	1

	Constructor	Pts
1	Ferrari	106
2	Renault	61
3	BAR-Honda	46
4	Williams-BMW	36
5	Sauber-Petronas	10
6	McLaren-Mercedes	5
7	Toyota	4
8	Jaguar-Cosworth	3
9	Jordan-Ford	2

Qualifying notes
Baumgartner Back 10 places for engine change
Bruni Back 10 places for engine change
Webber 1s added for yellow flag infringement

Fastest Lap
M Schumacher 1m29.468s,
on lap 7 (128.741mph)
New lap record

Fastest through speed trap
M Schumacher 199.584mph
Slowest through speed trap
Z Baumgartner 192.500mph

Fastest pit stop
F Alonso 22.888s
Slowest pit stop
G Pantano 33.629s

Giancarlo Fisichella

"Our target was to score points, but I never believed sixth was possible. The car was fantastic, the balance impeccable, our strategy perfect. The team did a great job."

Mark Webber

"Seventh place and two points in the bag was exactly what the doctor ordered. As the race wore on the balance of the car got better and it was good fun to drive."

Olivier Panis

"Everything was going well and I was retaining eighth, but it became rather difficult to hold onto the group in front of me. The tyres dropped off quite quickly."

Nick Heidfeld

"I was really happy with our performance over the weekend, especially in the race. I was pushing Felipe hard at the end which was really good fun. All very positive."

Gianmaria Bruni

"I was satisfied with the result – I had to try and maintain good lap times but also conserve my rear tyres. If I had pushed too hard I would have risked blistering them."

Felipe Massa

"When I let out the clutch at the start, nothing happened. Running behind the Minardis after that ruined my race since I lost so much time. It was a shame."

Christian Klien

"The start was great and I managed to overtake two cars by the first corner. The car felt good. I enjoyed my battle with Montoya: that's what we are all about."

Cristiano da Matta

"I didn't really see what happened, and there was not much I could do about the situation. There was nowhere for me to go, but these things occur from time to time."

Giorgio Pantano

"I was lucky to finish the race, to be honest, because for the final 25 laps I had a problem with the downshift. The first part of the race didn't go too badly."

Zsolt Baumgartner

"Generally we had a good, solid race. The biggest problem for me was actually the amount of time I lost under waved blue flags, having to let other drivers through."

Michael Schumacher is back in sixth, but he still raced through to the front of the field to win

STREET FIGHTER

Michael Schumacher was made to fight for this, especially by team-mate Rubens Barrichello, but still he came out in front for the seventh victory of his campaign

There were at least three drivers other than Michael Schumacher who *could* have won this race. But none of them did. So, for the second Canadian Grand Prix in succession Ferrari's lead driver made clinical capital from the shortcomings of others, thus becoming the first man in the sport's history to win the same event on seven occasions.

Of those who could conceivably have beaten him, perhaps the most intriguing was his team-mate Rubens Barrichello, who on a softer compound tyre made Michael fight, and looked for all the world as if he was actually quicker and would pull away if he could only get past. He wouldn't have needed to have overtaken had he not made a critical error in qualifying that left him behind Schumacher on the grid. But, even so, he might still have won. Had he been able to run longer than Michael at the first stint, which he completed right on Michael's gearbox, he would probably have got ahead. The whisper in the paddock was that he indeed had enough fuel on board to do this but was called in first by the team.

Of the other contenders, polesitter Ralf Schumacher – on a three-stop to the two of Ferrari – made his brother sweat for the win, the Williams well suited to the low-downforce track. But he, along with the other Williams and two Toyotas, was subsequently disqualified for brake duct infringements. Even more than the Williams cars, the Renaults appeared to have Ferrari-beating pace but both suffered driveshaft failures.

ROUND **8**

CANADA
FORMULA 1™
GRAND PRIX DU
CANADA 2004
Montréal

LAP BY LAP
ACTION

70 laps / 190 miles

Ralf Schumacher makes a flying start ahead of Button and Alonso

Start to lap 6

Sato and Bruni start from pitlane, the teams filling up the cars before the start. Trulli's transmission fails at the start and he pulls off. Ralf Schumacher leads from Button, Alonso, Montoya, Michael Schumacher, Räikkönen and Barrichello. Klien tips Coulthard into a spin, launching Klien into Jaguar team-mate Webber's car. Various drivers take evasive action and Webber pits with a puncture. At the end of lap 1, Ralf leads Button by 1.1s. Coulthard passes several cars on lap 2 to move to 13th, battling with Sato who is also making progress.

Coulthard's McLaren is tipped into a spin on lap 1 by Klien's Jaguar

Laps 7 to 17

Ralf's lead is up to 2.5s by lap 7 from Button and Alonso, with Montoya and Michael Schumacher next up. Barrichello passes Räikkönen for sixth, and Massa passes Klien for 15th. Webber pits and retires. On lap 8, Massa passes Sato for 14th. Ralf's lead has extended to 3.9s by lap 11. Coulthard pits. Räikkönen pits a lap later, dropping from seventh to ninth. Button and Montoya stop on lap 13. Alonso is second, Michael third and Barrichello fourth, with Button rejoining sixth behind da Matta but ahead of Montoya. On lap 15, Ralf Schumacher pits, and Alonso leads with Michael chasing and Barrichello third. Ralf rejoins fourth. Button passes da Matta for fifth. Alonso pits on lap 17, and Michael leads from Barrichello, with Ralf third and Button fourth. Da Matta pits, dropping from sixth to 11th. Glock and Klien also pit. Räikkönen is given a drive-through penalty for crossing the white line at the pit exit.

Close action as Coulthard and Sato attempt to make up lost ground

Laps 18 to 27

Barrichello pits on lap 18, rejoining behind Ralf, Button and Montoya. Klien pits again. On lap 19, Michael stops and Ralf leads with Button second. Michael rejoins third, with Montoya fourth and Barrichello fifth. Räikkönen comes in for his drive-through, dropping to 10th. Ralf leads Button by 4s on lap 20, with a 2.7s gap to Michael. Heidfeld pits from eighth, knocking over a Jordan mechanic as he departs. He is delayed, dropping to 18th. Luckily, the mechanic has no serious injuries. Klien pits again. On lap 21, Button closes on Ralf. Panis pits from seventh, rejoining 12th. Sato pits on lap 23, falling from 10th to 13th. On lap 25, Fisichella pits from seventh, rejoining 10th. Massa stops a lap later, dropping from eighth to 14th.

Barrichello appeared faster than Michael, but couldn't find a way by

Laps 28 to 43

Massa is back in again within two laps on lap 28, falling to 15th. Montoya pits two laps later, followed by Räikkönen. They rejoin seventh and eighth. On lap 31, Button pits, rejoining sixth, thus promoting Michael Schumacher to second. A lap after that, Coulthard pits, rejoining 12th. Ralf Schumacher's lead is 12s by lap 33 when he pits, rejoining third behind Michael and Barrichello. Rubens is obviously faster than Michael but is unable to pass. By lap 40, it's clear that the Ferraris are two-stopping. Heidfeld pits. On lap 42, 12th-placed Sato spins in front of the Ferraris, avoiding contact, then pitting and rejoining again. Panis pits, dropping from 10th to 11th. Glock also stops.

Massa's battered Sauber is cleared away after its shunt at the hairpin

Laps 44 to 62

Barrichello stops for a second time on lap 44, falling behind Ralf and Button. Da Matta pits, retaining eighth place. On lap 45, Räikkönen pits, rejoining seventh behind Fisichella. Sato passes Panis for 10th on lap 46. Then Michael Schumacher pits on lap 47, and Ralf leads. Ralf comes in a lap later, staying ahead of Barrichello. Button, Montoya and Fisichella all stop on lap 49, leaving Ralf second ahead of Barrichello, Button and Montoya. Sato's engine blows. On lap 53, Coulthard pits, re-emerging ninth. Massa pits two laps after that, retaining 12th. By lap 60, Michael is 8s ahead of Ralf, with a 5s gap to Barrichello. Button and Montoya fight over fourth, and sixth-placed Räikkönen pits for a steering wheel change, losing sixth place to Fisichella.

Michael Schumacher sets the Ferrari pit crew celebrating again

Lap 63 to the finish

Massa crashes at the hairpin on lap 63, hitting the tyres head-on after suspension failure. He is unhurt. Two laps later, Klien spins, albeit without losing his 13th place. The chequered flag is waved at Michael Schumacher on lap 70, with Ralf second, Barrichello third, Button fourth and Montoya fifth. Everyone else is lapped, with Fisichella sixth, Räikkönen seventh, da Matta eighth, Coulthard ninth and Panis 10th. The disqualification of Ralf, Montoya, da Matta and Panis elevates the drivers down to the final finisher, Minardi's Zsolt Baumgartner.

INSIDE LINE
RUBENS BARRICHELLO

This was a really great race for me. I was able to push Michael very hard, and I think that had things been just a little different I could have won the race. When everyone says I sit behind Michael and am happy, here they can see that I'm not: I'm fighting as hard as anybody to win. It was a good fight.

I decided to go for a softer tyre than Michael. It wasn't to do a different strategy, it was just that I preferred it and felt that it would be better for me. I think the race showed that I made the better choice, because there were two stages of the race when I was able to push him, when I could feel that I was quicker and that I would have pulled away if I'd got by him.

I made a small mistake in qualifying, and that meant that Michael was one place ahead of me on the grid and ahead in the race. We were on similar strategies, and the only way that I was going to beat him was by overtaking him or going a bit longer. I tried to pass at the hairpin. I

went for it but I went for it badly. It wasn't that I was backing off, but sometimes when you get inside if your brakes are working good, that's it. My pedal was a little long, though, so I couldn't do it like that. I went for the inside, hoping I had made him brake so late he wouldn't make the corner. I was saying to him 'ooh go straight, go straight'. But he was able to keep his line, and then I thought I might be able to pass him on the following straight by getting out of the corner better. It may have looked like I was backing off, but actually I was trying to get a better exit than him. Unfortunately, the bollard at that corner had come out and there were pieces of it everywhere, so it was difficult to know what part of the corner to take, and it didn't quite work.

After the last stops I was still pushing like crazy, but my brake pedal had got long by then and I wasn't able to get slowed down enough for Turn 8, so I went over the grass, losing me about 5s. After that, the fight was over really.

Both Williams entries flew, to second and fifth, but they, like the Toyotas, were ejected

Q THE BIG QUESTION

How did the brake ducts on the Williams and Toyota entries come to be the wrong shape?

Both Williams and both Toyotas were disqualified from the Canadian Grand Prix race results, after post-race scrutineering revealed that their brake ducts were in contravention of the technical regulations.

For Williams, it meant the loss of second and fifth places. Brake cooling is very marginal at Montreal, and illegally big ducts could give a significant advantage. However, it wasn't the size that was the problem.

"The duct was offset towards the centreline of the car," explained the team's technical director Sam Michael, "and that took it out of the prescribed 'box' laid down in the regs. There's a gap next to the tyre and that amount is what

is extra on the duct on the other side. Not only was there no improvement in performance, but it would've made it worse because the brake cooling would be the same, but the last thing you'd want to do is move the duct into the airflow that goes on to the diffuser off the back of the front wing. Yet illegal is illegal. We screwed up.

"A junior guy in the aero department drew it and didn't check its legality. It was released from the aero department without being checked. It went to the track and we didn't check it. There are normally three points at which it's checked and then a fourth at the circuit. It's obviously quite an embarrassing thing because, if you look at it, I should have realised and so should the other engineers because you can see it from miles away."

SAM MICHAEL
WILLIAMS TECHNICAL DIRECTOR

It's a race that we at Williams will remember for the wrong reasons but, before the disqualifications, we actually had a very strong performance, with Ralf [Schumacher] doing a really brilliant job for us by qualifying on pole position and then coming home a very close second.

Montreal is a low-downforce track that took us into a relatively more efficient part of our aero performance – where you run your ride heights, etc, is quite different. You move into a region where the diffuser works differently, and we really didn't know how we were going to be there until we turned up and saw what everyone else's aero packages were like. It turned out that in this configuration the FW26 was pretty good, certainly more competitive than on high-downforce tracks.

We ran Ralf on a three-stop strategy, whereas Ferrari, I assume because of their qualifying performance deficit, opted to run Michael on a two. Up until about halfway through the race, comparing Ralf and Michael and where each should have been given their strategies, Ralf was actually ahead by about 2s. But during the third stint Michael opened up a gap that was too big for us to cover. Their car on average was about 0.1s per lap quicker. That gave Michael 7s over the race – enough for him to keep just in front of us.

Actually, at the start you saw Ralf just storming away and that made us think initially that we were comfortably going to do it. But actually I think that early stint performance was coming from the Michelins. At Montreal you can run quite soft tyres because there are no fast corners, but it's very hard on traction and so you have to be careful you don't blister your tyres. But Michelin tend to be able push those limits a bit further [than Bridgestone] and so can run a bit softer. After the first four laps, the gap stabilised as [Ferrari's] tyres came up to temperature.

We got Juan to the finish in fifth, but he lost out really from Friday afternoon, which he'd lost to a fuel leak. He was playing catch-up after that. Ralf's always been good here. He's got this place pretty much sorted out.

Ralf Schumacher's early race pace flattered to deceive, but he only lost as the race unwound

PAT SYMONDS
RENAULT CHIEF OF ENGINEERING

It's a bit silly to extrapolate a race from a duration of 3s in the case of Jarno [Trulli], but I actually believe that the driveshaft failures we suffered on both cars cost us victory here.

We had both cars in front of Michael Schumacher on the grid, we were on the same two-stop strategy as him and we had the pace. Pace and positional advantage, plus the benefit of having two cars with which to control Michael, and I really think that we could have done it.

Montreal was one of those tracks where we had the speed in the car that we could run to an ideal strategy. We opted for two stops mainly on account of brake wear, which is always the primary consideration at this place.

Conventional wisdom says that running the car light will take less out of the brakes, but I'm not so sure. Over the course of a race you use around 180kg of fuel. On average you've got to accelerate it and brake it, so the integral of the braking energy is pretty similar. However, one of the reasons why braking is more marginal than it used to be is that we have a lot more tyre grip and there's no doubt if you've got a lot more tyre grip you're using the brakes harder.

That leads me to think that maybe doing a three-stop race here isn't a very clever idea. But I'm not sure whether I'm right! If you adopt a three-stop strategy the average tyre grip is better for the race, so you just wonder if that doesn't do a bit of harm

We had the choice of going for straightline speed or traction out of the hairpin, and we went for the latter as it meant we weren't vulnerable at the end of that straight.

Fernando's race was coming alive and he was just beginning to trouble Michael. Earlier, Michael had got ahead because of a problem at our first pit stop, but now he was coming back at him. It took a little while for Fernando's true pace to become apparent because he was suffering a little from front tyre graining initially, and that rather caught us by surprise. I think we had slightly better pace than Ferrari once that graining phase was over, but by then Fernando was behind them both because of the problem at the first stop, and realistically it would have been difficult to pass.

Alonso's recovery from tyre graining

	Alonso lap time	Difference to M.Schumacher lap
Lap 31	1m 15.105s	-0.2s
32	1m 15.166s	+0.3s
33	1m 15.934s	+1.0s
34	1m 15.201s	+0.5s
35	1m 15.162s	+0.8s
36	1m 14.868s	0s
37	1m 14.740s	-0.3s
38	1m 14.790s	0s
39	1m 14.656s	-0.1s
40	1m 14.292s	-0.2s
41	1m 14.179s	-1.5s
42	1m 14.615s	+0.2s
43	1m 14.323s	-0.3s
44	1m 14.183s	-0.1s
45	Retired	

Fernando Alonso would have been in with a shot at winning but for his fumbled first pit stop

RACE RESULTS
CANADA
MONTRÉAL

RACE DATE June 13th
CIRCUIT LENGTH 2.709 miles
NO. OF LAPS 70
RACE DISTANCE 189.694 miles
WEATHER warm and sunny, 25°C
TRACK TEMP 35°C
RACE ATTENDANCE 114,000
LAP RECORD Rubens Barrichello,
1m 13.622s, 132.515mph, 2004

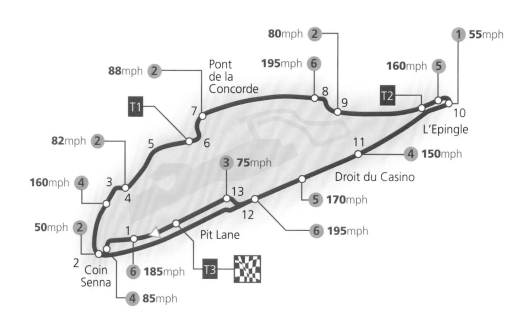

PRACTICE 1

	Driver	Time	Laps
1	M Schumacher	1m14.013s	15
2	R Barrichello	1m14.291s	13
3	A Davidson	1m14.519s	19
4	R Zonta	1m14.952s	23
5	J Trulli	1m15.428s	11
6	F Alonso	1m15.606s	14
7	J Button	1m15.905s	10
8	JP Montoya	1m15.928s	13
9	R Schumacher	1m15.948s	12
10	O Panis	1m15.997s	14
11	G Fisichella	1m16.240s	12
12	C da Matta	1m16.475s	13
13	K Räikkönen	1m16.570s	7
14	T Sato	1m16.655s	13
15	M Webber	1m16.820s	7
16	D Coulthard	1m16.947s	8
17	N Heidfeld	1m17.135s	17
18	F Massa	1m17.447s	6
19	T Glock	1m17.890s	27
20	C Klien	1m18.463s	23
21	G Bruni	1m18.828s	16
22	Z Baumgartner	1m18.959s	19
23	B Leinders	no time	1
24	B Wirdheim	no time	3
25	G Pantano	no time	0

PRACTICE 2

	Driver	Time	Laps
1	T Sato	1m14.086s	20
2	F Alonso	1m14.426s	29
3	M Schumacher	1m14.535s	26
4	K Räikkönen	1m14.581s	19
5	R Barrichello	1m14.705s	31
6	R Zonta	1m14.871s	33
7	C da Matta	1m15.146s	30
8	J Button	1m15.152s	21
9	D Coulthard	1m15.164s	19
10	G Fisichella	1m15.293s	28
11	J Trulli	1m15.492s	17
12	A Davidson	1m15.513s	21
13	O Panis	1m15.538s	28
14	R Schumacher	1m15.803s	22
15	M Webber	1m15.926s	14
16	F Massa	1m16.119s	25
17	G Bruni	1m16.235s	22
18	N Heidfeld	1m16.508s	23
19	T Glock	1m16.524s	28
20	JP Montoya	1m16.564s	6
21	C Klien	1m16.815s	27
22	Z Baumgartner	1m16.981s	17
23	B Leinders	1m17.697s	23
24	B Wirdheim	1m19.260s	18
25	G Pantano	no time	0

PRACTICE 3

	Driver	Time	Laps
1	M Schumacher	1m13.865s	13
2	F Alonso	1m13.946s	9
3	J Button	1m14.047s	10
4	R Barrichello	1m14.284s	12
5	J Trulli	1m14.421s	11
6	K Räikkönen	1m14.584s	7
7	D Coulthard	1m14.747s	7
8	JP Montoya	1m15.067s	17
9	R Schumacher	1m15.191s	13
10	G Fisichella	1m15.290s	10
11	C da Matta	1m15.573s	13
12	F Massa	1m15.764s	16
13	O Panis	1m15.843s	13
14	M Webber	1m15.854s	6
15	C Klien	1m16.124s	10
16	N Heidfeld	1m16.305s	15
17	T Glock	1m16.928s	13
18	G Bruni	1m18.409s	15
19	Z Baumgartner	1m18.711s	15
20	T Sato	no time	4

PRACTICE 4

	Driver	Time	Laps
1	J Trulli	1m12.629s	13
2	F Alonso	1m12.901s	14
3	J Button	1m13.026s	14
4	T Sato	1m13.235s	11
5	JP Montoya	1m13.320s	14
6	M Schumacher	1m13.420s	14
7	K Räikkönen	1m13.566s	14
8	D Coulthard	1m13.686s	13
9	R Barrichello	1m13.904s	10
10	C Klien	1m14.340s	20
11	C da Matta	1m14.521s	24
12	R Schumacher	1m14.697s	16
13	M Webber	1m14.835s	29
14	G Fisichella	1m14.902s	10
15	O Panis	1m14.916s	16
16	F Massa	1m15.332s	12
17	N Heidfeld	1m15.987s	14
18	T Glock	1m16.417s	17
19	Z Baumgartner	1m16.579s	17
20	G Bruni	1m16.825s	17

Best sectors – Qualifying

Sector 1	T Sato	20.136s
Sector 2	R Schumacher	23.022s
Sector 3	R Schumacher	28.867s

Speed trap – Qualifying

1	M Schumacher	211.835mph
2	R Schumacher	209.723mph
3	JP Montoya	209.350mph

Michael Schumacher
"I don't know why I have won so often here – I guess it's down to a good package and a bit of luck. Rubens pushed me very hard. I had no problems with the car."

Juan Pablo Montoya
"The team made a mistake. At the same time, when you go off track it's a mistake and the team don't go and slag you off. They didn't do it on purpose. It's racing."

Kimi Räikkönen
"I was given a drive-through penalty for touching the white line at the pit exit, and I had to make an additional stop to change steering wheels, which cost me sixth."

Fernando Alonso
"The car performed well during the first two stints, but then the left driveshaft failed – as I came down the straight I could feel it pulling to one side and had to stop."

Jenson Button
"I bogged down at the second pit stop after the anti-stall kicked in as I released the clutch. We felt a podium was possible and didn't expect to be behind Williams."

Rubens Barrichello
"This was a great race and I had fun fighting Michael. When I was pushing him I could feel the brake.pedal getting spongy. Then I realised that they were cooked."

Ralf Schumacher
"We were all disappointed, especially the mechanics. It was almost the result we were desperately looking for. It was just an unfortunate, unintentional incident."

David Coulthard
"Turn 2 is always difficult here and one of the Jaguars went into the back of my car and spun me around. I had a couple of lively laps as I regained positions."

Jarno Trulli
"My race was over as soon as it had started. I got a normal start but then suddenly the driveshaft failed. I pulled off straight away and that was that."

Takuma Sato
"We changed our plan so that I would start from the pit lane on a two-stopper. I tried really hard to make up places, but another engine failure ended my race."

POSITIONS LAP BY LAP

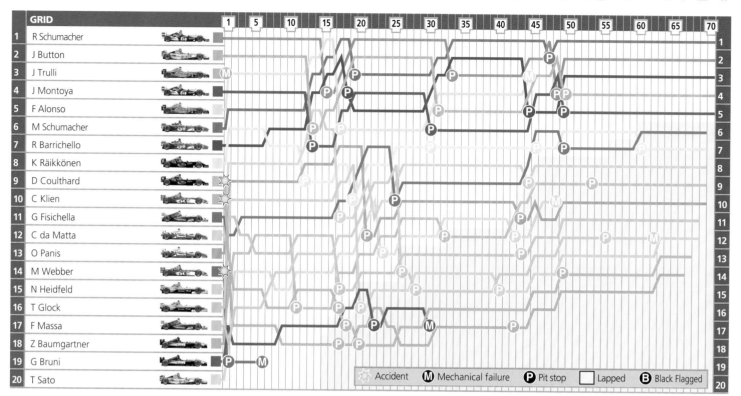

GRID		
1	R Schumacher	
2	J Button	
3	J Trulli	
4	J Montoya	
5	F Alonso	
6	M Schumacher	
7	R Barrichello	
8	K Räikkönen	
9	D Coulthard	
10	C Klien	
11	G Fisichella	
12	C da Matta	
13	O Panis	
14	M Webber	
15	N Heidfeld	
16	T Glock	
17	F Massa	
18	Z Baumgartner	
19	G Bruni	
20	T Sato	

Accident ⋆ Mechanical failure Ⓜ Pit stop Ⓟ Lapped ▢ Black Flagged Ⓑ

QUALIFYING

	Driver	Pre-qual time	Pos	Time
1	R Schumacher	1m12.441s	1	1m12.275s
2	J Button	1m13.333s	7	1m12.341s
3	J Trulli	1m13.149s	5	1m13.023s
4	JP Montoya	1m12.746s	2	1m13.072s
5	F Alonso	1m12.826s	3	1m13.308s
6	M Schumacher	1m13.463s	8	1m13.355s
7	R Barrichello	1m13.782s	11	1m13.562s
8	K Räikkönen	1m13.602s	9	1m13.595s
9	D Coulthard	1m13.206s	6	1m13.681s
10	C Klien	1m14.751s	16	1m14.532s
11	G Fisichella	1m13.663s	10	1m14.674s
12	C da Matta	1m13.807s	12	1m14.851s
13	O Panis	1m14.166s	13	1m14.891s
14	M Webber	1m14.715s	15	1m15.148s
15	N Heidfeld	1m15.657s	17	1m15.321s
16	T Glock	1m16.865s	18	1m16.323s
17	T Sato	1m12.989s	4	1m17.004s
18	Z Baumgartner	1m17.903s	19	1m17.064s
19	F Massa	1m14.392s	14	no time
20	G Bruni	no time	20	no time

RACE

	Driver	Car	Laps	Time	Fastest	Avg. mph	Stops
1	M Schumacher	Ferrari F2004	70	1h28m24.803s	1m13.630s	128.732	2
2	R Barrichello	Ferrari F2004	70	1h28m29.911s	1m13.622s	128.609	2
3	J Button	BAR-Honda 006	70	1h28m45.212s	1m14.246s	128.329	3
4	G Fisichella	Sauber-Petronas C23	69	1h28m44.952s	1m15.078s	126.413	2
5	K Räikkönen	McLaren-Mercedes MP4-19	69	1h29m05.165s	1m14.752s	125.935	5
6	D Coulthard	McLaren-Mercedes MP4-19	69	1h29m11.637s	1m15.478s	125.783	3
7	T Glock	Jordan-Ford EJ14	68	1h29m10.219s	1m16.300s	123.993	2
8	N Heidfeld	Jordan-Ford EJ14	68	1h29m10.556s	1m15.890s	123.985	3
9	C Klien	Jaguar-Cosworth R5	67	1h29m03.252s	1m15.731s	122.329	4
10	Z Baumgartner	Minardi-Cosworth PS04	66	1h29m25.857s	1m17.516s	119.995	2
R	F Massa	Sauber-Petronas C23	62	Accident	1m15.560s	-	3
R	T Sato	BAR-Honda 006	48	Engine	1m15.076s	-	2
R	F Alonso	Renault R24	44	Driveshaft	1m14.179s	-	1
R	G Bruni	Minardi-Cosworth PS04	30	Gearbox	1m18.025s	-	1
R	M Webber	Jaguar-Cosworth R5	6	Suspension	1m17.739s	-	1
R	J Trulli	Renault R24	0	Suspension	-	-	0
DQ	R Schumacher	Williams-BMW FW26	70	1h28m25.865s	1m14.010s		
DQ	JP Montoya	Williams-BMW FW26	70	1h28m46.003s	1m14.295s		
DQ	C da Matta	Toyota TF104	69	1h29m09.640s	1m15.652s		
DQ	O Panis	Toyota TF104	69	1h29m31.939s	1m16.045s		

CHAMPIONSHIP

	Driver	Pts
1	M Schumacher	70
2	R Barrichello	54
3	J Button	44
4	J Trulli	36
5	F Alonso	25
6	JP Montoya	24
7	R Schumacher	12
8	G Fisichella	10
9	T Sato	8
10	D Coulthard	7
11	F Massa	5
	K Räikkönen	5
13	C da Matta	3
	N Heidfeld	3
	M Webber	3

	Constructor	Pts
1	Ferrari	124
2	Renault	61
3	BAR-Honda	52
4	Williams-BMW	36
5	McLaren-Mercedes	15
6	Sauber-Petronas	12
7	Jordan-Ford	5
8	Toyota	4
9	Jaguar-Cosworth	3

Qualifying notes

Baumgartner	Back 10 places for engine change
Bruni	Back 10 places for engine change
Sato	Started race from pit lane

Fastest Lap
R Barrichello 1m13.622s,
on lap 68 (132.515mph)
New lap record

Fastest through speed trap
R Barrichello 216.174mph
Slowest through speed trap
M Webber 201.320mph

Fastest pit stop
R Schumacher 23.941s
Slowest pit stop
N Heidfeld 1m12.616s

Giancarlo Fisichella

"I wasn't very quick off the line, but that was a blessing after Coulthard and Klien tangled right in Turn 1. Our strategy was great and it was satisfying to score again."

Mark Webber

"As Christian made contact with David, the outcome was his R5 landing on my front wing. I could tell that some damage had been done: it was rear suspension."

Olivier Panis

"Unfortunately we had a lot of bad luck in the race – and after it. I got a good start, but the Jags crashed in front of me and I had to back off, which left me in ninth."

Nick Heidfeld

"My first pit stop really screwed up my race. The lollipop came up too early and I went over the guy on the fuel nozzle. He was okay but I lost nearly a minute."

Gianmaria Bruni

"A problem developed with the gearbox, and there was no choice but to retire. It was bad luck because the car had been handling well up to that point."

Felipe Massa

"I lost a lot of time in my first pit stop. As for the accident, I have no idea what happened – I was a passenger. I only went to hospital for a precautionary check-up."

Christian Klien

"I very quickly found myself in the thick of it. I was hit from behind and forced into the back of Coulthard. I did tried to avoid him but took off and landed on Mark."

Cristiano da Matta

"It was a tough race, but ultimately disappointing not to take a point away. We just had to put the frustration behind us as we headed off to Indianapolis."

Timo Glock

"I cannot describe how good it felt to find out I scored two points in my first ever F1 race. Perfect. It was great for the team. It was my target just to finish the race."

Zsolt Baumgartner

"I wrecked my first set of tyres avoiding several incidents on the first lap. Then Klien misjudged an overtaking move and hit my right front with his left rear, so I spun."

BANK ON MICHAEL

Even when a race doesn't appear to be going his way, Michael Schumacher somehow manages to come out in front, as he showed at Indianapolis

Even the hospitalisation of his brother Ralf and a team-mate who was demonstrably quicker than him failed to halt the Michael Schumacher steamroller. With the Ferrari team keeping Michael up to date on progress of Ralf's drawn-out rescue, he re-focussed himself on seeing off his only challenger, Rubens Barrichello.

Just as at the Canadian Grand Prix, Barrichello was clearly quicker, but Michael put himself in the positional driving seat – this time by slipstreaming past into the lead at the first restart. From then on, Barrichello was always trying to undo that development rather than controlling the race from the front.

Despite being used by Ferrari as a foil to hold up the rest of the field while Michael pitted during the second safety car period, Barrichello was still able to get himself on course to beat the reigning World Champion as he came up to

his final pit stop. But for hitting a piece of track debris on his in-lap, Barrichello would almost certainly have leapfrogged his team leader. As it was, Schumacher was able to aggressively repel Barrichello's fresh-tyre attack on him to settle the issue once and for all.

Pre-race, Ferrari had had concerns about blistering rear tyres and accepted that they may have needed to three-stop rather than two. This would have made them vulnerable to the BAR of an inspired Takuma Sato, but such concerns were not realised. Barrichello – who had outqualified Schumacher despite running with a much heavier fuel load – began the race on the understanding that he was two-stopping and Michael three-stopping, and so was initially dismayed when this turned out not to be the case. There was demonstrably a certain anger to the Brazilian's performance.

Michael Schumacher gets the jump on Barrichello as the first safety car withdraws

ROUND

9

USA
2004 FORMULA 1™
UNITED STATES
GRAND PRIX
Indianapolis

LAP BY LAP
ACTION

73 laps / 190 miles

Barrichello leads Schumacher through Turn 1 on the opening lap

Start to lap 3

Montoya swaps to his spare car just before the start of the parade lap, thus having to start from pitlane. The Ferraris lead away at the start while Alonso passes Sato for third. As they exit Turn 1, Barrichello leads Michael Schumacher, Alonso, Sato, Räikkönen, Button, Ralf Schumacher and Panis. Da Matta lifts off to avoid Panis and is hit by Klien, who is then thumped by Massa, both cars retiring along with Pantano and Bruni. A safety car is deployed, and Barrichello now leads Michael Schumacher, Alonso, Sato, Räikkönen, Button, Ralf Schumacher, Panis, Webber and Coulthard. Da Matta stops for repairs, and rejoins at the back. On lap 3, the Brazilian Toyota driver pits again.

Trouble at the back as Pantano and Bruni get into the thick of the action

Laps 4 to 10

The race restarts on lap 6. Michael Schumacher and Barrichello cross the line side-by-side and Michael leads into Turn 1. Coulthard overtakes Webber for ninth, and Montoya passes Fisichella and Bruni. The following lap, Montoya passes Heidfeld for 12th. On lap 9, at Turn 1, Alonso suffers a puncture and spins into the wall. He is uninjured, but Sato moves through to third. A lap later, Ralf Schumacher hits the wall at the final corner, going in backwards at high speed, spreading wreckage across the track. The safety car is deployed for a second time. Ralf tries to get out of the car but is in pain.

Alonso is pitched into the Turn 1 wall on lap 9 by a punctured tyre

Laps 11 to 27

Both Ferraris pit on lap 11, and Michael Schumacher rejoins before Sato arrives at the pit exit. Sato is second despite this, with Button third, Webber fourth and Montoya fifth. Räikkönen, Panis, Coulthard, Trulli, Heidfeld and Fisichella all stop as well. Webber pits on lap 17, dropping to the back of the field. On lap 18, Ralf Schumacher is lifted from his car. Da Matta retires. The race restarts on lap 20, and Webber passes Baumgartner for 12th. Only 13 cars remain in the race. On lap 24, the BARs put Michael Schumacher under pressure, but Button loses time by overshooting his pit. He rejoins 12th. Sato pits a lap later, falling to 10th. Then, on lap 27 Button retires with an engine problem. Sato passes Coulthard for ninth.

Ralf Schumacher spins to a halt after his hefty impact with the wall

Laps 28 to 41

On lap 28, Michael Schumacher leads Montoya by 8s. Räikkönen is third, with Barrichello fourth, Trulli fifth and Panis sixth. Räikkönen stops on lap 29, dropping to 11th. Sato passes Fisichella for eighth. A lap later, Sato overtakes Heidfeld for sixth. Räikkönen passes Webber to take 10th on lap 31, then passes Coulthard for ninth on the following lap. He makes an unscheduled pit stop on lap 34, dropping to the back. On lap 35, Montoya pits, falling from second to sixth. Michael Schumacher is 13s ahead of Barrichello, with Trulli third, 7s behind, then Panis fourth, Sato fifth and Montoya sixth. Heidfeld pits on lap 38, releasing a train of cars, and dropping from seventh to 10th. On lap 40, Sato passes Panis for fourth. Räikkönen fights back on lap 41 and passes Heidfeld for 10th place.

Zsolt Baumgartner gave Minardi reason to smile as he raced to eighth

Laps 42 to 58

Michael Schumacher pits on lap 42, rejoining behind Barrichello and Trulli. Sato pits on lap 45, falling from fourth to sixth. Heidfeld pulls off with an engine failure. Trulli pits on lap 46, rejoining fifth. Panis, briefly third on lap 47, pits, rejoining sixth. Coulthard pits, maintaining eighth. On lap 48, Fisichella has a puncture and pits, dropping from seventh to 10th. Barrichello pits on lap 50, and rejoins as Michael Schumacher passes to take the lead. Rubens then pressures Michael. Webber stops on lap 51, and Räikkönen passes Coulthard for eighth. Coulthard is next to pit, on lap 54, remaining 10th. Montoya stops on lap 57, but finds that he has been black-flagged for using the spare car at the start, and stops at the end of lap 58. Räikkönen passes Webber for seventh place.

Takuma shares his first podium visit with Rubens and Michael

Lap 59 to the finish

Räikkönen pits on lap 61, but remains sixth as Webber retires with engine failure. Sato passes Trulli for third in Turn 1 on lap 62, the two cars running on to the grass. Fisichella slows with a problem on lap 66, and is passed by Baumgartner. On lap 73, Michael Schumacher wins from Barrichello, with Sato third, Trulli fourth, Panis fifth, Räikkönen sixth and Coulthard seventh. The final point goes to Baumgartner, for Minardi's first of the year.

INSIDE LINE
MICHAEL SCHUMACHER

I guess that a critical part of this win was passing Rubens [Barrichello] at the first restart. When I knew the safety car was coming in, I slowed down enough to get into his slipstream. Having a long straight where you can slipstream made that move possible.

When they called me in after the safety car came out for a second time, I had no idea it was because of an accident to Ralf. They just said a car had gone off. So I rejoined, and even all the way around the lap I still didn't know. Then, as I came through the banking I saw it was a BMW and I knew Montoya was still in the race and I saw the angle that it had hit the wall and I thought 'oh no, please not something bad'. The team were telling me on the radio that he was ok and trying to reassure me, but I've heard that before and it has turned out differently. I was constantly in contact with the team. I was just asking questions like 'what's going on' or 'why is he still sitting there?' The worst thing was seeing Ralf in there for so long.

During the safety car phase it was explained to me by the team they were just being careful, and that he had wanted to get out of the car by himself but that they stopped him. That was a good message and I was less concerned after

hearing that. It was tough to keep concentration. It wasn't needed obviously, running behind the safety car, but imagine having to race normally. It wouldn't have been possible for me.

Looking back, it was crucial that it turned out to be quicker through the pits even with the pit stop than it was going through the accident. It meant I was still leading.

After that, it was really just about staying concentrated. We had flexibility in our strategy, but decided we could two-stop rather than three. There was the option before the last stop to go for another stop or to call it the last pit-stop, and it was a bit difficult because I didn't really have a good second stint. My tyres were completely gone at that stage and I couldn't really push very hard. Then putting in a lot of fuel, not knowing how much I could push, knowing Rubens was going as fast as he was, it was very difficult to manage the situation. Then, luckily for me, there was this debris for Rubens which put it into my favour.

We were at a different phase with our tyre wear, so I knew that he would be very quick on his new tyres when he came out. But, as long as I contained that, he would then be in the same phase as me.

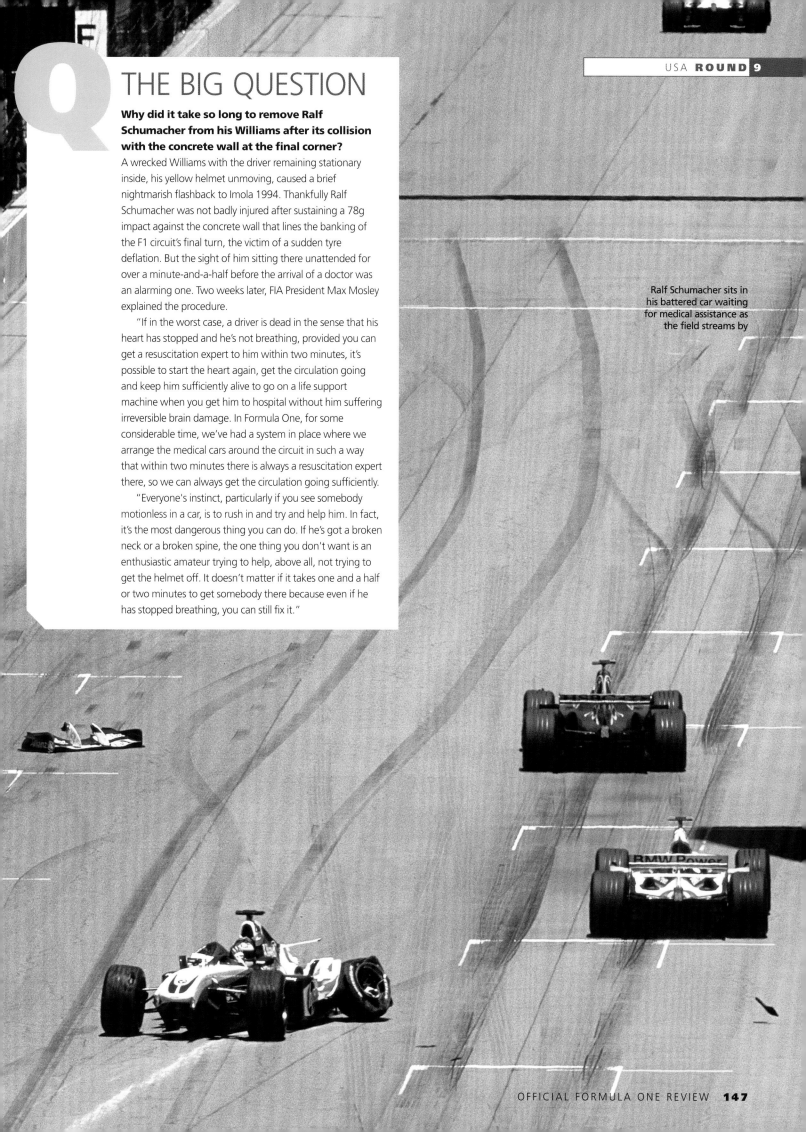

Q THE BIG QUESTION

Why did it take so long to remove Ralf Schumacher from his Williams after its collision with the concrete wall at the final corner?

A wrecked Williams with the driver remaining stationary inside, his yellow helmet unmoving, caused a brief nightmarish flashback to Imola 1994. Thankfully Ralf Schumacher was not badly injured after sustaining a 78g impact against the concrete wall that lines the banking of the F1 circuit's final turn, the victim of a sudden tyre deflation. But the sight of him sitting there unattended for over a minute-and-a-half before the arrival of a doctor was an alarming one. Two weeks later, FIA President Max Mosley explained the procedure.

"If in the worst case, a driver is dead in the sense that his heart has stopped and he's not breathing, provided you can get a resuscitation expert to him within two minutes, it's possible to start the heart again, get the circulation going and keep him sufficiently alive to go on a life support machine when you get him to hospital without him suffering irreversible brain damage. In Formula One, for some considerable time, we've had a system in place where we arrange the medical cars around the circuit in such a way that within two minutes there is always a resuscitation expert there, so we can always get the circulation going sufficiently.

"Everyone's instinct, particularly if you see somebody motionless in a car, is to rush in and try and help him. In fact, it's the most dangerous thing you can do. If he's got a broken neck or a broken spine, the one thing you don't want is an enthusiastic amateur trying to help, above all, not trying to get the helmet off. It doesn't matter if it takes one and a half or two minutes to get somebody there because even if he has stopped breathing, you can still fix it."

Ralf Schumacher sits in his battered car waiting for medical assistance as the field streams by

If the dice had rolled differently, BAR could have come away from Indy with their first win

DAVID RICHARDS
BAR TEAM PRINCIPAL

With hindsight, we would have finished closer to the Ferraris had we brought one or both of our guys in when the safety car was deployed while Ralf's accident was cleared up, but in the end it didn't lose us a place, and there were some very solid reasons for doing what we did.

Ralf's car came to rest right opposite us so we could see quite clearly that he was moving and wide awake. At the time we had to make the call whether to pit or not, it looked as though he was just waiting for the traffic to pass before he got out. Another thing driving that decision was that we felt if we did the same thing as Ferrari we would probably lose, whereas if we did something different we might give ourselves a chance.

We had the unusual situation here where Michael was able to pit and still come out leading the race, even against our guys who hadn't pitted. Partly, that was because they used Rubens to slow the pack while Michael was going flat-out, and that cost us a bit of time. Partly, it was because Taku [Sato] was very correct in the way he drove at the scene of the accident. He behaved very cautiously, just as we'd asked him to.

However, in a different scenario it could very well have turned out that Michael rejoined behind both our cars, and we might have found that Taku was able to blast away at the front while Jenson controlled Michael for us. Then our strategy would have looked very clever.

Takuma drove extremely well. We'd had a little talk on Friday about his approach after his practice tangle with Massa, and really that followed on from Montreal qualifying where he was trying to make up the 0.6s he'd lost from a mistake in the second sector, all in the final sector. That was never going to happen and he'd spun. But on Sunday at Indy he really was flawless and gave the sort of polished performance that we'd been looking for from him. He was out of synch on strategy, and that meant he had to come through the field a bit, getting past Panis and Trulli. The way he did that was unbelievable. We really couldn't have asked for more.

JOCK CLEAR
TAKUMA
SATO'S BAR
RACE ENGINEER

What does the data from the United States Grand Prix show us? Well, the data shows one thing, but perhaps experience tells us another.

The data shows that Takuma [Sato] was just 0.3s slower than the Ferraris if you look only at their fastest laps. Before the race, we were hoping that Ferrari were going to have to three-stop because of tyre wear. We knew that we could two-stop, which is by far the fastest way of doing a race

distance at Indianapolis, because the weight penalty is low and the pit lane is very, very long – and if you compared a three-stopping car that was 0.3s faster with a two-stopping car, the two-stopper would win the race every time.

As it happened, Ferrari two-stopped as well and so beat us comfortably. There was talk that if it hadn't been for all the slow laps behind the safety car they would have been forced to stop three times and would therefore have become beatable, but I don't buy that. Barrichello's second stint was for 38 laps, only eight of them under the safety car, and he had no tyre issues. If they'd been pushed hard, 38 may have become 32, but that's still almost half race distance. I think they could have two-stopped regardless.

The other thing is that when you analyse the season as a whole you see that Ferrari have a margin that they can use if needed. People have put

them under pressure – Alonso in France, Räikkönen at Silverstone and us at Indianapolis – but they really were never in any danger of losing those races. They just needed to dip into their reserves a little bit. For the same reasons, I'm convinced that Michael would have won at Monaco if he hadn't been taken out.

We went into this race thinking that we might realistically challenge Barrichello for second. Deciding to react differently to them during the first safety car period was worth trying,

but ultimately made sure we were third. But Taku drove a fantastic race here. He'd had a sequence of non-finishes with mechanical problems, and then he came to Indy and the car was quick and he just went with it. His sequence of laps from lap 30 to 37 was incredible. I think Indy should have been where the recovery to his season began, but unfortunately it then went back to the engine blowing, and psychologically, after all that had gone before, then the hope of Indy, that was very, very tough for him.

Fastest race laps	M.Schumacher	Barrichello	Sato
	1m 10.412s	1m 10.399s	1m 10.727s
Traffic-free Sato laps early in second stint			
Lap 30	1m 11.1s		
31	1m 11.2s		
32	1m 11.2s		
33	1m 11.3s		
34	1m 11.3s		
35	1m 11.3s		
36	1m 11.2s		
37	1m 11.1s		

Takuma Sato drove an excellent race with an astonishing sequence of quick and consistent laps

RACE RESULTS
USA
INDIANAPOLIS

RACE DATE June 20th
CIRCUIT LENGTH 2.605 miles
NO. OF LAPS 73
RACE DISTANCE 190.139 miles
WEATHER hot and sunny, 25°C
TRACK TEMP 40°C
RACE ATTENDANCE 110,000 (est)
LAP RECORD Rubens Barrichello,
1m 10.399s, 133.229mph, 2004

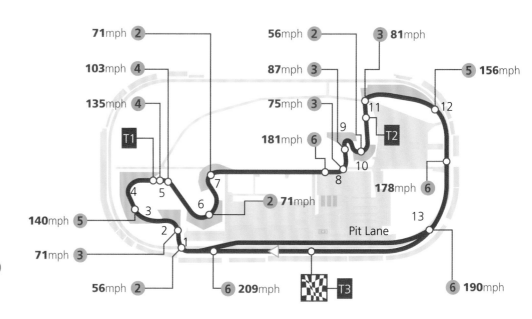

PRACTICE 1

	Driver	Time	Laps
1	R Barrichello	1m11.354s	16
2	M Schumacher	1m11.619s	16
3	A Davidson	1m11.693s	23
4	JP Montoya	1m12.008s	11
5	R Zonta	1m12.366s	25
6	B Wirdheim	1m12.454s	25
7	J Button	1m12.553s	14
8	G Fisichella	1m12.575s	12
9	O Panis	1m12.631s	16
10	R Schumacher	1m12.850s	14
11	F Alonso	1m12.989s	15
12	K Räikkönen	1m13.147s	8
13	J Trulli	1m13.351s	15
14	F Massa	1m13.371s	17
15	T Sato	1m13.532s	12
16	C da Matta	1m13.555s	18
17	M Webber	1m13.762s	10
18	D Coulthard	1m13.916s	10
19	C Klien	1m14.407s	26
20	T Glock	1m15.217s	25
21	N Heidfeld	1m15.020s	14
22	B Leinders	1m15.026s	20
23	G Pantano	1m15.260s	20
24	G Bruni	1m15.468s	9
25	Z Baumgartner	1m17.051s	16

PRACTICE 2

	Driver	Time	Laps
1	R Barrichello	1m10.365s	24
2	A Davidson	1m10.365s	42
3	JP Montoya	1m10.982s	29
4	M Schumacher	1m11.036s	28
5	J Button	1m11.230s	19
6	R Schumacher	1m11.530s	30
7	C da Matta	1m11.893s	35
8	O Panis	1m11.994s	30
9	R Zonta	1m12.019s	42
10	K Räikkönen	1m12.197s	20
11	M Webber	1m12.438s	33
12	J Trulli	1m12.441s	28
13	G Fisichella	1m12.537s	27
14	T Sato	1m12.601s	3
15	B Wirdheim	1m12.761s	30
16	C Klien	1m12.950s	31
17	F Massa	1m13.196s	32
18	Z Baumgartner	1m13.384s	18
19	T Glock	1m13.446s	33
20	F Alonso	1m13.732s	3
21	N Heidfeld	1m13.961s	18
22	G Pantano	1m14.407s	20
23	B Leinders	1m14.415s	21
24	G Bruni	1m14.428s	17
25	D Coulthard	no time	2

PRACTICE 3

	Driver	Time	Laps
1	R Barrichello	1m10.911s	9
2	J Button	1m11.071s	9
3	M Schumacher	1m11.207s	8
4	F Alonso	1m11.509s	12
5	R Schumacher	1m11.671s	14
6	J Trulli	1m11.723s	11
7	T Sato	1m11.989s	14
8	C da Matta	1m12.001s	12
9	K Räikkönen	1m12.015s	7
10	M Webber	1m12.128s	6
11	C Klien	1m12.147s	6
12	JP Montoya	1m12.240s	8
13	G Fisichella	1m12.405s	10
14	O Panis	1m12.451s	14
15	D Coulthard	1m12.584s	11
16	F Massa	1m12.911s	13
17	G Bruni	1m12.957s	12
18	Z Baumgartner	1m13.396s	12
19	N Heidfeld	1m13.454s	11
20	G Pantano	1m13.761s	12

PRACTICE 4

	Driver	Time	Laps
1	J Button	1m10.056s	17
2	M Schumacher	1m10.199s	16
3	T Sato	1m10.251s	23
4	R Barrichello	1m10.351s	16
5	JP Montoya	1m10.708s	13
6	F Alonso	1m10.749s	13
7	C da Matta	1m10.802s	19
8	R Schumacher	1m10.820s	9
9	J Trulli	1m10.848s	13
10	K Räikkönen	1m11.222s	14
11	O Panis	1m11.242s	20
12	D Coulthard	1m11.395s	13
13	C Klien	1m11.992s	20
14	N Heidfeld	1m12.524s	16
15	M Webber	1m12.590s	14
16	G Pantano	1m12.603s	9
17	G Fisichella	1m12.686s	10
18	F Massa	1m12.861s	9
19	Z Baumgartner	1m13.869s	13
20	G Bruni	1m13.915s	14

Best sectors – Qualifying

Sector 1	M Schumacher	21.401s
Sector 2	T Sato	29.024s
Sector 3	M Schumacher	19.516s

Speed trap – Qualifying

	Driver	Speed
1	F Massa	212.457mph
2	JP Montoya	211.773mph
3	O Panis	210.530mph

Michael Schumacher
"I took the lead as the safety car went in and I managed to slipstream Rubens. I was concerned to see Ralf in the car for so long but the team told me he was okay."

Juan Pablo Montoya
"I managed to run as high as second at one point but, realistically, we were on for a strong top-four position, then I got the black flag. But I was glad Ralf was okay."

Kimi Räikkönen
"I scored points but I strongly believe I could have finished on the podium. I had to make two unscheduled stops to top up the pneumatic air system on the engine."

Fernando Alonso
"I got a fantastic start. As for the accident it is difficult to explain because everything happened so fast, but I think it was a puncture. I lost the chance of a podium."

Jenson Button
"We decided to stay out instead of pitting under the second safety car, which was the right thing to do. The car was working well, so it was disappointing not to finish."

Rubens Barrichello
"I felt I could have won here and Canada. When the safety car came in my tyre pressures were low and I got wheelspin at the final corner, so Michael got past."

Ralf Schumacher
"I can't remember a thing about Indy. In my memory the race stopped before the start. Even if I see pictures now I basically just look at them as if I was a spectator."

David Coulthard
"In the early stages I picked up some debris, which damaged my deflector and upset the balance of the car, making it difficult to handle for the rest of the race."

Jarno Trulli
"I did my best from last on the grid. Sato caught me during the last stint. There were flags in the banking for oil on the track, I lifted off and he passed me into Turn 1."

Takuma Sato
"My first podium was an incredible feeling and a result we had worked so hard for. The car just felt beautiful. Jarno hesitated on the oil flags, so I took my opportunity."

POSITIONS LAP BY LAP

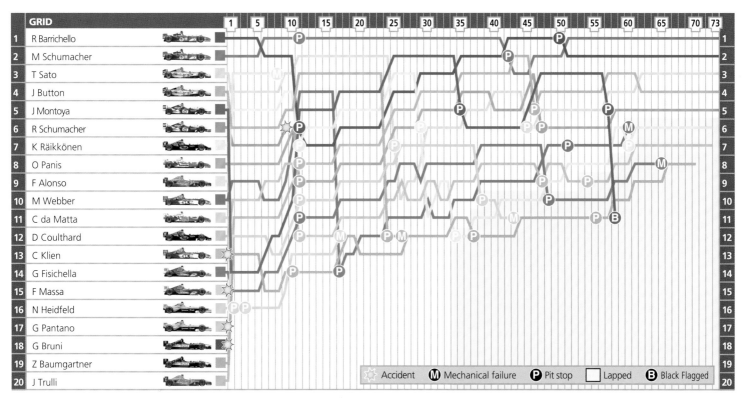

	GRID		
1	R Barrichello		
2	M Schumacher		
3	T Sato		
4	J Button		
5	J Montoya		
6	R Schumacher		
7	K Räikkönen		
8	O Panis		
9	F Alonso		
10	M Webber		
11	C da Matta		
12	D Coulthard		
13	C Klien		
14	G Fisichella		
15	F Massa		
16	N Heidfeld		
17	G Pantano		
18	G Bruni		
19	Z Baumgartner		
20	J Trulli		

Accident   M Mechanical failure   P Pit stop   ☐ Lapped   B Black Flagged

QUALIFYING

	Driver	Pre-qual time	Pos	Time
1	R Barrichello	1m09.454s	1	1m10.223s
2	M Schumacher	1m10.129s	9	1m10.400s
3	T Sato	1m10.002s	4	1m10.610s
4	J Button	1m10.115s	8	1m10.820s
5	JP Montoya	1m09.824s	2	1m11.062s
6	R Schumacher	1m10.003s	5	1m11.106s
7	K Räikkönen	1m11.415s	14	1m11.137s
8	O Panis	1m09.923s	3	1m11.167s
9	F Alonso	1m10.078s	6	1m11.185s
10	M Webber	1m11.444s	15	1m11.286s
11	C da Matta	1m10.108s	7	1m11.691s
12	D Coulthard	1m11.068s	12	1m12.026s
13	C Klien	1m11.777s	16	1m12.170s
14	G Fisichella	1m10.997s	11	1m12.470s
15	F Massa	1m11.315s	13	1m12.721s
16	N Heidfeld	1m12.329s	18	1m13.147s
17	G Pantano	1m12.017s	17	1m13.375s
18	G Bruni	1m13.776s	19	1m14.010s
19	Z Baumgartner	1m14.396s	20	1m14.812s
20	J Trulli	1m10.559s	10	no time

RACE

	Driver	Car	Laps	Time	Fastest	Avg. mph	Stops
1	M Schumacher	Ferrari F2004	73	1h40m29.914s	1m10.412s	113.529	2
2	R Barrichello	Ferrari F2004	73	1h40m32.864s	1m10.399s	113.473	2
3	T Sato	BAR-Honda 006	73	1h40m41.950s	1m10.727s	113.115	2
4	J Trulli	Renault R24	73	1h41m04.458s	1m11.187s	112.882	2
5	O Panis	Toyota TF104	73	1h41m07.448s	1m10.933s	112.826	2
6	K Räikkönen	McLaren-Mercedes MP4-19	72	1h40m57.710s	1m11.248s	111.460s	3
7	D Coulthard	McLaren-Mercedes MP4-19	72	1h41m24.532s	1m12.155s	110.968	3
8	Z Baumgartner	Minardi-Cosworth PS04	70	1h40m44.850s	1m14.097s	108.594	3
9	G Fisichella	Sauber-Petronas C23	68	Hydraulics	1m12.129s	108.073	2
R	M Webber	Jaguar-Cosworth R5	72	Engine	1m12.140s		2
R	N Heidfeld	Jordan-Ford EJ14	43	Engine	1m13.095s	-	2
R	J Button	BAR-Honda 006	26	Gearbox	1m11.025s	-	1
R	C da Matta	Toyota TF104	17	Gearbox	1m12.872s	-	2
R	R Schumacher	Williams-BMW FW26	9	Accident	1m11.982s	-	0
R	F Alonso	Renault R24	8	Accident	1m11.236s	-	0
R	C Klien	Jaguar-Cosworth R5	0	Accident	1m15.731s	-	0
R	F Massa	Sauber-Petronas C23	0	Accident	1m15.560s	-	0
R	G Pantano	Jordan-Ford EJ14	0	Accident	1m16.300s	-	0
R	G Bruni	Minardi-Cosworth PS04	0	Accident	1m18.025s	-	0
DQ	JP Montoya	Williams-BMW FW26	59	Grid error	-	-	3

CHAMPIONSHIP

	Driver	Pts
1	M Schumacher	80
2	R Barrichello	62
3	J Button	44
4	J Trulli	41
5	F Alonso	25
6	JP Montoya	24
7	T Sato	14
8	R Schumacher	12
9	G Fisichella	10
10	D Coulthard	9
11	K Räikkönen	8
12	F Massa	5
	O Panis	5
14	C da Matta	3
	M Webber	3

	Constructor	Pts
1	Ferrari	142
2	Renault	66
3	BAR-Honda	58
4	Williams-BMW	36
5	McLaren-Mercedes	17
6	Sauber-Petronas	15
7	Toyota	8
8	Jordan-Ford	5
9	Jaguar-Cosworth	3
10	Minardi-Cosworth	1

Race notes

Montoya Disqualified for switching cars within 15 minutes of the start of the race

Fastest Lap
R Barrichello 1m10.399s, on lap 7 (133.229mph)
New lap record

Fastest through speed trap
G Fisichella   221.580mph
Slowest through speed trap
G Pantano   189.145mph

Fastest pit stop
K Räikkönen   22.968s
Slowest pit stop
C da Matta   58.014s

Giancarlo Fisichella
"I picked up a puncture on lap 48 and having to drive so slowly back to the pits did some damage, so I subsequently had to retire because of a hydraulic leak."

Mark Webber
"I was racing a good race today when I was forced to retire after losing oil and catching fire. It was fun up to then and the pace of the car was encouraging."

Olivier Panis
"This was my 150th Grand Prix and I got a fantastic present of four points. I was very happy. The team gave me a consistent and competitive car and I drove a good race."

Nick Heidfeld
"My problem was the engine. The race was going better than expected: I was lucky not to be involved in the crash at the start. Later the tyres and car improved."

Gianmaria Bruni
"In Turn 2 a Jordan braked hard and chopped across me, hitting my right front wheel with his left rear. The impact bent the suspension and finished my race."

Felipe Massa
"I was trying to be very careful in Turn 1. Suddenly I found Klien broadside across the road after some other cars crashed and there was no way to avoid him."

Christian Klien
"It all came to an end too soon. Da Matta appeared to slow instantly on entering Turn 2 and I had nowhere to go other than into the back of him. Disappointing, yes."

Cristiano da Matta
"Coming into Turn 2 I was hit from behind by Klien. I had to pit, but the accident also resulted in me not being able to select first gear. I got stuck in gear and had to stop."

Giorgio Pantano
"What can I say? I got a great start but I was involved with the incident with Klien and da Matta. I had to stop because the front left suspension was totally broken."

Zsolt Baumgartner
"It was a great feeling to score a point – as if a miracle happened! There was some big pressure in those last few laps when I knew we were getting close to scoring."

RENAULT ROUTED

It looked as though Renault was set for a dream result in its home Grand Prix, but Ferrari played a masterstroke and pitted four times to end up in front

Ferrari's worst nightmare at Magny Cours was to be out-qualified by a Renault. The high tyre degradation induced by this circuit and its succession of hairpins means that in any tactical battle it's advantageous to pit before your rival, a reversal of the usual situation. Ferrari, relative to Renault, were slow at the start of a stint, fast at the end – fine if you're leading your rival, but disastrous if you're behind. Ferrari knew that if a Renault started from anywhere near the front row, the R24's electric getaway would ensure they were stuck behind it, unable to use the F2004's otherwise superior pace.

It duly happened, courtesy of Fernando Alonso, just as Ferrari had suspected it might.

But they had a 'get out of jail card', formulated by their ace strategist Luca Baldisserri: a four-stop strategy. The competitive circumstances of the race – Alonso leading the first two stints with Michael Schumacher unable to find a chink of overtaking light – triggered the plan into action.

For 11 laps, between Alonso's third stop and Schumacher's fourth, the World Champion gave the fastest car in the field its head and the Renault was left breathless. Schumacher's ninth win of the season was then a formality. To make matters worse for Renault, Jarno Trulli fell asleep and lost his distant third place to Rubens Barrichello's Ferrari two corners from home.

ROUND **10**

FRANCE
FORMULA 1™
MOBIL 1 GRAND PRIX
DE FRANCE 2004
Nevers Magny-Cours

The fans were out in
force, hoping to cheer
Renault to victory, but
Ferrari had other ideas

LAP BY LAP
ACTION

70 laps / 192 miles

Start to lap 6

Alonso leads away from Michael Schumacher, while Trulli bursts through from fifth place to third ahead of Button, Coulthard and Montoya, with a fast-starting Räikkönen up to seventh ahead of Sato, Barrichello and Webber. Panis is slow away and drops to the back of the field. At the end of lap 1, Alonso is 0.8s ahead of Michael, with Trulli 1s behind the Ferrari. A lap later, Alonso's lead is out to 1.2s. Barrichello passes Sato on lap 4 for eighth place.

Alonso blasts away ahead of Schumacher as Trulli passes Button

Laps 7 to 13

The gap between Alonso and Schumacher is stable at 1.5s by lap 7, with Trulli now 4s behind. By lap 10, Schumacher has closed the lead to 0.6s. The pit stops begin on lap 11, with Schumacher pitting unexpectedly, leaving Renault first and second with Button third. Schumacher rejoins in eighth. The stops continue on lap 12, with Coulthard dropping from fourth to ninth. On lap 13, Alonso stays in front but Trulli pits, which allows Button to move to second with Sato third after Montoya pits. Trulli rejoins in sixth place and Montoya drops to ninth.

Alonso stayed ahead, even though Michael Schumacher was faster

Laps 14 to 19

Alonso and Button pit on lap 14, and Alonso comes out in the lead with Sato second and Schumacher third. Webber is up to fourth ahead of Trulli. Button rejoins in sixth. Sato pits on lap 15, and Alonso is left with a lead of 2.8s over Schumacher. Webber also pits and so Trulli regains third with Button fourth, Coulthard fifth and Klien sixth. Montoya is next up ahead of Barrichello. On lap 16, Alonso pulls away from Schumacher while Klien pits and falls from sixth to 13th. Sato suffers an engine failure. On lap 17 Alonso continues to build his lead with Trulli dropping away. Montoya spins, dropping from sixth place to ninth.

Barrichello and Sato enjoy a tussle in the wake of their team-mates

Laps 20 to 31

By lap 20, the gap at the front has begun to close again. Räikkönen overtakes Massa for seventh. Schumacher has closed the gap to Alonso to less than 1s by lap 25, with Trulli 8s behind the Ferrari. Schumacher pits on lap 29. It's a quick stop and he rejoins fifth. Coulthard also stops, dropping from fifth to eighth. The Renaults are first and second again with Button third. Button pits on lap 30, rejoining fifth. Alonso stays at the front on lap 31, as Trulli and Barrichello pit. Schumacher grabs his opportunity, setting the fastest lap of the race on a clear stretch of track.

It's the end of the line for Sato as his Honda engine lets go on lap 16

Laps 32 to 45

Alonso pits on lap 32, crucially rejoining behind Schumacher. By lap 33, the gap between Schumacher and Alonso is 3s, with a 2s gap back to Trulli who has Button on his tail. Barrichello is next, while Webber pits and drops from sixth to 10th. Gené, deputising for Ralf Schumacher, also stops, falling from eighth to 11th. On lap 35, Alonso closes the gap to 2.1s, but Trulli begins to drop away, coming under pressure from Button on lap 37. Schumacher has a 5s lead by lap 40, and the order at the front is unchanged. There's a surprise on lap 42 as Schumacher pits again, suggesting that he's on a four-stop strategy. Thus Alonso regains the lead, but Michael rejoins ahead of Trulli.

Alonso holds off Barrichello in the closing laps, but it wasn't to last...

Lap 46 to the finish

Alonso pits for the third time on lap 46, rejoining more than 11s behind Schumacher. On lap 49, Trulli heads for pitlane, freeing up Button in third place, with Barrichello in pursuit. Trulli rejoins in sixth place. Then fifth-placed Montoya stops on lap 50, dropping to 10th. Barrichello pits on the same lap, rejoining behind Trulli. Button pits on lap 52 and rejoins fifth behind Trulli and Barrichello. Schumacher has pushed hard and, by lap 57, has built a lead of 22s over Alonso. Behind the leaders, there is a close battle for third place between Trulli, Barrichello and Button. The two McLarens run together in sixth and seventh places, Coulthard ahead of Räikkönen, with Montoya eighth. Schumacher pits on lap 58 and re-emerges still in the lead. And he stays there, crossing the finish line on lap 70 to take his ninth win in 10 Grands Prix. Alonso finishes second but, on the final lap, Trulli loses concentration and leaves a gap at the penultimate corner which Barrichello grabs for third. Button is fifth, with Coulthard sixth, Räikkönen seventh and Montoya eighth.

Alonso, Schumacher and Barrichello look happy with life

INSIDE LINE
FERNANDO ALONSO

I was very pleased with my pole position lap, as we were carrying quite a lot of fuel and so it was satisfying. The key for me was finding a good line through the chicane at the end of the lap. It's actually a very complicated corner and I was working through the practice sessions trying to find the right way.

I pushed the maximum from beginning to end, and second place in the race was the maximum target that we could achieve. I started well, got the lead and pushed. Then I saw Michael come into the pits quite early, and I kept pushing in the three laps I had before my first pit stop. I came out in the lead again and Michael stopped for a second time very early, and I think we were all a bit surprised by that. After my second stop, I was shocked that Michael was now ahead and with a good gap.

At this stage, he was pushing very hard and there was no way that I could run at that pace. It was only at Michael's third pit stop that we realised what was going on and that a fourth stop was coming, but I just couldn't get close enough to him.

For us, a four-stop wouldn't have been quicker. They were just quicker than us, quite a lot quicker, and really it wouldn't have mattered whether we stopped three times or four. We were getting two or three very good laps from our tyres at the beginning of each stint, but at the end we would be struggling a bit. This was the pattern at most of the races this year when you compare us to Ferrari. They seem to struggle for tyre grip in qualifying and that makes us look more competitive than we really are.

It might seem a disappointment to be only second after starting from pole and leading for two stints, but really we knew what to expect. Actually, it was better than we were expecting because at least we split the Ferraris.

Coulthard qualified well on the MP4-19B's debut, but a lack of running hampered his race form

THE BIG QUESTION

Is McLaren a team on the way back up?

A team with the profile and budget of Team McLaren Mercedes cannot operate indefinitely at the sorry level of performance it endured in the first half of 2004. The disastrous MP4-19 received a major update to become the MP4-19B and it made its debut here at Magny-Cours two races ahead of schedule.

The MP4-19B featured major aerodynamic revisions, with heavily cut-away sidepods visually similar to those of the Renault R24, a comprehensively revised rear suspension for greater stability, and a significantly revised Mercedes engine with superior oil flow plus an extra 20bhp. A great deal hung on the car's performance in the balance of the season.

The signs were promising as David Coulthard qualified a good third fastest, just 0.3s off pole, with a good representative fuel load

on board. Kimi Räikkönen messed up his lap, but had been similarly competitive in the practices.

"The rear end feels much better," reported Coulthard. "A lot of my time comes from being able to brake late. This car allows me to do that. It's much more stable and is better in high-speed corner entry."

In the race it wasn't quite so competitive, with Coulthard and Räikkönen coming home sixth and seventh, although Räikkönen set third fastest race lap, 0.4s off Michael Schumacher's best. Limited testing and the washing out of the Friday practice meant that the team hadn't got a full picture of tyre behaviour through a race stint, and both drivers found the grip falling away faster than ideal.

"We were still learning the car," said team principal Ron Dennis. "Kimi's poor qualifying performance and David's poor start – which wasn't his fault – masked what was actually quite a big step forward. We were also very encouraged to have got through a weekend with no engine problems."

LUCA BALDISSERRI
FERRARI RACE STRATEGIST

Well, we knew that we might have a problem getting the clean air at Magny-Cours. We felt confident that we could do a good race performance, but we couldn't be sure that we could qualify on the front row, and we suspected the Renault especially would be very fast, even more so in qualifying. The problem for us was finding a way to run out of synch if that happened, to find a window. This is what I was thinking in the week before the race, and I told Ross [Brawn] that maybe a four-stop strategy could do this for us. At first, I don't think he thought I was serious, but we looked at it and we agreed that, yes, in certain situations, it could work.

Michael ran behind Alonso for the first two stints. He had some traffic on his out-lap after the first stop and if it had not been for this, he could have got ahead then and we could have just stayed with a three-stop. There were other things pushing us to the four. Both Alonso and Michael were a long way clear of the others, so there was no threat from behind. If we did a four-stop, we weren't going to lose to those behind through track positioning. The other thing was that, compared to Renault, we were very quick at the end of the stints, but a bit slower at the beginning. So as we came to the second stops we decided that, yes, we would commit to the four-stop. The four-stop only had a window if you did a very short first stint. That window closed if you did normal three-stop first-stint length. So we'd kept the four option open from the start but didn't commit to it until the second stop.

It was made even better for us that Renault responded to our short stop, by short-stopping Alonso. Our short stop was because we were fitting another stint in, but they didn't know this. Because Alonso was light on his third stint it meant he had to be heavy for his last one.

After Alonso stopped, Michael had 11 laps in clear air on a light load to really use the performance of the car at a time when Alonso's car was heavy. That made it easier for Michael to pull out the time he needed after the third stop. When he came in for the last one we had over eight seconds to spare.

Serious thinking in the week before the race produced Ferrari's race-winning strategy

ROB WHITE
RENAULT
ENGINE
TECHNICAL
DIRECTOR

The fact that Ferrari did four stops gave the race a bit of a twist of drama, but we knew we were always defending a win, not attacking it. We knew they had significantly more race pace than us, and all we had was positional advantage from our qualifying advantage over them and our ability to make a quick start.

Fernando [Alonso] drove a spectacularly good race, but when you put it into the simulation programme afterwards you have to run several hundred scenarios before you find one in which Fernando wins. There's a solution with hindsight, but it always depends on you blocking a car that's fundamentally quicker.

On the face of it, it may seem odd that [Schumacher] wasn't able to pass us on the track, when the speed trap figures at the end of the long straight before the hairpin – the main recognised passing spot at Magny-Cours – show that he had a 10kph advantage there.

It's not necessarily the end speed that is critical, though. To understand it, you would need a speed profile of both cars from the exit of the previous corner all the way to the speed trap.

The physics of accelerating a car are well understood. At low car speeds, the cars are traction limited because the downforce is less and the wheel torque is high. Our traction is very good. Through the medium speeds, when the wheel torque is lower and the downforce is increasing, it becomes an engine power/car mass thing. Mass is always the same, so it becomes engine power. At high speeds, the wheel torque diminishes again as you change up, the drag starts to dominate and you get to be talking about aero efficiency drag comparison. For that kind of activity, the cars were very close on that day. This came as less of a surprise to us than it did to some other people.

Although the speed trap figures show our cars at 17th and 18th fastest, we were reasonably satisfied with that. It's less about speed differential at the fastest point of the straight than the nature of the event before and after. We're not too bad in straight drag races, and it's a tactical and strategic choice – the downforce at the end of the straight, and speed. It's quite tough to do it right a day and a half in advance, as a headwind or tailwind can make a big difference.

Race speed trap figures		
1	**Barrichello** (Ferrari)	324.4kph (**201.6mph**)
2	**M Schumacher** (Ferrari)	323.7kph (**201.1mph**)
17	**Trulli** (Renault)	315.6kph (**196.1mph**)
18	**Alonso** (Renault)	314.6kph (**195.5mph**)
19	**Baumgartner** (Minardi)	312.8kph (**194.4mph**)

Qualifying on pole gave Renault's crew great cheer, but they'd have preferred a race victory

RACE RESULTS

FRANCE
NEVERS MAGNY-COURS

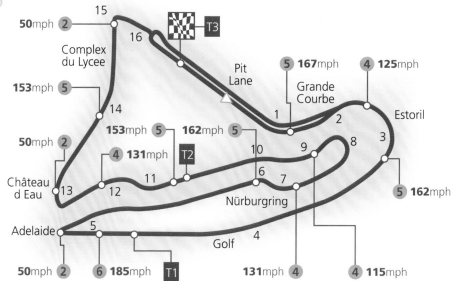

RACE DATE July 4th
CIRCUIT LENGTH 2.740 miles
NO. OF LAPS 70
RACE DISTANCE 191.800 miles
WEATHER dry and bright, 29°C
TRACK TEMP 44°C
RACE ATTENDANCE 70,000
LAP RECORD Michael Schumacher,
1m 15.377s, 130.932mph, 2004

PRACTICE 1

	Driver	Time	Laps
1	R Barrichello	1m15.487s	4
2	M Schumacher	1m15.713s	4
3	M Gené	1m19.348s	14
4	T Glock	1m19.428s	17
5	G Pantano	1m19.466s	12
6	N Heidfeld	1m20.531s	12
7	G Bruni	1m21.203s	13
8	B Leinders	1m22.767s	11
9	A Davidson	1m26.552s	17
10	C da Matta	1m26.757s	5
11	O Panis	1m27.449s	4
12	J Button	1m28.317s	5
13	R Zonta	1m29.085s	18
14	C Klien	1m29.626s	8
15	Z Baumgartner	1m29.877s	12
16	T Sato	1m30.092s	10
17	B Wirdheim	1m30.204s	17
18	J Trulli	1m39.392s	4
19	F Massa	no time	3
20	F Alonso	no time	3
21	G Fisichella	no time	1
22	D Coulthard	no time	1
23	JP Montoya	no time	3
24	K Räikkönen	no time	1
25	M Webber	no time	1

PRACTICE 2

	Driver	Time	Laps
1	C da Matta	1m15.518s	12
2	J Trulli	1m16.206s	9
3	A Davidson	1m16.231s	17
4	J Button	1m16.397s	8
5	M Schumacher	1m16.397s	7
6	F Alonso	1m16.454s	10
7	D Coulthard	1m16.464s	8
8	M Webber	1m16.745s	14
9	K Räikkönen	1m16.794s	10
10	R Barrichello	1m17.094s	5
11	O Panis	1m17.303s	10
12	G Fisichella	1m17.324s	13
13	JP Montoya	1m17.556s	5
14	M Gené	1m17.688s	17
15	R Zonta	1m17.735s	15
16	C Klien	1m17.936s	10
17	T Sato	1m17.967s	11
18	F Massa	1m18.614s	7
19	G Pantano	1m18.711s	10
20	B Wirdheim	1m19.179s	16
21	N Heidfeld	1m19.270s	12
22	G Bruni	1m19.349s	10
23	T Glock	1m19.490s	25
24	Z Baumgartner	1m19.636s	13
25	B Leinders	1m19.914s	16

PRACTICE 3

	Driver	Time	Laps
1	M Schumacher	1m14.944s	12
2	D Coulthard	1m15.402s	11
3	J Trulli	1m15.423s	11
4	F Alonso	1m15.434s	15
5	O Panis	1m15.478s	14
6	R Barrichello	1m15.500s	14
7	JP Montoya	1m15.529s	16
8	M Webber	1m15.907s	8
9	G Fisichella	1m15.910s	11
10	J Button	1m16.304s	15
11	C da Matta	1m16.384s	17
12	T Sato	1m16.569s	16
13	M Gené	1m16.608s	18
14	F Massa	1m16.619s	14
15	C Klien	1m16.669s	27
16	G Bruni	1m17.174s	15
17	G Pantano	1m17.399s	19
18	Z Baumgartner	1m17.731s	14
19	N Heidfeld	1m17.846s	16
20	K Räikkönen	no time	1

PRACTICE 4

	Driver	Time	Laps
1	K Räikkönen	1m14.513s	18
2	J Button	1m14.568s	14
3	M Schumacher	1m14.571s	14
4	T Sato	1m14.711s	18
5	R Barrichello	1m14.817s	12
6	O Panis	1m14.883s	23
7	C da Matta	1m14.885s	22
8	D Coulthard	1m14.977s	7
9	J Trulli	1m15.033s	12
10	F Alonso	1m15.096s	15
11	M Gené	1m15.179s	10
12	M Webber	1m15.350s	24
13	C Klien	1m15.449s	22
14	F Massa	1m16.062s	19
15	G Fisichella	1m16.161s	9
16	Z Baumgartner	1m16.861s	15
17	G Pantano	1m17.104s	12
18	N Heidfeld	1m17.162s	15
19	G Bruni	1m19.401s	8
20	JP Montoya	1m21.458s	8

Best sectors – Qualifying

Sector 1	JP Montoya	23.816s
Sector 2	F Alonso	25.641s
Sector 3	F Alonso	24.040s

Speed trap – Qualifying

1	M Gené	199.034mph
2	M Schumacher	198.102mph
3	JP Montoya	197.232mph

Michael Schumacher

"After the second stop, we decided to switch to a four-stop strategy. There wasn't much discussion once I was told I wouldn't be threatened from behind."

Juan Pablo Montoya

"It was a difficult race as I had an intense pain in my neck, having hurt it when I crashed on Friday. After 20 laps, I hit a kerb hard and spun, losing three places."

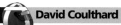

Kimi Räikkönen

"I made a good start and gained two places but it's difficult starting from ninth, and it wasn't enough. The 19B's speed is good and I'm confident for the rest of the year."

Fernando Alonso

"I've been waiting for this podium for a long time. The only disappointment I feel is for Jarno, as it would have been great to be on the podium in France together."

Jenson Button

"I'm very disappointed, as fifth isn't good enough. At the last pit stop, the car went into anti-stall mode and cost me the time advantage that could have left me third."

Rubens Barrichello

"From 10th to third, I had a lot of fun. On the final lap, Trulli slowed too much at Turn 13 and I was able to get alongside at 15. It was risky, but I thought it was worth a try."

Marc Gené

"I had a problem with the clutch, but as I didn't want to jump the start I released it slowly and lost three positions. Then Webber and I touched and I nearly spun."

David Coulthard

"I lost two positions to be fifth after the first corner, then I lost some grip in the middle of the race. However, it was an encouraging and reliable debut for the 19B."

Jarno Trulli

"I'm gutted. On the last lap Rubens was quicker on the exit of Turn 13 and passed me under braking for the next corner. I tried to close the door but couldn't."

Takuma Sato

"I immediately felt a loss of power after the pit stop and we knew there was a problem down the main straight, but there was nothing that we could do."

POSITIONS LAP BY LAP

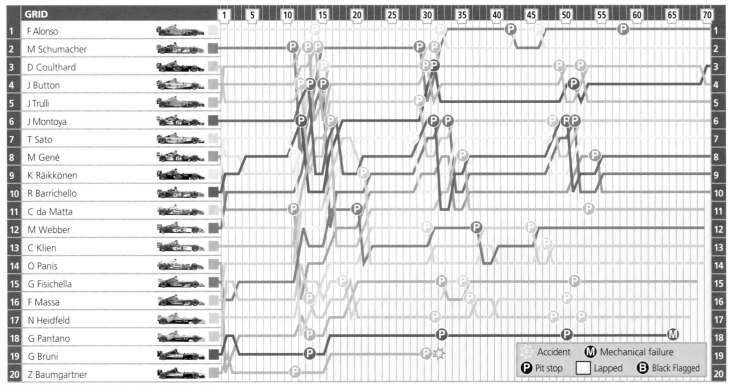

GRID		1	5	10	15	20	25	30	35	40	45	50	55	60	65	70	
1	F Alonso																1
2	M Schumacher																2
3	D Coulthard																3
4	J Button																4
5	J Trulli																5
6	J Montoya																6
7	T Sato																7
8	M Gené																8
9	K Räikkönen																9
10	R Barrichello																10
11	C da Matta																11
12	M Webber																12
13	C Klien																13
14	O Panis																14
15	G Fisichella																15
16	F Massa																16
17	N Heidfeld																17
18	G Pantano																18
19	G Bruni																19
20	Z Baumgartner																20

Accident **M** Mechanical failure **P** Pit stop ☐ Lapped **B** Black Flagged

QUALIFYING

	Driver	Pre-qual time	Pos	Time
1	F Alonso	1m13.750	5	1m13.698s
2	M Schumacher	1m13.541s	2	1m13.971s
3	D Coulthard	1m13.649s	3	1m13.987s
4	J Button	1m13.772s	6	1m13.995s
5	J Trulli	1m13.949s	7	1m14.070s
6	JP Montoya	1m13.377s	1	1m14.172s
7	T Sato	1m14.130s	8	1m14.240s
8	M Gené	1m14.133s	9	1m14.275s
9	K Räikkönen	1m13.736s	4	1m14.346s
10	R Barrichello	no time	20	1m14.478s
11	C da Matta	1m14.245s	10	1m14.553s
12	M Webber	1m15.332s	14	1m14.798s
13	C Klien	1m15.205s	13	1m15.065s
14	O Panis	1m14.540s	11	1m15.130s
15	G Fisichella	1m15.793s	15	1m16.177s
16	F Massa	1m14.627s	12	1m16.200s
17	N Heidfeld	1m16.366s	17	1m16.807s
18	G Pantano	1m15.913s	16	1m17.462s
19	G Bruni	1m18.070s	18	1m17.913s
20	Z Baumgartner	1m18.108s	19	1m18.247s

RACE

	Driver	Car	Laps	Time	Fastest	Avg. mph	Stops
1	M Schumacher	Ferrari F2004	70	1h30m18.133s	1m15.377s	127.409	4
2	F Alonso	Renault R24	70	1h30m26.462s	1m15.551s	127.213	3
3	R Barrichello	Ferrari F2004	70	1h30m49.755s	1m16.035s	1126.669	3
4	J Trulli	Renault R24	70	1h30m50.215s	1m16.248s	126.659	3
5	J Button	BAR-Honda 006	70	1h30m50.617s	1m15.971s	126.649	3
6	D Coulthard	McLaren-Mercedes MP4-19B	70	1h30m53.653s	1m16.203s	126.562	3
7	K Räikkönen	McLaren-Mercedes MP4-19B	70	1h30m54.363s	1m15.791s	126.488	3
8	JP Montoya	Williams-BMW FW26	70	1h31m01.552s	1m16.140s	126.396	3
9	M Webber	Jaguar-Cosworth R5	70	1h31m10.527s	1m15.956s	126.188	3
10	M Gené	Williams-BMW FW26	70	1h31m16.299s	1m16.070s	126.055	3
11	C Klien	Jaguar-Cosworth R5	69	1h30m28.235s	1m16.852s	125.354	3
12	G Fisichella	Sauber-Petronas C23	69	1h30m56.314s	1m16.699s	124.709	3
13	F Massa	Sauber-Petronas C23	69	1h31m10.148s	1n17.388s	124.393	2
14	C da Matta	Toyota TF104	69	1h31m19.703s	1m19.937s	124.176	3
15	O Panis	Toyota TF104	68	1h30m38.616s	1m17.039s	123.300	3
16	N Heidfeld	Jordan-Ford EJ14	68	1h31m22.115s	1m18.627s	122.322	4
17	G Pantano	Jordan-Ford EJ14	67	1h30m37.898s	1m17.641s	121.501	4
18	G Bruni	Minardi-Cosworth PS04	65	Gearbox	1m18.932s		3
R	Z Baumgartner	Minardi-Cosworth PS04	31	Spun off	1m19.659s	-	2
R	T Sato	BAR-Honda 006	15	Engine	1m16.809s	-	1

CHAMPIONSHIP

	Driver	Pts
1	M Schumacher	90
2	R Barrichello	68
3	J Button	48
4	J Trulli	46
5	F Alonso	33
6	JP Montoya	25
7	T Sato	14
8	D Coulthard	12
	R Schumacher	12
10	K Räikkönen	10
11	G Fisichella	10
12	F Massa	5
	O Panis	5
14	C da Matta	3
	N Heidfeld	3

	Constructor	Pts
1	Ferrari	158
2	Renault	79
3	BAR-Honda	62
4	Williams-BMW	37
5	McLaren-Mercedes	22
6	Sauber-Petronas	15
7	Toyota	8
8	Jordan-Ford	5
9	Jaguar-Cosworth	3
10	Minardi-Cosworth	1

Fastest race lap	Fastest through speed trap	Fastest pit stop
M Schumacher 1m15.377s,	R Barrichello 201.572mph	M Schumacher 19.036s
on lap 32 (130.932mph)	Slowest through speed trap	Slowest pit stop
New lap record	G Bruni 193.432mph	O Panis 25.832s

 **Giancarlo Fisichella**

"Our original strategy was to run two stops, but then we decided to go to three stops, as our pace wasn't fast enough and we were struggling for rear-end grip."

 Mark Webber

"The race was incredibly competitive, with most teams both fast and reliable. To see us finishing ninth and 11th after only one retirement is testament to our hard work."

Olivier Panis

"I had a problem at the start of the race when the clutch got stuck and the anti-stall was activated. Then we weren't quick enough to fight with cars in front of us."

Nick Heidfeld

"I had a poorer start than my team-mate, but I passed him after the first pit stop. Then I had a misunderstanding with my engineer so went through the pits again."

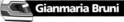 **Gianmaria Bruni**

"I had a good start. Right at the end, though, the telemetry indicated there was a gearbox oil leak, and the team asked me to come into the pits on the very last lap."

 Felipe Massa

"We figured it might be better for me to stick with two stops, but the tyre degradation is so high here that I had a really tough afternoon. It was a struggle."

 **Christian Klien**

"I feel everything is coming together for me. This was my best weekend so far, and I was very pleased to be able to stay with my team-mate through most of the race."

 **Cristiano da Matta**

"I can't really pinpoint why, but the car was a lot slower than it was on Friday and Saturday, and the only reason for this can be the higher temperature ."

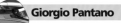 **Giorgio Pantano**

"It was good that we finished, as it's quite a long time since I did that. I had a really good start, but then I felt some problems with the car, especially with braking."

 **Zsolt Baumgartner**

"I was able to pass Gimmi at the start, but he repassed me at the Adelaide hairpin. Unfortunately, I made a mistake after my second stop and went off at Turn 3."

ANOTHER ILLUSION

Kimi Räikkönen really took the race to Michael Schumacher but, as almost everywhere else, it was the Ferrari driver who was in the lead when the flag fell

Kimi Räikkönen gave the 2004 FIA Formula One World Championship another of those moments of hope of relief from Michael Schumacher's dominance. But, just as with Jenson Button's performance at Imola or Fernando Alonso's in France, it was an illusion. Make no mistake, the McLaren MP4-19B, in just its second race, put in a very impressive performance, with Räikkönen taking pole position and never having any serious claim put upon his second position.

But the early picture that showed Räikkönen leading was skewed by Schumacher's heavier fuel load and the usual early-lap performance advantage of the Michelins over the Ferrari's Bridgestones. Schumacher chose to stop just twice compared to the three times of the leading Michelin cars, and the race then played out to the usual pattern of his dominance.

A safety car period because of a big shunt for Jarno Trulli out of Bridge late in the race actually put Michael under some pressure by allowing Räikkönen his third stop for free. But, as racing resumed, Schumacher was given some vital tyre-warming time as Räikkönen had first to find his way by two backmarkers before arriving on the Ferrari's tail. Game over and 10 wins from 11 for the reigning champion.

Kimi Raikkonen has the hammer down as he leads Schumacher on the sprint down to Copse

ROUND **11**

GREAT BRITAIN
2004 FORMULA 1 ™
FOSTER'S BRITISH
GRAND PRIX
Silverstone

LAP BY LAP
ACTION

60 laps / 192 miles

Räikkönen heads the field and is already stretching his advantage

Start to lap 8

The top six drivers hold station at the start, with Räikkönen leading away. Sato runs wide at the first corner, but maintains his position and during lap 1 passes Montoya for seventh place. Barrichello is unable to match Räikkönen's pace and ends the opening lap 3.5s behind, with Button and Schumacher chasing him. Räikkönen extends his lead to 4.3s on lap 2, with Barrichello still under pressure. On lap 3, the gap between Barrichello and Räikkönen stabilises. Sato runs over the grass, losing seventh place to Montoya. The two leaders begin to pull away from Button and Schumacher on lap 4, and by lap 8 the gap between the two leaders is down to 3.5s, with third-placed Button under pressure from Schumacher. There's then a gap back to Trulli, who has Coulthard and Montoya behind him, with a further gap to Sato, Webber and Massa.

Laps 9 to 15

Barrichello pits on lap 9, rejoining in 10th place and promoting Button to second. Coulthard stops on lap 10, dropping from sixth to 14th. Räikkönen, Button and Montoya all stop on lap 11. Schumacher takes the lead and reduces his lap times impressively. Räikkönen rejoins in fourth, with Button seventh. Schumacher continues to extend his lead, then on lap 13 second-placed Trulli pits and falls back to 13th. By lap 14, Schumacher has extended his lead over Räikkönen considerably to 21s. Sato, Webber and Massa are running third, fourth and fifth, but have yet to stop. Button is sixth. After another very fast lap, Schumacher pits on lap 15 and rejoins just ahead of Räikkönen. Behind him, Sato stops, dropping from fourth place to 14th. It becomes clear that there are several drivers running on two-stop strategies.

Button runs third ahead of Schumacher in the early laps

Laps 16 to 28

Third-placed Webber and fourth-placed Massa stop on lap 16. The Jaguar driver rejoins in 10th but Massa drops to 13th. On lap 17, the order at the front sees Schumacher leading Räikkönen, Button, Barrichello, Fisichella (who has yet to stop) and Montoya. By lap 23, Schumacher is under increasing pressure from Räikkönen, suggesting that Michael has a much bigger fuel load than Kimi and may be on a two-stop strategy. Fisichella finally pits for the first time, having moved up from last on the grid to fifth place. On lap 27, fourth-placed Button is the first of the two-stopping frontrunners to pit, rejoining in sixth. Räikkönen and Barrichello stop again on lap 28. Kimi maintains second place but Rubens drops behind Montoya and Coulthard.

Schumacher moves ahead of Räikkönen after his first pit stop

Laps 29 to 39

With Schumacher on his own at the front on lap 29, third-placed Montoya pits and drops to eighth. On lap 30, Schumacher is 23s ahead of Räikkönen, and the McLaren is just over 5s ahead of Barrichello. Coulthard stops and falls to 10th, promoting Button to fourth, Trulli to fifth and Fisichella to sixth. It's clear that Schumacher is on a two-stop strategy. Trulli pits on lap 32, falling from fifth to 11th. On lap 35, Barrichello begins to close on Räikkönen. Schumacher pits on lap 37 and again rejoins ahead of Räikkönen.

Mark Webber ran as high as third before making his first pit visit

Laps 40 to 45

By lap 40, as Schumacher and Räikkönen run together at the front, it's clear that Kimi will have to stop again. At the exit of Bridge Corner, Trulli spins to the inside of the track. The Renault then rolls when it hits the gravel trap, going on to hit the tyre wall. Trulli emerges unhurt, but the safety car is sent out. All the three-stop runners pit on lap 41, gaining an advantage over the two-stoppers. The order as the field forms up behind the safety car is Schumacher, da Matta and Klien (the pair a lap down), Räikkönen, Barrichello, Button, Montoya, Fisichella, Coulthard and Webber.

Suspension failure at Bridge put Jarno Trulli into the barriers, hard

Lap 46 to the finish

The race restarts on lap 46, and Schumacher pulls away from Räikkönen. Barrichello closes on the McLaren but is unable to challenge. On lap 60, Schumacher takes his 80th Grand Prix victory, with Räikkönen under pressure from Barrichello for second. Button finishes a lonely fourth, while behind him Montoya is chased home by Fisichella. Coulthard is seventh and Webber holds off Massa and Alonso for the final point.

Räikkönen is a rare McLaren driver among Ferrari's duo

INSIDE LINE
KIMI RÄIKKÖNEN

This was a really positive race, only the second time we ran the new car. It was quick and it was reliable, and this was great for the whole team and all of the people there after the difficult first part of the season we had. Pole position and second place we could only have dreamed about not long before the British Grand Prix.

We first tested the car at this track, and straight away it felt very good. It has a better rear end, the aerodynamics are better and the engine is stronger. Around here it was good everywhere but especially in the last sector, and through Bridge it was really good.

In the race, I just went flat-out right from the start and after the first lap there was already quite a big gap. I knew that Ferrari might be quicker than us over the race distance so I was just trying to build the gap as big as I could. Obviously, we were running a bit lighter [than Schumacher] and pitted before him. I was unlucky at this point to come out behind two

Minardis, and that allowed Michael to get enough time on me that he came out ahead after his stop. Without the traffic, I think I could have held him off for another stint, but probably not for the whole race.

I got caught in traffic again on my second stop. When you have the new tyres on, the Michelins find a lot of time over the Bridgestones, and so it cost us a lot hitting traffic and so losing that advantage. I was going to be well behind, but then the safety car gave us a window to do our third stop for free and then close right up to Michael. But there were two lapped cars between us in the queue and that just stopped me from being able to get to Michael in time. By the time I caught up with him, he had managed to get his tyres warm. Also, on my last set of tyres, I had more difficulty with the rear end than my other sets. Still, it was a good result and made me think that we could push for a win before the season was over.

Shaken but not stirred: Jarno Trulli was bemused by his 30g impact out of Bridge

Q THE BIG QUESTION

Why did Jarno Trulli's Renault R24's rear suspension break beneath him through Bridge?
An enormous accident for Jarno Trulli through the fifth gear Bridge corner brought out the safety car on lap 40. That he was totally unharmed after two high-speed roll-overs and a hefty 30g-plus impact with the tyre barriers was testimony to the passive safety of a modern Formula One car.

"There was no warning," he explained. "The car just suddenly went crazy. But I must say it didn't feel as big an accident from inside as it looked on the video."

A right rear suspension failure was identified by the Renault team as the likely cause of the accident, although confirmation of this was impossible because of the extensive nature of the damage inflicted by the accident itself. The right rear is actually the less heavily loaded side of the car as it turns into Bridge, and the failure was believed to be an internal fracture of the carbon-fibre wishbone. Immensely strong in the direction for which the loads are designed to feed through it, carbon-fibre can be vulnerable if it takes an impact from any other direction. Even the inadvertent dropping of a mechanic's spanner on to the unit may have been sufficient to weaken it invisibly.

From the following race, the German GP at Hockenheim, Renault took the step of replacing the R24's one-piece carbon-fibre wishbone with a titanium equivalent. "In performance terms that's a backwards step," said chief of engineering Pat Symonds, "but only a very marginal one, and we felt the lessons learned from Jarno's accident made it the responsible course of action."

It wasn't too much longer before it was mooted that such a material change may be made compulsory for all suspensions from 2005.

A 'free' final pit stop gave Kimi Räikkönen a chance to have a shot at Michael Schumacher

RON DENNIS
McLAREN TEAM PRINCIPAL

We had more knowledge of the MP4-19B than in France, but we were still getting to grips with its technical character. We knew very well how to get the best out of the car in high-speed corners, though, and therefore we were strong at Silverstone. The general stability of this car is much better than on the MP4-19 and that really was apparent here. We had ongoing engine developments race on race, and although we still had to limit our practice laps, the fact that this was the fourth successive race without an engine failure was a testament to Martin Whitmarsh and all the people on the engine programme to come to grips with change.

It's an inevitability in a tyre war that in some races you'll have a tyre advantage, and at others a tyre disadvantage, and I feel we were at a small disadvantage here, just as we were to enjoy a small advantage at Hockenheim.

Kimi was astounding in those early laps of the race. That was one of the best first laps that has ever been driven by anyone, and certainly the best first lap he's ever driven; he was just gone. But you can only do first laps like that when you start on the front row of the grid, and Kimi's pole and first lap was one of the upsides of the Michelins – their initial performance is very strong and Bridgestone tended to struggle in those laps.

I don't believe that Michael was two-stopping. They switched to a two-stop but, at the start of the race, their fuel loads were comparable. Kimi knew he had to push regardless. I don't get into planning the strategy with a driver, but it was one of those races where all I had to suggest was that the key would be racing from beginning to end. You can't know other people's strategy in advance and, even if you're leading someone by a healthy margin, they could be on a two-stop strategy and you're on a three, and the fact that they're staying with you means that they're going to win the race.

The late safety car gave us a second bite at the race, but the fact we were separated from Michael in the queue by two lapped cars proved critical.

WILLY RAMPF
SAUBER
TECHNICAL
DIRECTOR

This race saw the first major revision we did to our car and the first that had been developed in our new on-site wind tunnel. That it worked so well in its first race was obviously very satisfying for us, with Giancarlo [Fisichella] driving a great race to finish sixth. This was a better result than we were expecting, but we were still disappointed because we lost a place at the final pit stop when we needed to repressure the pneumatics and that cost us 4s. Otherwise we would have beaten Montoya's Williams. It was a simple component that caused the problem – one of the O-rings was leaking pressure.

The revision to the car was a new lower engine cover. We started the project even before the season began, but the tighter cover required different, v-shaped radiators. At Melbourne, we had the v-shape on the right-hand side with the water, and at Monaco we had it on the left-hand side for the oil. Only then could we finalise our work on the engine cover.

The wind tunnel suggested that this gave an aerodynamic efficiency improvement of around 3%. We also paid a lot of attention in the wind tunnel to aerodynamics in yaw, and this turned out to be very relevant at Silverstone, a track that often gives crosswind problems.

At the track, it immediately seemed to work well; in fact it was more of an improvement than the wind tunnel had suggested. The track and the conditions suited the Bridgestone tyres well, I think. They were fast and consistent.

Straight away Giancarlo and Felipe [Massa] said the balance was better, the traction was better and they could feel more downforce. Unfortunately, we had an engine problem with Giancarlo in one of the practices, so we had to change it and he started the race from the back, while Felipe was baulked by Panis's Toyota. We decided to run Giancarlo with a two-stop strategy with most of the others on a three, and it worked very well. From the first stops, he was fighting with Montoya and at the time of the final safety car we were ahead.

We hadn't expected to be faster than a Williams and so it was bitter-sweet to lose that place.

	Total pit time	Fastest race lap
Fisichella (Sauber)	50.153s	**1m 19.813s** (5th fastest overall)
Montoya (Williams)	66.853s	**1m 19.968s** (6th fastest overall)

Giancarlo Fisichella revelled in the revised car's handling, but ended up frustrated to be sixth

RACE RESULTS
GREAT BRITAIN SILVERSTONE

RACE DATE July 11th
CIRCUIT LENGTH 3.193 miles
NO. OF LAPS 60
RACE DISTANCE 191.580 miles
WEATHER dry and cloudy, 17°C
TRACK TEMP 27°C
RACE ATTENDANCE 100,000
LAP RECORD Michael Schumacher,
1m 18.739s, 146.059mph, 2004

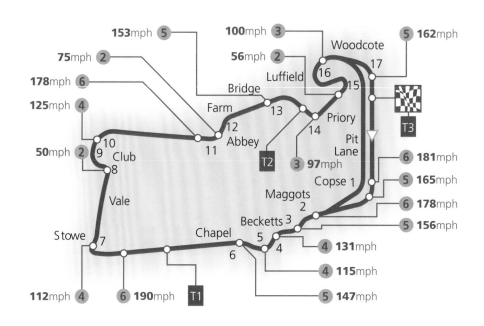

PRACTICE 1			
	Driver	Time	Laps
1	R Barrichello	1m19.138s	16
2	M Schumacher	1m19.214s	25
3	JP Montoya	1m19.502s	13
4	M Gené	1m19.687s	14
5	A Davidson	1m19.748s	23
6	D Coulthard	1m20.021s	6
7	F Massa	1m20.430s	17
8	G Fisichella	1m20.446s	10
9	K Räikkönen	1m20.633s	5
10	J Button	1m20.866s	8
11	R Zonta	1m21.095s	27
12	B Wirdheim	1m21.277s	24
13	T Sato	1m21.285s	13
14	M Webber	1m21.520s	6
15	J Trulli	1m21.792s	13
16	F Alonso	1m22.003s	5
17	C Klien	1m22.279s	11
18	C da Matta	1m22.466s	16
19	O Panis	1m22.520s	15
20	G Pantano	1m22.664s	20
21	N Heidfeld	1m22.716s	20
22	T Glock	1m23.149s	23
23	G Bruni	1m23.663s	19
24	Z Baumgartner	1m23.715s	20
25	B Leinders	1m24.887s	18

PRACTICE 2			
	Driver	Time	Laps
1	K Räikkönen	1m18.655s	16
2	G Fisichella	1m18.660s	20
3	M Schumacher	1m19.162s	14
4	D Coulthard	1m19.287s	17
5	J Button	1m19.401s	19
6	R Barrichello	1m19.473s	22
7	M Gené	1m19.540s	20
8	J Trulli	1m19.601s	21
9	T Sato	1m19.611s	13
10	F Massa	1m19.676s	23
11	JP Montoya	1m19.746s	20
12	F Alonso	1m19.874s	30
13	R Zonta	1m20.095s	35
14	O Panis	1m20.489s	25
15	C da Matta	1m20.829s	19
16	A Davidson	1m20.861s	14
17	C Klien	1m21.073s	30
18	M Webber	1m21.352s	27
19	B Wirdheim	1m21.353s	33
20	N Heidfeld	1m22.365s	13
21	T Glock	1m22.500s	24
22	G Bruni	1m22.516s	25
23	G Pantano	1m22.586s	14
24	B Leinders	1m22.792s	20
25	Z Baumgartner	1m23.436s	23

PRACTICE 3			
	Driver	Time	Laps
1	K Räikkönen	1m19.315s	5
2	J Button	1m19.468s	6
3	M Schumacher	1m19.571s	11
4	R Barrichello	1m19.585s	8
5	JP Montoya	1m19.699s	10
6	J Trulli	1m19.966s	5
7	D Coulthard	1m19.979s	5
8	T Sato	1m20.177s	6
9	F Alonso	1m20.482s	13
10	M Gené	1m20.552s	13
11	F Massa	1m20.685s	6
12	G Fisichella	1m20.759s	9
13	C da Matta	1m21.017s	11
14	M Webber	1m21.295s	5
15	O Panis	1m21.416s	15
16	C Klien	1m21.706s	6
17	G Pantano	1m21.984s	11
18	N Heidfeld	1m22.503s	12
19	Z Baumgartner	no time	0
20	G Bruni	no time	0

PRACTICE 4			
	Driver	Time	Laps
1	K Räikkönen	1m18.280s	14
2	J Button	1m18.414s	12
3	R Barrichello	1m18.623s	13
4	J Trulli	1m18.694s	14
5	M Gené	1m18.832s	10
6	JP Montoya	1m18.912s	11
7	D Coulthard	1m18.919s	11
8	M Schumacher	1m18.951s	8
9	F Alonso	1m19.169s	12
10	G Fisichella	1m19.895s	10
11	C da Matta	1m20.183s	19
12	F Massa	1m20.281s	6
13	M Webber	1m20.310s	23
14	O Panis	1m20.531s	16
15	N Heidfeld	1m20.726s	12
16	T Sato	1m20.837s	8
17	C Klien	1m20.913s	18
18	Z Baumgartner	1m21.980s	15
19	G Pantano	1m22.014s	11
20	G Bruni	1m23.941s	12

Best sectors – Qualifying		Speed trap – Qualifying	
Sector 1 R Barrichello	24.611s	1 M Gené	173.992mph
Sector 2 K Räikkönen	33.517s	2 R Barrichello	173.308mph
Sector 3 K Räikkönen	19.666s	3 JP Montoya	173.184mph

Michael Schumacher
"I wasn't worried by Kimi's pace at the start of the race, as I knew my strategy. I didn't want to overdo it and just let the potential of the car do the work."

Juan Pablo Montoya
"I made a mistake at the start, releasing the clutch too quickly, and it cost me a position to Sato. I tried to keep pushing but it wasn't possible to catch those in front."

Kimi Räikkönen
"All the hard work that went into the development of the 19B paid off. I made a very good start. Unluckily, I had a bit of traffic after my pit stops, but that's racing."

Fernando Alonso
"We missed the opportunity to pit directly after Jarno's accident. We had only two corners in which to react, otherwise I could have been in the points."

Jenson Button
"We came into this race expecting a lot more than we've been able to deliver. We really struggled with a lack of grip compared to the Ferraris."

Rubens Barrichello
"I had a good race but a tough one. At one point, I got stuck behind four or five cars fighting for position, and that probably lost me second place and maybe the win."

Marc Gené
"Alonso passed me in the first pit stop and after that I had to fight Sato and da Matta with our pit-stop strategy as I didn't have the pace to improve my track position."

David Coulthard
"Congratulations to Kimi on a great drive. Unfortunately, I'm not happy with my own performance, as I was struggling with my car's balance, especially in slow corners."

Jarno Trulli
"It was a big accident, but I gave the marshals the thumbs up straight away. Everything happened very quickly, but I think it was rear suspension failure."

Takuma Sato
"It was a risk to choose different strategies for the two cars, but we thought it would provide us with an opportunity to react to any change in the weather."

POSITIONS LAP BY LAP

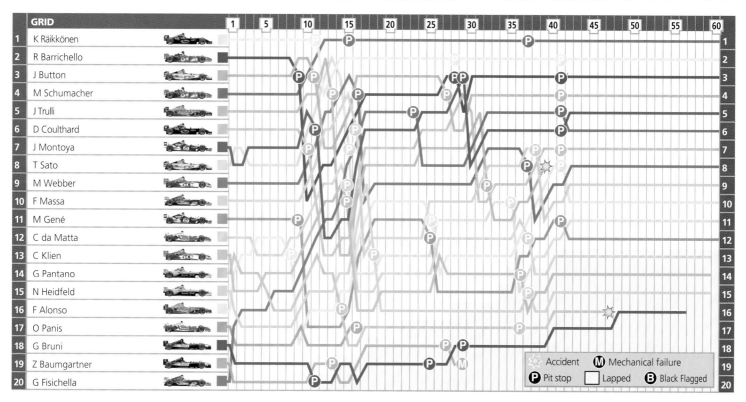

GRID		
1	K Räikkönen	
2	R Barrichello	
3	J Button	
4	M Schumacher	
5	J Trulli	
6	D Coulthard	
7	J Montoya	
8	T Sato	
9	M Webber	
10	F Massa	
11	M Gené	
12	C da Matta	
13	C Klien	
14	G Pantano	
15	N Heidfeld	
16	F Alonso	
17	O Panis	
18	G Bruni	
19	Z Baumgartner	
20	G Fisichella	

Legend: ☆ Accident — Ⓜ Mechanical failure — Ⓟ Pit stop — ☐ Lapped — Ⓑ Black Flagged

QUALIFYING

	Driver	Pre-qual time	Pos	Time
1	K Räikkönen	1m21.639s	6	1m18.233s
2	R Barrichello	1m24.817s	12	1m18.305s
3	J Button	1m18.872s	1	1m18.580s
4	M Schumacher	1m30.293s	14	1m18.710s
5	J Trulli	1m21.496s	5	1m18.715s
6	F Alonso	1m21.923s	7	1m18.811s
7	D Coulthard	1m23.521s	11	1m19.148s
8	JP Montoya	1m34.386s	15	1m19.378s
9	T Sato	1m28.910s	13	1m19.688s
10	M Webber	1m35.853s	17	1m20.004s
11	F Massa	1m19.317s	2	1m20.202s
12	O Panis	1m19.697s	3	1m20.335s
13	M Gené	1m34.981s	16	1m20.335s
14	C da Matta	1m22.507s	8	1m20.545s
15	C Klien	1m38.648s	18	1m21.559s
16	G Pantano	1m21.350s	4	1m22.458s
17	N Heidfeld	no time	20	1m22.677s
18	G Bruni	1m22.529s	9	1m23.437s
19	Z Baumgartner	1m23.116s	10	1m24.117s
20	G Fisichella	no time	19	no time

RACE

	Driver	Car	Laps	Time	Fastest	Avg. mph	Stops
1	M Schumacher	Ferrari F2004	60	1h24m42.700s	1m18.739s	135.716	2
2	K Räikkönen	McLaren-Mercedes MP4-19B	60	1h24m44.830s	1m19.554s	135.658	3
3	R Barrichello	Ferrari F2004	60	1h24m45.814s	1m19.296s	135.632	3
4	J Button	BAR-Honda 006	60	1h24m53.383s	1m19.488s	135.431	3
5	JP Montoya	Williams-BMW FW26	60	1h24m54.873s	1m19.968s	135.391	3
6	G Fisichella	Sauber-Petronas C23	60	1h24m55.588s	1m19.813s	135.372	2
7	D Coulthard	McLaren-Mercedes MP4-19B	60	1h25m02.368s	1m20.547s	135.192	3
8	M Webber	Jaguar-Cosworth R5	60	1h25m06.401s	1m20.768s	135.086	2
9	F Massa	Sauber-Petronas C23	60	1h25m06.723s	1m20.484s	135.077	2
10	F Alonso	Renault R24	60	1h25m07.535s	1m20.442s	135.056	3
11	T Sato	BAR-Honda 006	60	1h25m16.436s	1m20.790s	134.821	2
12	M Gené	Williams-BMW FW26	60	1h25m17.003s	1m20.434s	134.806	3
13	C da Matta	Toyota TF104	59	1h25m19.903s	1m20.768s	132.483	2
14	C Klien	Jaguar-Cosworth R5	59	1h25m20.971s	1m20.956s	132.455	2
15	N Heidfeld	Jordan-Ford EJ14	59	1h25m29.729s	1m21.730s	132.229	2
16	G Bruni	Minardi-Cosworth PS04	56	1h25m12.423s	1m24.296s	125.928	4
R	G Pantano	Jordan-Ford EJ14	47	Accident	1m22.146s	-	2
R	J Trulli	Renault R24	39	Accident	1m20.655s	-	2
R	Z Baumgartner	Minardi-Cosworth PS04	29	Engine	1m23.131s	-	2
R	O Panis	Toyota TF104	16	Extinguisher	1m24.317s	-	1

CHAMPIONSHIP

	Driver	Pts
1	M Schumacher	100
2	R Barrichello	74
3	J Button	53
4	J Trulli	46
5	F Alonso	33
6	JP Montoya	29
7	K Räikkönen	18
8	D Coulthard	14
	T Sato	14
10	G Fisichella	13
11	R Schumacher	12
12	F Massa	5
	O Panis	5
14	M Webber	4
15	C da Matta	3

	Constructor	Pts
1	Ferrari	174
2	Renault	79
3	BAR-Honda	67
4	Williams-BMW	41
5	McLaren-Mercedes	32
6	Sauber-Petronas	18
7	Toyota	8
8	Jordan-Ford	5
9	Jaguar-Cosworth	4
10	Minardi-Cosworth	1

Qualifying notes

Alonso, Baumgartner, Bruni & Fisichella Back 10 places for engine change

Panis Lost qualifying time for blocking a driver

Fastest race lap M Schumacher 1m18.739s, on lap 14 (146.059mph) New lap record

Fastest through speed trap M Schumacher 179.866mph

Slowest through speed trap Z Baumgartner 160.499mph

Fastest pit stop J Trulli 20.997s

Slowest pit stop G Bruni 1m11.727s

Giancarlo Fisichella

"I was able to pass several cars carrying less fuel than I was. But I lost time in my final stop as my pneumatics were topped up. Otherwise I'd have beaten Montoya."

Mark Webber

"I made a good start and enjoyed a great battle with Alonso and Massa for much of the race, and it was good to keep them at bay and get the last available point."

Olivier Panis

"Starting from 17th on the grid, it was never going to be easy, but the race finished far too early for me when my extinguisher exploded in the car."

Nick Heidfeld

"I nearly got by Klien at the start, but he touched me and a winglet broke on the left-hand side of the car. It didn't appear to have much effect. We were just too slow."

Gianmaria Bruni

"It was a difficult race for a number of reasons, including a drive-through penalty, but I'm pleased I was able to take the flag as a tribute to John [Walton]."

Felipe Massa

"I had a software problem in my stop on lap 38 and, initially, couldn't get first gear. Near the end, I dropped back from Webber then pressed hard, but his car was faster."

Christian Klien

"This wasn't an easy race as, once the safety car was deployed it was even more difficult to move up the order when I had to keep moving over for blue flags."

Cristiano da Matta

"I got held up a lot just before the safety car period, and we then lost ground because the three-stopping cars were able to use the safety car to their advantage."

Giorgio Pantano

"The second or third lap after my first stop, I had a spin. Later, I spun again. I don't know if I went onto the grass or whether rear locking caused me to get onto the grass."

Zsolt Baumgartner

"I'm upset that I wasn't able to finish the race and take the chequered flag today, as I'd promised myself that I would do it, both for John and for me."

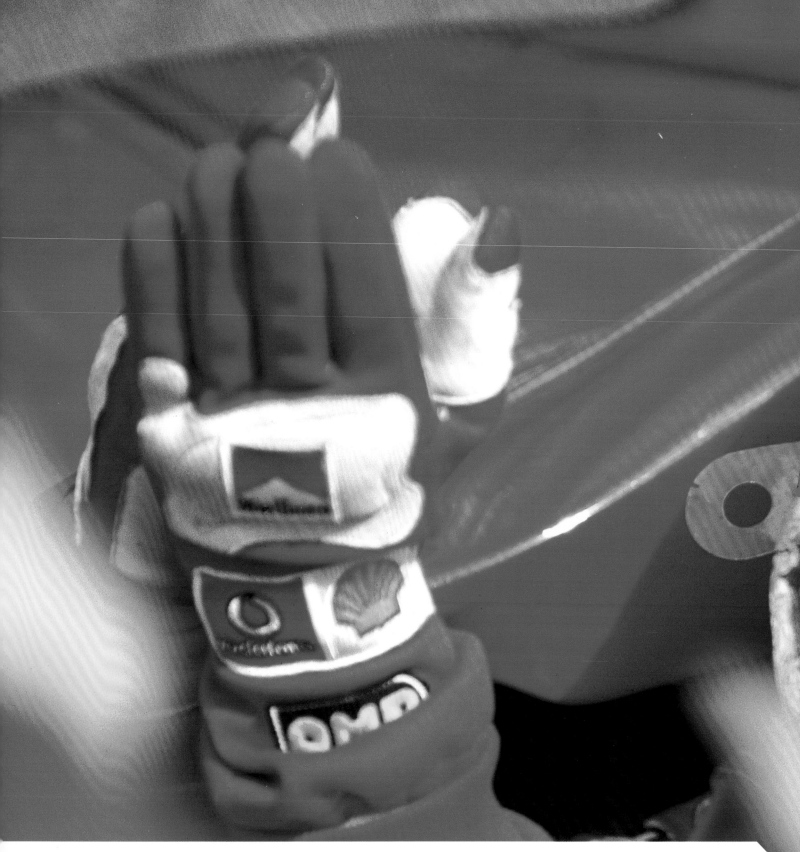

MICHAEL DELIVERS

Jenson Button was the star of the race, forcing his way up from 13th on the grid, but it was Michael Schumacher who laid claim to the spoils for Ferrari

Here was a race in which at least four drivers produced quite sensational performances. Unsurprisingly, one of these was Michael Schumacher and, despite a race widely reckoned as the best of the season to date, the end result was the same as in 10 of the previous 11 Grands Prix: a Michael Schumacher win.

Schumacher's cause was aided by taking a superb pole position. A new compound of Bridgestone that resolved the circuit's extreme demands on rear tyre heat degradation further assisted. However, he was possibly helped most of all by the dramatic retirement of the closely chasing McLaren-Mercedes of Kimi Räikkönen

on lap 14. When the silver car's rear wing failed and spun Räikkönen hard into the tyre barriers, it had more fuel on board than the Ferrari and yet had still been cutting into Schumacher's narrow lead.

With Räikkönen gone, Schumacher enjoyed a 10s lead over his pursuers and he simply maintained this gap to the flag.

The attention then shifted to a superb battle for second place between Fernando Alonso's Renault and Jenson Button's BAR-Honda, eventually settled in the latter's favour despite having started from 13th on the grid following a 10-place penalty for an engine change.

Wins in his home race have been rare for Michael, explaining the fans' delight at his lead

ROUND **12**

GERMANY
FORMULA 1™ GROSSER
MOBIL 1 PREIS VON
DEUTSCHLAND 2004
Hockenheim

LAP BY LAP
ACTION

66 laps / 188 miles

Schumacher leads the way from Alonso and Räikkönen on lap 1

Start to lap 3

At the end of the parade lap, Panis stalls and is sent to the back of the grid. As the field departs for the second parade lap, Panis stalls again and is pushed to start the race from pitlane. Montoya is slow away at the start from second on the grid, and Schumacher leads a fast-starting Alonso, Räikkönen, Trulli, Coulthard and Barrichello. Montoya is next, ahead of Webber. Barrichello runs into the back of Coulthard at the hairpin, losing his front wing, which bounces into Montoya's path. This enables Webber to pass the Williams. At the end of lap 1, Schumacher is 1s ahead of Alonso, with Räikkönen third, Trulli fourth, Coulthard fifth and Webber sixth. Next is Montoya, followed by Pizzonia (subbing at Williams for Ralf Schumacher), Sato and Klien. Barrichello pits for repairs. Schumacher leads by 2s by the end of lap 2, while Räikkönen passes Alonso at the hairpin for second. Further back, Button, demoted to 13th on the grid due to an engine change, passes da Matta for 11th.

Barrichello loses a wing against Coulthard's McLaren at the hairpin

Laps 4 to 13

Montoya passes Webber to take sixth on lap 4, while Button overtakes Klien for 10th. Räikkönen has been able to keep the pressure on Schumacher, but by lap 6 Schumacher pulls away again, increasing his lead by a second. On lap 9, Alonso is the first man to make a scheduled pit stop, followed by Pizzonia. Schumacher pits on lap 10, and Räikkönen leads. Also stopping are third-placed Trulli, Montoya, Sato and da Matta. Räikkönen and Montoya both stop on lap 11 and Webber takes the lead with Button following. Webber pits on lap 12, and Button moves into the lead. Klien pits from fourth on lap 13 and falls back down the order, while Button stays out with Schumacher second and Räikkönen third, Alonso up to fourth, Coulthard fifth and Trulli sixth.

Lap 2, and Button is working his way forward from 13th on the grid

Laps 14 to 33

At the start of lap 14, Räikkönen suffers a rear wing failure at the first corner and spins into the barriers at high speed. He is shaken, but unhurt. Button pits, and Schumacher assumes the lead. By lap 16, the German has a 10s lead, with Alonso second, Coulthard third, Montoya fourth, Button fifth and Trulli sixth under pressure from Webber. Montoya runs wide on lap 21 and loses fourth place to Button. Sato passes Trulli at the hairpin on lap 26, and Webber takes advantage of the situation to demote Trulli to eighth. Schumacher stops again on lap 28, allowing Alonso to lead with Button second. Alonso pits on lap 29, and Button takes the lead with Schumacher second. Alonso rejoins in third ahead of Coulthard. Fourth-placed Webber pits. Out front, Button pulls away from Schumacher, while Alonso can't make any impression on the two men ahead of him.

An angry Kimi Räikkönen struts away from his crashed McLaren

Laps 34 to 51

Button pits on lap 34, after building a 5s lead, rejoining just behind Alonso. So, Schumacher retakes the lead, 13s ahead of Alonso. Button and Alonso spend lap 36 side-by-side through several corners, but Fernando is unable to hold off the BAR driver. On lap 47, Schumacher, Alonso and Coulthard all pit, leaving Button in the lead with Schumacher rejoining behind him. Montoya is briefly up to third but stops on lap 48. The only major runner needing to stop again is now Button. On lap 49, Barrichello, who has been making steady progress through the field, passes Fisichella for eighth. Button stops finally on lap 50 and drops behind Alonso once again, rekindling the battle for second.

Alonso and Button spent most of the race's middle laps together

Lap 52 to the finish

Alonso has a problem on lap 52, and Button passes, the Renault falling back quickly. The order is now Schumacher, 10s clear of Button, with Alonso third and under pressure from Coulthard. There is then a gap back to Montoya, with Webber, Sato and Pizzonia scrapping over sixth. Button has to drive the final few laps with one hand holding his visor in place as the wind is lifting his helmet up, making it difficult for him to breathe. On lap 60, Pizzonia passes Sato for seventh and begins to attack Webber for sixth. Schumacher takes the chequered flag on lap 66, ahead of Button, Alonso, Coulthard, Montoya, Webber, Pizzonia and Sato.

Ferrari's Martinelli joins Button, Schuey and Alonso on the podium

INSIDE LINE
JENSON BUTTON

This was without doubt the best race of my F1 career to date. The car was working great here all weekend. In truth, the car and engine were fantastic, but my grid penalty made it a bit frustrating. I set third fastest time in qualifying and if I could have started from that place you naturally wonder if the race could have been a different story. I think I could certainly have put some pressure on Michael [Schumacher], which I would have enjoyed very much.

I got a good start, but at the first turn I got stuck behind Taku [Sato], on the outside, and that lost me a lot of the places I'd just gained, so I was still in 13th, where I'd started from. Then I just worked my way up bit by bit. We ran a little longer than the rest before pitting, and the team did a fantastic job at the first stop enabling me to rejoin in fifth. Then later I had a great little tussle with Fernando [Alonso]. He's not the easiest guy to overtake, but he's very fair and I really enjoyed it.

Alonso had good traction out of the hairpin so I would lose a bit of time to him there, but then I'd pull it back down the straight. Coming

into that hairpin, it's really difficult to know where to place the car to pass. Fernando went for the inside so I went outside first and tried to sweep back to the inside as we came out, but that didn't work because his traction was so good. So I tried the same thing a few different ways, but none of them quite worked. I eventually got him after the last round of pit stops, but I think he was in trouble by then.

After that last stop, I had a little problem with my helmet. The strap underneath had come a bit loose and was allowing the helmet to come up when the air got under it, which left the strap nearly choking me. The problem was, with the HANS device, you can't get your hand across to tighten the strap, so instead I was just having to hold the helmet down on every straight. It wasn't really a big thing, just a bit of a background worry.

It was great to come out of the recent tail-off in form and come back really hard. We'd made a lot of progress and to have such an exciting race made it all feel fantastic. However, I still had that little thing in my mind: if only I could have started the race from third on the grid.

Q THE BIG QUESTION

Why does overtaking happen here?

"When you make a move here, that's not the end of it," said BAR-Honda racer Jenson Button after his lengthy fight with Fernando Alonso for second place. "It continues for three or four more corners, which is great."

The solution to the general paucity of overtaking is something that has vexed F1 for years. Hockenheim, ever since being drastically shortened and revised in 2002, seems to have been able to generate the sort of passing action otherwise missing on the F1 calendar. The key is Turns 6, 7 and 8, a hairpin followed by a long straight, a kink, then a short straight into a switchback hairpin.

Turn 6 allows for distinct inside and outside lines, giving the following driver the opportunity to partly overlap the car he's chasing, thereby maintaining momentum on to the straight. Furthermore, if by positioning you can box in the car on the inside, you compromise its exit from the corner without hurting yours. Critically, the kink of Turn 7 allows cars to go through side-by-side, thus prolonging the opportunity of making an overtaking move work, and the advantageous inside line of Turn 7 automatically becomes the disadvantageous outside line for the following hairpin of Turn 9. These three interconnected corners were the battleground for Button and Alonso.

Renault's Pat Symonds, however, isn't convinced. "There was virtually no passing here in 2003. I think bad circuit design can screw the racing up, but good circuit design alone can't make for good racing. This sequence is clearly designed quite well from the point of view of overtaking, but we need to be looking elsewhere for the answers too. Perhaps Button's BAR being a fast car out of position was more to do with things than the circuit itself."

The hairpin at Turn 6 affords good overtaking possibilities, but Pat Symonds isn't so sure...

MARTIN WHITMARSH
McLAREN MANAGING DIRECTOR

To suffer a failure like that to Kimi's rear wing when actually fighting over the destiny of a race was doubly disappointing. Could we have won it? I don't know. Could we have put Michael [Schumacher] under a lot of pressure? Definitely, yes. I believe we had a tyre advantage [over Ferrari] here, our car was working very well and Kimi was very pumped up. At the time that Kimi retired, he had more fuel on board than Michael and was still catching. So it all looked very promising.

The moment that Kimi's wing failed was obviously very tense. We were relieved that Kimi was alright, but you then think about the other car. We have information on every component on the car at any given time, and so on the pit wall we were asking for the respective histories of the rear wings on each of the cars. What is this wing? What is our experience of it?

That design of wing was common to the MP4-19 and 19B and had done thousands of kilometres of testing and racing since the European Grand Prix in May without problems. We then looked at the records of each individual wing. That on Kimi's had done 480km before the start of the race – not a big distance, but not a case of infant mortality, where something was obviously wrong and breaks as soon as it's put under load. That on David's had done just 250km more than Kimi's. So both were relatively new components.

It was a main plane failure and it appeared to have broken on the right-hand side, probably four or five centimetres away from the right-hand endplate. Just before he braked you could see it come down on the right, at which point the main plane folded and ripped the rest off, with the two endplates still there as it was spinning.

At that moment, given the information at our disposal, we had to assume that the failure came from a quality issue or a damage issue of that particular wing. So we decided against calling DC in. Afterwards, you have to find a reason and if you can't, then you're obliged to strengthen the component.

We ran a thorough investigation on the Monday, and forensic analysis determined that it was a main plane failure, the precise cause of which is now understood. As a consequence, the wing was withdrawn from service. We didn't need a similar configuration of wing until the Chinese Grand Prix, by which time we had prepared a revised construction.

Failure of the main
plane on Räikkönen's
wing caused McLaren to
check the part's history

PAT SYMONDS
RENAULT CHIEF OF ENGINEERING

I can't remember another race quite like this one where both our cars were compromised by having caught various bits of debris from others.

Jarno [Trulli] had his problem first. He picked up part of Räikkönen's rear wing under his diffuser soon after his first pit stop and that badly hurt the car's performance. We were able to pull it out at the second stop, but he'd lost a lot of time and a few places by then. Getting the debris out from the car also meant we lost a further 7s or

so in the pits, and the combined result of all that dropped him out of contention. He finished 11th, having run fourth for most of the first stint.

Fernando had a similar problem but later in the race, and as such it wasn't quite so costly in terms of position, although it did lose us second place. Remarkably, Fernando's piece of debris eventually dislodged itself after he whacked a kerb and he was able to pick up his pace again.

He radioed in on lap 52 that something was seriously wrong with the car. He said it had no front-end grip and initially he thought there was a problem with a wheel or the front suspension. We have various on-board sensors to monitor many aspects of the car's performance, and the two critical ones here were those for the skid-plate temperatures and those for the aero loadings. We could see immediately that the skid plates were losing temperature rapidly, suggesting that the front of the car wasn't receiving much downforce. When we

looked at the aero loads we saw that the aero balance had moved 8% towards the rear. That's a massive amount on something as finely balanced as an F1 car.

He'd picked up debris in his left-hand barge board and the airflow was being wildly compromised. Knowing what we know from the data, I have absolutely no idea how Fernando kept

that car on the road, let alone how he dropped only a couple of seconds per lap. It was during this time that Jenson was able to pass him for second place. Fernando ran the next six laps with the car like that, during which time he was caught by Coulthard and Montoya. But it then dislodged itself and he pulled himself out of danger. It was a remarkable performance.

Alonso's lap times

Lap	
49	1m 15.312s
50	1m 15.281s
51	1m 15.635s (picked up debris near the end of this lap)
Aero balance shifts rearwards by 8%	
52	1m 17.221s
53	1m 18.201s
54	1m 18.518s
55	1m 17.699s
56	1m 18.138s
57	1m 17.021s (debris dislodged over kerb near end of this lap)
Aero balance reverts to normal	
58	1m 15.156s
59	1m 14.961s
60	1m 14.876s

Fernando Alonso adapted to his car's new-found poor balance after collecting debris

RACE RESULTS
GERMANY HOCKENHEIM

RACE DATE July 25th
CIRCUIT LENGTH 2.843 miles
NO. OF LAPS 66
RACE DISTANCE 187.638 miles
WEATHER dry and bright, 29°C
TRACK TEMP 45°C
RACE ATTENDANCE 101,000
LAP RECORD Kimi Räikkönen, 1m 13.780s, 138.685mph, 2004

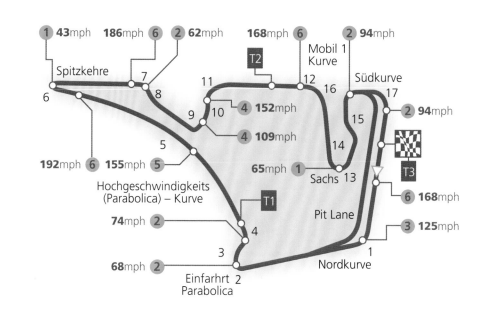

PRACTICE 1		
	Driver	Time	Laps
1	A Davidson	1m15.756s	32
2	M Schumacher	1m15.864s	11
3	K Räikkönen	1m16.318s	8
4	R Zonta	1m16.340s	36
5	G Fisichella	1m16.451s	11
6	O Panis	1m16.484s	20
7	R Barrichello	1m16.493s	16
8	J Button	1m16.544s	12
9	JP Montoya	1m16.795s	14
10	A Pizzonia	1m16.845s	14
11	D Coulthard	1m16.916s	8
12	C da Matta	1m17.111s	21
13	F Alonso	1m17.142s	11
14	F Massa	1m17.361s	18
15	J Trulli	1m17.487s	14
16	T Sato	1m17.526s	14
17	B Wirdheim	1m17.714s	20
18	C Klien	1m17.810s	15
19	N Heidfeld	1m18.257s	17
20	T Glock	1m18.768s	9
21	G Bruni	1m19.088s	17
22	B Leinders	1m19.270s	14
23	Z Baumgartner	1m19.959s	13
24	G Pantano	1m20.029s	17
25	M Webber	no time	1

PRACTICE 2		
	Driver	Time	Laps
1	M Schumacher	1m15.001s	27
2	K Räikkönen	1m15.045s	18
3	JP Montoya	1m15.167s	25
4	J Button	1m15.379s	23
5	A Pizzonia	1m15.470s	25
6	A Davidson	1m15.576s	33
7	T Sato	1m15.657s	21
8	F Alonso	1m15.677s	30
9	R Barrichello	1m15.738s	19
10	R Zonta	1m16.200s	38
11	D Coulthard	1m16.265s	18
12	B Wirdheim	1m16.342s	28
13	M Webber	1m16.514s	27
14	J Trulli	1m16.660s	32
15	C Klien	1m16.854s	31
16	F Massa	1m16.865s	30
17	G Fisichella	1m17.026s	26
18	C da Matta	1m17.300s	26
19	O Panis	1m17.419s	23
20	T Glock	1m17.724s	25
21	G Pantano	1m17.869s	24
22	Z Baumgartner	1m18.098s	21
23	B Leinders	1m18.224s	17
24	N Heidfeld	1m18.243s	23
25	G Bruni	1m18.309s	25

PRACTICE 3		
	Driver	Time	Laps
1	M Schumacher	1m15.066s	11
2	JP Montoya	1m15.277s	5
3	R Barrichello	1m15.354s	10
4	K Räikkönen	1m15.626s	6
5	J Button	1m15.839s	10
6	O Panis	1m15.882s	7
7	D Coulthard	1m15.919s	7
8	A Pizzonia	1m16.151s	12
9	G Fisichella	1m16.232s	9
10	J Trulli	1m16.334s	5
11	C da Matta	1m16.457s	8
12	F Alonso	1m16.462s	5
13	F Massa	1m16.532s	8
14	C Klien	1m16.650s	5
15	M Webber	1m16.961s	7
16	N Heidfeld	1m17.369s	10
17	G Bruni	1m18.198s	11
18	G Pantano	1m18.914s	4
19	Z Baumgartner	1m21.288s	9
20	T Sato	no time	4

PRACTICE 4		
	Driver	Time	Laps
1	J Button	1m13.676s	15
2	JP Montoya	1m13.976s	11
3	D Coulthard	1m14.064s	11
4	K Räikkönen	1m14.100s	14
5	F Alonso	1m14.320s	12
6	R Barrichello	1m14.393s	12
7	M Schumacher	1m14.459s	14
8	J Trulli	1m14.468s	15
9	A Pizzonia	1m14.766s	10
10	C da Matta	1m14.791s	19
11	O Panis	1m14.953s	16
12	M Webber	1m15.000s	25
13	C Klien	1m15.481s	20
14	G Fisichella	1m15.572s	10
15	F Massa	1m15.588s	10
16	N Heidfeld	1m16.832s	16
17	G Bruni	1m18.227s	13
18	Z Baumgartner	1m18.691s	15
19	T Sato	no time	0
20	G Pantano	no time	0

Best sectors – Qualifying		Speed trap – Qualifying	
Sector 1 D Coulthard	16.113s	1 M Schumacher	186.606mph
Sector 2 F Alonso	34.402s	2 D Coulthard	186.234mph
Sector 3 M Schumacher	22.501s	3 G Fisichella	185.923mph

Michael Schumacher
"I could feel the emotion from the fans and hear their noise above the engine as I crossed the line. To do this at home, where I've not been successful is just fabulous."

Juan Pablo Montoya
"I had so much wheelspin at the start that I lost a cool five positions. I also had some blistering problems, and it came to the point where driving the car was very hard."

Kimi Räikkönen
"I'm extremely disappointed. There was no doubt that we were in with a good chance of winning. But, all of a sudden, I lost downforce and was a passenger."

Fernando Alonso
"I had no grip at all in my final stint. I radioed the team to say I was coming in, but they told me to stay out. Then I hit a kerb and everything went back to normal."

Jenson Button
"Without doubt, this was the best race of my F1 career. I'm thrilled to finish second when I thought the best I could hope for was maybe fifth. The car felt fantastic."

Rubens Barrichello
"I had to protect my line at the start, as Montoya was very close. I tried to get inside Coulthard, but locked my rear wheels and guess that it was my fault."

Antonio Pizzonia
"I got stuck in a lot of traffic in the first two stints. When I was on my own, I could put in some quick laps, but it wasn't enough to catch Webber in the last few laps."

David Coulthard
"I had balance problems after Barrichello hit me from behind at the first corner. Also, I picked up debris from Kimi's accident that broke the deflector on my front wing."

Jarno Trulli
"Just like Fernando, I hit debris that stuck to the car. The car wouldn't turn in to corners, so we changed the nose and front wing and everything was okay again."

Takuma Sato
"Unfortunately, there was an incident at the hairpin on lap 1 and I lost a few places. I also had problems with my HANS device slipping from under my shoulder straps."

POSITIONS LAP BY LAP

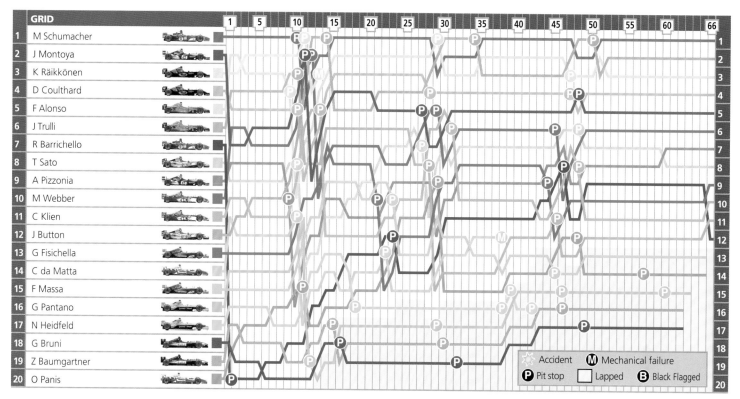

GRID

1	M Schumacher	
2	J Montoya	
3	K Räikkönen	
4	D Coulthard	
5	F Alonso	
6	J Trulli	
7	R Barrichello	
8	T Sato	
9	A Pizzonia	
10	M Webber	
11	C Klien	
12	J Button	
13	G Fisichella	
14	C da Matta	
15	F Massa	
16	G Pantano	
17	N Heidfeld	
18	G Bruni	
19	Z Baumgartner	
20	O Panis	

Legend: ☆ Accident Ⓜ Mechanical failure Ⓟ Pit stop ☐ Lapped Ⓑ Black Flagged

QUALIFYING

	Driver	Pre-qual time	Pos	Time
1	M Schumacher	1m14.042s	11	1m13.306s
2	JP Montoya	1m13.391s	1	1m13.668s
3	J Button	1m13.535s	3	1m13.674s
4	K Räikkönen	1m13.842s	8	1m13.690s
5	D Coulthard	1m13.640s	5	1m13.821s
6	F Alonso	1m13.582s	4	1m13.874s
7	J Trulli	1m13.737s	7	1m14.134s
8	R Barrichello	1m14.111s	12	1m14.278s
9	T Sato	1m14.465s	13	1m14.287s
10	O Panis	1m13.641s	6	1m14.368s
11	A Pizzonia	1m13.422s	2	1m14.556s
12	M Webber	1m15.093s	15	1m14.802s
13	C Klien	1m15.090s	14	1m15.011s
14	G Fisichella	1m13.914s	10	1m15.395s
15	C da Matta	1m15.119s	16	1m15.454s
16	F Massa	1m13.899s	9	1m15.616s
17	G Pantano	1m16.167s	17	1m16.192s
18	N Heidfeld	1m16.538s	18	1m16.310s
19	G Bruni	1m17.283s	19	1m18.055s
20	Z Baumgartner	1m17.515s	20	1m18.400s

RACE

	Driver	Car	Laps	Time	Fastest	Avg. mph	Stops
1	M Schumacher	Ferrari F2004	66	1h23m54.848s	1m13.783s	134.130	3
2	J Button	BAR-Honda 006	66	1h24m03.236s	1m14.117s	133.907	3
3	F Alonso	Renault R24	66	1h24m11.199s	1m14.265s	133.696	3
4	D Coulthard	McLaren-Mercedes MP4-19B	66	1h24m14.079s	1m14.558s	133.619	3
5	JP Montoya	Williams-BMW FW26	66	1h24m17.903s	1m14.446s	133.519	3
6	M Webber	Jaguar-Cosworth R5	66	1h24m35.956s	1m14.833s	133.043	3
7	A Pizzonia	Williams-BMW FW26	66	1h24m36.804s	1m14.586s	133.022	3
8	T Sato	BAR-Honda 006	66	1h24m41.690s	1m14.585s	132.894	3
9	G Fisichella	Sauber-Petronas C23	66	1h25m01.950s	1m15.635s	132.366	2
10	C Klien	Jaguar-Cosworth PS04	66	1h25m03.426s	1m15.045s	132.328	3
11	J Trulli	Renault R24	66	1h25m05.106s	1m14.386s	132.284	3
12	R Barrichello	Ferrari F2004	66	1h25m08.100s	1m14.963s	132.207	3
13	F Massa	Sauber-Petronas C23	65	1h24m15.001s	1m16.248s	131.572	2
14	O Panis	Toyota TF104B	65	1h24m29.351s	1m14.247s	131.199	4
15	G Pantano	Jordan-Ford EF14	63	1h23m58.555s	1m16.058s	127.939	4
16	Z Baumgartner	Minardi-Cosworth PS04	62	1h24m07.080s	1m18.760s	125.696	3
17	G Bruni	Minardi-Cosworth PS04	62	1h25m09.155s	1m18.372s	124.169	3
R	N Heidfeld	Jordan-Ford EJ14	42	Handling	1m16.903s	-	3
R	C da Matta	Toyota TF104B	38	Puncture	1m15.145s	-	2
R	K Räikkönen	McLaren-Mercedes MP4-19B	13	Accident	1m13.780s	-	1

CHAMPIONSHIP

	Driver	Pts
1	M Schumacher	110
2	R Barrichello	74
3	J Button	61
4	J Trulli	46
5	F Alonso	39
6	JP Montoya	33
7	D Coulthard	19
8	K Räikkönen	18
9	T Sato	15
10	G Fisichella	13
11	R Schumacher	12
12	M Webber	7
13	F Massa	5
	O Panis	5
15	C da Matta	3

	Constructor	Pts
1	Ferrari	184
2	Renault	85
3	BAR-Honda	76
4	Williams-BMW	47
5	McLaren-Mercedes	37
6	Sauber-Petronas	18
7	Toyota	8
8	Jaguar-Cosworth	7
9	Jordan-Ford	5
10	Minardi-Cosworth	4

Qualifying notes

Button Back 10 places for engine change

Panis Started from back of grid after stalling at outset of the parade lap

Fastest race lap
K Räikkönen 1m13.780s, on lap 10 (138.685mph) New lap record

Fastest through speed trap
G Fisichella   211.576mph
Slowest through speed trap
G Bruni   199.956mph

Fastest pit stop
O Panis   19.895s
Slowest pit stop
G Bruni   1m14.061s

Giancarlo Fisichella

"I got blocked at the start then, in my second stop, we weren't able to change the left rear. It was stuck on, so I had to go back into the race with the same tyre."

Mark Webber

"I started from 11th, made a good start and, at the end of the first lap, was up to sixth. I then battled it out with the best of them and the car was feeling really good."

Olivier Panis

"I'm disappointed that I stalled and was forced to start last. Sometimes, drivers make mistakes but, as the problem has recurred, we should check for a technical problem."

Nick Heidfeld

"I had to do an extra stop so the team could check the tyres and suspension. It was then difficult to hold the car on the track, so we decided that I should retire."

Gianmaria Bruni

"My engine was a little over-full with oil for the first seven or so laps, but it cleaned up after that. Then I had a problem with my bargeboards, delaying my first stop."

Felipe Massa

"My first and third sets of tyres were okay, but the second set was horrible. I don't know why, but they made the car very difficult to drive and blistered badly."

Christian Klien

"The car's balance has been helped by our new aero package and I could really feel the difference. Near the end, I had Trulli on my tail and was able to keep him at bay."

Cristiano da Matta

"My retirement was sudden, although I had felt an increasing vibration at the rear. But the right rear went down suddenly and it's hard to know what made it blow."

Giorgio Pantano

"A lap before I planned to make my first stop, we had a flat tyre so I had to slow right down. Just before the end, I had another flat tyre at the same corner."

Zsolt Baumgartner

"I got by Gimmi on the first lap and pulled away a little. The last 20 laps were hard, particularly through the stadium, and I've got the blisters on my hands to prove it."

TOP TYRE CHOICE

Finding the right tyre made the world of difference to Ferrari as they went from losers in 2003 to dominant winners, Michael Schumacher again to the fore

It was definitely the least eventful race of the year – the order barely changed after the third corner of lap one – but it was far from the least significant. Ferrari clinched their sixth consecutive constructors' championship, breaking their own record, and mathematically confirmed that one of their drivers would become World Champion. Michael Schumacher's 12th victory of the season broke his own record of 2002. It was, however, perhaps the stark contrast between this race and the one 12 months earlier – when Schumacher had finished a lapped eighth – that really gave the red team its greatest satisfaction.

In that defeat of 2003, tyre supplier Bridgestone had come in for some criticism. Its wares of 2004 had proved generally more competitive than the year before, but Hungary – the nadir of the '03 campaign – was the real

litmus test. Accordingly, an all-new rear tyre had been designed for this track, with its high demands on a tyre's chemical grip. With a stiffer construction from more steel in its casing, it allowed a softer compound to be used. On the high-downforce, beautifully balanced Ferrari F2004 it worked brilliantly, although Michelin's Pierre Dupasquier – his tail tweaked after public rows with Renault's Flavio Briatore and Fernando Alonso – was quick to point out that on other Bridgestone-equipped cars, the tyre didn't look so special.

That wasn't the concern of Schumacher and team-mate Rubens Barrichello, though, as they cruised to a crushing 1–2. As if to underline the point of their progress from one year before, in third place and fully half a minute behind was the man who had lapped the champion on his way to victory here in 2003: Alonso.

Ferrari's flags weren't waving in Hungary in '03, but they were flying high this time around

ROUND 13

HUNGARY
FORMULA 1™
MARLBORO MAGYAR
NAGYDIJ 2004
Budapest

LAP BY LAP
ACTION

70 laps / 191 miles

Schumacher and Barrichello lead Alonso and Sato into the first corner

Start to lap 2

Barrichello is slow away at the start of the parade lap, but is underway before the last car passes him and so retakes his position. Bruni has a problem and drops to the back of the grid. The Ferraris get away well at the start, with Schumacher and Barrichello leading into the first corner comfortably ahead of the fast-starting Alonso. Sato is fourth ahead of Montoya and Button but, by the end of the first lap, Sato has fallen back to eighth. There is excitement in the midfield as Ricardo Zonta, replacing da Matta at Toyota, is tipped into a spin by Pantano after he is caught out by a rapidly slowing Webber. Zonta rejoins at the back. The order as they cross the line to start lap 2 is Schumacher from Barrichello, Alonso, Montoya, Button, Trulli, Räikkönen, Sato, Fisichella, Pizzonia, Coulthard and Webber.

Zonta's first start of 2004 is spoiled by Pantano pitching him into a spin

Laps 3 to 13

By lap 3, Schumacher is 2.5s ahead of Barrichello, who is 2.2s ahead of Alonso. The Ferraris extend their lead and by lap 6 Schumacher's lead is up to 3.1s with Barrichello 3.9s ahead of Alonso. On lap 10, with Schumacher now leading by 5s, Alonso is the first pit caller, promoting Montoya to third. Räikkönen also pits and drops from seventh to 11th. Barrichello, Montoya, Button, Trulli and Coulthard all pit on lap 11. Schumacher pits on lap 12, emerging still in the lead. Third-placed Sato also stops, while further back Räikkönen, Panis and Massa all pit. By lap 13, Schumacher and Barrichello are first and second, more than 10s ahead of Pizzonia (who has still to pit). Alonso is fourth, with Webber fifth, Montoya sixth, Button seventh and Trulli eighth. Then Räikkönen pits and retires with an electrical problem.

Schumacher soon extended his lead over Barrichello as Alonso faded

Laps 14 to 27

Pizzonia stops on lap 14, dropping back to ninth. On lap 16, Webber, now up to fourth, stops, falling to 11th. Massa calls at the pits on lap 18 to have the nose of his Sauber replaced, falling back to 17th, but on lap 21 he returns to the pits to retire. At the same time, the Ferrari mechanics are seen to be working on one of the refuelling rigs, Barrichello's. By lap 24, the order is unchanged with Schumacher's lead up to 6.7s and his team-mate Barrichello 17s ahead of Alonso.

Action in Ferrari's pit as Barrichello's refuelling rig is fixed

Laps 28 to 32

The second round of pit stops begins on lap 28, with Sato calling in. On lap 29, Alonso stops and Montoya is promoted to third place. Montoya pits on lap 30, followed into pitlane by Button and Fisichella. On lap 31, the pit-stops continue with Barrichello, Trulli, Webber and Panis all calling in. Schumacher makes his second stop on lap 32, and emerges 8.5s ahead of Barrichello. Alonso is still third, now almost half a minute behind Barrichello. Zonta slows and stops beside the track.

Pizzonia ran as high as fourth by staying out for a long second stint

Laps 33 to 50

Pizzonia stays out longer than anyone else once again, and so is briefly fourth before pitting on lap 33 and falling back to seventh place. On lap 41, the race order is still the same, with Schumacher 13s ahead of Barrichello, who is more than half a minute in front of Alonso. Montoya is fourth ahead of Button and Sato, with Pizzonia seventh. Trulli slows and comes into the pits to retire. The final pit-stops begin on lap 46, with Webber dropping from 10th to 11th. Sato pits on lap 47 and drops behind Pizzonia. The pit-stop sequence continues on lap 50, with Barrichello and Pizzonia stopping. This does nothing to change the order.

What a difference a year makes: Schumacher acknowledges his win

Lap 51 to the finish

Schumacher makes his final stop on lap 51. Alonso also pits. On lap 52 Montoya is the last driver to stop, and he rejoins in fourth place. By lap 53, Schumacher's lead is 18s with Barrichello 30s ahead of Alonso. The order behind is unchanged all the way to the finish, although Pizzonia goes off at one point but doesn't lose a place. On lap 70, Ferrari complete another dominant 1–2 finish to win the constructors' championship. Alonso finishes third, with Montoya fourth, Button fifth and Sato sixth, followed by Pizzonia and Fisichella.

INSIDE LINE
RUBENS BARRICHELLO

It means a great deal to me to be involved in another championship for the team. Ever since I joined Ferrari in 2000, the team have won the championship and that is just phenomenal. Michael [Schumacher] has had difficult times in the past building the team, and I've been there when the work has been done already and it's been fantastic. The work we do together in terms of chassis set-up and pushing each other helps a lot. We never stop.

As for my race, finishing second to Michael, people might say I was happy with that and I just went out and knew I was going to be second. But really, it's not like that. In qualifying, I came close to taking the pole from [Schumacher] and had I started from there I might have won the race. As it was, Michael was able to lead into the first corner and after that it became very difficult. I was on a softer tyre than Michael and although it was good, it really came right on my fourth set when the track's grip had built up and then I finally found I was maybe a little bit quicker than Michael had been, although by then the race

was lost for me. Had there not been the heavy rain on Saturday that washed the track clean, I think I could maybe have had that level of performance from the start.

In qualifying, the temperatures were very low for Hungary in August, the coolest I can remember here. That gave us a bit of understeer, and I guess Michael dealt with that just a little bit better than me and he got the pole. That was really the critical part of the weekend between us, more than the tyre.

I was the one who pushed to use the soft tyre. It wasn't a case of the team imposing the choice on me. When we ran on Friday I thought it was the better tyre. The team analysed the situation and said that it was alright. Obviously, Michael was happier with the harder tyres. I had in my mind that I might have some problems with graining at the start, but actually for some reason I didn't really have that problem until I was on my third set of tyres. But then, on the final set, it was better than ever and I was really able to drive the car again.

THE BIG QUESTION

Williams: why no 'walrus' nose?

When the Williams-BMW FW26 had been unveiled on the eve of the season, it had quickly gained the nickname of 'the walrus' because of its radical-looking short, drooping nose with its curved, drooping pillars down to the wing. This had been designed to take maximum aerodynamic advantage of the car's new twin-keel front suspension, permitting a clean flow of air under the nose. At the Hungarian Grand Prix, though, the car appeared with a conventional nose and 'the walrus' was consigned to history.

"The original nose had shown a good gain aerodynamically," said Williams Technical Director Sam Michael, "and was something we thought we could develop into more again, but it didn't really develop as we expected it to." The expected aero gains were supposed to overcome the inherent drawbacks of the design, which centred around the weight necessary for such a short a nosecone to pass the front impact tests.

"Yes, there was a problem with weight," conceded Michael. "To get that crash performance from such a short space made it not only heavy but also moved the weight quite high up in the car, affecting the centre of gravity. The weight also meant that we couldn't carry as much ballast as we would have liked, and that restricts how adjustable your weight distribution can be from circuit to circuit."

There had been no time before the summer testing ban to try the new configuration, and at Hungary the team were still learning about it. The revised cars qualified sixth and seventh in the hands of Antonio Pizzonia and Juan Pablo Montoya respectively, and finished fourth (Montoya) and seventh (Pizzonia) in the race. Results that were, at best, inconclusive.

For Hungary, Williams adopted a narrow nose, but came away unsure of whether it was better

Jean Todt accepts the plaudits after a race result that confirmed Ferrari as constructors' champions

JEAN TODT
FERRARI
SPORTING
DIRECTOR

On this day we clinched the constructors' championship and confirmed that the winner of the drivers' championship would be a Ferrari driver. Obviously, it was a very satisfying conclusion, especially if you think back to how Ferrari struggled in Hungary in 2003.

You try not to think of figures and statistics as you are working, because thinking about them doesn't help you beat them! But this was clearly a historical time because Michael scored his 12th win out of 13 races and that's a record. Ferrari became World Champions for a sixth

consecutive time and that's another record. So these records do give us a lot of pleasure, but we tackled this race just as we would any other.

There are always many ingredients in a victory but clearly, with Bridgestone, we have been doing a good job on tyre construction, on tyre consistency, and it helped us a lot to be competitive here.

It's true that we had a tough race at the Hungaroring in 2003, but Michael was still in the lead of the Drivers' World Championship after the Hungarian Grand Prix last year. The year ended well, too, because in 2003 Ferrari were World Constructors' winners for the fifth time in succession and Michael was World Drivers' Champion for the fourth successive year. This year, one could say that Ferrari has dominated hugely in Formula One, so have Bridgestone and so has Michael, which means that if you compare the 2003 Hungarian Grand Prix and the 2004 Hungarian Grand Prix you have two races which were fundamentally very different.

Basically, all weekend we saw a very competitive Bridgestone-shod Ferrari from Friday, and this was finally confirmed in qualifying when we had to do one quick lap as opposed to the race, where we have been strong all year.

You saw in the race that our fuel load in qualifying was not low and yet we still qualified in first and second places on the grid. It's just simply that we've been working in the right direction and we have understood the problem that had been causing us not to be competitive enough [in qualifying], but I must say it was mainly a tyre problem.

If there is a secret to our success, it is people and partners. However, everybody has partners and everybody has human resources in the company. But maybe the way we handle them, the way we deal with the people, our style, maybe that is the secret.

But I was under no illusions about how the others were all crazy about how they would beat us, and when...

ROSS BRAWN
FERRARI
TECHNICAL
DIRECTOR

For the team, the constructors' title is the thing we work towards. The drivers' title has more kudos to the public, but the thing we're proud of is the constructors' title.

In a way, it was nice to win the constructors' championship separately from the drivers' one. I was brought up with Williams, where winning the constructors' championship was everything and the drivers' championship didn't matter too much, and I tend to still have that view, to a degree. After all, it shows that we're the best team.

When I came to Ferrari I thought that winning a championship would be pretty special. If I'd been told we could win six, I would have thought that beyond comprehension.

It was particularly satisfying to clinch it with a performance like this, and much of the credit for this race really must go to Bridgestone. They have done us proud this year, but the Hungaroring required something special and they produced it. We had a new rear tyre construction which was very, very good.

Consistency was the key. The tyre had an incredibly consistent performance. You can see that when looking at the pattern of Michael's pace and that of our closest rival here, Alonso. Early in the stint, Michael was around 1.0s quicker. By the middle of the stint, it was more like 0.6s and, by the end, it was up to over 1s again.

Michael was able to just reel off a pace and the tyres just took it, whereas it appears the others had to have more compromise in their set-up to allow for the balance change through a stint. Usually, you begin with understeer, move through neutrality and end up with oversteer, but that was hardly evident here and to achieve that at the Hungaroring is really saying something.

It's no secret that one of the differences between Bridgestone and Michelin is that the Bridgestones run at a higher temperature. The tyre we used in Hungary was a tyre that ran at a lower temperature as its philosophy, and that meant it was more consistent.

The only hint of a drama we had was with Rubens' refuelling rig. There's a flangeable coupling on the bottom of the fuel rig which cracked and let the fuel out. We think we must have stressed them somewhere. The amount of fuel wasn't excessive: it was just the residual fuel left in the hose that leaked out. So we simply put new parts on after the stop.

Stint 1 lap times reflecting bigger balance change on Renault compared to consistency of Ferrari			
	Schumacher	Alonso	Difference
EARLY STINT (understeer phase)			
Lap 2	1m 20.128s	1m 21.134s	**1.006s**
Lap 3	1m 19.921s	1m 21.208s	**1.287s**
MID STINT (neutral phase)			
Lap 4	1m 20.479s	1m 21.073s	**0.594s**
Lap 5	1m 20.258s	1m 21.040s	**0.782s**
Lap 6	1m 20.067s	1m 20.993s	**0.926s**
LATE STINT (oversteer phase)			
Lap 7	1m 19.678s	1m 21.189s	**1.511s**
Lap 8	1m 19.506s	1m 21.079s	**1.573s**
Lap 9	1m 19.737s	1m 20.919s	**1.182s**
Lap 10	1m 19.412s	Pits	-----

Bridgestone had a major role to play in Ferrari ending up with the constructors' trophy

RACE RESULTS
HUNGARY BUDAPEST

RACE DATE August 15th
CIRCUIT LENGTH 2.722 miles
NO. OF LAPS 70
RACE DISTANCE 190.540 miles
WEATHER dry and bright, 26°C
TRACK TEMP 35°C
RACE ATTENDANCE 110,000
LAP RECORD Michael Schumacher,
1m 19.071s, 123.966mph, 2004

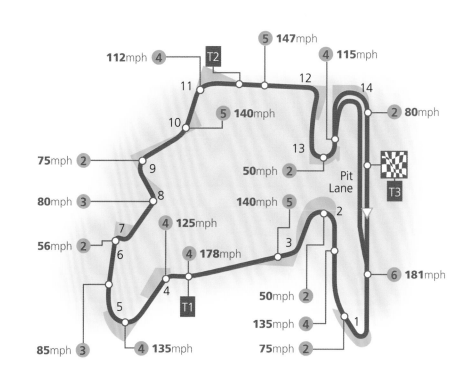

	PRACTICE 1		
	Driver	**Time**	**Laps**
1	M Schumacher	1m21.552s	10
2	R Barrichello	1m21.938s	11
3	A Davidson	1m21.951s	24
4	K Räikkönen	1m23.024s	5
5	D Coulthard	1m23.100s	8
6	JP Montoya	1m23.753s	8
7	O Panis	1m23.827s	8
8	R Briscoe	1m24.103s	20
9	J Trulli	1m24.124s	13
10	J Button	1m24.140s	14
11	F Alonso	1m24.191s	13
12	G Fisichella	1m24.198s	13
13	R Zonta	1m24.236s	14
14	B Wirdheim	1m24.265s	23
15	G Pantano	1m24.353s	15
16	A Pizzonia	1m24.381s	13
17	N Heidfeld	1m24.462s	13
18	T Glock	1m24.843s	22
19	T Sato	1m25.071s	13
20	F Massa	1m25.218s	17
21	C Klien	1m25.834s	10
22	B Leinders	1m26.074s	18
23	Z Baumgartner	1m28.296s	11
24	G Bruni	1m28.893s	12
25	M Webber	no time	4

	PRACTICE 2		
	Driver	**Time**	**Laps**
1	K Räikkönen	1m20.884s	20
2	M Schumacher	1m21.009s	30
3	JP Montoya	1m21.185s	24
4	D Coulthard	1m21.203s	19
5	O Panis	1m21.352s	23
6	T Sato	1m21.364s	22
7	A Pizzonia	1m21.574s	26
8	J Button	1m21.685s	19
9	R Barrichello	1m21.712s	19
10	F Alonso	1m21.948s	22
11	M Webber	1m21.999s	33
12	A Davidson	1m22.356s	34
13	B Wirdheim	1m22.559s	23
14	N Heidfeld	1m22.651s	19
15	T Glock	1m22.697s	21
16	G Fisichella	1m22.743s	23
17	J Trulli	1m22.788s	28
18	R Zonta	1m22.808s	28
19	G Pantano	1m22.937s	22
20	C Klien	1m23.003s	30
21	R Briscoe	1m23.170s	22
22	F Massa	1m23.188s	20
23	B Leinders	1m25.339s	17
24	Z Baumgartner	1m25.450s	16
25	G Bruni	1m26.365s	4

	PRACTICE 3		
	Driver	**Time**	**Laps**
1	M Schumacher	1m20.216s	10
2	A Pizzonia	1m20.482s	14
3	JP Montoya	1m20.696s	15
4	J Button	1m20.731s	11
5	R Barrichello	1m20.830s	12
6	J Trulli	1m21.257s	10
7	F Alonso	1m21.392s	8
8	D Coulthard	1m21.555s	8
9	F Massa	1m21.593s	6
10	K Räikkönen	1m21.825s	8
11	O Panis	1m21.838s	15
12	R Zonta	1m21.927s	17
13	G Fisichella	1m22.013s	9
14	M Webber	1m22.068s	9
15	C Klien	1m22.421s	6
16	G Pantano	1m22.709s	11
17	G Bruni	1m23.112s	14
18	N Heidfeld	1m23.242s	13
19	Z Baumgartner	1m24.233s	14
20	T Sato	no time	4

	PRACTICE 4		
	Driver	**Time**	**Laps**
1	J Button	1m19.556s	15
2	M Schumacher	1m19.747s	18
3	R Barrichello	1m19.768s	10
4	A Pizzonia	1m19.913s	11
5	J Trulli	1m20.130s	10
6	T Sato	1m20.363s	12
7	F Alonso	1m20.363s	20
8	JP Montoya	1m20.480s	15
9	R Zonta	1m20.606s	18
10	K Räikkönen	1m20.614s	13
11	O Panis	1m20.689s	12
12	D Coulthard	1m20.914s	13
13	M Webber	1m21.112s	24
14	G Fisichella	1m21.165s	12
15	C Klien	1m21.390s	22
16	N Heidfeld	1m21.712s	14
17	F Massa	1m21.989s	4
18	G Pantano	1m23.083s	12
19	G Bruni	1m23.979s	14
20	Z Baumgartner	1m24.522s	13

Best sectors – Qualifying		Speed trap – Qualifying	
Sector 1 R Barrichello	28.172s	1 M Schumacher	186.606mph
Sector 2 M Schumacher	28.346s	2 D Coulthard	186.234mph
Sector 3 J Button	22.402s	3 G Fisichella	185.923mph

 **Michael Schumacher**

"To win in style here compared to last year shows why we won the constructors' title so early. It may have looked easy from the outside, but I was flat-out for this race."

 Juan Pablo Montoya

"I gained three places immediately and climbed up to fourth, keeping that position until the end. We made the best of the car and couldn't really have asked for more."

Kimi Räikkönen

"I gained a few positions on the first lap to be seventh, and was getting into the race. Then the engine kept cutting out, so there was nothing for me to do but retire."

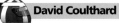 **Fernando Alonso**

"It was a pretty calm race for me, maybe a little bit lonely even. Once I was third, it was just a matter of managing the gap to Montoya and maintaining my pace."

Jenson Button

"My start was reasonable but I lost places to Alonso and Montoya. Then I was able to get past Taku when he went a bit off line. The main thing is we both scored points."

 **Rubens Barrichello**

"The previous night's rain made my side of the track less dirty, so I had a good start and was able to follow Michael. I had a slight problem with my third set of tyres."

 **Antonio Pizzonia**

"For most of the race I was behind Sato, trying to get close enough to pass him, but I never had the right opportunity. I scored two points and that is what matters."

David Coulthard

"We suffered from making the wrong tyre decision, as the ambient temperature remained relatively low. There was not a lot I could do in the race from so far back."

 Jarno Trulli

"My retirement was caused by the engine. I lost power then it cut out. I was already having difficulties at that stage with the front of the car, understeering so much."

 Takuma Sato

"At Turn 1, I was outside Alonso and put a wheel off-line and into the dusty area. I lost traction and several cars came by as I lost momentum. I did my best to recover."

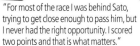

POSITIONS LAP BY LAP

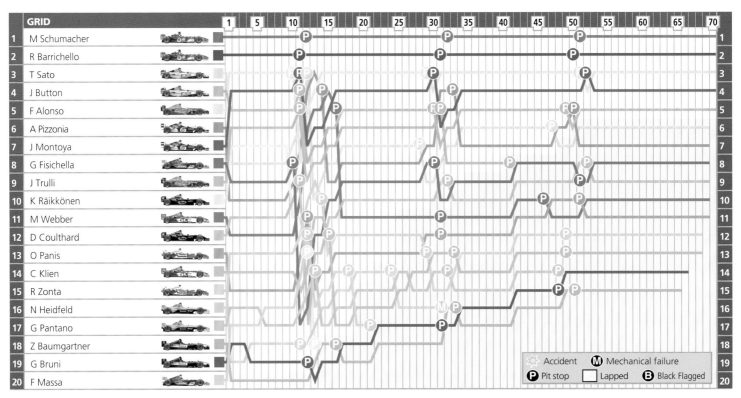

GRID

	Driver
1	M Schumacher
2	R Barrichello
3	T Sato
4	J Button
5	F Alonso
6	A Pizzonia
7	J Montoya
8	G Fisichella
9	J Trulli
10	K Räikkönen
11	M Webber
12	D Coulthard
13	O Panis
14	C Klien
15	R Zonta
16	N Heidfeld
17	G Pantano
18	Z Baumgartner
19	G Bruni
20	F Massa

Legend: ☼ Accident   Ⓜ Mechanical failure   Ⓟ Pit stop   ☐ Lapped   Ⓑ Black Flagged

QUALIFYING

	Driver	Pre-qual time	Pos	Time
1	M Schumacher	1m19.107s	2	1m19.146s
2	R Barrichello	1m18.436s	1	1m19.323s
3	T Sato	1m19.695s	5	1m19.693s
4	J Button	1m19.878s	7	1m19.700s
5	F Alonso	1m20.135s	11	1m19.996s
6	A Pizzonia	1m20.019s	9	1m20.170s
7	JP Montoya	1m19.821s	6	1m20.199s
8	G Fisichella	1m19.668s	4	1m20.324s
9	J Trulli	1m19.879s	8	1m20.411s
10	K Räikkönen	1m20.066s	10	1m20.570s
11	M Webber	1m21.452s	17	1m20.730s
12	D Coulthard	1m21.192s	16	1m20.897s
13	O Panis	1m20.491s	14	1m21.068s
14	C Klien	1m21.510s	18	1m21.118s
15	R Zonta	1n20.199s	12	1m21.135s
16	N Heidfeld	1m20.439s	13	1m22.180s
17	G Pantano	1m21.187s	15	1m22.356s
18	Z Baumgartner	1m24.656s	20	1m24.329s
19	G Bruni	1m23.362s	19	1m24.679s
20	F Massa	1m19.658s	3	no time

Qualifying notes
Massa   Back 10 places for engine change

RACE

	Driver	Car	Laps	Time	Fastest	Avg. mph	Stops
1	M Schumacher	Ferrari F2004	70	1h35m26.131s	1m19.071s	119.805	3
2	R Barrichello	Ferrari F2004	70	1h35m30.827s	1m19.213s	119.706	3
3	F Alonso	Renault R24	70	1h36m10.730s	1m20.275s	118.878	3
4	JP Montoya	Williams-BMW FW26	70	1h36m28.744s	1m20.715s	118.508	3
5	J Button	BAR-Honda 006	70	1h36m33.570s	1m20.425s	118.410	3
6	T Sato	BAR-Honda 006	69	1h35m26.613s	1m21.030s	118.083	3
7	A Pizzonia	Williams-BMW FW26	69	1h35m27.748s	1m20.501s	118.060	3
8	G Fisichella	Sauber-Petronas C23	69	1h35m53.595s	1m21.022s	117.529	3
9	D Coulthard	McLaren-Mercedes MP4-19B	69	1h35m55.652s	1m21.134s	117.489	3
10	M Webber	Jaguar-Cosworth R5	69	1h36m21.740s	1m20.825s	116.957	3
11	O Panis	Toyota TF104B	69	1h36m38.075s	1m21.310s	116.627	3
12	N Heidfeld	Jordan-Ford EJ14	68	1h35m59.009s	1m21.518s	115.717	3
13	C Klien	Jaguar-Cosworth R5	68	1h36m37.631s	1m22.530s	114.946	3
14	G Bruni	Minardi-Cosworth PS04	66	1h36m46.632s	1m24.601s	111.392	3
15	Z Baumgartner	Minardi-Cosworth PS04	65	1h36m04.389s	1m24.855s	110.509	3
R	G Pantano	Jordan-Ford EJ14	48	Gearbox	1m22.927s	-	3
R	J Trulli	Renault R24	41	Engine	1m20.705s	-	3
R	R Zonta	Toyota TF104B	31	Electronics	1m22.525s	-	2
R	F Massa	Sauber-Petronas C23	21	Brakes	1m21.856s	-	2
R	K Räikkönen	McLaren-Mercedes MP4-19B	13	Electrics	1m21.678s	-	1

Fastest race lap
M Schumacher 1m19.071s,
on lap 29 (123.966mph)
New lap record

Fastest through speed trap
M Schumacher   194.985mph
Slowest through speed trap
G Bruni   184.236mph

Fastest pit stop
T Sato   20.605s
Slowest pit stop
F Massa   41.537s

CHAMPIONSHIP

	Driver	Pts
1	M Schumacher	120
2	R Barrichello	82
3	J Button	65
4	J Trulli	46
5	F Alonso	45
6	JP Montoya	38
7	D Coulthard	19
8	K Räikkönen	18
9	T Sato	18
10	G Fisichella	14
11	R Schumacher	12
12	M Webber	7
13	F Massa	5
	O Panis	5
15	A Pizzonia	4

	Constructor	Pts
1	Ferrari	202
2	Renault	91
3	BAR-Honda	83
4	Williams-BMW	54
5	McLaren-Mercedes	37
6	Sauber-Petronas	19
7	Toyota	8
8	Jaguar-Cosworth	7
9	Jordan-Ford	5
10	Minardi-Cosworth	1

Giancarlo Fisichella
"The car had very good pace and balance. The sole problem was the tyres graining two or three laps after each stop. I really pushed and didn't make any mistakes."

Mark Webber
"In Turn 1, I was hit from behind by Zonta. The car suffered no damage and I was lucky only to lose one place. I had a spin at Turn 9 later on but didn't lose any places."

Olivier Panis
"It was a shame we started from 13th, because we looked good during the race. I didn't get a very good start, but did my best from then on to recover positions."

Nick Heidfeld
"All in all a relatively positive weekend. I had a good race, although I didn't finish in the points. I lost a bit of time in my second stop when the car fell off the front jack."

Gianmaria Bruni
"I was really pleased to have taken the chequered flag. The engine stalled before the formation lap but, once the race got going, there were no real problems."

Felipe Massa
"Unfortunately, after my first stop I had a problem with a 'long' brake pedal at the end of the straight. We couldn't fix the problem so I stopped for safety reasons."

Christian Klien
"It was a difficult race – and good to see the chequered flag after 70 laps. The R5 was generally feeling good, but my expectations for this race were higher."

Ricardo Zonta
"This wasn't how I'd planned my debut for the team. A Jordan hit me in Turn 1, which sent me into a spin and to the back of the field, but I made progress before I retired."

Giorgio Pantano
"I think the gearbox problem maybe caused my two outings off the track: when I changed down the rear locked up and I went off. The car wasn't bad though."

Zsolt Baumgartner
"I lost a lot of time in this race allowing faster cars through, so I didn't really have a chance to show what I could do. I was disappointed for all the Hungarian fans."

ICE MAN COMETH

To win, Kimi Räikkönen had to work his way to the front from 10th on the grid and then keep his cool as Michael Schumacher put him under pressure

Thirteen years after his Formula One debut here, a dozen years after his first Grand Prix victory here, Michael Schumacher clinched an astonishing seventh World Championship at Spa-Francorchamps. The Belgian track has always had a special resonance with him and it was an appropriate venue at which to wrap up his remarkable 2004 title campaign. He might have wished to do it in a more resounding manner, though, as the race represented just the second time that he had been beaten all season.

Schumacher on this day simply had no answer for the flying Kimi Räikkönen in the resurgent McLaren-Mercedes MP4-19B, despite the Finn having started from 10th. The characteristics of Kimi's Michelin tyres, which were much quicker to reach working temperature than the Ferraris' Bridgestones, played very much to McLaren's advantage in a race interrupted three times by safety car periods. Ironically, one of these was for an accident caused by one of three Michelin tyre failures.

Circumstances were not entirely on Räikkönen's side, though, as he had to fight against a couple of key technical problems – a faulty downchange and damaged diffuser, both from a first corner hit by Felipe Massa – and also had a 12s advantage over Schumacher erased by the timing of the second safety car period. But even with the World Champion sitting in his wheeltracks, with the safety car about to come in – a situation that he faced twice – Räikkönen never looked like losing the race and fully lived up to his Ice Man moniker.

Kimi Räikkönen put McLaren back on the map by mastering Schumacher and how to handle the safety car periods

ROUND **14**

BELGIUM
2004 FORMULA 1™
BELGIAN
GRAND PRIX
Spa-Francorchamps

LAP BY LAP
ACTION
44 laps / 191 miles

Schumacher tries to keep clear of the chaos at the first corner

Start and first lap
Alonso makes a better start than Schumacher and claims second behind Trulli before the first corner. Coulthard takes advantage of the situation to grab third while, behind them, Räikkönen tries to go around the outside of Massa and they hit, with Button hitting the back of the Sauber. Webber dives inside Fisichella and slides into the back of Barrichello, losing his front wing. As they go down the hill, Webber is rather slow and through Eau Rouge Sato tries to pass him. They touch and Montoya tries to pass the pair of them. Sato spins at the exit of Raidillon. Bruni hits Sato and Pantano runs into the stationary Minardi. Button, Massa, Baumgartner, Barrichello, Heidfeld and Panis all stop for repairs and the safety car is dispatched while the track is cleared.

Laps 2 to 11
Trulli, Alonso, Coulthard, Schumacher, Montoya, Fisichella and Pizzonia lead onto lap 2, at the end of which Massa and Barrichello stop for further repairs. The race restarts on lap 5, with the Renaults staying ahead as Räikkönen passes Schumacher at Eau Rouge. Montoya then overtakes Michael with an outside pass at the Bus Stop. Räikkönen passes Coulthard at Kemmel on lap 6 to take third. On lap 9, Klien is the first to make a scheduled stop, falling from ninth to 14th. Trulli pits on lap 10 and so Alonso takes the lead.

Renault duo Alonso and Trulli bide their time behind the safety car

Laps 12 to 19
Alonso spins out on lap 12, putting Räikkönen into the lead. Coulthard has a puncture and has to go slowly to the pits, falling to the back. Räikkönen pits on lap 13, and Montoya takes over with Schumacher behind him. Fisichella reaches third with Pizzonia fourth, Räikkönen fifth and Button sixth. Fisichella pits on lap 14 and Pizzonia moves to third. Montoya stops on lap 15 and Schumacher takes the lead with Pizzonia second. Schumacher pits on lap 16 and rejoins fifth, leaving Pizzonia in front, Räikkönen second and Button third. Trulli is back to fourth, Schumacher fifth. Montoya and Massa enter Eau Rouge side-by-side and Montoya has to back off. On lap 17, Pizzonia pits, leaving Räikkönen in the lead with Button second. Schumacher passes Trulli on the run into the chicane on lap 18. Räikkönen's lead is up to 4.6 by lap 19, when Massa pits, falling to ninth.

Montoya completes the move of the race, overtaking Schumacher

Laps 20 to 28
Fisichella bounces over the grass at Les Combes on lap 20 and loses his bargeboards. At the chicane, Montoya and Trulli collide, Trulli spinning and falling from fouth to eighth, as Pizzonia passes Montoya for fourth. Button pits on lap 21 and falls to seventh. Trulli pits on lap 22, and Barrichello passes Fisichella for fifth. Barrichello pits a lap later and falls to 10th. At the front on lap 24, Räikkönen is able to maintain his lead over Pizzonia, while Pizzonia is third with Montoya right with him. Button is next from Fisichella, Zonta, Massa, Panis, Barrichello, Klien, Trulli and Coulthard. Fisichella pits again on lap 26 and falls to 11th.

Coulthard had to pit twice for repairs, costing him a top finish

Laps 29 to 34
Räikkönen pits on lap 29, and Schumacher takes the lead with Pizzonia second. Fourth-placed Montoya also stops. On the run up to Les Combes on lap 30, Button suffers a blow-out and spins into Baumgartner. A safety car is deployed and Schumacher, Pizzonia, Zonta, Massa and Panis benefit as Räikkönen and Fisichella lose ground. Coulthard and Heidfeld also pit. Pizzonia stops on lap 32 with a gearbox problem.

Trulli is pitched into a spin by Montoya at the reshaped Bus Stop

Lap 35 to the finish
The race is on again on lap 35, and Räikkönen slows the lap before the safety car's withdrawal so that the Bridgestone runners lose heat from their tyres. He's thus able to make a break from Schumacher. On lap 36, Coulthard passes Panis for ninth. Montoya has a blow-out on lap 37 and retires. On lap 39, Coulthard tries to pass Klien and clips him. A safety car is sent out and Coulthard pits for repairs. Räikkönen repeats the same trick on lap 41, slowing the cars right down before the race is restarted at the start of lap 42. Zonta retires from fourth with engine failure. Coulthard passes Trulli again then, on lap 43, takes Panis for seventh. Räikkönen claims McLaren's first victory of 2004 on lap 44. Second-placed Schumacher wins his seventh drivers' title. Barrichello is third ahead of Massa, Fisichella, Klien, Coulthard and Panis.

Räikkönen becomes the second driver to beat Ferrari in 2004

INSIDE LINE
MICHAEL SCHUMACHER

It took a while for me to know how to feel about this one, to be honest. On the one hand, it was very special. We were in Spa-Francorchamps, which does mean a lot to me, and to clinch the seventh constructors' title at the 700th Grand Prix for Ferrari is something very special of course. On the other hand, we were beaten in the race and at the time I didn't feel anywhere near as good as I did when we won it for the fifth or sixth time. Obviously, afterwards, when I came to the motorhome it was a great atmosphere and then I had good feelings.

The safety cars made this a tough race for us. We weren't strong enough at the right moments. Each time the safety car went in it took us a long time before my tyres got going and got temperature and pressure, which was the opposite of the Michelin runners. We have seen this very often, so it wasn't a surprise and here the conditions were especially cruel to us. The tyres were great in terms of general consistency – and before the last safety car I thought I was in with a chance of putting some pressure on Kimi – but they were not so good in the moments after a safety car and that meant in these circumstances I had no chance to win.

After the start, there was nothing I could do against David [Coulthard] – he just out-accelerated me after the first corner due to the same problem we had after every safety car. The same happened with Kimi [Räikkönen], when he out-accelerated me. With Juan Pablo [Montoya], it was a lot more exciting, but he did a very good move on me [at the Bus Stop] which I didn't expect. He passed me in a moment where I didn't think there was enough space, and when he was beside me it was too late to react.

If we hadn't had all the safety cars, if we had had a clean, normal race, I think then our situation would have been a lot more competitive, considering as well the starting position Kimi came from – because if you think he overtook me because of the safety car, which he wouldn't have done otherwise. He would have then been behind me and I'd always had one lap more than him for the pit-stops, so I think we could have driven certainly a completely different race. But there are so many ifs, there's no point to talk too much about the ifs.

I still love the sport. It's in my blood to compete and to fight, to try and beat the opponents and to win. That's just what I'm living for in a way and, as long as I can live that dream, I want to live it.

THE BIG QUESTION

Why were the Michelins blowing?

There were three spectacular tyre blow-outs here. Every one of them was a Michelin right rear – the less loaded of the rear tyres over a lap – and every one of them happened on the stretch of track between Eau Rouge and Les Combes.

On lap 12, David Coulthard, lying in third place, suffered the first of the blow-outs. He made it back to the pits for a replacement and, despite a later high-speed incident with Christian Klien on the exit of Raidillon, finished seventh.

On lap 30, Jenson Button had his tyre blow as he approached Les Combes at 200mph. The BAR turned sharp right into the side of Zsolt Baumgartner's Minardi, the accident bringing out the second safety car.

Finally, on lap 37, Juan Pablo Montoya lost fourth place when his tyre exploded with such force that his rear suspension was terminally damaged.

In addition to these, Toyota test driver Ryan Briscoe had suffered an accident during Friday practice at Eau Rouge when a left rear Michelin blew.

Michelin conducted a thorough post-race analysis and afterwards technical manager Pascal Vasselon said: "We noticed the existence of a small step between the inside of the kerb and the grass at the entry of the Bus Stop; the edge of the step was blackened, showing the frequent passage of tyres. We noticed that Briscoe pinched the kerb at the exit of the corner and we noticed a small step when we went there to inspect the corner. The organisers sorted it out before qualifying, but we didn't think that the same problem was also at the chicane's entry."

All three tyres showed damage to their inner shoulder. After being damaged on the chicane step, the right-rear wouldn't then be under extreme load until the high-speed left-right-left sequence of Eau Rouge. It was speculated that the Bridgestone, with a stiffer, less flexible sidewall, was less susceptible to damage over the chicane.

Three blow-outs in the race caused Michelin to inspect both their tyres and the circuit's kerbs

RON DENNIS
McLAREN
TEAM
PRINCIPAL

Silverstone had given us the belief that we could win, Hockenheim we should have won and here we finally did it.

It was our first victory since Malaysia in 2003, but it was special for more reasons than that. Sometimes you leave a circuit with a race victory and feel that circumstances have contributed to your result. But this was a race won from 10th on the grid, from a first-lap collision that damaged the car, through to the team contributing to optimise the car with diff controls and other parameters that are permitted under the regulations, and then to see a lead wiped out twice with the deployment of the safety car. Finally, Kimi's fastest lap came just two laps from the end, which was just a sensation.

Kimi's handling of the safety car periods showed that his determination was just amazing, and it just shows

that if you put Kimi in a position to win he wins, and the only thing spoiling an even better result was David's puncture. Button's accident brought out the second safety car and that effectively gave Michael [Schumacher] his second stop for free, wiping out Kimi's 12s advantage. In this situation it is extremely difficult to see your lead eroded, but deployment of the safety car was the right thing.

The pit lane entrance is such at Spa that there was part of the circuit immediately after where we knew we were vulnerable [to Schumacher's car], and so it was essential each time on the restart that we emerged out of La Source with some sort of a lead, and Kimi played it just right. He was very calm and did a fantastic job.

We have won two World Championships against Michael and so know that he isn't invincible. He has done a tremendous job, and congratulations to him on his World Championship, but what was particularly satisfying, and a small bonus for McLaren, was that Kimi's victory here meant Ferrari now couldn't win all but one of the races, which is something we did in 1988.

Hopefully, this is the start of their decline, but they are a tough, well-run team with very competent drivers, and you know they are never going to be easy to beat.

HISAO SUGANUMA
BRIDGESTONE TECHNICAL MANAGER

Although Michael [Schumacher] clinched the drivers' championship title, this was a disappointing race for us after such a very strong season. It showed that there were still areas of performance that we needed to work on, specifically the performance after the safety car periods.

The tyres lose between 40 and 50% of their pressure during a long period at reduced safety car speeds and need around two to three laps at racing speed to get back to normal temperatures and pressures. It meant that we were very vulnerable to safety car periods and unfortunately this race had three of them.

If you look at Michael's lap time performance after each of the safety cars, you see he struggles against Räikkönen for the following two or three laps. The first time was the most serious because it was at the start of the race, and so the tyres had not even reached normal temperatures before the safety car came out. He is maybe 2s a lap slower, although he loses more time than this because he is being overtaken and it takes three laps before he is on a pace with Kimi.

The second time was less severe because the tyres were up to temperature before the safety car came out. He is not so far away and it takes less time before he is up to full speed, two laps rather than three.

After the final safety car period, the race was already lost so I don't think Michael's times were representative.

We believe we have a solution to this problem and we were at the time working on a different generation of rear tyre, but it was not ready for this sort of high-speed circuit.

On the positive side, I think we showed that once under normal race conditions we were very competitive and also we didn't suffer any failures – and durability has to be considered as part of a tyre's performance.

Time Schumacher lost to Räikkönen in immediate aftermath of safety car periods			
Safety car comes in end lap 4	**Räikkönen**	**Schumacher**	
Lap **5**	1m 46.982s	1m 50.930s	**+4.0s** (being passed)
Lap **6**	1m 45.647s	1m 47.418s	**+1.8s**
Lap **7**	1m 46.161s	1m 47.249s	**+1.1s**
Lap **8**	1m 46.317s	1m 46.885s	**+0.6s**
Second safety car in end lap 34			
Lap **35**	1m 45.984s	1m 46.518s	**+0.5s**
Lap **36**	1m 45.938s	1m 46.186s	**+0.3s**
Lap **37**	1m 46.228s	1m 46.114s	**- 0.1s**
Lap **38**	1m 46.415s	1m 46.054s	**- 0.4s**
Third safety car in end lap 41			
Lap **42**	1m 45.108s*	1m 46.681s	**+1.6s**
Lap **43**	1m 45.351s	1m 46.403s	**+1.1s**
* Race's fastest lap			

Bridgestone admit that work is still needed to make their tyres quicker after safety car restarts

RACE RESULTS
BELGIUM
SPA-FRANCORCHAMPS

RACE DATE August 29th
CIRCUIT LENGTH 4.333 miles
NO. OF LAPS 44
RACE DISTANCE 190.476 miles
WEATHER dry and overcast, 18°C
TRACK TEMP 22°C
RACE ATTENDANCE 57,000
LAP RECORD Kimi Räikkönen,
1m 45.108s, 148.472mph, 2004

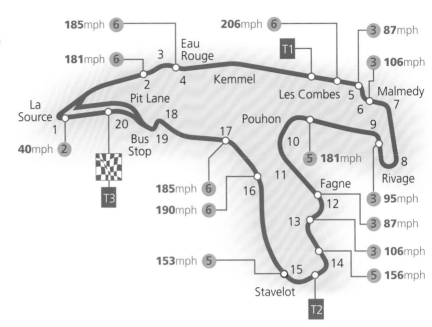

185mph 6   206mph 6   3 87mph
181mph 6   Eau Rouge   T1   3 106mph
3   Kemmel   Malmedy
2   4   Les Combes 5   7
Pit Lane   6
La Source   18   Pouhon   9
1   20   19   17   10   8
40mph 2   Bus Stop   5 181mph   Rivage
185mph 6   16   11   Fagne   3 95mph
190mph 6   12   3 87mph
13   3 106mph
153mph 5   15   14   5 156mph
Stavelot
T2
T3

PRACTICE 1

	Driver	Time	Laps
1	A Davidson	1m45.104s	12
2	M Schumacher	1m45.408s	10
3	R Barrichello	1m45.605s	8
4	B Wirdheim	1m46.658s	20
5	K Räikkönen	1m46.674s	6
6	F Alonso	1m46.679s	10
7	M Webber	1m46.782s	16
8	C Klien	1m46.809s	18
9	A Pizzonia	1m47.083s	10
10	R Briscoe	1m47.506s	21
11	J Button	1m47.511s	6
12	JP Montoya	1m47.560s	13
13	T Sato	1m47.618s	5
14	G Fisichella	1m47.648s	12
15	D Coulthard	1m47.650s	6
16	F Massa	1m47.765s	11
17	J Trulli	1m47.829s	9
18	R Zonta	1m48.642s	12
19	O Panis	1m48.834s	10
20	G Pantano	1m50.165s	9
21	B Leinders	1m50.311s	13
22	T Glock	1m50.317s	19
23	G Bruni	1m50.531s	12
24	N Heidfeld	1m50.805s	10
25	Z Baumgartner	1m50.950s	10

PRACTICE 2

	Driver	Time	Laps
1	K Räikkönen	1m44.701s	14
2	J Button	1m45.015s	15
3	M Schumacher	1m45.137s	16
4	A Davidson	1m45.437s	25
5	T Sato	1m45.451s	20
6	D Coulthard	1m45.507s	13
7	A Pizzonia	1m45.559s	14
8	R Barrichello	1m45.625s	20
9	F Alonso	1m45.658s	20
10	JP Montoya	1m45.678s	17
11	F Massa	1m45.960s	20
12	G Fisichella	1m45.978s	19
13	M Webber	1m46.471s	10
14	O Panis	1m46.528s	17
15	R Zonta	1m46.902s	20
16	J Trulli	1m46.912s	21
17	B Wirdheim	1m47.265s	23
18	C Klien	1m47.370s	8
19	R Briscoe	1m47.634s	9
20	Z Baumgartner	1m48.687s	16
21	N Heidfeld	1m48.803s	18
22	T Glock	1m48.817s	21
23	G Pantano	1m48.962s	17
24	B Leinders	1m49.480s	16
25	G Bruni	1m49.742s	16

PRACTICE 3

Session cancelled

PRACTICE 4

	Driver	Time	Laps
1	R Barrichello	1m57.085s	6
2	M Schumacher	1m57.906s	6
3	K Räikkönen	1m57.975s	6
4	G Fisichella	1m58.138s	4
5	D Coulthard	1m58.434s	6
6	F Massa	1m58.864s	5
7	J Button	1m59.182s	6
8	J Trulli	1m59.519s	6
9	T Sato	2m00.088s	6
10	F Alonso	2m01.475s	5
11	R Zonta	2m02.175s	6
12	C Klien	2m02.411s	6
13	M Webber	2m02.501s	6
14	JP Montoya	2m02.559s	5
15	O Panis	2m02.592s	6
16	N Heidfeld	2m03.556s	5
17	G Pantano	2m04.131s	6
18	G Bruni	2m05.485s	4
19	A Pizzonia	2m07.337s	4
20	Z Baumgartner	2m09.428s	4

Best sectors – Qualifying

Sector 1	F Alonso	31.091s
Sector 2	R Barrichello	52.333s
Sector 3	F Alonso	32.162s

Speed trap – Qualifying

1	D Coulthard	181.325mph
2	J Button	178.093mph
3	M Schumacher	177.969mph

 **Michael Schumacher**
"Of course I would have preferred to have taken the drivers' title with a win, but it was not possible. The better man won, but I was happy with what we had achieved."

 **Juan Pablo Montoya**
"The car was really good and I was having a great race, running third with a few laps to go, but then the right rear tyre failed, causing damage that forced me to retire."

Kimi Räikkönen
"I couldn't have hoped for a better result! The race was tough: I suffered a little damage to the floor after Massa hit me, and I had downshift problems from lap 8."

 Fernando Alonso
"To retire from the lead of a race is never good. We looked competitive compared to Kimi, and I was just beginning to run at full pace when I spun off with oil on my tyres."

Jenson Button
"I was hit by Pizzonia and went wide and into the back of Massa at Turn 1. I lost my front wing and had to pit. I was pleased with the balance until my rear tyre let go."

 **Rubens Barrichello**
"If I was unlucky with the accident at the start, I was lucky with the safety car. To finish third after that was a magic feeling. I kept pushing hard all the way to the end."

 **Antonio Pizzonia**
"I hadn't had the smallest problem with my car all race and then, suddenly, I lost all the gears when I was running third. A bad day for the team, but that's motor racing."

David Coulthard
"It was an eventful race, having lost a tyre before my first stop from third. I'd got up to eighth when I lost my front wing colliding with Klien, so seventh was reasonable."

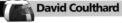 **Jarno Trulli**
"I don't know what happened. Things seemed good in the first stint, but after my first stop the car became undriveable and I had no confidence in high-speed corners."

 Takuma Sato
"Webber was going into Eau Rouge very slowly so I hit the brakes to avoid him. Montoya was overtaking me to the right, I became sandwiched and Webber hit me."

POSITIONS LAP BY LAP

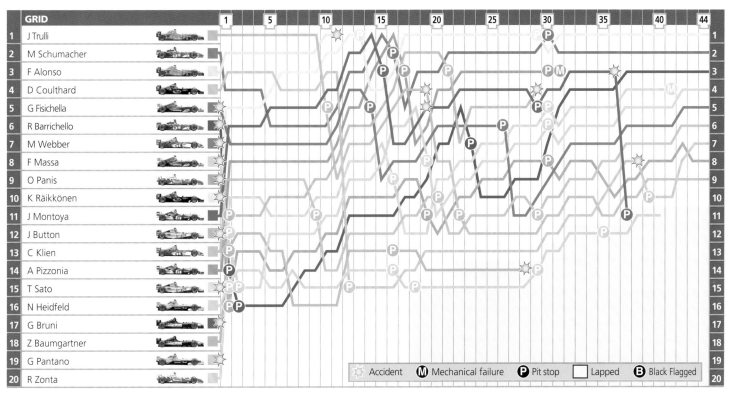

GRID					
1	J Trulli				1
2	M Schumacher				2
3	F Alonso				3
4	D Coulthard				4
5	G Fisichella				5
6	R Barrichello				6
7	M Webber				7
8	F Massa				8
9	O Panis				9
10	K Räikkönen				10
11	J Montoya				11
12	J Button				12
13	C Klien				13
14	A Pizzonia				14
15	T Sato				15
16	N Heidfeld				16
17	G Bruni				17
18	Z Baumgartner				18
19	G Pantano				19
20	R Zonta				20

☆ Accident Ⓜ Mechanical failure Ⓟ Pit stop ☐ Lapped Ⓑ Black Flagged

QUALIFYING

	Driver	Pre-qual time	Pos	Time
1	J Trulli	1m58.606s	9	1m56.232s
2	M Schumacher	1m53.755s	1	1m56.304s
3	F Alonso	1m58.242s	8	1m56.686s
4	D Coulthard	1m56.994s	7	1m57.990s
5	G Fisichella	1m56.068s	5	1m58.040s
6	R Barrichello	1m54.913s	2	1m58.175s
7	M Webber	1m59.437s	13	1m58.729s
8	F Massa	1m56.057s	4	1m59.008s
9	O Panis	2m01.472s	18	1m59.552s
10	K Räikkönen	1m55.371s	3	1m59.635s
11	JP Montoya	1m56.842s	6	1m59.681s
12	J Button	1m58.837s	10	2m00.237s
13	C Klien	1m59.997s	15	2m01.246s
14	A Pizzonia	1m59.100s	12	2m01.447s
15	T Sato	1m58.929s	11	2m01.872s
16	N Heidfeld	2m00.166s	16	2m02.645s
17	G Bruni	2m03.226s	19	2m02.651s
18	Z Baumgartner	2m01.195s	17	2m03.303s
19	G Pantano	1m59.442s	14	2m03.833s
20	R Zonta	No time	20	2m03.895s

RACE

	Driver	Car	Laps	Time	Fastest	Avg. mph	Stops
1	K Räikkönen	McLaren-Mercedes MP4-19B	44	1h32m35.274s	1m45.108s	123.595	2
2	M Schumacher	Ferrari F2004	44	1h32m38.406s	1m45.503s	123.526	2
3	R Barrichello	Ferrari F2004	44	1h32m39.645s	1m45.666s	123.498	3
4	F Massa	Sauber-Petronas C23	44	1h32m47.778s	1m47.624s	123.318	4
5	G Fisichella	Sauber-Petronas C23	44	1h32m49.378s	1m46.758s	123.282	2
6	C Klien	Jaguar-Cosworth R5	44	1h32m49.888s	1m47.509s	123.271	3
7	D Coulthard	McLaren-Mercedes MP4-19B	44	1h32m53.244s	1m46.579s	123.197	3
8	O Panis	Toyota TF104B	44	1h32m53.967s	1m47.765s	123.181	3
9	J Trulli	Renault R24	44	1h32m57.389s	1m45.898s	123.106	2
10	R Zonta	Toyota TF104B	41	Engine	1m47.576s	122.067	2
11	N Heidfeld	Jordan-Ford EJ14	40	1h32m59.249s	1m50.471s	111.876	5
R	JP Montoya	Williams-BMW FW26	37	Suspension	1m46.547s		2
R	A Pizzonia	Williams-BMW FW26	31	Gearbox	1m46.740s		2
R	J Button	BAR-Honda 006	29	Accident	1m47.151s		2
R	Z Baumgartner	Minardi-Cosworth PS04	28	Accident	1m51.031s		2
R	F Alonso	Renault R24	11	Accident	1m45.870s		0
R	M Webber	Jaguar-Cosworth R5	0	Accident			0
R	T Sato	BAR-Honda 006	0	Accident			0
R	G Bruni	Minardi-Cosworth PS04	0	Accident			0
R	G Pantano	Jordan-Ford EJ14	0	Accident			0

CHAMPIONSHIP

	Driver	Pts
1	M Schumacher	128
2	R Barrichello	88
3	J Button	65
4	J Trulli	46
5	F Alonso	45
6	JP Montoya	38
7	K Räikkönen	28
8	D Coulthard	21
9	T Sato	18
10	G Fisichella	18
11	R Schumacher	12
12	F Massa	10
13	M Webber	7
14	O Panis	6
15	A Pizzonia	4

	Constructor	Pts
1	Ferrari	216
2	Renault	91
3	BAR-Honda	83
4	Williams-BMW	54
5	McLaren-Mercedes	49
6	Sauber-Petronas	28
7	Jaguar-Cosworth	10
8	Toyota	9
9	Jordan-Ford	5
10	Minardi-Cosworth	1

Fastest race lap
K Räikkönen 1m45.108s,
on lap 42 (148.472mph)
New lap record

Fastest through speed trap
A Pizzonia 199.708mph
Slowest through speed trap
N Heidfeld 184.540mph

Fastest pit stop
N Heidfeld 31.609s
Slowest pit stop
N Heidfeld 4m46.457s

Giancarlo Fisichella
"Someone hit me at Turn 1, damaging the rear wing and diffuser. I lost downforce and on lap 20 momentarily went off. To see our cars fourth and fifth was great."

Mark Webber
"I braked too late into La Source and hit Rubens, losing my front wing. I was going up Eau Rouge when I lost steering and, through no fault of his own, Sato hit me."

Olivier Panis
"At the start I hit one of the Saubers and had to pit for a front wing and tyre change, so I was at the back of the field. The car ran quite well and I took away a point."

Nick Heidfeld
"At the first corner I was pushed to the outside, lost my front wing and had to pit. After that the balance was very poor – that's why I nearly went off at Eau Rouge."

Gianmaria Bruni
"I was 14th going into Eau Rouge. Then Sato spun, and as he was coming back on the circuit I lifted off and my team-mate hit me from behind. It was very unfortunate."

Felipe Massa
"I locked up at La Source at the start and didn't see Kimi on the outside until we touched. I stopped twice before lap 3 but was then able to attack and finish fourth."

Christian Klien
"This was an amazing race for me! I managed to avoid a few incidents at the start and my three-stop strategy worked well enough to score my first ever points."

Ricardo Zonta
"After a difficult qualifying it was good to run fourth before my engine blew. I was certain that we had the car to hold on to that position, so I was very disappointed."

Giorgio Pantano
"As I arrived at the top of Eau Rouge on lap 1 I saw Sato go off, so I slowed down. Then a Minardi appeared and spun in front of me; there was nowhere to go."

Zsolt Baumgartner
"We had a very good race and were consistently quicker than the Jordans, but I was really unlucky that Button was right next to me when his tyre exploded."

RUBENS RULES

It looked as though Ferrari had got it all wrong on home ground, but through came the red cars, this time with Rubens Barrichello scoring his first win of 2004

It was another Ferrari 1–2, but this time there was a big difference. For one, it was Rubens Barrichello who came out on top. For another, the uncertain unfolding of the order towards the end made for a thriller of a race.

As is so often the case in great races, the variables were mixed by the weather. Up to an hour-and-a-half before the start, Monza was laid siege by a terrific rainstorm. Although it had stopped as 14:00 approached, the track was still wet enough that everyone drove to the grid on wet weather tyres. The drivers noted that although parts of the circuit were still extremely treacherous, from the Lesmos onward it was beginning to dry. In the 10-minute wait on the grid, almost everyone changed to dries.

But not poleman Barrichello. One of only three drivers – and the only front-running one – to remain on wets, he built up a huge lead in the first couple of laps. By the third lap, though, it was obvious that he was on the wrong tyres and would need to pit extremely prematurely. By this time, though, team-mate Michael Schumacher was battling down among the lower order, having spun at the Roggia chicane on the opening lap.

So, with the two Ferraris out of position, the race was very definitely on. Yet, such was their speed advantage that they were each able to overcome their dramas, and using three- and two-stop strategies respectively, Barrichello and Schumacher pounced on the race-leading BAR-Honda of Jenson Button almost simultaneously in the late stages.

Rubens Barrichello made up for starting on wet weather tyres to come through for victory

ROUND **15**

ITALY
FORMULA 1™ GRAN
PREMIO VODAFONE
D'ITALIA 2004
Monza

LAP BY LAP
ACTION

53 laps / 191 miles

Michael Schumacher runs across the first chicane on the opening lap

Start to lap 2

With a damp but drying track, Heidfeld starts from the pits. Coulthard pits at the end of the formation lap to switch from wet to dry tyres. The majority of the field start on dry tyres but, at the start, Barrichello – on wets – storms into the lead and pulls 6.9s clear of Alonso, followed by Montoya, Räikkönen, Button and Massa. Michael Schumacher runs wide at the first chicane and passes Montoya, but eases up and cedes the place. The German then spins at the second chicane (rejoining 15th), where Panis and Pizzonia tangle. Pizzonia rejoins at the back, while Panis retires. Barrichello extends his lead on lap 2, while Schumacher advances to 14th.

Schumacher finds himself facing backwards at the second chicane

Laps 3 to 10

The performance differential between wet and dry tyres begins to equalise and, on lap 4, Alonso slashes Barrichello's advantage. Montoya runs wide at the second chicane, while fending off Button, losing a place. Barrichello pits on lap 5, elevating Alonso to the lead as Barrichello drops to ninth. The wet-shod Massa also stops. On lap 7, Webber passes Trulli for seventh at the first chicane. Alonso leads Button, Montoya, Räikkönen, Sato and Klien. Schumacher is up to 11th. Massa stops for a fresh nose on lap 9, after a chop from Heidfeld at the second chicane. Then leader Alonso makes the race's first scheduled pit stop on lap 10.

Pizzonia and Barrichello get close as they fight for position on lap 12

Laps 11 to 20

Running ninth on lap 11, Schumacher is lapping fastest of all. On lap 12, Pizzonia runs wide at the first chicane while trying to pass Barrichello. Trulli pits. On lap 13, Montoya, Sato and Räikkönen all stop – the first two for fuel, the latter to retire. Pizzonia passes Barrichello at the Parabolica. Leader Button pits on lap 14, and rejoins ahead of Alonso and Schumacher. Schumacher outbrakes Alonso at the first chicane for second on lap 15, but pits at the end of the lap, slipping back to 10th. Pizzonia pits from fifth on lap 16, and rejoins 10th, behind Schumacher. Fisichella, up to sixth, makes his first stop on lap 19. Schumacher passes Webber for seventh place on lap 20, after the Australian makes a mistake.

A flash fire enveloped Bruni's Minardi during his stop on lap 31

Laps 21 to 33

The order on lap 21 sees Button leading Alonso – who is closing gradually – Montoya, Barrichello, Sato and Coulthard, who has yet to make his first stop. On lap 22, Pizzonia passes Webber for eighth. Coulthard pits on lap 26, dropping from sixth to 10th. By lap 28, Button is 1s clear of Alonso, with a 0.5s gap back to Montoya. Sixth-placed Schumacher sets the fastest lap of the race. Barrichello – out of synch with his rivals following his early tyre stop – refuels on lap 29, rejoining sixth, behind his team-mate. Bruni pits on lap 31 and his car is briefly enveloped in a flash fire. It is swiftly extinguished but he retires. Barrichello sets a new fastest lap. Alonso, Montoya and Sato pit on lap 33, rejoining in the same order, holding down fifth to seventh places. The Ferraris move up to second and third.

Schumacher dives past Button into second place at the start of lap 43

Laps 34 to 42

Leader Button comes in again on lap 34, and rejoins third, behind Schumacher and Barrichello. A lap later, Schumacher sets another fastest lap as Pizzonia pits from fifth. Schumacher pits on lap 36, while Montoya loses ground, dropping behind Sato and Fisichella, with the Sauber driving pitting on lap 37. Barrichello leads Button by 12.1s, with Alonso and Schumacher next, from Sato and Montoya. Barrichello stretches his lead to 19.3s on lap 40, a lap before Alonso spins into retirement at the second chicane. Barrichello pits on lap 42 but retains his lead.

Ferrari ran 1–2 to the finish, this time with Barrichello in front

Lap 43 to the finish

Schumacher passes Button on the approach to the first chicane on lap 43, to give Ferrari a 1–2. Barrichello leads Schumacher by 3.2s at the end of the lap, from Button, Sato, Montoya and Coulthard. Pizzonia and Fisichella complete the top eight. By lap 47, Schumacher sits 1s behind his team-mate, but Button and Sato are losing touch. Montoya is well clear of Coulthard, who comes under pressure from Fisichella, with Fisichella still ninth. Barrichello crosses the line 0.9s clear of Schumacher at the end of lap 53 to score his first win since Japan 2003. Button, Sato, Montoya, Coulthard, Pizzonia and Fisichella complete the scorers.

INSIDE LINE
JENSON BUTTON

There were elements of this third place that were very satisfying but, in the end, we had nowhere near the pace of the Ferraris. I didn't think they were going to be as strong towards the end of the race, but the pace of those two guys was just untouchable.

The first part of the race was fantastic. Getting up to third before the first pit stop wasn't too bad considering where I was in the first corner – about seventh.

When I turned in to the second chicane, I thought I must be going the wrong way because everyone else seemed to be going straight on! In the second part of the corner, I was overlapping with Michael. I was on the outside, which is normally a bit more grippy on turn-in because you don't use that line in the dry, so I had quite a lot of grip, but I knew that Michael was a little bit out of control on the inside. I had to try and make the corner and I did, but his wheel touched my sidepod and he came off worse.

Catching the others was thrilling. I got by Takuma [Sato] straight after the Michael incident, I got Kimi early on and I got past Juan. Then, once I got up with Fernando, I knew I had the low-fuel stage, where our car is extremely good, to come so I was just biding my time and looking after the tyres. The car seemed to run much better on low fuel towards the end of the stints. That's when I was able to pull out a gap over Alonso and Montoya. The last three or four laps before the stop I pushed a bit harder and was able to get a gap. That brought me out in the lead of the race.

At this stage, I actually thought we had a chance of a win but, as I said, I didn't know those two [Ferrari] guys would be so strong. Their performance in the dry was staggering.

When Michael was coming past me I was a bit confused because the team on the radio was shouting about Rubens 'ah, he's going to come out in front', and I wasn't sure if Michael was Rubens and had pitted a lap earlier than expected. When I then saw Michael alongside me I was thinking 'ah, that means there's two of them in front', and then I saw Rubens coming out of the pits and I was third.

It was wet before the
race, but it was soon to
dry, leaving a decision to
be made on the grid

THE BIG QUESTION

Dry- or wet-weather tyres?

Immediately after completing their wet-weather-tyred lap to
the grid, most of the 20 drivers were fairly convinced that
dry-weather tyres would soon be coming into their own. The
track was still treacherous through the first two chicanes and
on the approach to Lesmo 1 but, thereafter, away from the
shade of the trees, the track was already drying. The sun
breaking cover during the 10-minute wait on the grid just
confirmed things.

At least that's how it was for the Michelin runners. The
French company's dry-weather tyre is notoriously able to
cope with conditions of marginal wet far better than the
equivalent Bridgestone.

"That was the big concern for us," said Ferrari's Ross
Brawn. "If we have a problem with the dry-weather
Bridgestone, it's that it takes a while to get up to
temperature and that problem gets exacerbated if the track
is damp, as obviously it is then cooler. We knew that we
were going to be very uncompetitive in the early laps if we
went with the dry tyre.

"The Bridgestone wet is a fantastic tyre with a very wide
operating band of conditions, but we didn't know how fast
the track was going to dry. We were thinking that if the track
stayed within the wet tyres' operating band for, say, eight
laps, a window would then appear in which we could come
in and combine our first fuel stop with a switch to dry tyres.
That is in fact what Rubens [Barrichello] chose to try. We left
the choice entirely up to the drivers because they were the
ones who'd been in the car during the reconnaissance laps.
Rubens made the choice first and Michael [Schumacher] I
think just waited to see what Rubens did, then did the
opposite simply because he didn't know which was going to
be better either, and at least this way the team was covered."

ROSS BRAWN
FERRARI TECHNICAL DIRECTOR

We went about this one the long way, but got the result in the end. As it turned out, Michael was struggling badly for grip and spun down almost to the back on the first lap. Rubens, as expected, built up a big early lead but the track dried very quickly and as early as lap three the dry-weather tyres became much quicker. We called him in the following lap, but there was some confusion over the radio and he ended up coming in the lap after that. We fuelled him to run until lap 30, the plan being to keep him on a two-stop.

At that stage I really wasn't thinking about a win. I thought we could realistically get some points, a podium maybe at a push. However, as Michael began to make progress through the field and as the track settled in, we saw a pattern we hadn't been expecting. We could see that our car was very fast – we couldn't yet see that with Rubens

because he'd been heavily refuelled and also had some understeer – and also that the Michelin cars weren't as fast as we'd been expecting.

We then began to think again about Rubens' strategy. He'd got back up to fourth place, close behind Alonso, Button and Montoya, but we weren't going to be able to pass all of them at the stops. We decided to switch him to a three-stop strategy, with just a small amount of fuel for a very fast penultimate stint that would then buy him the time to make the extra stop. He responded fantastically.

It worked to perfection in that he got out of the pits just ahead of Button. But at the same time Michael was passing Button! We hadn't expected that he would be able to pass him pretty much immediately. Had Michael managed to get by ahead of Rubens, everyone would have said we'd put Rubens on a three-stop in order to hand the race to Michael!

Rubens wasn't quite sure where he stood as he came out of the pits, and he was asking what position he was in. We then lost radio contact. He asked me again later in the lap and I said 'you're in P1', and he screamed in Portuguese down the radio.

After that, we asked them to turn the engines down as this is the hardest engine track of the season and we'd been using them to the max for longer than we usually do.

Michael Schumacher congratulates Rubens Barrichello on heading home a Ferrari 1–2

MARIO THEISSEN
BMW
MOTORSPORT
DIRECTOR

For a time, we were looking quite strong with Juan Pablo [Montoya], and it appeared we were in with a chance of the win. He was running very close behind Alonso and Button, and it seemed like it would all hang on the second stops. But that was to ignore a couple of things: the Ferraris' pace, and a problem that we encountered with Juan's car that put him out of contention. There was a sensor failure that prevented us from knowing how much fuel was in the tank. It meant that we had to be conservative in terms of when we fuelled and how much fuel we put in at both stops.

So, Juan was running heavier than he needed to be in the last stint of the race, in addition to which he reported a technical problem on the overrun. All of this made the car very difficult – he complained massively of the handling – and this is reflected in the comparison in his lap times at this stage with those before the second stop.

Unfortunately, the car that didn't suffer any technical issues – Antonio Pizzonia's – ended up at the back after being hit on the first lap by another competitor. This was a real shame because his pace was very good. He set the fastest time behind the Ferraris, and his best lap was a full 0.4s faster than the next best Michelin runner. Antonio completed the first lap 33s behind the leader, and finished the last lap still 33s behind the leader. To do that while fighting his way through the field suggests he could have been running right at the front.

Furthermore, for the last 12 laps or so he was stuck behind Coulthard's McLaren, which was holding him up by quite a lot.

Data comparison of Montoya and Pizzonia			
	Stint 1	Stint 2	Stint 3
Montoya's best lap	1m 23.015s (excess fuel)	1m 22.929s (excess fuel + tech prob)	1m 23.730s
Pizzonia's best lap	1m 22.994s	1m 22.246s	1m 22.483s
Actual sector comparison: Pizzonia running less wing than Montoya, which theoretically gives faster sector 1 and 3 times, but slower sector 2 time (because of Lesmo corners)			
	Sector 1	Sector 2	Sector 3
Montoya's fastest	26.591s	28.327s	27.357s
Pizzonia's fastest	26.389s	28.163s	27.471s

Montoya would have been in with a shot at winning but for having to run fuel-heavy

RACE RESULTS
ITALY
MONZA

RACE DATE September 12th
CIRCUIT LENGTH 3.596 miles
NO. OF LAPS 53
RACE DISTANCE 190.588 miles
WEATHER dry and cloudy, 23°C
TRACK TEMP 26°C
RACE ATTENDANCE 100,000
LAP RECORD Rubens Barrichello,
1m 21.046s, 159.726mph, 2004

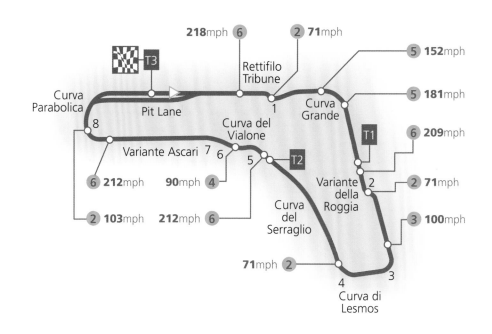

	PRACTICE 1				PRACTICE 2				PRACTICE 3				PRACTICE 4		
	Driver	**Time**	**Laps**		**Driver**	**Time**	**Laps**		**Driver**	**Time**	**Laps**		**Driver**	**Time**	**Laps**
1	M Schumacher	1m20.526s	10	1	K Räikkönen	1m20.846s	13	1	JP Montoya	1m21.700s	6	1	R Barrichello	1m20.555s	11
2	R Barrichello	1m20.861s	4	2	R Barrichello	1m20.899s	21	2	F Alonso	1m21.705s	9	2	JP Montoya	1m20.653s	11
3	A Davidson	1m20.902s	25	3	M Schumacher	1m21.080s	20	3	A Pizzonia	1m21.723s	8	3	J Button	1m20.734s	13
4	K Räikkönen	1m21.637s	5	4	J Button	1m21.124s	16	4	R Barrichello	1m21.855s	9	4	F Alonso	1m20.773s	11
5	F Alonso	1m21.778s	10	5	A Pizzonia	1m21.264s	18	5	T Sato	1m21.867s	7	5	T Sato	1m20.805s	11
6	J Button	1m21.904s	5	6	T Sato	1m21.313s	20	6	M Schumacher	1m21.962s	7	6	K Räikkönen	1m20.856s	11
7	J Trulli	1m22.052s	11	7	JP Montoya	1m21.419s	17	7	K Räikkönen	1m22.018s	5	7	M Schumacher	1m20.898s	10
8	B Wirdheim	1m22.065s	24	8	A Davidson	1m21.544s	37	8	J Button	1m22.062s	9	8	A Pizzonia	1m20.921s	10
9	A Pizzonia	1m22.159s	9	9	F Alonso	1m21.630s	18	9	D Coulthard	1m22.097s	6	9	D Coulthard	1m21.058s	11
10	JP Montoya	1m22.232s	9	10	D Coulthard	1m22.052s	12	10	F Massa	1m22.284s	6	10	J Trulli	1m21.506s	8
11	T Sato	1m22.245s	8	11	J Trulli	1m22.191s	19	11	G Fisichella	1m22.369s	5	11	F Massa	1m21.859s	14
12	D Coulthard	1m22.248s	5	12	R Briscoe	1m22.197s	35	12	J Trulli	1m22.774s	9	12	O Panis	1m21.889s	18
13	F Massa	1m22.259s	13	13	F Massa	1m22.258s	18	13	M Webber	1m22.784s	70	13	G Fisichella	1m21.929s	9
14	G Fisichella	1m22.460s	11	14	R Zonta	1m22.298s	22	14	R Zonta	1m22.867s	9	14	R Zonta	1m22.114s	20
15	O Panis	1m22.487s	8	15	G Fisichella	1m22.302s	12	15	O Panis	1m23.103s	9	15	C Klien	1m22.230s	18
16	R Zonta	1m22.607s	10	16	T Glock	1m22.332s	17	16	C Klien	1m23.332s	8	16	M Webber	1m22.490s	15
17	R Briscoe	1m22.815s	21	17	M Webber	1m22.392s	24	17	G Bruni	1m24.411s	14	17	N Heidfeld	1m23.146s	13
18	M Webber	1m23.071s	7	18	O Panis	1m22.813s	15	18	G Pantano	1m24.526s	11	18	G Bruni	1m23,794s	14
19	T Glock	1m23.333s	28	19	B Wirdheim	1m22.914s	26	19	N Heidfeld	1m24.669s	12	19	G Pantano	no time	2
20	B Leinders	1m23.696s	16	20	C Klien	1m23.199s	25	20	Z Baumgartner	1m26.114s	10	20	Z Baumgartner	no time	2
21	C Klien	1m23.723s	7	21	G Pantano	1m23.818s	17								
22	N Heidfeld	1m24.000s	11	22	B Leinders	1m24.045s	19								
23	G Pantano	1m24.412s	10	23	Z Baumgartner	1m24.063s	17								
24	G Bruni	1m26.062s	11	24	G Bruni	1m24.225s	23								
25	Z Baumgartner	1m26.161s	13	25	N Heidfeld	no time	2								

Best sectors – Qualifying			Speed trap – Qualifying		
Sector 1	M Schumacher	25.927s	1	J Trulli	225.630mph
Sector 2	R Barrichello	27.150s	2	M Schumacher	225.630mph
Sector 3	R Barrichello	26.922s	3	G Fisichella	224.947mph

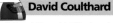

Michael Schumacher
"At the first chicane I couldn't stop in time, and at the second chicane I got a four-wheel slide, but Button was outside me, we touched and it spun me around."

Juan Pablo Montoya
"I didn't have enough grip at the start of the race and lost a place to Alonso. Then, in the third stint, my car became very difficult to drive as it developed a gearbox problem."

Kimi Räikkönen
"After only two laps it became clear that my engine was losing water pressure. It's a shame, as I made a good start and gained a few places. I think a podium finish was on."

Fernando Alonso
"Monza was the worst circuit for us, but I was fighting with BAR. We made the right decision on tyres, but I spun when I took too much kerb at the second chicane."

Jenson Button
"We came very close to our first victory here, but third and fourth for myself and Taku is amazing. But all credit to Ferrari for turning things around in the closing stages."

Rubens Barrichello
"I loved every moment of this weekend. It was difficult regarding the tyres at the start, but I felt it was best to fit rain tyres and to push as hard as possible."

Antonio Pizzonia
"My race was basically compromised on the first lap when I got hit from behind and spun off. I was lucky to get out of the gravel, but had dropped to 19th place."

David Coulthard
"I thought it would still be damp in the forest section and decided to start on intermediates. But it became clear on the out lap that dries were the right choice."

Jarno Trulli
"I struggled in the opening stages when grip levels were low. I was quick towards the end of my stints, though, although it was too late to make up any positions."

Takuma Sato
"My start was good, but I couldn't pull away at the exit of the first chicane, so lost a few places. Once the track dried, though, I was able to get back onto the pace."

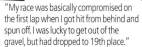

POSITIONS LAP BY LAP

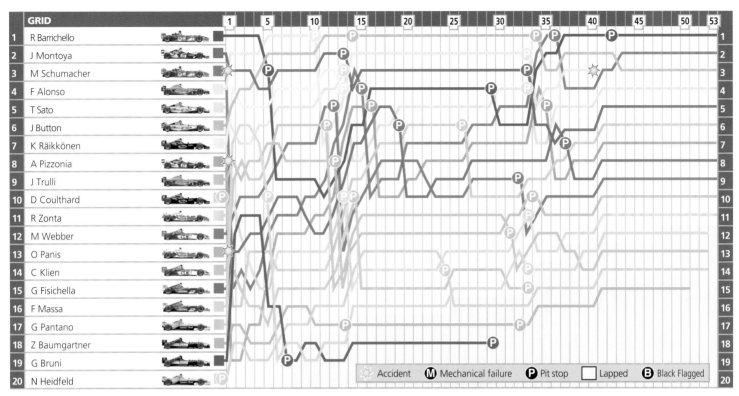

GRID				1	5	10	15	20	25	30	35	40	45	50	53	
1	R Barrichello															1
2	J Montoya															2
3	M Schumacher															3
4	F Alonso															4
5	T Sato															5
6	J Button															6
7	K Räikkönen															7
8	A Pizzonia															8
9	J Trulli															9
10	D Coulthard															10
11	R Zonta															11
12	M Webber															12
13	O Panis															13
14	C Klien															14
15	G Fisichella															15
16	F Massa															16
17	G Pantano															17
18	Z Baumgartner															18
19	G Bruni															19
20	N Heidfeld															20

Accident   Ⓜ Mechanical failure   Ⓟ Pit stop   ☐ Lapped   Ⓑ Black Flagged

QUALIFYING

	Driver	Pre-qual time	Pos	Time
1	R Barrichello	1m20.552s	10	1m20.089s
2	JP Montoya	1m19.525s	1	1m20.620s
3	M Schumacher	1m20.528s	9	1m20.637s
4	F Alonso	1m20.341s	5	1m20.645s
5	T Sato	1m19.733s	3	1m20.715s
6	J Button	1m19.856s	4	1m20.786s
7	K Räikkönen	1m20.501s	8	1m20.788s
8	A Pizzonia	1m19.671s	2	1m20.888s
9	J Trulli	1m21.011s	12	1m21.027s
10	D Coulthard	1m20.414s	7	1m21.049s
11	R Zonta	1m21.829s	14	1m21.520s
12	M Webber	1m21.783s	13	1m21.602s
13	O Panis	1m22.169s	16	1m21.841s
14	C Klien	1m22.114s	15	1m21.989s
15	G Fisichella	1m20.357s	6	1m22.239s
16	F Massa	1m20.571s	11	1m22.287s
17	G Pantano	1m23.264s	17	1m23.239s
18	G Bruni	1m23.963s	18	1m24.940s
19	Z Baumgartner	1m25.082s	19	1m25.808s
20	N Heidfeld	no time	20	1m22.301s

RACE

	Driver	Car	Laps	Time	Fastest	Avg. mph	Stops
1	R Barrichello	Ferrari F2004	53	1h15m18.448s	1m21.046s	151.854	3
2	M Schumacher	Ferrari F2004	53	1h15m19.795s	1m21.361s	151.809	2
3	J Button	BAR-Honda 006	53	1h15m28.645s	1m22.671s	151.512	2
4	T Sato	BAR-Honda 006	53	1h15m33.818s	1m22.660s	151.339	2
5	JP Montoya	Williams-BMW FW26	53	1h15m50.800s	1m22.929s	150.774	2
6	D Coulthard	McLaren-Mercedes MP4-19B	53	1h15m51.887s	1m22.889s	150.738	1
7	A Pizzonia	Williams-BMW FW26	53	1h15m52.200s	1m22.246s	150.728	2
8	G Fisichella	Sauber-Petronas C23	53	1h15m53.879s	1m22.615s	150.672	2
9	M Webber	Jaguar-Cosworth R5	53	1h16m15.209s	123.090s	149.970	2
10	J Trulli	Renault R24	53	1h16m24.764s	1m22.855s	149.657	2
11	R Zonta	Toyota TF104B	53	1h16m40.979s	1m23.410s	149.130	2
12	F Massa	Sauber-Petronas C23	52	1h15m22.268s	1m22.941s	148.860	2
13	C Klien	Jaguar-Cosworth R5	52	1h15m40.224s	1m23.432s	148.271	3
14	N Heidfeld	Jordan-Ford EJ14	52	1h16m06.392s	1m24.168s	147.422	2
15	Z Baumgartner	Minardi-Cosworth PS04	50	1h15m23.973s	1m26.356s	143.075	2
R	F Alonso	Renault R24	40	Spun off	1m22.881s		2
R	G Pantano	Jordan-Ford EJ14	33	Spun off	1m24.061s		2
R	G Bruni	Minardi-Cosworth PS04	29	Pit fire	1m26.371s		1
R	K Räikkönen	McLaren-Mercedes MP4-19B	13	Engine	1m23.365s		0
R	O Panis	Toyota TF104B	0	Spun off			0

CHAMPIONSHIP

	Driver	Pts
1	M Schumacher	136
2	R Barrichello	98
3	J Button	71
4	J Trulli	46
5	F Alonso	45
6	JP Montoya	42
7	K Räikkönen	28
8	D Coulthard	24
9	T Sato	23
10	G Fisichella	19
11	R Schumacher	12
12	F Massa	10
13	M Webber	7
14	O Panis	6
	A Pizzonia	6

	Constructor	Pts
1	Ferrari	234
2	BAR-Honda	94
3	Renault	91
4	Williams-BMW	60
5	McLaren-Mercedes	52
6	Sauber-Petronas	29
7	Jaguar-Cosworth	10
8	Toyota	9
9	Jordan-Ford	5
10	Minardi-Cosworth	1

Qualifying notes
Heidfeld Back 10 places for engine change
Coulthard Started from pit lane

Fastest race lap
R Barrichello 1m21.046s,
on lap 41 (159.726mph)
New lap record

Fastest through speed trap
A Pizzonia   229.844mph
Slowest through speed trap
N Heidfeld   218.038mph

Fastest pit stop
C Klien   15.321s
Slowest pit stop
N Heidfeld   31.386s

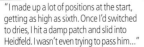

Giancarlo Fisichella
"A point was what I expected, but also not what I expected given the conditions at the start. At the end, I saw Pizzonia and Coulthard collide and hoped for more."

Mark Webber
"I was keen to stay out of the collision zone at the second chicane and did so. The car then felt good, although I suffered from understeer, making it hard to drive."

Olivier Panis
"I think we made a good decision to start on slicks despite the damp track. I was racing Pizzonia into the second chicane, but hit his car and broke my front wing."

Nick Heidfeld
"I think we managed to get the maximum from our resources. Massa tried to pass me and ran into the back of my car, but this had no big influence on the car's balance."

Gianmaria Bruni
"When the refuelling nozzle was placed on the car at the second stop, it seems that a small amount of fuel leaked out, hit the hot parts of the car and there was fire."

Felipe Massa
"I made up a lot of positions at the start, getting as high as sixth. Once I'd switched to dries, I hit a damp patch and slid into Heidfeld. I wasn't even trying to pass him..."

Christian Klien
"I had to do a drive-through penalty, as it appears that I'd been speeding in the pitlane at one of my stops, but I passed Trulli at one point and that was great fun."

Ricardo Zonta
"It was difficult to raise the temperature of the tyres when the track was still damp. Every time I was behind another car, I lost downforce and the tyres didn't perform."

Giorgio Pantano
"I don't know what happened, but at the Parabolica very soon after my second stop, I found perhaps some water on the track and the car just suddenly spun."

Zsolt Baumgartner
"I lost a little time on the damp track in the first few laps, but then the grip came in. I then had a good, fair dice with Gimmi before he had his unfortunate pit fire."

GOLDEN DEBUT

A full house at Formula One's most stunning new facility saw Barrichello win a three-way battle as his team-mate Schumacher followed error with error

For the second time in the season Formula One charted new territory, on this occasion with the inaugural Chinese Grand Prix held on a spectacular new no-expense-spared circuit. In front of a packed-to-capacity Shanghai audience, the sport gave a pretty good account of itself on-track, as Ferrari's Rubens Barrichello emerged on top of a tense three-car battle involving Kimi Räikkönen's McLaren-Mercedes and Jenson Button's BAR-Honda. The Chinese might have been forgiven for wondering what all the fuss around Michael Schumacher was about, as the World Champion finished only 12th after a succession of errors and incidents that had begun with him spinning away his qualifying lap on Saturday.

Victory in Shanghai brought Barrichello into quite an exclusive club as a driver who has won two consecutive Grands Prix – and he did it in fine style, taking immediate command of the race from pole, then fighting hard to repulse the challenges of his two rivals. This was no easy job, as the Ferrari went through a very notable drop in its tyre performance early in each of its four stints. Räikkönen would have been able to pull away at these stages if only he could have passed. But the McLaren's straightline speed deficit to the Ferrari ensured he wasn't able to do this. McLaren's attempt at using strategy to overcome the stalemate – they short-fuelled Räikkönen for his third of four stints – backfired, as it allowed the two-stopping Button to leapfrog him. Ultimately, Button's BAR didn't have the necessary pace to beat the Ferrari, but came home a fine second.

Barrichello made it two wins on the trot, but was pushed hard by Räikkönen then Button

ROUND **16**

CHINA
2004 FORMULA 1™
SINOPEC CHINESE
GRAND PRIX
Shanghai

LAP BY LAP ACTION

56 laps / 190 miles

Barrichello leads away from Räikkönen as Alonso grabs third

Villeneuve got back into the action for Renault, tussling with Montoya

Ralf Schumacher was also back, in his case returning from injury

Räikkönen pressed Barrichello hard but couldn't find a way past

Michael Schumacher completed a race he'd rather forget with a spin

Button and Barrichello appear delighted, Räikkönen frustrated

Start to lap 2

Michael Schumacher was due to start from the back of the grid after a spin in qualifying, joining Sato and Baumgartner who'd line up there after having engine changes. However, the Ferrari driver elected to top up with fuel and start from the pits. At the start of the race, Barrichello and Räikkönen lead from the front row. Alonso sprints through from sixth to third. Button fights with Massa, but the Brazilian ends lap 1 ahead. Fisichella, Ralf Schumacher and Coulthard complete the top eight, with Michael Schumacher running last.

Laps 3 to 11

Button passes Massa on lap 3, by which time Michael Schumacher has advanced to 16th. On lap 5, Fisichella and Ralf Schumacher pass Massa, behind whom a queue has formed. Räikkönen is pressing hard, and on lap 6 is within 0.2s of Barrichello. On the same lap, Coulthard overtakes Massa. Button demotes Alonso on lap 7, and Zonta passes Massa. On lap 8, Barrichello leads by half a second, and on lap 9 Montoya briefly passes Villeneuve, before being repassed. Massa and Panis pit on lap 10, then Fisichella, Zonta and Coulthard pit a lap later. Michael Schumacher hits Klien as he attempts to pass him for 15th place. He gets by, but the Austrian retires.

Laps 12 to 23

Barrichello and Räikkönen pit on lap 12, rejoining in the same order, 1.1s apart. By staying out, Button now leads. Second-placed Alonso pits on lap 13, a lap before Button comes in. He rejoins third. Villeneuve also pits. Ralf Schumacher stays out until lap 15, while brother Michael spins at Turn 13 and drops from 10th to 12th, resuming behind Coulthard. Montoya pits on lap 16, and Michael Schumacher gets by Coulthard after a frantic battle. Sato pits from fourth on lap 18, and Michael Schumacher sets the race's fastest lap. Two laps later, Michael Schumacher passes his brother for fifth, then pits. On lap 21, with the first stops over, Barrichello leads by less than 1s from Räikkönen, Button, Alonso, Ralf Schumacher, Fisichella, Coulthard, Zonta, Massa, Sato, Montoya, Webber and Villeneuve, with Michael Schumacher back in 14th place.

Laps 24 to 34

By lap 24, the gap between Räikkönen and Barrichello is 0.9s, with Button another 12s behind. Michael Schumacher is trapped in 13th, behind Villeneuve. Räikkönen pits on lap 27, but is delayed by Bruni, rejoining third. Fisichella also pits. Coulthard comes in on lap 28, and Barrichello a lap later, rejoining more than 1s clear of Räikkönen. Button leads once more. By lap 32, it's clear that Button intends to pit only twice, with Barrichello and Räikkönen running a three-stop strategy. Fourth-placed Alonso pits on lap 33, dropping to seventh. On lap 34, Ralf Schumacher pits from fourth. Villeneuve also stops, finally releasing Michael Schumacher.

Laps 35 to 44

Button makes his second stop on lap 35. Michael Schumacher limps to the pits with a puncture. With Barrichello leading on lap 36, Räikkönen makes his final stop, leaving Barrichello leading Button by 21.7s on lap 37. Ralf Schumacher spins at Turn 14 after a nudge from Coulthard, and pits to retire. On lap 38, Coulthard's front left deflates and he crawls back to the pits. Barrichello has a lead of 25.4s by lap 39, and he makes his final stop on lap 42, retaining a comfortable lead. By the end of the following lap, he's 8.2s clear of Button, who is 6.3s up on Räikkönen. Alonso is a distant fourth from Massa, Montoya, Sato, Fisichella, Coulthard, Webber, Villeneuve and Michael Schumacher, the last unlapped runner.

Lap 45 to the finish

By lap 45, Barrichello, Button, Räikkönen, Alonso, Montoya, Sato, Fisichella and Massa run in the top eight, while Michael Schumacher is pressing Villeneuve for 11th. Michael Schumacher finally passes Villeneuve on lap 48, then pits immediately, rejoining 12th. Räikkönen has closed to within 1.6s of Button by lap 53, with Barrichello only 3.2s in front, and all three coming up to lap Webber and Villeneuve. Barrichello laps the Canadian on lap 54, but his lead is cut to 2.0s, with Räikkönen now only 0.6s behind Button. Barrichello takes the chequered flag on lap 56, 1s clear of Button and Räikkönen. Alonso takes fourth from Montoya, Sato, Fisichella and Massa, who just holds off Coulthard, while the lapped Michael Schumacher languishes in 12th.

INSIDE LINE
RUBENS BARRICHELLO

For me, that was a tough race because there was pressure all the way through. I think we still had the fastest car, but not like at Monza where we were fastest by a lot. Here it was only a little, and there were phases in the race where we certainly were not quick – and in those times it took a lot of effort and concentration to keep Kimi [Räikkönen] behind me. Then we had to pull out everything to make sure that we had enough in hand to make our extra pit stop over Jenson [Button].

Michael spinning in qualifying meant he wasn't able to threaten my pole, and really that decided our weekend. It's been a season where I've been playing catch-up to Michael. He started on a higher level, but here I was going through a good phase. All weekend in China I was quick and I found a good set-up.

Because no-one had been here before, the Bridgestone guys had to make an educated guess on compounds, and we had something that was very quick but which went through a bit of a graining phase for the fronts early in the stint. That took a bit of managing but, other than that, they were great. Kimi could probably have gone faster than me early in the stints, and I had three or four laps each stint when I had to hold him up. Then the tyres would come good and it was easier.

At one time, I was a bit worried about Jenson. We needed about 23s for our extra pit stop over him and after he had pitted the gap was 21s. Then the lap after that it was only 21.7s, and I didn't have many laps left before I had to come in. At that point I said to myself 'oh, I'm in trouble', but then suddenly the gap was up to 25s and at that stage things became a bit calmer.

I think the reception we got from the people in China was fantastic. It was a great place to come, but I think next year I will try to find a hotel close to the circuit or rent a bed at the track, because the roads are pretty scary. They overtake anywhere!

Q THE BIG QUESTION

Three stops or two?

Among the three cars fighting for victory, one was on a two-stop strategy, while the others were on a three-stop. Ultimately, Barrichello's three-stopping Ferrari won the race over Button's two-stopping BAR. So, was three-stop correct and two-stop incorrect?

It's not that simple. Without taking tyre degradation into account, Shanghai's succession of low-gear corners meant it was a track where lap time was highly sensitive to fuel load. That being the case, a light three-stopping car could theoretically more than make up the time needed to make an extra pit-stop over a heavier two-stopping car, even taking into account the track's long pit lane.

But enter tyre behaviour into the equation and the picture can change. The Michelins were generally reckoned to be too hard a compound for the track. As such, they were very consistent but didn't give their usual performance boost when new. There was not much tyre performance to offset the fuel load in the early laps of a stint, and the benefits of three-stopping were therefore reduced. In fact, the simulations of almost all of the Michelin teams said two-stopping was faster.

McLaren were an exception. Running more downforce than the others, they were able to work the hard compound tyres hard enough to get a performance boost from them in the early laps. They were therefore able to three-stop.

At Ferrari, the Bridgestone had an early-lap performance boost, but this was more than offset by the subsequent four-lap trough as the front tyres grained. This too should have suggested a two-stopping strategy. But the plain fact was that the wear rates of the Bridgestone front-lefts didn't allow for long two-stopping stints.

Like most Michelin users, BAR went for a two-stop strategy, as their tyres weren't fast when fresh

SAM MICHAEL
WILLIAMS TECHNICAL DIRECTOR

It was not a good day for Williams in terms of results. However, the car pace and strategy was not bad. At least Juan Pablo drove through the field and picked up some points. He had a good start, but then had to avoid a Toyota and lost a few positions.

The most costly thing for us was Ralf's incident with Coulthard on lap 37, because Ralf had run ahead of Juan Pablo all weekend. Ralf was hit from behind by the McLaren and suffered a punctured right rear tyre as a result. He immediately pitted but, unfortunately, we were at that very moment waiting for Juan Pablo to make his scheduled second stop. We didn't know whether Ralf's car had been damaged in the incident, and we knew a damage check and repair could easily have

resulted in Juan Pablo coming in for his stop and us still being busy with Ralf's car – in which case both our cars would have been delayed rather than just one. So we asked Ralf to go back out again and pit the following lap, but he didn't want to and got out of the car.

We serviced Juan Pablo at his stop, then replaced the tyre on Ralf's car and checked for damage. We found there wasn't any and asked him to get back in the car but he was two laps down by then and chose to retire.

At least Juan Pablo was able to drive through the field. His delay at the start held him up badly through the first stint when he was stuck down the field fighting with Jacques Villeneuve's Renault. It was only in the second stint that he began to make progress. He came through to fifth place in the end. Had we been able to have a clean race with Ralf, we could probably have taken fourth place and maybe even challenged for third.

Ralf's pace after his long lay-off was pretty impressive, I must say. He was quick in the Silverstone test before this race and was immediately on the pace at Shanghai. He found a balance with his car more quickly than Juan Pablo and performed well. It certainly showed that there had been no ill effects after his Indianapolis accident.

Ralf was right back on the pace on his return, but chose not to go on after being hit by Coulthard

GEOFF WILLIS
BAR TECHNICAL DIRECTOR

For a little while, after our final stop, it crossed my mind that we might win. But you never know with Ferrari if you've got them, and ultimately they had the extra pace they needed to pull out that vital gap on us. Then, after Rubens had made his final stop, we were catching him again. If we'd managed to close up three or four laps earlier maybe we could've had a go.

But you don't know whether Rubens was conserving his tyres.

At the first stop, getting Jenson out ahead of Webber was pretty critical, giving him a clear track. Had that gone wrong, it could have changed the whole complexion of the race for us [see data]. It was a big relief when he got out just ahead.

McLaren chose to do a short third stint for Räikkönen, but it didn't work for them at all. As soon as they did that we thought 'that's made our life much easier'. Even if they hadn't done that I don't know whether it would have changed the result. We would have been 1s ahead of Kimi at the last stop instead of 9s, so Kimi would still have had to pass Jenson on track. I'm not sure whether he could've done that, because we were stronger on straightline speed and we were also very strong on the brakes.

In looking at where we lost out to

the Ferrari, it was our pace after the stops. They were three-stopping and we were two-stopping, and I suspect in both cases those strategies were driven by the characteristics of the respective tyres. Even allowing for the increased weight after the stops, we were not as quick as we really needed to be to take advantage of our strategy in terms of track positioning. Jenson reported that the car had quite a lot of oversteer when it was fuelled up, and that made the difference.

Ferrari needed around 23s over us for their extra stop if they were to get out ahead. With seven laps to go to their stop, they were only 20s ahead, and for a couple of laps it looked as though we might be able to peg it at that. But ultimately they were able to increase their pace and we weren't, and that gave them the necessary time for their pit stop.

I think our strategy was spot-on, but their edge in pace was just enough to swing it for them.

Shanghai pit stop time = 17s plus stationary time
Button's first stop = 9.7s
Total approximation = 27s

Button therefore needed at least 27s in hand over the first car in the traffic he would fall into if he wasn't to be held up. This car was Webber's sixth-placed Jaguar. Button's stop would be on lap 14. At end of lap 13, before stopping, Button was 27.3s ahead of the Jaguar. After pitting, he exited less than 1s in front of the Jaguar and had to defend for two corners. Had he emerged from the pits behind, Button would have lost approx 0.5s (the Jaguar's low fuel time vs the BAR's high fuel time) over the lap, as the Jaguar pitted on lap 15. During this time, Button would also have been vulnerable to attack from the Williams of the closely following Montoya.

Jenson Button really had to push before his first pit stop to come back out onto a clear track

RACE RESULTS
CHINA
SHANGHAI

FIA Formula 1
WORLD CHAMPIONSHIP™

RACE DATE September 26th
CIRCUIT LENGTH 3.387 miles
NO. OF LAPS 56
RACE DISTANCE 189.672 miles
WEATHER dry and bright, 29°C
TRACK TEMP 40°C
RACE ATTENDANCE 150,000
LAP RECORD Michael Schumacher,
1m 32.238s, 132.202mph, 2004

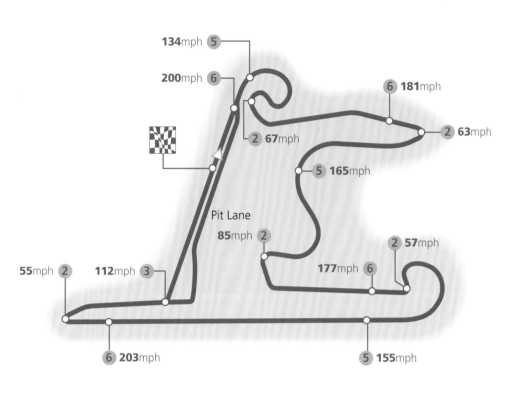

134mph 5
200mph 6
181mph 6
2 67mph
2 63mph
5 165mph
Pit Lane
85mph 2
2 57mph
55mph 2
112mph 3
177mph 6
6 203mph
5 155mph

PRACTICE 1

	Driver	Time	Laps
1	A Davidson	1m35.369s	22
2	R Schumacher	1m35.455s	13
3	JP Montoya	1m35.761s	13
4	F Massa	1m36.086s	12
5	R Briscoe	1m36.394s	21
6	J Button	1m36.475s	11
7	R Barrichello	1m36.660s	14
8	F Alonso	1m36.884s	15
9	G Fisichella	1m36.944s	9
10	R Zonta	1m36.970s	16
11	K Räikkönen	1m37.102s	5
12	B Wirdheim	1m37.142s	19
13	O Panis	1m37.191s	14
14	J Villeneuve	1m37.240s	20
15	M Schumacher	1m37.300s	11
16	T Sato	1m37.438s	9
17	T Glock	1m37.587s	15
18	D Coulthard	1m37.976s	5
19	N Heidfeld	1m38.132s	14
20	C Klien	1m38.504s	15
21	M Webber	1m38.761s	11
22	G Bruni	1m38.8.05s	13
23	R Doornbos	1m39.244s	23
24	B Leinders	1m39.529s	15
25	Z Baumgartner	1m42.795s	12

PRACTICE 2

	Driver	Time	Laps
1	A Davidson	1m33.289s	22
2	J Button	1m34.174s	19
3	K Räikkönen	1m34.289s	16
4	D Coulthard	1m34.362s	15
5	R Barrichello	1m34.448s	21
6	G Fisichella	1m34.680s	23
7	R Schumacher	1m34.714s	23
8	M Schumacher	1m34.776s	25
9	R Zonta	1m34.868s	23
10	O Panis	1m34.870s	25
11	R Briscoe	1m34.881s	29
12	F Massa	1m34.959s	23
13	F Alonso	1m35.514s	27
14	JP Montoya	1m35.646s	22
15	J Villeneuve	1m35.851s	25
16	M Webber	1m35.886s	22
17	B Wirdheim	1m36.363s	19
18	N Heidfeld	1m36.630s	19
19	Z Baumgartner	1m37.076s	15
20	C Klien	1m37.111s	25
21	G Bruni	1m37.431s	19
22	T Glock	1m37.728s	15
23	B Leinders	1m38.522s	18
24	R Doornbos	1m39.051s	15
25	T Sato	no time	1

PRACTICE 3

	Driver	Time	Laps
1	R Schumacher	1m34.380s	7
2	JP Montoya	1m34.679s	7
3	M Schumacher	1m34.844	9
4	R Barrichello	1m34.854s	8
5	G Fisichella	1m35.049s	14
6	K Räikkönen	1m35.532s	5
7	R Zonta	1m35.597s	8
8	J Button	1m35.660s	9
9	D Coulthard	1m35.930s	5
10	J Villeneuve	1m35.965s	9
11	M Webber	1m36.002s	6
12	T Sato	1m36.226s	13
13	F Alonso	1m36.243s	8
14	F Massa	1m36.539s	18
15	O Panis	1m36.623s	6
16	C Klien	1m37.160s	4
17	N Heidfeld	1m37.166s	10
18	G Bruni	1m37.533s	12
19	Z Baumgartner	1m37.552s	13
20	T Glock	1m38.128s	11

PRACTICE 4

	Driver	Time	Laps
1	M Schumacher	1m33.448s	13
2	R Barrichello	1m33.796s	12
3	K Räikkönen	1m34.042s	11
4	J Button	1m34.233s	15
5	G Fisichella	1m34.286s	10
6	N Heidfeld	1m34.404s	12
7	JP Montoya	1m34.458s	12
8	D Coulthard	1m34.470s	10
9	R Zonta	1m34.518s	19
10	F Massa	1m34.607s	12
11	F Alonso	1m34.627s	12
12	R Schumacher	1m34.769s	9
13	T Sato	1m35.155s	16
14	O Panis	1m35.211s	14
15	J Villeneuve	1m35.309s	12
16	M Webber	1m35.354s	20
17	C Klien	1m35.869s	17
18	G Bruni	1m36.748s	10
19	T Glock	1m37.158s	14
20	Z Baumgartner	1m38.014s	9

Best sectors – Qualifying

Sector 1	F Massa	24.697s
Sector 2	R Barrichello	27.777s
Sector 3	J Button	41.312s

Speed trap – Qualifying

1	F Massa	205.248mph
2	O Panis	204.627mph
3	G Fisichella	204.565mph

Michael Schumacher
"This was a slightly more interesting race than I would have wanted! I tried to pass Christian but he turned in – just a racing incident. Then I spun and had a puncture."

Juan Pablo Montoya
"In the first part of the race I was stuck in traffic, but the second part was better. It was good to finish fifth from where we started and score points for the team."

Kimi Raikkonen
"From where I was sitting, this was a close and exciting debut race for China. I was able to keep up with Rubens but just lacked that final speed to get past him."

Fernando Alonso
"It was a pretty good race. We started the weekend with quite a lot of problems, but we improved the car throughout and it got even better during the race."

Jenson Button
"It was fantastic to finish on the podium in the first ever Chinese Grand Prix. Losing two places off the grid was disastrous, but our two-stop strategy was really good."

Rubens Barrichello
"Everything went well all weekend. I had a very good start and was amazed by the amount of grip I had on lap 1. Kimi pushed me quite hard, and later so did Jenson."

Ralf Schumacher
"My car had a puncture following contact with Coulthard after he tried to overtake me. It was a shame because I had been fighting up in the top five positions."

David Coulthard
"On lap 37 I had a coming together with Ralf at the hairpin and damaged my left front wheel. I was very sorry for him, but it also affected my race, costing us points."

Jacques Villeneuve
"To be honest, I just needed too long to get into the rhythm at the start of the race. I made a good start but I hadn't warmed up the tyres enough and lost positions."

Takuma Sato
"I was delighted to start from the back and still score good points. I fought a hard battle with heavy fuel on board, but I was able to enjoy the race and finish sixth."

POSITIONS LAP BY LAP

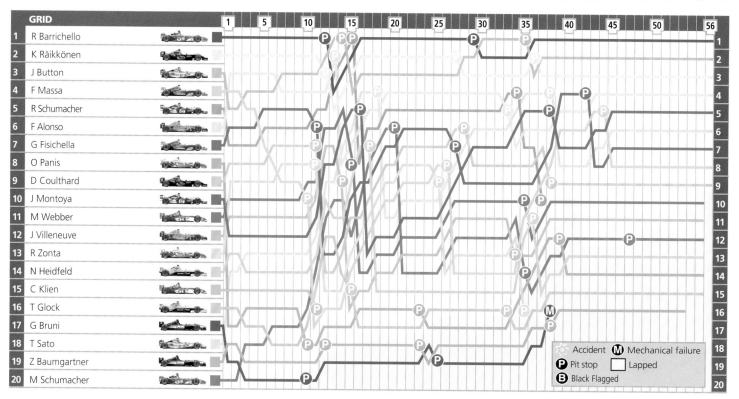

GRID			
1	R Barrichello		
2	K Räikkönen		
3	J Button		
4	F Massa		
5	R Schumacher		
6	F Alonso		
7	G Fisichella		
8	O Panis		
9	D Coulthard		
10	J Montoya		
11	M Webber		
12	J Villeneuve		
13	R Zonta		
14	N Heidfeld		
15	C Klien		
16	T Glock		
17	G Bruni		
18	T Sato		
19	Z Baumgartner		
20	M Schumacher		

Legend:
- ☀ Accident
- Ⓜ Mechanical failure
- Ⓟ Pit stop
- ☐ Lapped
- Ⓑ Black Flagged

QUALIFYING

	Driver	Pre-qual time	Pos	Time
1	R Barrichello	1m33.787s	4	1m34.012s
2	K Räikkönen	1m33.499s	2	1m34.178s
3	J Button	1m34.273s	10	1m34.295s
4	F Massa	1m33.816s	5	1m34.759s
5	R Schumacher	1m33.849s	6	1m34.891s
6	F Alonso	1m34.599s	14	1m34.917s
7	G Fisichella	1m33.738s	3	1m34.951s
8	O Panis	1m34.153s	9	1m34.975s
9	D Coulthard	1m34.355s	12	1m35.029s
10	JP Montoya	1m34.016s	7	1m35.245s
11	M Webber	1m34.334s	11	1m35.286s
12	J Villeneuve	1m34.425s	13	1m35.384s
13	R Zonta	1m34.958s	16	1m35.410s
14	N Heidfeld	1m34.808s	15	1m36.507s
15	C Klien	1m35.447s	17	1m36.535s
16	T Glock	1m37.143s	19	1m37.140s
17	Z Baumgartner	1m37.510s	20	1m40.240s
18	M Schumacher	1m33.185s	1	no time
19	T Sato	1m34.051s	8	1m34.293s
20	G Bruni	1m36.623s	18	no time

RACE

	Driver	Car	Laps	Time	Fastest	Avg. mph	Stops
1	R Barrichello	Ferrari F2004	56	1h29m12.420s	1m32.455s	127.502	3
2	J Button	BAR-Honda 006	56	1h29m13.455s	1m32.935s	127.477	2
3	K Räikkönen	McLaren-Mercedes MP4-19B	56	1h29m13.889s	1m32.876s	127.467	3
4	F Alonso	Renault R24	56	1h29m44.930s	1m33.625s	126.732	2
5	JP Montoya	Williams-BMW FW26	56	1h29m57.613s	1m33.108s	126.434	2
6	T Sato	BAR-Honda 006	56	1h30m07.211s	1m33.533s	126.210	2
7	G Fisichella	Sauber-Petronas C23	56	1h30m17.884s	1m33.520s	125.961	3
8	F Massa	Sauber-Petronas C23	56	1h30m32.500s	1m33.483s	125.622	3
9	D Coulthard	McLaren-Mercedes MP4-19B	56	1h30m33.039s	1m33.727s	125.610	3
10	M Webber	Jaguar-Cosworth R5	55	1h29m12.531s	1m34.893s	125.221	2
11	J Villeneuve	Renault R24	55	1h29m12.708s	1m34.950s	125.217	2
12	M Schumacher	Ferrari F2004	55	1h29m22.312s	1m32.238s	124.993	3
13	N Heidfeld	Jordan-Ford EJ14	55	1h29m40.248s	1m34.717s	124.576	2
14	O Panis	Toyota TF104B	55	1h29m41.045s	1m34.603s	124.557	3
15	T Glock	Jordan-Ford EJ14	55	1h30m11.738s	1m34.931s	123.851	2
16	Z Baumgartner	Minardi-Cosworth PS04	53	1h30m38.646s	1m37.578s	118.754	3
R	G Bruni	Minardi-Cosworth PS04	38	Lost wheel	1m37.377s		2
R	R Schumacher	Williams-BMW FW26	37	Crash damage	1m33.546s		2
R	R Zonta	Toyota TF104B	35	Gearbox	1m34.269s		2
R	C Klien	Jaguar-Cosworth R5	11	Crash damage	1m36.888s		0

CHAMPIONSHIP

	Driver	Pts
1	M Schumacher	136
2	R Barrichello	108
3	J Button	79
4	F Alonso	50
5	J Trulli	46
6	JP Montoya	46
7	K Räikkönen	34
8	D Coulthard	24
9	T Sato	23
10	G Fisichella	21
11	R Schumacher	12
12	F Massa	11
13	M Webber	7
14	O Panis	6
	A Pizzonia	6

	Constructor	Pts
1	Ferrari	244
2	BAR-Honda	105
3	Renault	96
4	Williams-BMW	64
5	McLaren-Mercedes	58
6	Sauber-Petronas	32
7	Jaguar-Cosworth	10
8	Toyota	9
9	Jordan-Ford	5
10	Minardi-Cosworth	1

Qualifying notes
Sato Back 10 places for engine change

Fastest race lap
M Schumacher 1m32.238s, on lap 55 (132.202mph) New lap record

Fastest through speed trap
G Fisichella 211.762mph
Slowest through speed trap
G Bruni 202.255mph

Fastest pit stop
K Räikkönen 23.555s
Slowest pit stop
Z Baumgartner 32.020s

Giancarlo Fisichella
"I was happy with seventh because my tyres were graining really badly. The car was very, very competitive on new tyres, but two seconds slower under graining."

Mark Webber
"I knew this race was going to be tough. I made a good start, taking Juan by Turn 1, and did all I could to make up places, but points were always going to be difficult."

Olivier Panis
"At the start the anti-stall kicked in and the car wouldn't get going, ending a good chance for a points-scoring result. I was at the back of the pack heading into Turn 1."

Nick Heidfeld
"I was pleasantly surprised at how well I was able to keep up with the cars in front. I just worked really hard to keep Panis behind me and was really happy to do so."

Gianmaria Bruni
"Glock blocked me at the start and Zsolt got ahead. I suffered a puncture on lap 10. I was able to reduce the gap to Zsolt until my front wheel came loose and I retired."

Felipe Massa
"I had a fantastic first lap and enjoyed my fight with Button. I was very happy to overtake him again after he had passed me, but then I suffered bad tyre graining."

Christian Klien
"On lap 12 on the long straight I could see Michael's Ferrari a long way behind me. I looked again, couldn't see him and turned in, only to make contact with his car."

Ricardo Zonta
"I was happy with the performance of the car; my speed was competitive enough, able to fight with Coulthard and Fisichella, but I lost fifth gear after my final pit stop."

Timo Glock
"The first five laps I experienced graining and watched Nick speed away from me. The tyres came back but I pushed too hard and spun. My aim was to finish and I did."

Zsolt Baumgartner
"For me, this was one of the most difficult races of the season. I struggled with the balance of the car after each stop, but this gradually improved as the stints wore on."

TYPHOON MICHAEL

Typhoon 22 threatened to wipe out the Japanese GP, but it blew by without damage, allowing Michael Schumacher to race to his record 13th win of the year

Typhoon 22 was all set to hit Suzuka on Saturday, and so severe was it expected to be that all of the day's track activities were cancelled. Which meant qualifying had to be postponed until Sunday morning. As it happened, the typhoon missed Suzuka by 40 miles, but still the weather had juggled the variables surely? No-one had done any dry-track running going into the race – the two qualifying sessions having been held on a damp but drying track that put those out late in pre-qualifying at a big advantage – and no-one had been able to establish baseline data for fuel consumption, tyre usage or car set-up.

Yet what unfolded was a remarkably standard-looking 2004 race, with Michael Schumacher's Ferrari running away from pole position and hiding from the rest of the field, once brother Ralf's Williams-BMW had made an early first stop from only a few seconds behind. The Williams went on to finish runner-up, comfortably beating the BAR-Hondas of Jenson Button and Takuma Sato, although third and fourth places virtually guaranteed BAR runner-up spot in the constructors' championship ahead of Renault.

The only man who might have threatened Schuey, his team-mate Rubens Barrichello, had fought through the midfield (where his poor grid position had put him) when he tried to pass David Coulthard for fifth place. Into the chicane, the McLaren man didn't budge and both protagonists were forced to retire with deranged front suspensions.

The Renaults weren't as quick as normal, but Fernando Alonso drove a relentless race to take fifth. This was much better than team-mate Jacques Villeneuve, who continued to struggle in his comeback and held up a train of out-of-position faster cars for much of the race before finishing 10th. Behind Alonso were Kimi Räikkönen, Juan Pablo Montoya and Giancarlo Fisichella, all of whom had been delayed as they tried to find a way past the 1997 champion.

When Typhoon 22 had passed, the sun shone, particularly on Michael Schumacher who won as he pleased for Ferrari

ROUND **17**

JAPAN
2004 FORMULA 1™ FUJI
TELEVISION JAPANESE
GRAND PRIX
Suzuka

LAP BY LAP ACTION

53 laps / 191 miles

Schumachers to the fore as Michael leads away from Ralf et al

Panis and Barrichello spent the early laps jousting with each other

Alonso, Montoya, Räikkönen and Barrichello enjoy a fierce battle

Toyota debutant Trulli holds off Montoya and Barrichello mid-race

Barrichello limps back to the pits to retire after clashing with Coulthard

Bouncing back from two poor races, Michael claims his 13th win

Start to lap 4
Before the start, the FIA declares an official change in meteorological conditions, enabling those who qualified on wet tyres – Bruni and both Jordan drivers – to switch to dry tyres. Baumgartner elects to start from pitlane. The Schumacher brothers make clean starts from the front row – Michael ahead of Ralf – and sweep into the lead. The World Champion opens up a 1.1s gap during the course of lap 1. Ralf easily holds on to second from Button, Sato, Trulli, Webber (a tardy start from third on the grid), Coulthard, Villeneuve, Fisichella, Alonso, Räikkönen, Montoya, Barrichello, Panis, Heidfeld, Klien, Glock, Massa, Bruni and Baumgartner. On lap 2, Panis passes Barrichello for 13th, and a lap later Fisichella dives past Villeneuve at Turn 1 to claim eighth.

Laps 5 to 12
By lap 5, Michael Schumacher's lead is out to 2.7s. Barrichello retakes 13th from Panis. A colossal traffic jam is forming behind eighth-placed Villeneuve. On lap 7 Alonso dives out of Villeneuve's slipstream at Turn 1, snatching eighth. Sato passes Button for third on lap 8, while an epic battle rages between Räikkönen, Montoya, Barrichello and Villeneuve. Montoya passes Räikkönen into Turn 1. Ralf pits on lap 9, as does Panis. The German rejoins in ninth, and on lap 10 Michael Schumacher leads Sato by 17.2s. On lap 11, Fisichella overtakes Webber for sixth. Webber, Montoya and Massa – up to 14th from the back of the grid – all pit, as does Bruni. A lap later, Sato, Trulli, Fisichella, Barrichello and Heidfeld head for the pits.

Laps 13 to 21
Michael pits on lap 13, rejoining 2.8s ahead of Button, and Alonso and Räikkönen make their first stops on lap 14. Button and Coulthard pit from second and third on lap 15, rejoining fourth and fifth. Villeneuve comes in, too. Klien and Baumgartner stop on lap 16, as the final runners to do so. The order on lap 17 sees the elder Schumacher ahead of his brother, followed by Sato, Button, Coulthard, Alonso, and then a fierce battle between Trulli, Webber, Montoya and Barrichello. On lap 18, Montoya passes Webber at Turn 1, then Webber pits, rejoining 18th, before retiring on lap 21.

Laps 22 to 31
By lap 22, Michael's lead over Ralf is 20.2s. Montoya passes Trulli on the approach to the chicane, but runs wide and loses places to both Trulli and Barrichello. On the next lap, Barrichello passes Trulli at Turn 1, and Montoya loses out to Fisichella at the same spot. Ralf Schumacher makes his second stop on lap 24, and resumes in fifth. Massa passes Villeneuve for 12th. Trulli pits on lap 25, followed by Michael Schumacher and Sato on lap 26, 36.1s apart. They rejoin in first and sixth respectively. Massa (11th) and Heidfeld (14th) come in, too. Fisichella pits from seventh on lap 27, and slips to 11th. Barrichello and Montoya, seventh and eighth, head for pitlane on lap 28. They re-emerge eighth and 10th.

Laps 32 to 41
Third-placed Coulthard makes his second pit stop on lap 32, and rejoins sixth. Alonso stops a lap later, slipping from fourth to eighth. On lap 34, Villeneuve makes his second, and final, stop. Button pits on lap 35, and rejoins in fourth, 3.3s behind Sato. On lap 36, Räikkönen makes his second stop, Panis his third. Coulthard and Barrichello clash on lap 38 while battling for fifth, and both retire. Michael and Ralf Schumacher both pit on lap 39. They resume first and third, split by Sato, who drops back, to the disappointment of the fans, when he makes his final stop on lap 41, resuming behind Button. Montoya and Fisichella stop, too.

Lap 42 to the finish
Their stops behind them, the Schumachers are split by 23.7s on lap 42. Button runs third from Sato, Alonso, Räikkönen, Montoya, Fisichella, Villeneuve, Massa (the last unlapped runner), Trulli, Klien, Heidfeld, Panis, Glock, Bruni and Baumgartner. By lap 49, Sato is seen rubbing his neck. Alonso is catching him at about 0.5s per lap. Massa tries to pass Villeneuve for ninth at the chicane, but fails, finally succeeding on lap 50. Michael Schumacher cements his 13th win of the season on lap 53, beating Ralf by 14.0s. Button, Sato, Alonso, Räikkönen, Montoya and Fisichella complete the scorers.

INSIDE LINE
DAVID COULTHARD

It was the second successive collision in a row for me, though this time I was the attacked rather than the attacker. I was running in a strong fifth place and felt that Sato's fourth was a realistic target, but Rubens [Barrichello] was coming through the field.

We came flat through 130R up to the braking zone for the chicane. I think what he tried to do was similar to what I had tried to do to Ralf [Schumacher] in China. If you can make a pass the instant you catch someone, it often works because you don't get caught in their rhythm. He tried to use that, but just like me in China, I think he was a bit optimistic.

The difficulty for him here was how strong our car is on the brakes. It really is very good under braking, and that's where we find a lot of our lap time. So he happened to catch me going into the very area where we are really strong. I guess he didn't remember that as he made the dive.

It was a bit frustrating because things had gone quite well up to this point. Qualifying was a bit of a lottery, and I started from eighth but soon made progress. I passed Mark [Webber] for sixth going into the chicane, then lost a bit of time behind Trulli for a few laps until he pitted. It was then going to be a question of holding Rubens behind while attacking Sato.

Although I ended up taking no points away, I was happy with my performance. I was quicker than Kimi [Räikkönen], just as I was here last year. It's funny; this used to be a track where I struggled when I was a right-foot braker. I would always be three or four tenths slower than Mika here. But then, when I swapped, I was on a par with Mika and I've always been quicker here than Kimi. There's a lot of time to be found through the Esses, obviously, but there are other places where it's not so obvious where you can push, and others where it looks like you can but it's actually quicker to be patient.

It was nice to be on the front foot here and leading the team challenge. As soon as you're in that position your confidence goes up and you find time from that too. It all snowballs and I feel I gave a good account of myself to anyone who was thinking of employing me in 2005.

THE BIG QUESTION

Had F1 stumbled upon a better format?

Precautions against the expected typhoon meant no Saturday track activity, so giving Sunday a real wham-bam programme with pre-qualifying starting at 9am, followed by qualifying one hour later. With this compacted programme, the gap between the end of qualifying and the beginning of the race was only three-and-a-half hours.

The Sunday spectators got a very full day of entertainment, and the forcible re-jigging had no visible impact on the performances of teams and drivers. Was this accident of nature therefore a pointer to how things should be planned in future? With cost-cutting very much on F1's agenda, could F1 in the future have two-day meetings with Saturday becoming simply a test and practice day, with Sunday following the format we saw in Suzuka?

"Yes, why not?" said Flavio Briatore. "I have been saying for a long time we shouldn't be testing away from the races, because it costs money but doesn't add value."

Michael Schumacher was less certain. "It was very interesting," he said, "but I don't think it would be a good idea as a regular feature. It makes things very awkward from an operational point of view, and of knowing whether you've made the correct choices. Also, if you damaged your car in qualifying, it could be very awkward given how little time there is. It all puts a lot of stress on the mechanics and the preparation. It was exciting, but I prefer the old style."

However, the drastic reduction in time for team debriefs and strategy simulations that concerned Michael may well be the very thing in its favour in terms of mixing up the order from race to race. Then again, looking at how this race panned out, that ain't necessarily so either.

Fernando Alonso splashes around, trying to learn as much as possible in a restricted timetable

ROSS BRAWN
FERRARI TECHNICAL DIRECTOR

We've seen pretty often this year that we can be very quick straight away, and that was a real advantage here at Suzuka when there had been so little prior running because of the weather. It's down to the quality of our engineers and the simulation.

It wasn't a straightforward task to be ready either, because we brought a different sort of tyre to Japan. It was similar to that used in Hungary and China, but with a different compound, one that was fairly soft by the standards of this track – which is very hard on tyres – but which we chose because we knew it would perform well in damp conditions. However, setting the car up around this tyre is very different than with the type of tyre we used for most of the races this year. Basically, we had to extrapolate from our Hungary set-up.

It worked perfectly. Bridgestone did a terrific job with it. It came up to temperature quickly, yet was consistently fast. There was a little bit of graining in the first stint, as I think there was with everyone on such a green track, but thereafter it was really good. The choice of compound committed us to a three-stop race, which was fine for Michael starting from the front, but it meant that Rubens, starting from 15th, was up against it. The fact that Michael had finished so far back in China really worked to his advantage here, with qualifying being held on a damp but drying track. Rubens almost overcame the running slot disadvantage his China win gave him, but ran wide at the chicane. The conditions were very tricky. Michael had watched Rubens do this and so had taken it on board when he came to do his run near the end.

With Michael, we monitored Ralf early on, but when he made his first stop four laps earlier than us, it became quite straightforward. With Rubens, we were trying to tailor his strategy to the traffic, but he had a job on his hands. Once he got clear of the pack that had been held up by Villeneuve, he was able to lap just as fast as Michael, but he was a long way behind by then. Had he not had the collision with Coulthard, I reckon he would have finished fifth, maybe even fourth. The accident was just one of those things. I don't think Coulthard expected him to be there.

Michael benefitted from starting on pole, and from Ralf making his first stop four laps earlier

JAMES ROBINSON
JORDAN
HEAD OF
ENGINEERING

It was a hard race, and we had a number of technical problems on the way to 13th place with Nick [Heidfeld] and 15th with Timo [Glock]. We had to limit Timo's performance part-way through the race because of an engine problem.

Nick did his usual very professional job while, for Timo, it was very tough coming to this track new and then getting very little prior running on it because of the weather during the practice days. His first ever dry lap of the place was the first lap of the race, so we feel he came through okay.

Because of the tyre characteristics, we were obliged to three-stop. Nick got off to a good start and was pushing Panis's Toyota for most of the first stint. Because everyone had done a best guess for set-up, invariably there were compromises, and Nick was reporting that he had excessive oversteer during this time. There was also some issue with the electronics that were giving him occasional gear selection problems. But he stayed hard on it, and was very quick and consistent throughout.

We adjusted his front wing at the first stop, and his pace picked up by an average of 0.4s per lap in the second stint. It was during this time that he was able to pass Panis on-track, something quite satisfying for us given the difference in budget between the two teams. With some further adjustments of the software, he was a couple of tenths quicker still in the third stint. We were at this stage fighting with Klien's Jaguar for 12th, but they were on a two-stop strategy so we had to try to pull out enough time to give us the extra stop. Unfortunately, we couldn't quite do that. But it was a great effort from Nick. He really has been superb all year, both in his driving and his feedback. A really big asset.

Timo never got a balance he was happy with, even though we were making changes for him at the stops. He also had some gearbox problems, and that may have contributed towards his quick spin mid-race. Towards the end, he was hit a glancing blow as he was lapped by Räikkönen. So it was a very busy afternoon for him.

	Heidfeld	Glock
Stint 1 avg. lap time	1m 37.0s Front wing changed	1m 38.3s Front wing changed
Stint 2 avg. lap time	1m 36.6s	1m 38.1s Engine map turned down
Stint 3 avg. lap time	1m 36.4s	1m 38.6s
Stint 4	Positions decided	

Nick Heidfeld leads
Timo Glock in a race that
improved as it went on
for the team leader

RACE RESULTS

JAPAN
SUZUKA

RACE DATE October 10th
CIRCUIT LENGTH 3.608 miles
NO. OF LAPS 53
RACE DISTANCE 191.126 miles
WEATHER warm and dry, 27°C
TRACK TEMP 32°C
RACE ATTENDANCE 156,000
LAP RECORD Rubens Barrichello, 1m 32.730s, 139.998mph, 2004

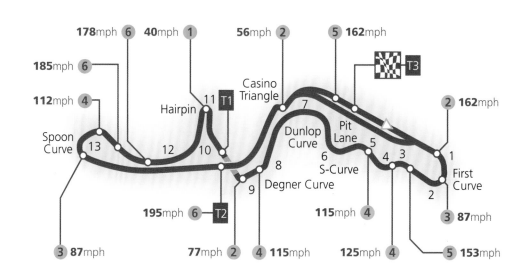

PRACTICE 1

	Driver	Time	Laps
1	M Schumacher	1m47.906s	5
2	G Fisichella	1m48.362s	8
3	R Barrichello	1m49.846s	4
4	J Button	1m49.937s	5
5	N Heidfeld	1m51.438s	7
6	K Räikkönen	1m51.530s	5
7	T Glock	1m52.602s	8
8	JP Montoya	1m53.517s	4
9	R Doornbos		10
10	F Alonso	1m54.012s	4
11	B Leinders		10
12	R Schumacher	1m55.632s	5
13	J Villeneuve	1m57.547s	5
14	J Trulli	1m58.351s	10
15	A Davidson		4
16	G Bruni	2m02.825s	5
17	Z Baumgartner	2m03.955s	7
18	D Coulthard	no time	3
19	T Sato	no time	1
20	F Massa	no time	3
21	M Webber	no time	2
22	C Klien	no time	3
23	O Panis	no time	1
24	B Wirdheim		0
25	R Briscoe		0

PRACTICE 2

	Driver	Time	Laps
1	M Schumacher	1m45.388	5
2	G Fisichella	1m46.102	4
3	K Räikkönen	1m46.749	5
4	R Barrichello	1m46.874	5
5	D Coulthard	1m48.033	7
6	T Glock	1m49.277	8
7	N Heidfeld	1m49.286	4
8	T Sato	1m49.370	6
9	A Davidson		12
10	J Villeneuve	1m49.672	8
11	F Alonso	1m49.712	7
12	R Schumacher	1m49.736	4
13	JP Montoya	1m50.060	3
14	J Trulli	1m50.386	7
15	M Webber	1m50.666	9
16	R Doornbos		11
17	C Klien	1m52.232	9
18	B Leinders		8
19	G Bruni	1m53.194	6
20	J Button	1m53.842	3
21	Z Baumgartner	1m54.703	8
22	F Massa	no time	2
23	O Panis	no time	1
24	B Wirdheim		0
25	R Briscoe		0

PRACTICE 3

Driver	Time	Laps
Session cancelled		

PRACTICE 4

Driver	Time	Laps
Session cancelled		

Best sectors – Qualifying

Sector 1	M Schumacher	31.677s
Sector 2	R Schumacher	41.536s
Sector 3	M Schumacher	20,124s

Speed trap – Qualifying

1	M Schumacher	179.585mph
2	R Schumacher	179.585mph
3	G Fisichella	178.901mph

Michael Schumacher
"This was a historic day for F1, taking pole and the win on the same day. It was certainly exciting but I think I prefer the normal system! I had a trouble-free race."

Juan Pablo Montoya
"My starting position compromised my race. I got stuck in traffic and lost between one and two seconds every lap. The best I could do was score a couple of points."

Kimi Räikkönen
"A fairly uneventful race for me. I was struggling with the car and from 12th on the grid it's fairly limited what you can do. It was a race to forget to be honest."

Fernando Alonso
"From 11th the only thing I could do was to go maximum attack. From the back you never have clear track, so only at the end of my first stint could I run at my true pace."

Jenson Button
"Another podium was a fantastic result to celebrate BAR's 100th Grand Prix. As we got further into the race the car felt great and two-stopping really paid off for me."

Rubens Barrichello
"I was having a great race. It was a shame about the incident with Coulthard. I think I caught him by surprise, he closed the door and we touched. It was a racing incident."

Ralf Schumacher
"The start went okay and I was surprised I was able to follow Michael. I pitted four laps earlier, so he was obviously heavier, but our car and strategy were both good."

David Coulthard
"We were looking to score points, but on lap 38 I had a coming together with Rubens at the chicane while he was trying to pass. I don't think anybody is to blame."

Jacques Villeneuve
"After the start we quickly found that the set-up was not ideal for the dry conditions. The car was understeering a lot, so we added front downforce at both pitstops."

Takuma Sato
"It was extremely difficult to work out the set-up. As it turned out I was not able to get the podium I wanted, but at the end of the day it was a great result for the team."

POSITIONS LAP BY LAP

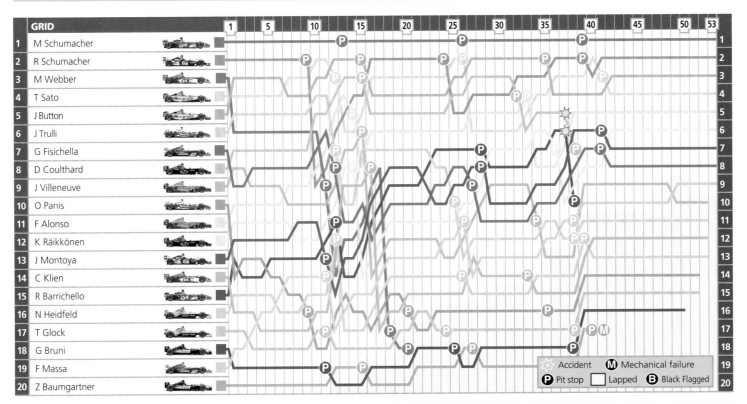

GRID			
1	M Schumacher		
2	R Schumacher		
3	M Webber		
4	T Sato		
5	J Button		
6	J Trulli		
7	G Fisichella		
8	D Coulthard		
9	J Villeneuve		
10	O Panis		
11	F Alonso		
12	K Räikkönen		
13	J Montoya		
14	C Klien		
15	R Barrichello		
16	N Heidfeld		
17	T Glock		
18	G Bruni		
19	F Massa		
20	Z Baumgartner		

☆ Accident   Ⓜ Mechanical failure
Ⓟ Pit stop   ☐ Lapped   Ⓑ Black Flagged

QUALIFYING

	Driver	Pre-qual time	Pos	Time
1	M Schumacher	1m38.397s	2	1m33.542s
2	R Schumacher	1m38.864s	3	1m34.032s
3	M Webber	1m39.170s	4	1m34.571s
4	T Sato	1m40.135s	6	1m34.897s
5	J Button	1m41.423s	10	1m35.157s
6	J Trulli	1m37.716s	1	1m35.213s
7	G Fisichella	1m40.151s	7	1m36.136s
8	D Coulthard	1m41.126s	9	1m36.156s
9	J Villeneuve	1m41.857s	13	1m36.274s
10	O Panis	1m40.029s	5	1m36.420s
11	F Alonso	1m42.056s	15	1m36.663s
12	K Räikkönen	1m41.517s	11	1m36.820s
13	JP Montoya	1m44.370s	18	1m37.653s
14	C Klien	1m42.054s	14	1m38.258s
15	R Barrichello	1m41.001s	8	1m38.637s
16	N Heidfeld	1m42.434s	16	1m41.953s
17	T Glock	1m43.682s	17	1m43.533s
18	G Bruni	1m45.415s	19	1m48.069s
19	F Massa	1m41.707s	12	no time
20	Z Baumgartner	no time	20	no time

RACE

	Driver	Car	Laps	Time	Fastest	Avg. mph	Stops
1	M Schumacher	Ferrari F2004	53	1h24m26.985s	1m32.796s	135.791	3
2	R Schumacher	Williams-BMW FW26	53	1h24m41.083s	1m33.467s	135.414	3
3	J Button	BAR-Honda 006	53	1h24m46.647s	1m33.819s	135.266	2
4	T Sato	BAR-Honda 006	53	1h24m58.766s	1m33.742s	134.944	3
5	F Alonso	Renault R24	53	1h25m04.752s	1m34.279s	134.787	2
6	K Räikkönen	McLaren-Mercedes MP4-19B	53	1h25m06.347s	1m33.920s	134.744	2
7	JP Montoya	Williams-BMW FW26	53	1h25m22.332s	1m33.779s	134.324	3
8	G Fisichella	Sauber-Petronas C23	53	1h25m23.261s	1m33.850s	134.299	3
9	F Massa	Sauber-Petronas C23	53	1h25m56.641s	1m33.614s	133.430	3
10	J Villeneuve	Renault R24	52	1h24m28.973s	1m35.290s	133.175	2
11	J Trulli	Toyota TF104B	52	1h24m35.505s	1m34.626s	133.004	3
12	C Klien	Jaguar-Cosworth R5	52	1h25m01.022s	1m35.261s	132.338	2
13	N Heidfeld	Jordan-Ford EJ14	52	1h25m09.577s	1m35.524s	132.117	3
14	O Panis	Toyota TF104B	51	1h24m30.991s	1m34.438s	130.560	3
15	T Glock	Jordan-Ford EJ14	51	1h25m08.892s	1m36.667s	129.592	3
16	G Bruni	Minardi-Cosworth PS04	50	1h25m20.899s	1m39.352s	126.751	3
R	Z Baumgartner	Minardi-Cosworth PS04	41	Spun off	1m39.434s		3
R	D Coulthard	McLaren-Mercedes MP4-19B	38	Accident	1m33.917s		2
R	R Barrichello	Ferrari F2004	38	Accident	1m32.730s		2
R	M Webber	Jaguar-Cosworth R5	20	Driver pain	1m34.229s		2

CHAMPIONSHIP

	Driver	Pts
1	M Schumacher	146
2	R Barrichello	108
3	J Button	85
4	F Alonso	54
5	JP Montoya	48
6	J Trulli	46
7	K Räikkönen	37
8	T Sato	31
9	D Coulthard	24
10	G Fisichella	22
11	R Schumacher	20
12	F Massa	11
13	M Webber	7
14	O Panis	6
	A Pizzonia	6

	Constructor	Pts
1	Ferrari	254
2	BAR-Honda	116
3	Renault	100
4	Williams-BMW	74
5	McLaren-Mercedes	61
6	Sauber-Petronas	33
7	Jaguar-Cosworth	10
8	Toyota	9
9	Jordan-Ford	5
10	Minardi-Cosworth	1

Fastest Lap
R Barrichello 1m32.730s, on lap 30 (139.998mph)
New lap record

Fastest through speed trap
F Massa 196.500mph
Slowest through speed trap
Z Baumgartner 178.000mph

Fastest pit stop
JP Montoya 20.816s
Slowest pit stop
M Webber 38.215s

Giancarlo Fisichella
"My only problem came on lap 16 when I ran off at the Spoon Curve. I was radioing the pits and left my braking late as I lost concentration, but I recovered quite well."

Mark Webber
"My start wasn't as good as I'd have liked and I lost three places. On lap 7 I noticed the cockpit becoming increasingly hot. It was soon excruciatingly hot and I retired."

Olivier Panis
"I had a lot of graining and couldn't push, but I'm happy I could complete my last F1 race in front of the Japanese fans. To stop after 11 years was a special moment."

Nick Heidfeld
"In the circumstances, given that we did not have a lot of time to practice here, I was happy with our starting set-up and what we managed to achieve in the race."

Gianmaria Bruni
"It turned out to be quite an uneventful race, and we struggled with oversteer, but it was good to finish at Suzuka because that is always the team's first ambition."

Felipe Massa
"It was fantastic! I really enjoyed myself. I was able to push hard right from the start and I did a lot of overtaking. I pulled some great moves so it was really satisfying."

Christian Klien
"I had not had any dry practice on this track, so the race was really my first chance to learn it. I was pleased that the race went smoothly and I was able to finish."

Jarno Trulli
"I was up to fifth at the end of the first lap. Unfortunately there was a big tyre drop-off, but it was my race debut for Toyota and I gathered a lot of valuable experience."

Timo Glock
"Overall it was a difficult day. The car set-up wasn't that good and I had over- and understeer. I had big problems and just couldn't find rhythm. All in all, a bad race."

Zsolt Baumgartner
"Overall it was not my weekend, although my pace in the race was not too bad. I made a mistake after pushing really hard after my final stop and went off track."

São Paulistas hoped for a win at last for Barrichello, but Montoya was best on the day

GRAND FINALE

The final race of the campaign was a cracker, with Juan Pablo Montoya pipping Räikkönen to win on his final Williams outing

Here was as great a race as we saw all season, a fitting way to end the year. It was also a fitting farewell present to Williams from Juan Pablo Montoya, who exorcised the ghost of his retirement from the lead here in 2001 with a great win over his future McLaren team-mate Kimi Räikkönen. From the moment that they ran side-by-side down pitlane on lap five, to the finish 66 laps later, these two were locked in combat. It was a flat-out struggle for supremacy the whole way.

Rubens Barrichello, after exciting the partisan fans with pole position, again had circumstances conspire against him in his quest to finally win his home Grand Prix. A steady drizzle just before the start ensured that the early stages of the race were definitely Michelin territory, and he lost a lot of time in his Bridgestone-shod Ferrari. Third place was the maximum he could have hoped for on this day, and he achieved that. It was certainly better than team-mate Michael Schumacher, who was a quiet seventh from a penalised 18th on the grid.

Arguably the drive of the race was that of Fernando Alonso in fourth place. The Renault was one of only three cars to start on dry-weather tyres, enabling him to take the lead when the wet-shod cars had to make their switch early in the race. The R24 didn't have the pace to allow him to maintain that position, though, and he was on an unsuitable compound of tyre that led the team to double-stint the fronts, leaving him with a severe grip problem for most of the last stint. He was nonetheless flawless in his defence from a whole train of much quicker cars, and his securing of the place clinched him fourth place in the championship, one point ahead of Montoya.

ROUND **18**

BRAZIL
FORMULA 1™
GRAND PRÊMIO DO
BRASIL 2004
São Paulo

LAP BY LAP
ACTION

71 laps / 190 miles

Barrichello leads away for Ferrari from Räikkönen and Montoya

Start and lap 1

Light rain begins to fall 45 minutes before the start, and the FIA declares a change in climatic conditions. Alonso (eighth), Coulthard (12th) and Villeneuve (13th) are the only drivers to start on dry tyres. Local hero Barrichello leads from pole position, but Räikkönen passes him at Turn 3. Massa lies third, but Button overhauls him before the end of the lap. Montoya, Sato, Ralf Schumacher, Trulli, Klien, Michael Schumacher (up from 18th after a 10-position grid penalty), Zonta, Heidfeld, Webber, Glock, Alonso, Villeneuve, Coulthard, Fisichella, Bruni and Baumgartner complete the order.

Laps 2 to 6

Villeneuve runs wide at Turn 1 on lap 2, but rejoins. Montoya passes Massa who, in turn, passes Button. On lap 3, Michael Schumacher spins at Turn 2, dropping to 13th. Button slips to ninth place. Barrichello repasses Räikkönen for the lead at Turn 1 on lap 4. Button stops amid a trail of engine smoke. Ralf Schumacher pits for dry tyres. The dry-shod Alonso – running 15th – sets the fastest lap so far. On lap 5, Barrichello and Massa press on, as Räikkönen, Montoya, Sato, Trulli and Michael Schumacher pit for dries. Räikkönen and Montoya exit the pits side-by-side, but the Finn stays in front... until Turn 4, where Montoya slices ahead. Barrichello pits a lap later, and Massa leads. Jaguar team-mates Klien and Webber pit at the same time with Zonta also in.

Michael Schumacher found himself in the pack, fighting with Zonta...

Laps 7 to 25

On lap 7, Massa is the last wet-shod front-runner to stop. The order settles down on lap 9, with Alonso leading Montoya, Räikkönen, Ralf Schumacher, Sato, Barrichello, Villeneuve, Massa, Coulthard and Michael Schumacher. One lap on, Coulthard and Michael Schumacher pass Massa. Schumacher moves up another place on lap 14, as Coulthard pits. On lap 16, Heidfeld goes off-track and retires. Alonso makes his first stop on lap 18, rejoining sixth, and Montoya leads. The order on lap 20 is Montoya, Räikkönen, Ralf Schumacher, Sato, Barrichello and Alonso, as Villeneuve pits from seventh. Michael Schumacher is next up. On lap 24, battling for 10th, Klien and Webber collide at Turn 1 when the Australian dives inside his team-mate. Webber retires, and Klien pits for repairs.

...before he rotated on lap 3, forcing Webber to hit the brakes

Laps 26 to 53

On lap 26, Ralf Schumacher makes his second stop, from third, rejoining seventh. On the following lap, Sato and Barrichello pit from third and fourth. Montoya pits to cede the lead to Räikkönen on lap 28. Michael Schumacher (fifth) and Trulli (ninth) also stop. Räikkönen pits on lap 29, and Montoya retakes the lead. He rejoins second ahead of Alonso, Ralf Schumacher, Sato, Barrichello, Massa, Fisichella, Michael Schumacher and Villeneuve. On lap 33, Sato runs wide at Turn 1, dropping to sixth. Two laps later, Montoya leads by 5.3s, controlling the gap to Räikkönen. Alonso pits from third on lap 47, and on the following lap Ralf Schumacher pits from fourth. Barrichello pits on lap 49, and vaults both Alonso and Ralf Schumacher. Montoya stops on lap 50, as does Michael Schumacher. Räikkönen leads again. Massa pits on lap 53.

Just four laps in, Button's race was run, his Honda engine blown

Laps 54 to 64

Sato pits on lap 54, rejoining ahead of Ralf Schumacher and gaining a place. Räikkönen pits on lap 55, but can't quite get out ahead of Montoya. Barrichello runs third, and Alonso heads Sato, Ralf and Michael Schumacher. Massa lies a distant eighth. On lap 56, Montoya leads by 1.4s, but by lap 59 Räikkönen cuts his deficit to 0.5s. Then, Montoya edges away again. Only 1.8s covers Alonso to Michael Schumacher, running fourth to seventh. On lap 64, Michael Schumacher has a pop at Ralf approaching Turn 4, but there's no way through.

The wrong impact for Jaguar, as Webber meets Klien at Turn 1...

Lap 65 to the finish

On lap 65, Montoya retains a 1s cushion. Barrichello is a lonely third. Räikkönen closes to within 0.6s on lap 68. Ralf Schumacher passes Sato for fifth on lap 70. On lap 71, Montoya wins his final race for Williams – the fourth F1 victory of his career – by 1s from Räikkönen. Barrichello takes third, his best result on home soil, from Alonso, Ralf Schumacher, Sato, Michael Schumacher and Massa. Fisichella is the last unlapped runner.

Montoya signs out from Williams in style before heading to McLaren

INSIDE LINE
JUAN PABLO MONTOYA

That was an unbelievable end to my time at Williams. What a way to go! Plus, it came at the place where I was robbed of a victory in just my third race with the team. It's been four years at Williams, we've had ups and downs, and to close all that with a win was fantastic.

When the rain came before the start, there was really no question of starting on dries. The full width of the track was wet all around the circuit. Plus, we were thinking about Kimi [Räikkönen]. We heard that he had a lot of fuel on board, and we didn't want to be stuck behind in the early stages. To make our strategy work, we needed track position, and we wouldn't have had that if we started on dries.

It was difficult to get temperature in the tyres at the beginning, and I didn't get a good start, but then the grip came and it was okay. Sam Michael and the team did a great job, calling me in early for dries, and that really played into my hands. I went side-by-side with Kimi as we came

down pitlane together, and though he had the inside line for the turn at the end of pitlane, I was able to get better momentum for the straight down to Turn 4, and that's where I did him. From there, I was in front of him the whole time, but he was always pushing, and I was flat-out pretty much the whole time.

After we made that first stop for the dries, and Alonso took the lead because he'd started on dries, I was a bit concerned. But then I began to think that in all the running during the weekend he hadn't been competitive with us, so I thought we would probably be fast enough to overcome his stop advantage, and we were.

Up to the final pit stops, Kimi was running a bit longer than us, so right before my stop I managed to do a couple of laps that gave me enough of a gap to stay ahead. He came out just behind, then I made a little mistake and I thought "whoa, don't do anything stupid, just keep it on the road," and I did.

Q THE BIG QUESTION

Can Rubinho ever win at home?

This was Rubens Barrichello's 12th home Grand Prix – and, for the 12th time, he failed to win it. Yet during qualifying, just as in 2003, it was looking as though the fairy story was about to slot into place.

Rubens was the fastest man around almost from the moment the cars first took to the track on Friday. The local hero seemed to have a small but decisive edge over team-mate Michael Schumacher. It was difficult to escape from the conclusion that Michael was getting rattled by this in the closing moments of Saturday practice. He was out on a hot lap, trying for the third time to beat Barrichello's earlier benchmark. Approaching Turn 6, the World Champion's Ferrari got out of shape and hit the tyre barriers side-on very hard. A brief engine fire ensured that Michael would have to be in the T-car and have a fresh engine fitted, the latter ensuring that he would have to take a 10-place grid penalty.

With Michael effectively out of the equation, fuelled heavy and penalised, Rubens duly reeled off a lap good enough for pole. All was right with his world until about half an hour before the start on race day. That's when the dark clouds began depositing a steady drizzle on to the track. Because of the characteristics of his Bridgestone tyres, Rubens needed it either to remain dry or rain heavily. "In the dry we're fastest, in the wet we're fastest," he said. "But in the damp we're in trouble." And so it proved.

Although Rubens took the lead from Kimi Räikkönen on the third lap, and held it until being forced to change to dry-weather rubber three laps later, the Bridgestone dries did not come into their operating band until around lap 17, by which time he had fallen a long way behind the Michelin-shod cars of Montoya and Räikkönen.

"I think I can leave here with my head held high," he said after finishing third. "That was the maximum possible today, and I achieved it. The win will just have to wait another year."

Barrichello looks happy enough, happy even for Montoya, but inside he must be hurting

NORBERT HAUG
MERCEDES SPORTING DIRECTOR

First of all, I would like to say thank you to David Coulthard, who was having his last race for us after 150 Grands Prix, a record for any driver/team combination. In that time, he has scored 12 victories and has been on the podium on average one race in three, a record that he can be very proud of and for which we are very grateful.

As for Kimi [Räikkönen], he drove a great race and pushed for victory the whole way, only narrowly missing out. It was very close, and could easily have been the other way around. The encouraging thing is that both ourselves and Williams showed that Ferrari are beatable. All through the early part of the year, people thought it couldn't happen, but we just kept pushing with our development, and since we brought in the 19B we have been on the front row six times from nine races.

The appearance of the rain before the start perhaps hurt us a little bit. We were all-set for a two-stop strategy, which in the dry I think would have given us the victory. As it was, everyone had to make their first pit stops very early to get on to dry-weather tyres, and that forced us to three-stop like everyone else. Kimi was faster than Juan in the end, but there was no chance by then to overtake him.

For sure, it was nice to see both of our 2005 drivers fighting for the victory, and obviously that's something we hope to see repeated next year, when Juan will also be in a McLaren-Mercedes.

On the podium one race in three for McLaren, Coulthard was unable to achieve this in Brazil

PAT SYMONDS
RENAULT
CHIEF OF
ENGINEERING

Although we lost out on second place in the constructors' championship, Fernando's drive here secured him fourth in the drivers' championship. It was one of his best drives of the year, all things considered. He had to contend with a lot of factors that made his race very difficult, and he came through superbly.

The tyre choice at the start of the race, with drizzle falling, was very difficult. The circuit seemed very slippery but, on the other hand, there wasn't a great deal of water falling, and so when it stopped it was likely to dry quite quickly. Furthermore, the Michelin dry-weather tyre is very good in how early it begins to work on a damp track. That being the case, we put both Fernando and Jacques [Villeneuve] on dries.

It was very difficult for them in the early laps, and Fernando actually spun on the first lap, while Jacques fell a long way back. Fernando was able to respond very quickly as the grip came up in the early laps, though, and you can see he was the fastest on the track as early as lap 4, quicker than all the wet-tyred runners. After they all made their stops, Fernando was able to lead and stay there until our first planned pit stop on lap 18.

We didn't have the pace to be able to continue at the front, and just pushed as hard as we could within those constraints. We had chosen the softer of the tyre compounds available to us, and it turned out to be the wrong choice. During his middle stint, Fernando got fairly severe graining of the fronts, and he did extremely well to keep up the pace that he did. As we came up to our second stop, it was important we retained track position, and so we couldn't afford to go through the graining process again. So we kept the same front tyres on. It kept him in fourth – which was as high as we could've got, given our pace – but he was soon in trouble, as the tyres were by now very worn. Fernando had to defend for over 20 laps from three faster cars, and he did it in masterful fashion. It was a superb drive.

Jacques was going quite quickly by the end of the race, but he suffered from his early delays in traffic.

Early lap dry-weather tyre performance comparison to fastest wet-tyre lap time

		Lap 1	2	3	4	5
Alonso	(soft compound)	+14.9s	+10.0s	+2.0s	-2.2s	-4.0s
Villeneuve	(hard compound)	+16.7s	+11.8s	+6.9s	+2.3s	-2.7s

Alonso had to make his tyres last, and impressed the team hugely as he clung on to fourth place

RACE RESULTS

BRAZIL
SÃO PAULO

RACE DATE October 24th
CIRCUIT LENGTH 2.677 miles
NO. OF LAPS 71
RACE DISTANCE 190.067 miles
WEATHER damp and cloudy, 25°C
TRACK TEMP 28°C
RACE ATTENDANCE 69,203
LAP RECORD Juan Pablo Montoya,
1m 11.473s, 134.837mph, 2004

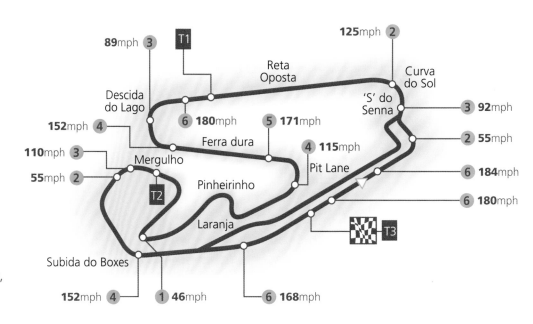

T1	89mph 3
Reta Oposta	
Curva do Sol	125mph 2
Descida do Lago	
'S' do Senna	3 92mph
6 180mph	5 171mph
152mph 4	
Ferra dura	2 55mph
110mph 3	4 115mph
Mergulho	Pit Lane
55mph 2	6 184mph
T2	Pinheirinho
	6 180mph
Laranja	T3
Subida do Boxes	
152mph 4	1 46mph
6 168mph	

PRACTICE 1

	Driver	Time	Laps
1	JP Montoya	1m12.547s	11
2	R Briscoe	1m12.614s	25
3	R Schumacher	1m12.873s	12
4	K Räikkönen	1m13.150s	4
5	A Davidson	1m13.232s	22
6	D Coulthard	1m13.277s	6
7	J Trulli	1m13.512s	15
8	T Sato	1m13.839s	10
9	R Barrichello	1m13.855s	13
10	F Alonso	1m13.990s	12
11	M Schumacher	1m14.042s	13
12	G Fisichella	1m14.118s	14
13	M Webber	1m14.147s	9
14	J Button	1m14.187s	13
15	R Zonta	1m14.207s	14
16	F Massa	1m14.479s	13
17	J Villeneuve	1m14.585s	13
18	R Doornbos	1m14.966s	27
19	B Wirdheim	1m15.065s	24
20	N Heidfeld	1m15.414s	12
21	C Klien	1m15.476s	15
22	Z Baumgartner	1m15.490s	12
23	T Glock	1m15.647s	18
24	G Bruni	1m16.406s	13
25	B Leinders	no time	1

PRACTICE 2

	Driver	Time	Laps
1	R Barrichello	1m11.166s	25
2	M Schumacher	1m11.334s	28
3	K Räikkönen	1m11.526s	20
4	J Button	1m11.731s	25
5	A Davidson	1m11.920s	31
6	T Sato	1m11.988s	23
7	F Alonso	1m12.005s	30
8	F Massa	1m12.183s	24
9	R Briscoe	1m12.209s	34
10	R Schumacher	1m12.235s	26
11	JP Montoya	1m12.280s	24
12	J Villeneuve	1m12.316s	31
13	R Doornbos	1m12.345s	27
14	R Zonta	1m12.347s	30
15	D Coulthard	1m12.430s	24
16	J Trulli	1m12.545s	36
17	G Fisichella	1m12.631s	29
18	M Webber	1m12.816s	35
19	N Heidfeld	1m13.114s	24
20	G Bruni	1m13.467s	31
21	C Klien	1m13.509s	32
22	T Glock	1m13.966s	24
23	Z Baumgartner	1m13.979s	25
24	B Wirdheim	1m14.303s	28
25	B Leinders	1m14.754s	10

PRACTICE 3

	Driver	Time	Laps
1	J Button	1m11.466s	9
2	T Sato	1m11.580s	11
3	K Räikkönen	1m11.591s	7
4	R Barrichello	1m11.641s	6
5	R Schumacher	1m11.714s	8
6	M Schumacher	1m11.740s	9
7	G Fisichella	1m11.985s	6
8	F Massa	1m12.064s	5
9	D Coulthard	1m12.085s	7
10	JP Montoya	1m12.208s	7
11	J Trulli	1m12.263s	5
12	M Webber	1m12.356s	8
13	F Alonso	1m12.563s	8
14	C Klien	1m12.612s	8
15	R Zonta	1m13.025s	10
16	N Heidfeld	1m13.327s	8
17	Z Baumgartner	1m14.284s	10
18	G Bruni	1m14.336s	11
19	T Glock	1m14.805s	11
20	J Villeneuve	no time	2

PRACTICE 4

	Driver	Time	Laps
1	R Barrichello	1m10.229s	15
2	M Schumacher	1m10.352s	15
3	K Räikkönen	1m10.385s	15
4	D Coulthard	1m10.413s	11
5	J Button	1m10.480s	16
6	F Alonso	1m10.683s	11
7	R Schumacher	1m10.997s	9
8	T Sato	1m11.127s	18
9	M Webber	1m11.130s	23
10	F Massa	1m11.142s	10
11	JP Montoya	1m11.157s	12
12	J Villeneuve	1m11.321s	18
13	G Fisichella	1m11.425s	5
14	R Zonta	1m11.688s	16
15	J Trulli	1m11.711s	15
16	C Klien	1m12.248s	21
17	N Heidfeld	1m12.299s	12
18	Z Baumgartner	1m12.990s	17
19	T Glock	1m13.818s	17
20	G Bruni	1m14.411s	16

Best sectors – Qualifying

Sector 1	R Barrichello	17.883s
Sector 2	R Barrichello	36.071s
Sector 3	R Schumacher	16.609s

Speed trap – Qualifying

	Driver	Speed
1	M Schumacher	201.520mph
2	F Massa	201.396mph
3	F Alonso	200.402mph

 Michael Schumacher

"When I realised it was raining, at first I thought it would be a good opportunity for me. But to be honest, it was never wet enough for us to have an advantage."

Juan Pablo Montoya

"It was unbelievable to end four years at Williams with a win. The race was decided by a good strategy and by Sam Michael calling me for slicks at just the right time."

Kimi Räikkönen

"I was close to winning, but just not close enough. After my first stop, I did what I could to keep Juan Pablo behind; perhaps I could have been a bit more aggressive."

 **Fernando Alonso**

"Starting on dry tyres was a risk – I went off on the first lap but, as the track dried, I was able to take the lead. After my first stop I didn't have the pace for a podium."

Jenson Button

"From the first red light at the start, I knew I had some kind of problem. There was a lot of smoke and fire as I left the grid. I tried to continue but the damage was done."

Rubens Barrichello

"The final result was disappointing after I had been dominant all weekend. The weather just didn't play into our hands, but I was still happy to be on the podium."

Ralf Schumacher

"Owing to the rain, my strategy did not pay off at all. But I have to say I was not fast enough to overtake Alonso, and as a consequence I missed out on a podium."

David Coulthard

"It took me a few laps to feel comfortable with the dry Michelin tyres. It was quite slippery. It was an emotional moment to say goodbye to the team after nine years."

 **Jacques Villeneuve**

"My race pace was actually very good. I lost time when the track was wet, and it was too risky to try to overtake Alonso. We were quick in the second and third stints."

Takuma Sato

"We chose to start on wets, but I was on a two-stop strategy, so lost time pitting for dries. After my last stop I had a great battle with Alonso, Ralf and Michael."

POSITIONS LAP BY LAP

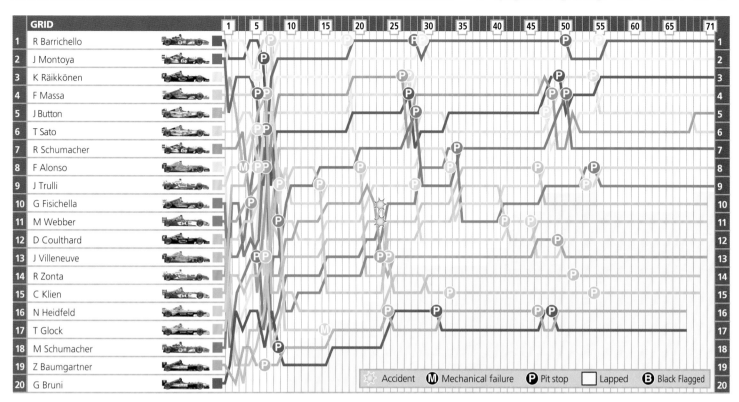

	GRID		1	5	10	15	20	25	30	35	40	45	50	55	60	65	71	
1	R Barrichello																	1
2	J Montoya																	2
3	K Räikkönen																	3
4	F Massa																	4
5	J Button																	5
6	T Sato																	6
7	R Schumacher																	7
8	F Alonso																	8
9	J Trulli																	9
10	G Fisichella																	10
11	M Webber																	11
12	D Coulthard																	12
13	J Villeneuve																	13
14	R Zonta																	14
15	C Klien																	15
16	N Heidfeld																	16
17	T Glock																	17
18	M Schumacher																	18
19	Z Baumgartner																	19
20	G Bruni																	20

Legend: ✷ Accident Ⓜ Mechanical failure Ⓟ Pit stop ▢ Lapped Ⓑ Black Flagged

QUALIFYING

	Driver	Pre-qual time	Pos	Time
1	R Barrichello	1m09.822s	1	1m10.646s
2	JP Montoya	1m09.862s	2	1m10.850s
3	K Räikkönen	1m10.440s	8	1m10.892s
4	F Massa	1m09.930s	3	1m10.922s
5	J Button	1m10.607s	11	1m11.092s
6	T Sato	1m10.373s	6	1m11.120s
7	R Schumacher	1m10.258s	5	1m11.131s
8	M Schumacher	1m10.192s	4	1m11.386s
9	F Alonso	1m10.637s	12	1m11.454s
10	J Trulli	1m10.478s	10	1m11.483s
11	G Fisichella	1m10.467s	9	1m11.571s
12	M Webber	1m11.230s	14	1m11.665s
13	D Coulthard	1m10.418s	7	1m11.750s
14	J Villeneuve	1m10.708	13	1m11.836s
15	R Zonta	1m11.315s	15	1m11.974s
16	C Klien	1m11.912s	17	1m12.211s
17	N Heidfeld	1m11.394s	16	1m12.829s
18	T Glock	1m12.242s	18	1m13.502s
19	Z Baumgartner	1m13.032s	20	1m13.550s
20	G Bruni	1m12.916s	19	no time

RACE

	Driver	Car	Laps	Time	Fastest	Ave mph	Stops
1	JP Montoya	Williams-BMW FW26	71	1h28m01.451s	1m11.473s	129.572	0
2	K Räikkönen	McLaren-Mercedes MP4-19B	71	128m02.473s	1m11.562s	129.547	0
3	R Barrichello	Ferrari F2004	71	1h28m25.550s	1m11.672s	128.983	0
4	F Alonso	Renault R24	71	1h28m50.359s	1m12.118s	128.383	0
5	R Schumacher	Williams-BMW FW26	71	1h28m51.191s	1m11.764s	128.363	0
6	T Sato	BAR-Honda 006	71	1h28m51.699s	1m11.941s	128.351	0
7	M Schumacher	Ferrari F2004	71	1h28m52.077s	1m11.763s	128.342	0
8	F Massa	Sauber-Petronas C23	71	1h29m03.761s	1m12.066s	128.061	0
9	G Fisichella	Sauber-Petronas C23	71	1h29m05.293s	1m11.877s	128.025	0
10	J Villeneuve	Renault R24	70	1h28m04.721s	1m12.210s	127.668	0
11	D Coulthard	McLaren-Mercedes MP4-19B	70	1h28m198.905s	1m12.522s	127.326	0
12	J Trulli	Toyota TF104B	70	1h28m32.201s	1m12.435s	127.007	0
13	R Zonta	Toyota TF104B	70	1h28m56.280s	1m12.961s	126.434	0
14	C Klien	Jaguar-Cosworth R5	69	1h28m12.131s	1m12.891s	125.668	0
15	T Glock	Jordan-Ford EJ14	69	1h29m03.524s	1m13.905s	124.459	0
16	Z Baumgartner	Minardi-Cosworth PS04	67	1h28m02.126s	1m14.743s	122.256	0
17	G Bruni	Minardi-Cosworth PS04	67	1h28m18.523s	1m14.756s	121.878	0
R	M Webber	Jaguar-Cosworth R5	23	Accident	1m13.197s	-	0
R	N Heidfeld	Jordan-Ford EJ14	15	Clutch	1m15.855s	-	1
R	J Button	BAR-Honda 006	3	Engine	1m24.440s	-	0

CHAMPIONSHIP

	Driver	Pts
1	M Schumacher	148
2	R Barrichello	114
3	J Button	85
4	F Alonso	59
5	JP Montoya	58
6	J Trulli	46
7	K Räikkönen	45
8	T Sato	34
9	R Schumacher	24
10	D Coulthard	24
11	G Fisichella	22
12	F Massa	12
13	M Webber	7
14	O Panis	6
15	A Pizzonia	6

	Constructor	Pts
1	Ferrari	262
2	BAR-Honda	119
3	Renault	105
4	Williams-BMW	88
5	McLaren-Mercedes	69
6	Sauber-Petronas	34
7	Jaguar-Cosworth	10
8	Toyota	9
9	Jordan Ford	5
10	Minardi-Cosworth	1

Qualifying notes
M Schumacher Back 10 places for engine change
G Bruni Back 10 places for engine change
Z Baumgartner Started race from pit lane

Fastest race lap
JP Montoya 1m11.473s,
on lap 49 (134.837mph)
New lap record

Fastest through speed trap
F Massa 203.068mph
Slowest through speed trap
N Heidfeld 188.710mph

Fastest pit stop
R Barrichello 23.354s
Slowest pit stop
Z Baumgartner 36.145s

Giancarlo Fisichella
"I was running very close to another car early on, and was caught out when it braked early. I took to the grass and lost time. A frustrating last race at Sauber."

Mark Webber
"I went to overtake Christian on lap 24. Unfortunately we tangled as he appeared not to see me coming. It was a sad end to what should have been a rewarding race."

Jarno Trulli
"I got a good start and was up to sixth, but I struggled every time the track was damp. As the track dried, I got more competitive and the car was better than at Suzuka."

Nick Heidfeld
"I had a good start and made up a couple of places, but I had to retire quite early with a clutch problem. It was a shame not to end the season with a good last race."

Gianmaria Bruni
"It wasn't a very good day for me. When I changed to dry tyres with the set-up we had, the car developed a lot of oversteer. I just concentrated on getting to the finish."

Felipe Massa
"It was a fantastic feeling, leading the race. I will never forget that lap. Early on, the car was very fast, but when the track dried it was hard to find grip in each stint."

Christian Klien
"Mark was getting closer, and I saw him in my mirror but I didn't think he was close enough to overtake. But he tried it and we collided. I was pleased to finish though."

Ricardo Zonta
"It was great to race in front of my home crowd. I think we did a good job. In the damp the speed of the car was good, but I had some balance problems at the end."

Timo Glock
"I didn't get a good line through the first corner, and then it was really slippery – the car was pretty nervous. After the first and second pit stops the car was much better."

Zsolt Baumgartner
"I'd picked up a cold in Brazil, and was a little worried about how I would be during the race. As it turned out, I was able to push hard to the end with a consistent pace."

DRIVER RESULTS

	Driver	Nationality	Car	ROUND 1 AUSTRALIAN GP March 6	ROUND 2 MALAYSIAN GP March 20	ROUND 3 BAHRAIN GP April 3	ROUND 4 SAN MARINO GP April 24	ROUND 5 SPANISH GP May 8	ROUND 6 MONACO GP May 22
1	M Schumacher	GER	Ferrari F2004	1PF	1P	1PF	1F	1PF	RF
2	R Barrichello	BRA	Ferrari F2004	2	4	2	6	2	3
3	J Button	GBR	BAR-Honda 006	6	3	3	2P	8	2
4	F Alonso	SPA	Renault R24	3	7	6	4	4	R
5	J Montoya	COL	Williams-BMW FW26	5	2F	13	3	R	4
6	J Trulli	ITA	Renault R24 / Toyota TF104B	7	5	4	5	3	1P
7	K Räikkönen	FIN	McLaren-Mercedes MP4-19 / McLaren-Mercedes MP4-19B	R	R	R	8	11	R
8	T Sato	JAP	BAR-Honda 006	9	15	5	16	5	R
9	R Schumacher	GER	Williams-BMW FW26	4	R	7	7	6	10
10	D Coulthard	GBR	McLaren-Mercedes MP4-19 / McLaren-Mercedes MP4-19B	8	6	R	12	10	R
11	G Fisichella	ITA	Sauber-Petronas C23	10	11	11	9	7	R
12	F Massa	BRA	Sauber-Petronas C23	R	8	12	10	9	5
13	M Webber	AUS	Jaguar-Cosworth R5	R	R	8	13	12	R
14	O Panis	FRA	Toyota TF104 / Toyota TF104B	13	12	9	11	R	8
15	A Pizzonia	BRA	Williams-BMW FW26						
16	C Klien	AUT	Jaguar-Cosworth R5	11	10	14	14	R	R
17	C da Matta	BRA	Toyota TF104 / Toyota TF104B	12	9	10	R	13	6
18	N Heidfeld	GER	Jordan-Ford EJ14	R	R	15	R	R	7
19	T Glock	GER	Jordan-Ford EJ14						
20	Z Baumgartner	HUN	Minardi-Cosworth PS04	R	16	R	15	R	9
	J Villeneuve	CDN	Renault R24						
	R Zonta	BRA	Toyota TF104B						
	M Gené	SPA	Williams-BMW FW26						
	G Pantano	ITA	Jordan-Ford EJ14	14	13	16	R	R	R
	G Bruni	ITA	Minardi-Cosworth PS04	NC	14	17	R	R	R

RACE SCORING

1st	10	POINTS
2nd	8	POINTS
3rd	6	POINTS
4th	5	POINTS
5th	4	POINTS
6th	3	POINTS
7th	2	POINTS
8th	1	POINT

DATA KEY

D	DISQUALIFIED
F	FASTEST LAP
NC	NON-CLASSIFIED
NS	NON-STARTER
P	POLE POSITION
R	RETIRED
W	WITHDRAWN

Race results for both drivers, ie. first and second listed as 1/2 with team's best result listed first

CONSTRUCTOR RESULTS

1	Ferrari
2	BAR-Honda
3	Renault
4	Williams-BMW
5	McLaren-Mercedes
6	Sauber-Petronas
7	Jaguar-Cosworth
8	Toyota
9	Jordan-Ford
10	Minardi-Cosworth

Drivers' Championship (Rounds 7–18)

R7 European GP (May 29)	R8 Canadian GP (June 12)	R9 United States GP (June 19)	R10 French GP (July 3)	R11 British GP (July 10)	R12 German GP (July 24)	R13 Hungarian GP (Aug 14)	R14 Belgian GP (Aug 28)	R15 Italian GP (Sept 11)	R16 Chinese GP (Sept 25)	R17 Japanese GP (Oct 9)	R18 Brazilian GP (Oct 23)	TOTAL POINTS
1PF	1	1	1F	1F	1P	1PF	2	2	12F	1P	7	148
2	2F	2PF	3	3	12	2	3	1PF	1P	RF	3P	114
3	3	R	5	4	2	5	R	3	2	3	R	85
5	R	R	2P	10	3	3	R	R	4	5	4	59
8	D	D	8	5	5	4	R	5	5	7	1F	58
4	R	4	4	R	11	R	9P	10		11	12	46
R	5	6	7	2P	RF	R	1F	R	3	6	2	45
R	R	3	R	11	8	6	R	4	6	4	6	34
R	DP	R							R	2	5	24
R	6	7	6	7	4	9	7	6	9	R	11	24
6	4	9	12	6	9	8	5	8	7	8	9	22
9	R	R	13	9	13	R	4	12	8	9	8	12
7	R	R	9	8	6	10	R	9	10	R	R	7
11	D	5	15	R	14	11	8	R	14	14		6
					7	7	R	7				6
12	D	R	11	14	10							3
R	D	R	14	13	R	R	10	11	R		13	3
10	8	R	16	15	R	12	11	14	13	13	R	3
						13	6	13	R		14	3
	7								15	15		2
15	10	8	R	R	16	15	R	15	16	R	16	1
									11	10	10	
			10	12								
13		R	17	R	15	R	R	R				
14	R	R	18	16	17	14	R	R	R	16	17	

Constructors' Championship (Rounds 1–18)

R1 Australian GP (Mar 6)	R2 Malaysian GP (Mar 20)	R3 Bahrain GP (Apr 3)	R4 San Marino GP (Apr 24)	R5 Spanish GP (May 8)	R6 Monaco GP (May 22)	R7 European GP (May 29)	R8 Canadian GP (June 12)	R9 United States GP (June 19)	R10 French GP (July 3)	R11 British GP (July 10)	R12 German GP (July 24)	R13 Hungarian GP (Aug 14)	R14 Belgian GP (Aug 28)	R15 Italian GP (Sept 11)	R16 Chinese GP (Sept 25)	R17 Japanese GP (Oct 9)	R18 Brazilian GP (Oct 23)	TOTAL POINTS
1/2	1/4	1/2	1/6	1/2	3/R	1/2	1/2	1/2	1/3	1/3	1/12	1/2	2/3	1/2	1/12	1/R	3/7	262
6/9	3/15	3/5	2/16	5/8	2/R	3/R	3/R	3/R	5/R	4/11	2/8	5/6	R/R	3/4	2/6	3/4	6/R	119
3/7	5/7	4/6	4/5	3/4	1/R	4/5	R/R	4/R	2/4	10/R	3/11	3/R	9/R	10/R	4/11	5/10	4/10	105
4/5	2/R	7/13	3/7	6/R	4/10	8/R	D/D	R/D	8/10	5/12	5/5	4/7	R/R	5/7	5/R	2/7	1/5	88
8/R	6/R	R/R	8/12	10/11	R/R	R/R	5/6	6/7	6/7	2/7	4/R	9/R	1/7	6/R	3/9	6/R	2/11	69
10/R	8/11	11/12	9/10	7/9	5/R	6/9	4/R	9/R	12/13	6/9	9/13	8/R	5/4	8/12	7/8	8/9	8/9	34
11/R	10/R	8/14	13/14	12/R	R/R	7/12	9/R	R/R	9/11	8/14	6/10	10/13	6/R	9/13	10/R	12/R	14/R	10
12/13	9/12	9/10	11/R	13/R	6/8	11/R	D/D	5/R	14/15	13/R	14/R	11/R	8/10	11/R	14/R	11/14	12/13	9
14/R	13/R	15/16	R/R	R/R	7/R	10/13	7/8	R/R	16/17	15/R	15/R	12/R	11/R	14/R	13/15	13/15	15/R	5
NC/R	14/16	17/R	15/R	R/R	9/R	14/15	10/R	8/R	18/R	16/R	16/17	14/15	R/R	15/R	16/R	16/R	16/17	1

FORMULA ONE STATISTICS

STARTS

256	Riccardo Patrese
213	Michael Schumacher
210	Gerhard Berger
208	Andrea de Cesaris
204	Nelson Piquet
201	Jean Alesi
199	Alain Prost
198	Rubens Barrichello
194	Michele Alboreto
187	Nigel Mansell
176	Graham Hill
175	David Coulthard
	Jacques Laffite
171	Niki Lauda
164	Thierry Boutsen
162	Mika Häkkinen
	Johnny Herbert
161	Ayrton Senna
159	Heinz-Harald Frentzen
158	Martin Brundle
	Olivier Panis
152	John Watson
149	René Arnoux
147	Eddie Irvine
	Derek Warwick
146	Carlos Reutemann
144	Emerson Fittipaldi
142	Giancarlo Fisichella
135	Jean-Pierre Jarier
134	Jacques Villeneuve
132	Eddie Cheever
	Clay Regazzoni
130	Jarno Trulli
128	Mario Andretti
127	Ralf Schumacher
126	Jack Brabham
123	Ronnie Peterson
119	Pierluigi Martini
116	Damon Hill
	Jacky Ickx
	Alan Jones
114	Keke Rosberg

OTHERS

85	Nick Heidfeld
84	Jenson Button
68	Juan Pablo Montoya
	Kimi Räikkönen
51	Fernando Alonso
50	Mark Webber
37	Ricardo Zonta
36	Marc Gené
	Takuma Sato
34	Felipe Massa
28	Cristiano da Matta
20	Zsolt Baumgartner
18	Gianmaria Bruni
	Christian Klien
15	Antonio Pizzonia
14	Giorgio Pantano
4	Timo Glock

CONSTRUCTORS

704	Ferrari
577	McLaren
496	Williams
490	Lotus
418	Tyrrell
409	Prost
394	Brabham
383	Arrows
322	Minardi
317	Benetton
231	Jordan
230	March
198	Sauber
197	BRM

OTHERS

174	Renault
134	Jaguar
101	BAR
51	Toyota

WINS

83	Michael Schumacher
51	Alain Prost
41	Ayrton Senna
31	Nigel Mansell
27	Jackie Stewart
25	Jim Clark
	Niki Lauda
24	Juan Manuel Fangio
23	Nelson Piquet
22	Damon Hill
20	Mika Häkkinen
16	Stirling Moss
14	Jack Brabham
	Emerson Fittipaldi
	Graham Hill
13	Alberto Ascari
	David Coulthard
12	Mario Andretti
	Alan Jones
	Carlos Reutemann
11	Jacques Villeneuve
10	Gerhard Berger
	James Hunt
	Ronnie Peterson
	Jody Scheckter

OTHERS

9	Rubens Barrichello
6	Ralf Schumacher
4	Juan Pablo Montoya
2	Kimi Räikkönen
1	Giancarlo Fisichella
	Olivier Panis
	Jarno Trulli

CONSTRUCTORS

182	Ferrari
138	McLaren
113	Williams
79	Lotus
35	Brabham
27	Benetton
23	Tyrrell
17	BRM
	Renault
16	Cooper
10	Alfa Romeo

OTHERS

4	Jordan
1	Jaguar

IN 2004

13	Michael Schumacher
2	Rubens Barrichello
1	Juan Pablo Montoya
	Kimi Räikkönen
	Jarno Trulli

CONSTRUCTORS

15	Ferrari
1	McLaren
	Renault
	Williams

WINS IN ONE SEASON

13	Michael Schumacher	2004
11	Michael Schumacher	2002
9	Nigel Mansell	1992
	Michael Schumacher	1995
	Michael Schumacher	2000
	Michael Schumacher	2001
8	Mika Häkkinen	1998
	Damon Hill	1996
	Michael Schumacher	1994
	Ayrton Senna	1988
7	Jim Clark	1963
	Alain Prost	1984
	Alain Prost	1988
	Alain Prost	1993
	Ayrton Senna	1991
	Jacques Villeneuve	1997

CONSTRUCTORS

15	Ferrari	2002
	Ferrari	2004
	McLaren	1988
12	McLaren	1984
	Williams	1986
11	Benetton	1995
10	Ferrari	2000
	McLaren	1989
	Williams	1992
	Williams	1993

POLE POSITIONS

65	Ayrton Senna
63	Michael Schumacher
33	Jim Clark
	Alain Prost
32	Nigel Mansell
29	Juan Manuel Fangio
26	Mika Häkkinen
24	Niki Lauda
	Nelson Piquet
20	Damon Hill
18	Mario Andretti
	René Arnoux
17	Jackie Stewart
16	Stirling Moss
14	Alberto Ascari
	James Hunt
	Ronnie Peterson

OTHERS

13	Rubens Barrichello
12	David Coulthard
11	Juan Pablo Montoya
5	Ralf Schumacher
3	Fernando Alonso
	Kimi Räikkönen
2	Jarno Trulli
1	Jenson Button
	Giancarlo Fisichella

CONSTRUCTORS

178	Ferrari
124	Williams
115	McLaren
107	Lotus
39	Brabham
36	Renault
16	Benetton
14	Tyrrell
12	Alfa Romeo

OTHERS

2	Jordan
1	BAR
	Jaguar

IN 2004

8	Michael Schumacher
4	Rubens Barrichello
2	Jarno Trulli
1	Fernando Alonso
	Jenson Button
	Kimi Räikkönen
	Ralf Schumacher

CONSTRUCTORS

12	Ferrari
3	Renault
1	BAR
	McLaren
	Williams

FASTEST LAPS

66	Michael Schumacher
41	Alain Prost
30	Nigel Mansell
28	Jim Clark
25	Mika Häkkinen
24	Niki Lauda
23	Juan Manuel Fangio
	Nelson Piquet
21	Gerhard Berger
19	Damon Hill
	Stirling Moss
	Ayrton Senna
18	David Coulthard
15	Rubens Barrichello
	Clay Regazzoni
	Jackie Stewart
14	Jacky Ickx

13	Alberto Ascari
	Alan Jones
	Riccardo Patrese
12	René Arnoux
	Jack Brabham
11	Juan Pablo Montoya
	John Surtees

OTHERS

9	Jacques Villeneuve
7	Ralf Schumacher
6	Kimi Räikkönen
1	Fernando Alonso
	Giancarlo Fisichella

CONSTRUCTORS

180	Ferrari
128	Williams
114	McLaren
71	Lotus
40	Brabham
38	Benetton
20	Tyrrell
19	Renault
15	BRM
	Maserati

OTHERS

2	Jordan

IN 2004

10	Michael Schumacher
4	Rubens Barrichello
2	Juan Pablo Montoya
	Kimi Räikkönen

CONSTRUCTORS

14	Ferrari
2	McLaren
	Williams

POINTS

1186	Michael Schumacher
798.5	Alain Prost
614	Ayrton Senna
485.5	Nelson Piquet
482	Nigel Mansell
475	David Coulthard
451	Rubens Barrichello
420.5	Niki Lauda
420	Mika Häkkinen
386	Gerhard Berger
360	Damon Hill
	Jackie Stewart
310	Carlos Reutemann
289	Graham Hill
281	Emerson Fittipaldi
	Riccardo Patrese
277.5	Juan Manuel Fangio
274	Jim Clark
261	Jack Brabham
259	Ralf Schumacher
255	Jody Scheckter

OTHERS

221	Juan Pablo Montoya
219	Jacques Villeneuve
169	Kimi Räikkönen

130	Jenson Button
116	Giancarlo Fisichella
	Jarno Trulli
114	Fernando Alonso
76	Olivier Panis
39	Takuma Sato
28	Nick Heidfeld
26	Mark Webber
16	Felipe Massa
13	Cristiano da Matta
6	Antonio Pizzonia
4	Marc Gené
3	Christian Klien
2	Timo Glock
1	Zsolt Baumgartner

CONSTRUCTORS

3344.5	Ferrari
2858.5	McLaren
2435.5	Williams
1352	Lotus
887.5	Benetton
854	Brabham
617	Tyrrell
528	Renault
439	BRM
424	Prost
333	Cooper

OTHERS

275	Jordan
182	BAR
176	Sauber
88	Jaguar
31	Minardi
27	Toyota

LAPS LED

4867	Michael Schumacher
2931	Ayrton Senna
2683	Alain Prost
2058	Nigel Mansell
1940	Jim Clark
1918	Jackie Stewart
1633	Nelson Piquet
1590	Niki Lauda
1490	Mika Häkkinen
1363	Damon Hill
1347	Juan Manuel Fangio
1164	Stirling Moss
1106	Graham Hill
926	Alberto Ascari
894	David Coulthard

OTHERS

699	Rubens Barrichello
634	Jacques Villeneuve
386	Ralf Schumacher
382	Juan Pablo Montoya
209	Kimi Räikkönen
157	Fernando Alonso
141	Jarno Trulli
70	Jenson Button
36	Giancarlo Fisichella
17	Cristiano da Matta

16	Olivier Panis
2	Felipe Massa
	Takuma Sato
	Mark Webber
1	Antonio Pizzonia

IN 2004

728	Michael Schumacher
89	Jarno Trulli
60	Fernando Alonso
52	Jenson Button
51	Rubens Barrichello
	Juan Pablo Montoya
50	Kimi Räikkönen
30	Ralf Schumacher
2	Felipe Massa
	Takuma Sato
1	Antonio Pizzonia

CONSTRUCTORS

779	Ferrari
149	Renault
82	Williams
54	BAR
50	McLaren
2	Sauber

MILES LED

13753	Michael Schumacher
8345	Ayrton Senna
7751	Alain Prost
6282	Jim Clark
5905	Nigel Mansell
5789	Juan Manuel Fangio
5692	Jackie Stewart
4820	Nelson Piquet
4475	Mika Häkkinen
4386	Niki Lauda
3939	Damon Hill
2962	Graham Hill
2821	Jack Brabham
2607	David Coulthard

OTHERS

2106	Rubens Barrichello
1846	Jacques Villeneuve
1152	Ralf Schumacher
1112	Juan Pablo Montoya
666	Kimi Räikkönen
445	Fernando Alonso
358	Jarno Trulli
196	Jenson Button
109	Giancarlo Fisichella
54	Cristiano da Matta
33	Olivier Panis
6	Takuma Sato
5	Felipe Massa
	Mark Webber
4	Antonio Pizzonia

IN 2004

2243	Michael Schumacher
213	Jarno Trulli
188	Kimi Räikkönen
174	Rubens Barrichello
171	Fernando Alonso

146	Jenson Button
87	Juan Pablo Montoya
6	Takuma Sato
5	Felipe Massa
4	Antonio Pizzonia

CONSTRUCTORS

2416	Ferrari
384	Renault
188	McLaren
152	BAR
91	Williams
5	Sauber

DRIVERS' TITLES

7	Michael Schumacher
5	Juan Manuel Fangio
4	Alain Prost
3	Jack Brabham
	Niki Lauda
	Nelson Piquet
	Ayrton Senna
	Jackie Stewart
2	Alberto Ascari
	Jim Clark
	Emerson Fittipaldi
	Mika Häkkinen
	Graham Hill
1	Mario Andretti
	Giuseppe Farina
	Mike Hawthorn
	Damon Hill
	Phil Hill
	Denny Hulme
	James Hunt
	Alan Jones
	Nigel Mansell
	Jochen Rindt
	Keke Rosberg
	Jody Scheckter
	John Surtees
	Jacques Villeneuve

CONSTRUCTORS' TITLES

14	Ferrari
9	Williams
8	McLaren
7	Lotus
2	Brabham
	Cooper
1	Benetton
	BRM
	Matra
	Tyrrell
	Vanwall

NB. To avoid confusion, the Renault stats listed are based on the team that evolved from Benetton in 2002 and include those stats that have happened since plus those from Renault's first spell in F1 between 1977 and 1985. The figures for Benetton and the Toleman team from which it metamorphosed in 1986 are listed as Benetton. Conversely, the stats for Jaguar include those of the Stewart team from which it evolved in 2000.

FERRARI
TECHNICAL DEVELOPMENT

Ferrari's F2004 was perhaps one of the greatest cars in F1 history. It won all but a handful of the 18 races, but that doesn't give credit to its level of dominance. To Technical Director Ross Brawn, Chief Designer Rory Byrne and Engine Director Paolo Martinelli – maximum respect. They took the F2003-GA as a starting point and, according to Michael Schumacher, improved it in every way. The chassis was small, the 053 V10 was all but unbreakable, and the Bridgestone tyres a leap forward from 2003 in hot weather.

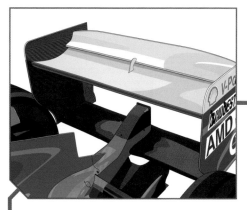

Ferrari produced numerous permutations for its rear wing in 2004. This one is as used by the team at Montréal and Indianapolis, with its trailing edge being curved in shape to control and stabilise air flow over the wing. The wing that had been used at Barcelona and the Nürburgring had a flat top edge

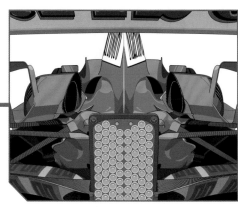

This close-up view of the F2004's rear end shows how much attention designer Byrne has applied to the cooling of the engine bay, with eight hot air outlets, ranging from sidepod gills, to eyelets in the engine cover, to the exhaust chimneys and two tucked away neatly in the area ahead of the rear suspension

The F2004's nose wing was seen in many forms through the season, according to the type of circuit visited. The wing below is a three-plane wing as used at Imola, with a two-plane wing being used at high-speed Monza. Note the shape of the barge boards and radiator intakes behind it

This slatted section of sidepod bodywork has a clear purpose, namely to help remove hot air from around the radiator. This is crucial when you consider that for every extra 5°C of heat the engine is robbed of 1bhp. By pressurising the water system, its boiling point is raised to close on 120°C, thus requiring less venting

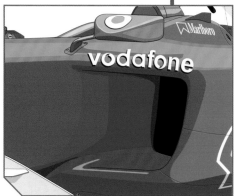

Surprisingly, in a year in which engines had to last all meeting, the F2004 sported relatively small openings to its sidepods, even in Malaysia where keeping engines cool was a massive job. What is radical in this drawing, though, is that the mirrors have long arms to put them where the designer wants them

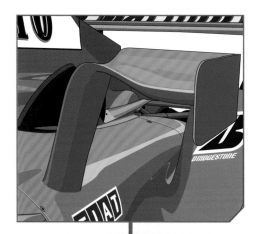

Ferrari plumped for curved winglets atop the sidepods (right) in their quest to achieve the best compromise between downforce and drag. By having only one support, the winglet can be mounted as close as possible to the edge of the car. Note too the treatment of the wing at the rear of the sidepod (below right), with its kick-up at the tail just ahead of the rear wheels. For Monaco, these winglets found their environment changed by the introduction of a narrow chimney exhaust right in front of them (bottom right), these replacing the 'shark gills' shown in the drawing at the foot of the opposite page. These chimney exhausts work in conjunction with the winglet, and help by directing the hot air out of the side of the car rather than back over the rear wing

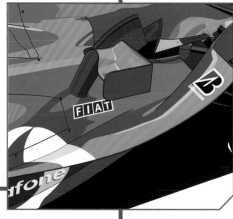

The F2004 started the season with a 60cm-wide wing mounted on the top of its airbox in order to improve air flow over the car. By the third race, at Imola, this wing had been trimmed to 40cm (as above)

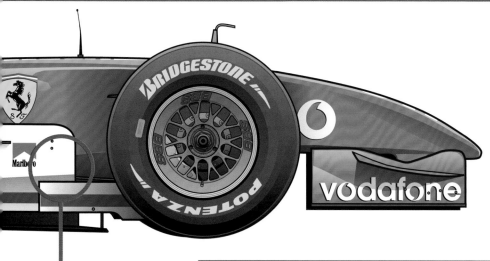

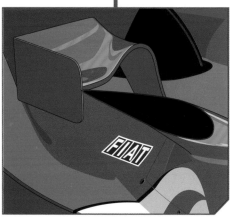

Ferrari stuck with the double barge-board style they had introduced in 2003, but always with a difference, as shown by this one with the jagged-edged second barge board, as fitted for the season-opening Australian GP in Melbourne

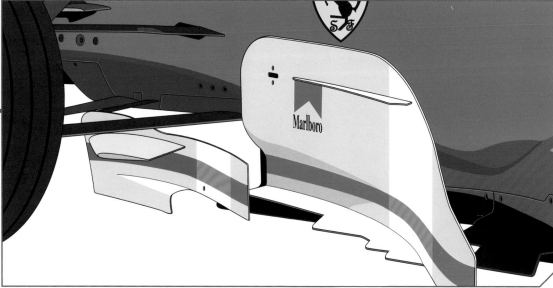

BAR HONDA
TECHNICAL DEVELOPMENT

BAR's 006 was the surprise package of 2004. This was the first true product of Geoff Willis's involvement with BAR, after spending his first year sorting the team's technical structure. After changing from Bridgestone to Michelin, it flew in testing and kept up that pace through the season as Honda found 960bhp from its V10, being the only car to run Ferrari close. The team's torque-transfer braking system broke cover at the German GP but was banned, with a simpler version introduced at the Italian GP.

There are few flat planes in F1: even wing endplates are sculpted, as shown by this version run on the 006. Made larger than before by a change in the rules, the designers were eager to reduce the amount of drag they caused, with BAR's the most sculpted of all

In a bid to counter the effects of the gusting cross-winds that were prevalent at Silverstone, BAR introduced this support beneath the flick-up at the rear of the sidepods, with the express purpose of conditioning the air flow around the rear wheels

The ever changing aerodynamic packages produced by Geoff Willis and his team included this updated front wing for the 006 seen at the Chinese GP. Note the sculpted planes and endplates

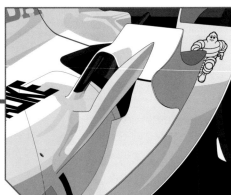

The 006 was fitted at the French GP with a fin in front of its sidepod winglet to channel air onto the winglet. It was modified for the British GP, then removed to undergo further testing, as it wasn't reproducing the results that it had achieved in the wind tunnel

The problem with the fin in front of the sidepod winglet (above and left) is that it was affected by cross-winds, which are common at Silverstone. This left the car experiencing 'apparent yaw', rotation about a vertical axis through its centre

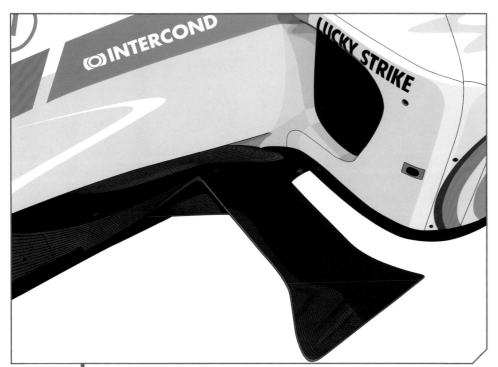

Guiding vanes are used to tidy up air flow that was made turbulent by passing over the front wheels, so that it can be directed under the car. The 006's curved guiding vanes were notably bulky, having been beefed up with extra carbonfibre

The 006 sported a bespoke new wing for the Chinese GP (above right), this intended to cure likely understeer through the first three corners. It had an unusual square front edge, and an unusual additional flap under the main flap at its rear (right)

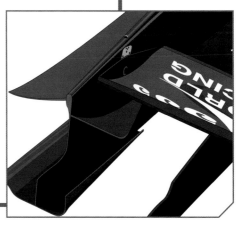

BAR's major technical interest of 2004 was its torque-transfer braking system. The aim is to cancel out uneven torque between the front wheels under braking, transferring it from the loaded outside to the more lightly loaded inside. Introduced at the German GP, it was instantly banned

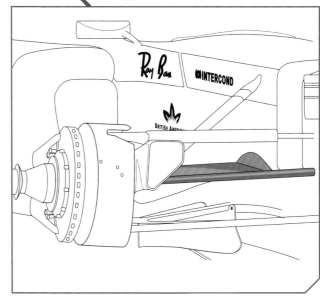

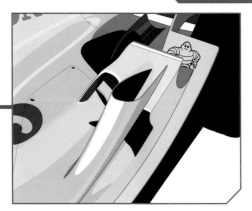

The sidepod fins were superseded at the Chinese GP by the introduction of a chimney in front of the winglet. It was fitted to the left-hand side of the car due to the separation of the oil and water cooling systems, having been used on both sides in previous races

RENAULT
TECHNICAL DEVELOPMENT

The Renault R24 was the fruit of the Mark Smith-led design team under technical director Bob Bell. It earned the accolade of being the first car to beat Ferrari when Trulli won at Monaco in May. Although the move from a wide-angled V10 to a 72-degree unit left the drivers short on power, the engine's strong torque characteristic and longer-than-usual gearbox, which shifted the centre of gravity towards the rear wheels, helped the R24 shine in the sprint off the starting grid.

At first glance, the rear wing shown above and that on the right look quite similar, with their clever wing endplate arrangement. However, contrast the simple single element of the wing above used on the R24s at Monza with the wing shown on the right that was used in Montréal, and the difference is obvious

This high-downforce rear wing used in the Canadian GP offers two strakes and a steep rear flap, in order to harness the airflow to create more downforce around The Esses in particular. Note, too, the small vertical slit cut towards the rear of the endplate of this high-downforce wing, a device used to reduce drag

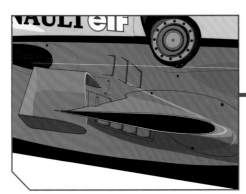

Venting hot air out through the top of the sidepod has been around in F1 since the late 1990s, but this sleek chimney, as seen on the R24 at Bahrain, showed how narrow they have become. Note the slotted openings cut into the sidepod, with these being taped over at circuits where cooling was less essential

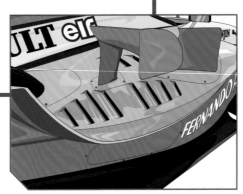

Williams appeared to follow Renault's lead in the shape of the side wings that it used in 2004, aping the kick-up wing ahead of the rear wheels, and raising the tail of the sidepod, contrasting to the sidepod's predominant Coke-bottle shape. This is the sidepod and side wing as raced on the R24s at the French GP

Renault worked hard in its quest for maximum downforce, and this double-winged engine cover, as used at Monaco, is a typical example. For low-downforce circuits such as Silverstone, these four winglets were positioned differently, with the forward set placed below the television camera mounting

This third version of the R24's rear wing was used at the Chinese GP, offering a rounder treatment of its rear corners, as the top flap flows into the endplates without a right-angle junction. One of the reasons for the continued change was the quest for a balanced car under acceleration out of Shanghai's slow corners

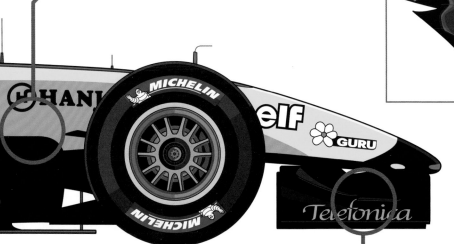

As ever, barge boards kept changing in shape. Take this duo from Renault, with the former (top) as raced at Bahrain and the latter (above) as introduced at the Monaco GP. Renault had followed Ferrari's lead on barge-board shape in 2003, adopting the double barge-board approach, and took this on a step or two this year. The biggest change was the Monaco barge board, with a scooped blade at its tail

The marked difference between the nose-wing treatments sported by the R24 in 2004 show how the car's needs change according to the format of the circuits visited. The upper one of this pair is as used at the first race of the season, up until the San Marino GP. At Barcelona, in a bid to make the car less nervous and more consistent in handling, the team reintroduced a selection of its 2003 noses, with a more rounded shape and narrower centre profile (below right), before introducing a couple of extra tabs on each endplate for the Hungarian GP

WILLIAMS
TECHNICAL DEVELOPMENT

Taking the twin-keel route with its FW26 was a brave move for Williams, with its 'walrus-tusked' nose. Yet, the sums that worked in CFD (Computational Fluid Dynamics) failed to do the same on the track, with a lack of downforce hampering turn-in. Having taken over the reins from Patrick Head, new Tech Director Sam Michael opted for a more standard nose from the Hungarian GP, but results didn't improve until Ralf Schumacher finished second in the Japanese GP.

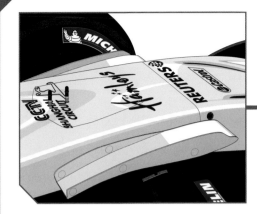

Before consigning its 'walrus' nose to history, Williams fitted these winglets on either side of the short, high nose, just above the front suspension. Rather than being for downforce, their shape suggests that they were added to push air lower down the side of the car

The wide-mounted tusks of the original 'walrus' nose FW26 were robust if nothing else, with turning vanes mounted on struts from the side of the keel to divert air both between the keels, and towards the edge of the car and on to the radiators in the sidepods

Changes flowed once Williams opted for a standard nose. Note the difference between this wing (below), as raced in Italy, with its deeper central section and curved edges, and the one in Hungary (far right). It helped Antonio Pizzonia hit 230mph at Monza

The FW26's rear-wing endplates followed the lead set by others as early as the opening round, by having slots shaped into them. Two curving slots and one vertical were introduced in an attempt to reduce drag by accelerating air over the top of the wing

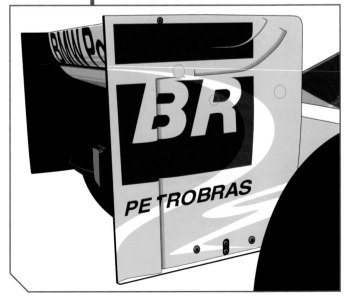

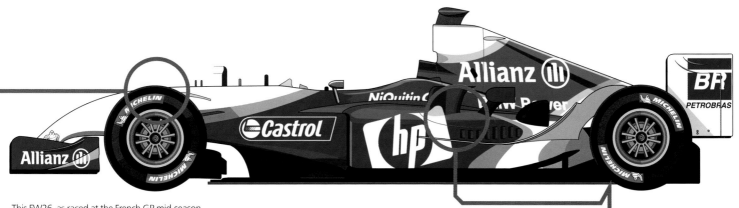

This FW26, as raced at the French GP mid-season, shows a marked difference to the car as it had been at its launch (below), with the rounding of its sidepods the major change. Note how the kick-up in front of the rear wheels extends further backwards

Williams matched Renault in the style of its sidepods, chimneys, flick-ups and gills. The sidepods themselves became increasingly flowing in shape and lower, changing to this format for the French GP, having been flat-topped when launched. Note the flick-ups at the rear of the floor

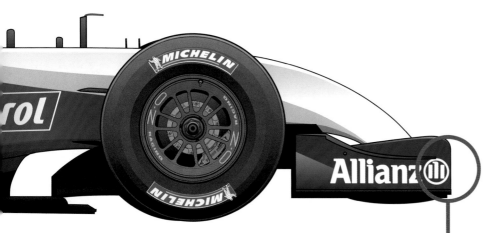

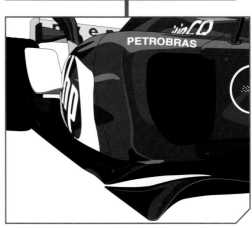

This view shows just how curvaceous the FW26's sidepods became by mid-season, tailing away from a chunky front to a svelte tail, with just one flick-up at their rear, rather than the more commonplace pair

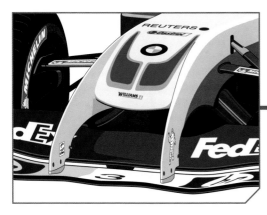

The FW26 started the year with this 'walrus' nose, to help it extract the most from its twin-keel chassis by leaving a clear passage for air under the short, high nose. But it didn't work as wished, leaving the drivers struggling for downforce at high-downforce tracks

Aerodynamicist Antonia Terzi's 'walrus' nose was replaced for the Hungarian GP, with this longer, narrower and more standard nose, similar to that on the 2003 FW25. The team used the occasion to introduce a more swoopy front wing as well

McLAREN
TECHNICAL DEVELOPMENT

McLaren's twin-keel MP4-19 was the car that was supposed to propel McLaren back to the sharp end of the grid. That it was replaced by the MP4-19B, shortly after mid-season, is clear evidence that it didn't. Adrian Newey led the rescue attempt, affecting changes to the shape of the sidepods, barge boards and engine cover that made the MP4-19B more stable under braking, so that the drivers could feel confident carrying speed into the corners. Then Räikkönen turned it into a Grand Prix winner.

This noticeably curved rear wing was used by the MP4-19 on medium- to low-downforce circuits, such as the Circuit Gilles Villeneuve for the Canadian GP. On such occasions, its spooned shape was echoed by that of its front wing

The MP4-19B (below) superseded the MP4-19 (main graphic) from the French GP. It can be identified from the side by its different barge-board lay-out, extended engine cover and more Ferrari-shaped sidepods. The MP4-19B could also be differentiated by its superior speed on the track...

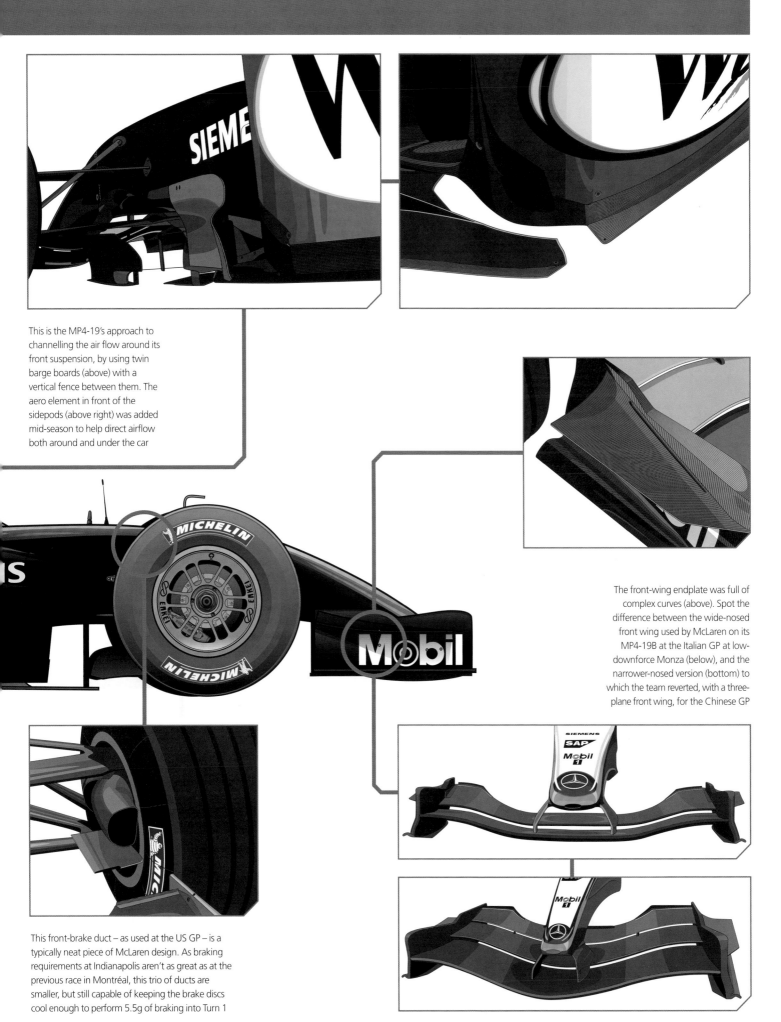

This is the MP4-19's approach to channelling the air flow around its front suspension, by using twin barge boards (above) with a vertical fence between them. The aero element in front of the sidepods (above right) was added mid-season to help direct airflow both around and under the car

The front-wing endplate was full of complex curves (above). Spot the difference between the wide-nosed front wing used by McLaren on its MP4-19B at the Italian GP at low-downforce Monza (below), and the narrower-nosed version (bottom) to which the team reverted, with a three-plane front wing, for the Chinese GP

This front-brake duct – as used at the US GP – is a typically neat piece of McLaren design. As braking requirements at Indianapolis aren't as great as at the previous race in Montréal, this trio of ducts are smaller, but still capable of keeping the brake discs cool enough to perform 5.5g of braking into Turn 1

TOYOTA
TECHNICAL DEVELOPMENT

Toyota failed to perform to expectations in their third season, and a lack of results in the first half of the year, save for Panis's fifth in the US GP, had Toyota working on a new spec of engine, and Tech Director Mike Gascoyne on a host of modifications. These were launched with the TF104B at the German GP in July, after which form improved – but unfortunately good results remained scarce.

Toyota's TF104 (above right) was the team's starting point, and the changes for the TF104B (below) are clear to see, with a chimney atop its sidepod and a narrower engine cover, with the flick-up starting lower down its flanks. The TF104B sported a winglet that had been given an unusual curved support (right). Also, the pillars between the nose and the front wing (far right) were changed from straight to arched in shape

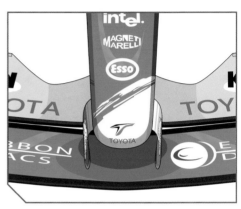

SAUBER
TECHNICAL DEVELOPMENT

Sauber's C23 was the last car from the Swiss team before the full fruits of their wind tunnel will be harnessed by Willy Rampf's designers. However, it showed its worth in development parts, producing the revised engine cover that was a step forward when it made its debut mid-year.

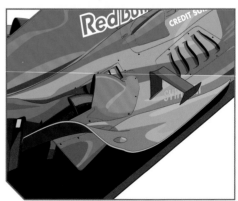

This is the tail end of the Sauber C23's Coke bottle-shaped sidepod, as it appeared for the season-opener in Melbourne, with a simple uni-support winglet, a cowling in front of the hot-air chimney, and a regular flick-up in front of the rear wheels

By the time Sauber attended the British GP at Silverstone, the fruits of time spent in its new state-of-the-art wind tunnel had produced changes, such as the ventilation gills on the right, revised bodywork in front of the chimney and a cutaway at its tail

FOSTER'S®

Number 1 for flavour.

The crisp, clean taste of Foster's is
a favourite of race fans worldwide.

FOSTER'S, OFFICIAL BEER OF FORMULA 1™

JAGUAR
TECHNICAL DEVELOPMENT

Jaguar Racing's R5 – the work of Ben Agathangelou, Ian Pocock and Robert Taylor – was a tidy design, but much of its progress was blighted by a series of mechanical breakages in testing, and the departure of Rob White from Cosworth pre-season.

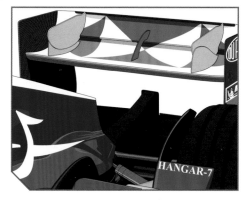

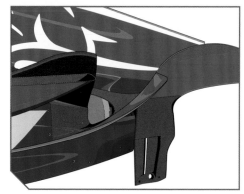

After FIA Technical Delegate Charlie Whiting clarified at Imola what was acceptable in rear wing design, Jaguar produced this design for the Spanish GP, with one fence fixed to the top plane, the other to the bottom, only to have it banned from future races

Little vertical louvres cut into the struts supporting the flick-ups in front of the R5's rear wheels appeared at the Belgian GP. They were introduced to help reduce drag, much as other teams, such as Williams and Renault, cut louvres into their rear-wing endplates

JORDAN
TECHNICAL DEVELOPMENT

John McQuilliam took the reins of the design team at Jordan after the departure of Gary Anderson and Henri Durand, but a lack of budget was Jordan's chief restraint as they sought to develop the single-keel EJ14. A supposed lack of grunt from its Ford-badged Cosworth V10s was a bugbear.

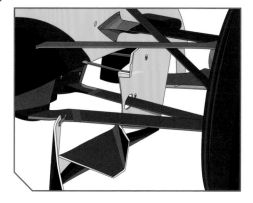

This clever tweak to the underside of the EJ14 was first seen at the season-opening Australian GP. The graphic shows how the front suspension is mounted on to the single central keel at its front mounting point, and yet to a vestigial twin keel further back

The EJ14 sported some of the largest winglets seen all year. They were mounted ahead of the sidepod's shoulders. First seen at the German GP, they were thought to be there to reduce drag and to clean up airflow around the chimney-winglet area behind

MINARDI
TECHNICAL DEVELOPMENT

Minardi's PS04 was little changed from its predecessor, and then changed remarkably little through the season, restricted like Jordan both by a lack of budget and a lack of testing. Technical Director Gabriele Tredozi did what he could, but their best hope was reliability not speed.

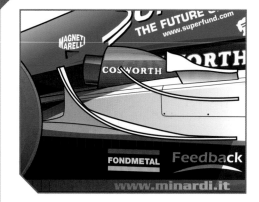

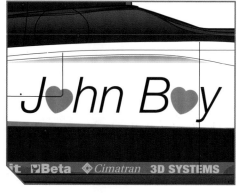

Minardi ran two flick-ups and a winglet in a quest for downforce and helping the air over the rear wheels on to the wing, something that was vitally important: with the Cosworth CR-3L short on grunt, they needed all the aero efficiency they could find

Changes to the PS04 were few and far between through 2004. The most notable was this change of livery for the British GP, where the team carried this message to team manager John Walton, who'd died of a heart attack in the lead-up to the event

TESTING, TESTING'

Often invisible, sometimes unsung, test drivers do thousands of miles per year to help teams hone their cars and, hopefully, land a race seat

A re-jig of Formula One's sporting regulations for 2004 meant that those teams finishing outside the top four in the previous year's constructors' championship could run a third car in the Friday practice sessions at Grands Prix, potentially aiding their tyre choice and set-up. There were certain restrictions on the choice of third driver: a superlicence was required, but the driver must not have scored World Championship points in the previous two years.

Among those teams eligible to run a third car in 2004 there were some interesting variations in strategy. Sauber was the only team not to take up the opportunity, feeling that the budget necessary to run the extra car could be better allocated elsewhere.

BAR and Jaguar committed to the scheme and paid two up-and-coming drivers, Anthony Davidson and Bjorn Wirdheim respectively. Toyota already had on their books one of the few men with extensive recent F1 experience who was eligible: Ricardo Zonta. The financially strapped Jordan and Minardi teams used the third driver option as an opportunity to raise much needed further budget.

As well as giving the lower six teams the opportunity of a head-start to the weekend over the top four, it also allowed the Friday test drivers a shop window for their talents as they looked to gain entry into a prized race seat. However, gauging their performances relative to their race-driving team-mates was a difficult task because of the differing circumstances.

Unlike the race drivers, though, the Friday test drivers weren't subject to any restrictions on engine mileage or on the number of tyres used. In the case of all of these teams except Minardi, more revs, tyres and laps put the Friday men at a significant advantage over their race team-mates in the same practice sessions. At Minardi, the restrictions imposed on the third car by lack of budget probably overcame the theoretical benefits.

FRIDAY MEN

RYAN BRISCOE

Ryan Briscoe has been F1 testing for Toyota on and off since 2002. This year the Australian got a brief promotion from general tester to Friday tester when the man who'd filled that role, Ricardo Zonta, was promoted to a race seat.

Ryan made his Friday debut at Hungary and immediately showed that he was a far more confident performer than when he'd tested regularly in 2002, when he'd been out of his depth through lack of experience. Two weeks later at Spa-Francorchamps he was genuinely impressive, being quick and error-free, also shrugging aside a scary tyre failure-induced accident through Eau Rouge. His Toyota-backed title-winning campaign in European F3 in 2003 seemed to have done a great deal for his confidence.

Unsurprisingly, Ryan lacked Zonta's polish initially as he sought to impress, rendering his data not quite as useful as it could have been. That was cured by a bit of guidance from the team and by Monza his runs were the models of consistent and race representative speed.

Ironically for a driver who was pushed into F1 testing before he was ready, now that he has the experience there's no Friday role for him in 2005, although he continues as a general test driver for the team. At 23, it's a near-certainty that he has an F1 future ahead of him, although maybe not initially with Toyota. Ryan can only be judged definitively when he gets into a race seat, but he made a big stride towards that goal in 2004, doing himself a lot of favours.

ANTHONY DAVIDSON

With the BAR-Honda 006 beneath him, Anthony Davidson had what was comfortably the fastest car of the Friday testers. However, the English driver made wonderful use of it for not only was he a big asset to the team in terms of tyre choice and set-up, but he pasted the biggest possible advertisement for his own talents in that Friday shop window. Anthony was very quick, comfortably on a par with BAR's two race drivers, analytical and virtually error-free. There was an accident in Montréal, where the car behaved strangely over a bump under braking, but otherwise he put not a scratch on the car.

Remarkably, this included Monaco and its magnetic barriers, a track on which he'd never driven before. Even more remarkably, he was fastest of all in the second session, shaving barriers like he'd been racing there for years.

Unfathomably, there were question marks about Anthony as he came into this year with his BAR make-or-break opportunity. For the paddock cynics, he'd not been

sufficiently close to team-mate Mark Webber in 2002 when guesting for Minardi for a couple of races. No matter that he was being measured against a driver who'd been in the car all year, no matter that he'd been closing down on a Toyota in the Belgian GP when he went off.

In such a fickle and unrealistically demanding environment, he'd been virtually written off at the age of 24 on the strength of two Grands Prix in an uncompetitive car. He all but obliterated those doubts in 2004 though.

Anthony hasn't done a full season of racing since his rookie F3 season of 2001, when he was often the class of the field and by the end of the year usually quicker than team-mate Takuma Sato, ironically one of the men for whom he was doing the donkey work this year. Since then, aside from his brief Minardi foray, Anthony has been a BAR F1 test driver.

TIMO GLOCK

Twenty-two-year-old German Timo Glock took his backing to Jordan, securing his place as a Friday tester and thereby continuing his education direct from European F3, where he'd been a front-runner in 2003.

It was an even bigger leap for Timo than for his erstwhile rival Christian Klien, as the Jordan team was so financially limited that there was precious little in the way of pre-event testing.

However, it was soon apparent that he had little fear of an F1 car as he threw the difficult and nervous Jordan EJ14 around with considerable gusto. In fact his initial adaptation to F1 looked rather more impressive than that of the more experienced Giorgio Pantano.

At Montréal, Timo got a fairytale promotion to race driver as Pantano was forced to duck out of the weekend to sort out a managerial problem. What's more, he made excellent use of the opportunity. Despite a somewhat wild-looking run, he was impressively close to Nick Heidfeld in

qualifying and then took full advantage of heavy attrition in the race to finish in seventh place, becoming one of only a handful of drivers in the sport's history to have scored points on their Grand Prix debut.

Thereafter, it was back to reality and continued pounding around on Fridays. Timo's inexperience meant that his data wasn't as solid as those performing the same role in better-funded teams, but he scored heavily for effort and spirit, and very rarely left the road despite looking like he was about to most of the time. He then rounded this off with three solid outings in the last three Grands Prix of the year, commendably bringing his car home on each occasion.

BAS LEINDERS

Like Timo Glock, a pay-tester, 29-year-old Belgian Leinders has struggled with financial shortfall since the days when he was a coming man. Since winning the British and European Formula Ford series in 1995, the GM Euroseries in '96 and German F3 title in '98, his career momentum had petered out, leaving him on the flaky edges of the subsequent steps of the ladder. It was appropriate that he should choose a Friday test seat with Minardi as the next precarious move.

Bas didn't do a bad job at all considering his limited running and prior F1 experience that amounted to 16 laps with Jordan and a few laps at a wet day at Fiorano in an old Minardi PS01. Apart from the Fridays, he did a single test where he shared a car with his two team-mates.

Although it took until Indianapolis before Bas was the fastest of the three Minardis on a Friday, which was hardly surprising given the circumstances, thereafter he achieved the feat quite regularly. Underlining the struggle of a team at this level of the F1 grid, Bas's car was not to the same specification as the other two and he would run on high-mileage engines (usually about 20bhp down on the race units) and even on the discarded brakes of the two race drivers. It often took many races for updates to reach his car.

What was important for the team was that Bas didn't drive over his head and yet still went fast enough to give worthwhile data. This he accomplished with ease and didn't once leave the track all year, illustrating a very mature and disciplined approach. The engineers report that his speed in the medium-fast corners was often faster than either of the two race drivers.

It's extremely difficult to gauge drivers in such circumstances but Bas did nothing to suggest that he wasn't worthy of his place in F1, and his early-career pedigree – more distinguished than either of the Minardi race drivers' – would tend to back this up.

BJORN WIRDHEIM

Reigning Formula 3000 champion Bjorn Wirdheim was drafted in by Jaguar Racing for his first full season as an F1 tester, although he had performed the role for Jordan at the 2003 American Grand Prix.

The Swede had nowhere near the prior F1 mileage of, say, Davidson or Zonta, and as such was noticeably more conservative, particularly so early in the season. He was very aware of how disruptive any incident would be of the team's weekend programme and this, combined with his initial lack of experience, meant that he rarely looked like the super-confident performer of his title-winning F3000 year.

Initially this meant he couldn't be of as much value as those drivers in similar roles at BAR and Toyota, and early in the season Mark Webber would often conduct his own Friday-long runs for tyre evaluation.

Bjorn's confidence did pick up as he gained experience, however, and by mid-season we began to see some flashes of his true potential: he was sixth quickest in the first session at Indianapolis, for instance. Thereafter, Bjorn was usually on a par with Christian Klien, a driver who'd done ten times as much testing with the team over the winter.

As he developed, so the team began to rely on him more and he ended up conducting a lot more of the between-races testing than had originally been envisaged. In reality, Bjorn has now reached the experience baseline that would enable more direct comparison with the likes of Anthony Davidson and Ricardo Zonta.

RICARDO ZONTA

A return to the tracks on Grand Prix weekends came Ricardo Zonta's way after Toyota decided to take advantage of the Friday testing option for 2004. This in turn led to his late-season promotion as replacement race driver following the termination of Cristiano da Matta's contract.

As would be expected of someone with two years' experience as an F1 racer – with BAR in 1999-2000 – the Brazilian was quick and error-free during his Friday performances. Having tested with the team (away from Grands Prix) throughout 2003, he was a known quantity. The extra revs and tyre allocation over the race drivers often saw him as quickest of the Toyotas on Fridays. His feedback tied in strongly with that of Olivier Panis and da Matta.

Da Matta's disappointing form appeared to give Ricardo's race career a lifeline, although in reality the team's 2005 driver line-up had already been decided. Ricardo was simply a stand-in, reckoned by the team to be more likely to score championship points than da Matta.

On his way up, Ricardo had looked destined for more than the journeyman role that has fallen to him. Formula 3000 champion in 1997 and FIA GT champion the year after, he looked more than ordinarily promising. However, a dispiriting couple of years in an uncompetitive BAR alongside Jacques Villeneuve wasn't the ideal start to his F1 career and his motivation appeared to sag, not helped by a succession of big accidents, most of them induced by mechanical failure. He restarted his career by becoming Formula Nissan champion in 2002, this being the prelude to his recruitment by Toyota. The peculiarity of the regulations that dictate who can and can't be a Friday tester – the candidate has to have a superlicence but can't have scored World Championship points in the previous two years – meant he was one of the few drivers with F1 experience who qualified, and this made him the man for the role.

LOST BOYS

The test drivers who covered
the greatest mileage did their
runs not at Grands Prix, but
hidden away at private tests

Take a stroll around a Grand Prix paddock and you see a sub-community of drivers in team gear who never got behind the wheel, not even on a Friday. Yet in between races, these guys in some cases racked up more F1 miles than the regular race stars. These were the official team test drivers.

The tyre war has made layers and layers of testing *de rigueur* for the top teams. Compound and construction testing ahead of the races has come to take up more time than the traditional aero, engine and set-up work. For this reason, Ferrari, Williams and McLaren sometimes have two test teams in addition to their race teams, and testing can occur at two different venues on the same day. Even slightly less well-funded teams have more test days than their race drivers can comfortably handle. It bleeds money but it means gainful employment for a roster of drivers comprising old hands who never quite made it and potential stars of the future, with the balance stacked in favour of the former.

Luca Badoer was the season's champion tester, with more than 70 days under his belt. Employed by Ferrari in this role since his Grand Prix career came to an end after the 1999 season with Minardi, his Ferrari links actually go back to 1993 and his season in the lamentable Lola-Ferrari. A fast F3 and Formula 3000 racer in the early-1990s (F3000 champion in '92), Badoer's F1 race performances never quite demanded the attention of anyone not requiring that a driver bring a budget. With his F1 race career set to peter out anyway, hooking up with Ferrari was a very wise career move.

In his years there he has come to be the testing backbone of the team, a very safe pair of hands whose feedback on the cars tallies well with the race drivers'. There are rarely any days where his pace raises an eyebrow from Michael Schumacher or Rubens Barrichello, but he seems at peace now with his role as an essential lynchpin in one of the greatest teams F1 has ever seen. Living up to the 'test' driver label more closely than he would have liked, Badoer took a couple of light injuries in big shunts believed to have been caused by mechanical failures.

Pre-season, there was so much work to be got through between tyre testing and new car testing that Badoer was supplemented by Luciano Burti and Felipe Massa – contracted Ferrari test drivers in 2002 and '03 respectively. Once into the season, however, the programme was entrusted almost solely to Badoer. If there was any overlap of requirements, the donkey work of electronics systems checks and suchlike was handled by Andrea Bertolini, a sports car driver for Ferrari's sister company Maserati. He is not a potential Grand Prix driver.

At Williams, the culture is that money is invested in technology rather than big-name drivers. As such, they are more pro-active than Ferrari in looking for new driving talent. The test driving role is an ideal opportunity for this and it's significant that in Antonio Pizzonia they had one of only three up-and-coming men in the ranks of the regular testers (the others being Renault's Franck Montagny and Toyota's Ryan Briscoe).

However, senior to Pizzonia at Williams was Marc Gené, a driver with a distinguished but not outstanding racing career. He conducted roughly twice as many miles in testing as Pizzonia and was first in line as race stand-in when Ralf Schumacher was injured at Indianapolis. However, the Spaniard's disappointing pace in his two races led to Pizzonia being given a crack thereafter, and the

Brazilian made rather more use of the opportunity. Gené is a highly intelligent and effective technical analyst, but Pizzonia is quicker and may even have brought his F1 race career back from the brink after a disastrous half-season with Jaguar Racing in 2003. In fact, in the races that he did in 2004, Pizzonia was actually faster than race star Juan Pablo Montoya, and team insiders reckon that whenever Montoya tested his preoccupation was with how quick Pizzonia was.

During the off-season, up-and-coming 'sons-of', Nico Rosberg and Nelson Piquet Jnr, each enjoyed four days of testing with the team and showed themselves capable of extracting the necessary speed from the car, although Rosberg was rather better prepared than Piquet and impressed the engineers with his consistency and attitude.

Indy Racing League champion of 2003, Scott Dixon, was seriously considered as a 2005 Williams race driver and, as such, conducted a few days' testing early in the year. He hadn't had time to prepare his neck for the braking loads but nonetheless impressed by getting to within a few tenths of Ralf Schumacher.

Because of their extremely challenging engine reliability, McLaren were not able to conduct as many miles of testing as they would have liked. Alex Wurz and

Left: Ricardo Zonta pounds around Paul Ricard for Toyota. Above: Ferrari's Luca Badoer continued to record more test laps than anyone else. Below: Alex Wurz was one of a pair of experienced F1 racers who tried to sort out McLaren's chassis problems

Above: Franck Montagny was extremely busy for Renault, but judging his form is hard to do until he goes head-to-head with his team's race drivers. Below: Anthony Davidson tested both at Grands Prix, on Fridays, as well as out of the public glare with the other hidden boys

Pedro de la Rosa, two highly competent F1 race drivers whose careers never made the jump from promising to dazzling, shared the duties almost equally between them. Wurz is nominally senior of the pair only on account of having been with the team since 2001, two years earlier than de la Rosa. Both would dearly love to be back in race seats and could still give a good account of themselves but time is ticking away and paid race seats in F1 are becoming fewer. They continue therefore to pound around in the silver cars out of sight of the crowds.

At Renault, Franck Montagny – dominant Formula Nissan champion in 2003 – was the third busiest F1 tester of the season, just a couple of days behind Gené. Signed up to a Flavio Briatore management deal, he was the obvious choice for the team. He was quick and consistent enough to be an asset, but no-one will really know just how quick he is until he's stacked up against the regulars over a race weekend. Even the Friday testers were easier to gauge than him. Promising Finnish Formula Nissan racer Heikki Kovalainen – also on the Briatore roster – did occasional days for the team and settled in well.

BAR used their race drivers and Friday driver Anthony Davidson to cover their testing needs, but late in the season tested Enrique Bernoldi – who had an unremarkable two-season stint with Arrows in 2001-2 – for reasons assumed to be sponsorship-related. Bernoldi was generally around 0.7s slower than Davidson, which was competent but hardly suggestive of a ride on merit.

Sauber cut its cloth according to its budget and, as such, tested only around 30 days in total, all but two of them with their race drivers. The exceptions were a run for young Swiss driver Neel Jani early in the year and for dominant F3000 champion Vitantonio Liuzzi towards the season's end. Jaguar Racing used a combination of its racers and Friday driver Bjorn Wirdheim for its requirements.

At Toyota, young Australian Ryan Briscoe conducted as much test work as the regular race drivers and Friday man Zonta. Fresh from his title win in European F3, he was able to dial himself into F1 away from the limelight and was soon on a par with his senior team colleagues. When there was a late-season driver shuffle, it made his brief promotion to Friday tester an easy and risk-free decision.

Such was the financial plight of Jordan and Minardi that their rare tests were invariably conducted by the race drivers or Friday men. If there were exceptions to that, the drivers brought money for the privilege – Russian Sergey Zlobin and Tiago Monteiro each tested under these terms.

TESTING STATISTICS

DRIVERS RANKED IN ORDER OF MILES RUN IN TESTING

	Driver	Team	Miles	Laps	Tests	Days	'Fastest' days
1	Luca Badoer	Ferrari	13,953	5004	41	83	51
2	Franck Montagny	Renault	12,879	4701	20	52	5
3	Ricardo Zonta	Toyota	12,856	4551	23	58	9
4	Marc Gené	Williams	11,220	4005	23	51	3
5	Takuma Sato	BAR	10,412	3654	24	45	10
6	Jenson Button	BAR	8963	3127	22	41	13
7	Anthony Davidson	BAR	8794	3079	21	43	5
8	Alexander Wurz	McLaren	8632	3039	17	48	4
9	Pedro de la Rosa	McLaren	8488	2978	17	41	6
10	Fernando Alonso	Renault	8072	2702	14	32	7
11	Michael Schumacher	Ferrari	8032	3089	21	41	28
12	David Coulthard	McLaren	7620	2679	16	38	6
13	Ryan Briscoe	Toyota	7528	2724	18	37	5
14	Felipe Massa	Ferrari/Sauber	7405	2653	20(4/16)	39(11/28)	6(1/5)
15	Ralf Schumacher	Williams	7360	2592	16	39	14
16	Olivier Panis	Toyota	6960	2344	18	30	1
17	Antonio Pizzonia	Williams	6809	2340	14	30	11
18	Mark Webber	Jaguar	6684	2360	13	27	1
19	Jarno Trulli	Renault/Toyota	6495	2250	13(11/2)	32(28/4)	2(2/0)
20	Christian Klien	Jaguar	6398	2245	12	28	0
21	Kimi Räikkönen	McLaren	6362	2228	13	31	7
22	Rubens Barrichello	Ferrari	6316	2261	18	33	15
23	Cristiano da Matta	Toyota	6306	2236	17	30	1
24	Juan Pablo Montoya	Williams	6172	2189	14	34	7
25	Giancarlo Fisichella	Sauber	5508	1909	13	25	7
26	Nick Heidfeld	Jordan	4035	1316	11	24	5
27	Bjorn Wirdheim	BAR/Jaguar	2669	954	7(1/6)	12(1/11)	0
28	Giorgio Pantano	Jordan	2451	786	8	15	0
29	Timo Glock	Jordan	1883	590	7	9	0
30	Heikki Kovalainen	Renault/Minardi	1687	631	5(4/1)	9(8/1)	1(0/1)
31	Enrique Bernoldi	BAR	1372	497	3	6	0
32	Gianmaria Bruni	Minardi	1291	485	6	8	2
33	Luciano Burti	Ferrari	904	391	5	9	3
34	Scott Dixon	Williams	805	286	2	4	0
35	Nico Rosberg	Williams	744	263	2	4	0
36	Zsolt Baumgartner	Minardi	743	266	4	5	1
37	Nelsinho Piquet	Williams	648	230	2	4	0
38	Andrea Bertolini	Ferrari	642	331	8	10	4
39	Jacques Villeneuve	Renault	585	191	2	3	0
40	Jose Maria Lopez	Renault/Minardi	443	187	2(1/1)	4(2/2)	1(0/1)
41	Bas Leinders	Jordan/Minardi	359	155	3(1/2)	3(1/2)	0
42	Justin Wilson	Jaguar	316	127	1	1	0
43	Jarek Janis	Jordan	308	112	1	2	0
44	Neel Jani	Sauber	259	94	1	1	0
45	Olivier Beretta	Williams	239	87	1	1	0
46	Franck Perera	Toyota	198	72	1	1	0
47	Satoshi Motoyama	Renault	190	69	1	1	0
48	Vitantonio Liuzzi	Sauber	165	60	1	1	0
49	Townsend Bell	Jaguar	154	62	1	1	0
50	Sergey Zlobin	Minardi	140	70	1	1	0
51	Katsuyuki Hiranaka	Toyota	140	51	1	1	0
52	Ralph Firman	Jordan	132	48	1	1	0
53	Ho-Pin Tung	Williams	116	42	1	1	0
54	Norbert Siedler	Minardi	93	47	1	1	0
55	Tiago Monteiro	Minardi	92	46	1	1	1
56	Chanoch Nissany	Jordan	80	25	1	1	0
57	Fabrizio del Monte	Minardi	66	33	1	2	0
58	Darren Turner	McLaren	49	17	1	1	0
59	Valentino Rossi	Ferrari	n/a	n/a	1	1	0
60	Narain Karthikeyan	Minardi	n/a	n/a	1	1	0

TEAMS RANKED IN ORDER OF MILES RUN IN TESTING

	Team	Miles	Laps	Tests	Driver days	'Fastest' days
1	Toyota	34,887	12,291	28	159	16
2	Williams	34,114	12,034	26	168	35
3	Ferrari	31,858	11,791	63	188	102
4	McLaren	31,150	10,941	26	159	23
5	BAR	29,756	10,435	26	136	28
6	Renault	29,067	10,224	24	126	14
7	Jaguar	16,007	5670	15	68	1
8	Sauber	11,325	4005	15	55	12
9	Jordan	8941	2895	13	53	5
10	Minardi	3119	1278	8	24	3

TYRE COMPANIES RANKED IN ORDER OF MILES RUN IN TESTING

Tyre company	Miles	Laps	Tests	Driver days	'Fastest' days
Michelin	174,982	61,595	145	816	117
Bridgestone	55,242	19,948	99	320	122

MOST-USED CIRCUITS RANKED IN ORDER OF TESTS PER VENUE

Circuit	Tests	Days	Best lap	Driver	Car	Date set
Fiorano	32	54	55.999s	M Schumacher	Ferrari F2004	1 Feb 2004
Jerez	9	40	1m15.629s	M Schumacher	Ferrari F2004	30 Sep 2004
Silverstone	9	25	1m16.150s	K Raikkonen	McLaren MP4-19B	15 Sep 2004
Mugello	8	26	1m18.704s	R Barrichello	Ferrari F2004	9 Feb 2004
Valencia	8	25	1m09.001s	K Raikkonen	McLaren MP4-19	19 Feb 2004
Barcelona	7	26	1m13.797s	T Sato	BAR'04-concept	3 Feb 2004
Paul Ricard	7	24	1m06.301s	J Button	BAR 006	15 Apr 2004
Monza	4	14	1m19.659s	L Badoer	Ferrari F2004	4 Jun 2004
Imola	3	9	1m19.664s	M Schumacher	Ferrari F2004	25 Feb 2004
Vallelunga	3	6	56.335s	L Badoer	Ferrari F2004	15 Oct 2004
Estoril	1	2	1m30.390s	R Zonta	Toyota TF103	16 Apr 2004
Misano	1	2	1m09.627s	G Bruni	Minardi PS04B	11 Feb 2004
Varano	1	2	n/a	A Bertolini	Ferrari F2004	14 Apr 2004

Masterful...

DESIGNED TO
SPECTATOR
SPECIFICATION

THE GRAND PRIX MASTERS WORLD SERIES

GP
MASTERS

www.gpmasters.com

TESTING CALENDAR

COMPLETE TESTING CALENDAR 25 NOVEMBER 2003 TO BRAZILIAN GRAND PRIX 2004

Date	Circuit	Teams present	Best lap	Driver	Team
25-27 Nov 2003	Barcelona	F,B,S	1m17.291s	L Badoer	Ferrari
25-28 Nov 2003	Valencia	W,Mc,R,Ja,T	1m10.021s	D Coulthard	McLaren
25-28 Nov 2003	Paul Ricard	T	n/a	R Zonta	Toyota
2-4 Dec 2003	Barcelona	Mc,R,Ja,T	1m16.296s	F Montagny	Renault
2-5 Dec 2003	Jerez	F,W,B,Jo	1m17.453s	R Schumacher	Williams
8-12 Dec 2003	Jerez	F,W,Mc,R,B,S,Ja,T	1m16.203s	P de la Rosa	McLaren
9-12 Dec 2003	Fiorano	F	58.594s	L Burti	Ferrari
10-12 Dec 2003	Vallelunga	Mi	1m02.216s	G Bruni	Minardi
5 Jan 2004	Valencia	W	n/a	R Schumacher	Williams
7-13 Jan 2004	Jerez	F,W,Mc,R,B,T	1m16.074s	K Räikkönen	McLaren
14-16 Jan 2004	Valencia	S	1m10.530s	G Fisichella	Sauber
19-23 Jan 2004	Barcelona	F,W,R,B,S,Ja,T,Jo	1m14.588s	J Button	BAR
20-23 Jan 2004	Valencia	Mc	1m09.697s	D Coulthard	McLaren
27-29 Jan 2004	Valencia	F,W,R,B,S,Ja,T,Mi	1m09.165s	A Pizzonia	Williams
29-30 Jan 2004	Barcelona	T	n/a	R Zonta	Toyota
30 Jan-1 Feb 2004	Fiorano	F	55.999s	M Schumacher	Ferrari
2-6 Feb 2004	Barcelona	F,W,Mc,R,B,S,T	1m13.797s	T Sato	BAR
4-5 Feb 2004	Imola	F	1m21.231s	M Schumacher	Ferrari
4-5 Feb 2004	Silverstone	Jo	n/a	T Glock	Jordan
7-9 Feb 2004	Mugello	F	1m18.704s	R Barrichello	Ferrari
9-13 Feb 2004	Paul Ricard	T	n/a	R Zonta	Toyota
10 Feb 2004	Fiorano	F	57.113s	M Schumacher	Ferrari
10-11 Feb 2004	Misano	Mi	1m09.627s	G Bruni	Minardi
10-15 Feb 2004	Jerez	F,Mc,W,R,B,S,Ja,Jo	1m16.907s	R Schumacher	Williams
11-13 Feb 2004	Mugello	F	1m18.902s	M Schumacher	Ferrari
17-19 Feb 2004	Imola	F,R,S,Jo,Mi	1m20.480s	F Alonso	Renault
17-19 Feb 2004	Mugello	F	1m19.060s	M Schumacher	Ferrari
17-20 Feb 2004	Valencia	W,Mc,B,Ja,T	1m09.001s	K Räikkönen	McLaren
21-22 Feb 2004	Mugello	F	1m25.842s	R Barrichello	Ferrari
23-25 Feb 2004	Silverstone	Mc,R,B,Ja,Jo	1m19.542s	T Sato	BAR
23-26 Feb 2004	Imola	F,W,Mc,T	1m19.664s	M Schumacher	Ferrari
27 Feb 2004	Fiorano	F	1m03.887s	L Badoer	Ferrari
5-7 Mar 2004	**AUSTRALIAN GRAND PRIX, MELBOURNE**				
9-12 Mar 2004	Valencia	F,W,Mc,R,B,T	1m09.979s	P de la Rosa	McLaren
11 Mar 2004	Fiorano	Mi	n/a	B Leinders	Minardi
15 Mar 2004	Fiorano	F	57.840s	L Badoer	Ferrari
19 Mar 2004	Fiorano	F	n/a	L Burti	Ferrari
19-21 Mar 2004	**MALAYSIAN GRAND PRIX, SEPANG**				
23-25 Mar 2004	Mugello	F	1m20.106s	M Schumacher	Ferrari
23-26 Mar 2004	Paul Ricard	W,Mc,R,B,T	1m10.860s	J Button	BAR
25-27 Mar 2004	Fiorano	F	57.398s	L Badoer	Ferrari
31 Mar 2004	Fiorano	F	n/a	L Badoer	Ferrari
2-4 Apr 2004	**BAHRAIN GRAND PRIX, SAKHIR**				
6-9 Apr 2004	Barcelona	F,W,Mc,R,B,S,T,Ja	1m14.686s	T Sato	BAR
7-8 Apr 2004	Valencia	B	1m25.647s	A Davidson	BAR
12-16 Apr 2004	Fiorano	F	56.060s	M Schumacher	Ferrari
13-15 Apr 2004	Silverstone	Jo	1m22.04s	N Heidfeld	Jordan
13-16 Apr 2004	Paul Ricard	W,Mc,R,B,Ja,T	1m06.301s	J Button	BAR
14-15 Apr 2004	Varano	F	n/a	A Bertolini	Ferrari
15-16 Apr 2004	Estoril	T	1m30.390s	R Zonta	Toyota
21 Apr 2004	Fiorano	F	58.433s	L Badoer	Ferrari
21-23 Apr 2004	**SAN MARINO GRAND PRIX, IMOLA**				
27-29 Apr 2004	Fiorano	F	57.090s	G Fisichella	Sauber
27-29 Apr 2004	Monza	F	1m21.626s	L Badoer	Ferrari
27-30 Apr 2004	Mugello	F,B,T,Mi	1m19.150s	T Sato	BAR
27-30 Apr 2004	Silverstone	W,Mc,R	1m18.291s	A Pizzonia	Williams
3-5 May 2004	Fiorano	F	59.684s	L Badoer	Ferrari
7-9 May 2004	**SPANISH GRAND PRIX, BARCELONA**				
11 May 2004	Silverstone*	S	40.380s	F Massa	Sauber

Denotes Silverstone's National Circuit was used for this test rather than the full Grand Prix circuit

Date	Circuit	Teams present	Best lap	Driver	Team
11-12 May 2004	Paul Ricard	W,Mc,R,B,T,Jo	1m32.460s	P de la Rosa	McLaren
11-13 May 2004	Silverstone	S	1m18.382s	G Fisichella	Sauber
11-14 May 2004	Fiorano	F	56.342s	M Schumacher	Ferrari
11-14 May 2004	Mugello	F	1m19.370s	L Badoer	Ferrari
13-14 May 2004	Paul Ricard	W,Mc,R,B,T,Jo	1m10.472s	T Sato	BAR
17-18 May 2004	Fiorano	F	57.477s	L Badoer	Ferrari
20-23 May 2004	**MONACO GRAND PRIX, MONTE CARLO**				
26 May 2004	Fiorano	F	57.746s	L Badoer	Ferrari
28-30 May 2004	**EUROPEAN GRAND PRIX, NÜRBURGRING**				
1-3 Jun 2004	Silverstone	F,W,Mc,R,B,Ja,T,Jo	1m17.636s	M Webber	Jaguar
1-4 Jun 2004	Monza	F,W,Mc,B,S,T	1m19.659s	L Badoer	Ferrari
4 Jun 2004	Fiorano	F	57.844s	L Badoer	Ferrari
8 Jun 2004	Fiorano	F	n/a	A Bertolini	Ferrari
11-13 Jun 2004	**CANADIAN GRAND PRIX, MONTRÉAL**				
18-20 Jun 2004	**USA GRAND PRIX, INDIANAPOLIS**				
22-25 Jun 2004	Barcelona	F,R,S,Ja	1m14.679s	M Schumacher	Ferrari
22-25 Jun 2004	Jerez	W,Mc,B,T	1m17.098s	P de la Rosa	McLaren
29-30 Jun 2004	Fiorano	F	58.184s	L Badoer	Ferrari
2-4 Jul 2004	**FRENCH GRAND PRIX, MAGNY-COURS**				
5 Jul 2004	Fiorano	F	59.113s	L Badoer	Ferrari
9-11 Jul 2004	**BRITISH GRAND PRIX, SILVERSTONE**				
13-15 Jul 2004	Silverstone	Mc,Jo	1m17.649s	K Räikkönen	McLaren
13-15 Jul 2004	Paul Ricard	T	n/a	R Briscoe	Toyota
13-16 Jul 2004	Jerez	F,W,Mc,R,B,Ja,T	1m17.383s	M Schumacher	Ferrari
13-16 Jul 2004	Monza	F	1m21.603s	L Badoer	Ferrari
20 Jul 2004	Fiorano	F	57.096s	L Badoer	Ferrari
23-25 Jul 2004	**GERMAN GRAND PRIX, HOCKENHEIM**				
26 Jul-31 Aug 2004	**SUMMER TESTING BAN** (NB Ferrari dates during this time were shakedowns only)				
6 Aug 2004	Fiorano	F	58.854s	L Badoer	Ferrari
13-15 Aug 2004	**HUNGARIAN GRAND PRIX, HUNGARORING**				
23 Aug 2004	Fiorano	F	59.798s	L Badoer	Ferrari
27-29 Aug 2004	**BELGIAN GRAND PRIX, SPA-FRANCORCHAMPS**				
1-2 Sep 2004	Fiorano	F	57.340s	L Badoer	Ferrari
1-3 Sep 2004	Monza	F,W,Mc,R,B,S,Ja,T,Jo,Mi	1m20.027s	A Pizzonia	Williams
2-3 Sep 2004	Vallelunga	Mi	1m03.750s	T Monteiro	Minardi
8 Sep 2004	Fiorano	F	1m00.273s	L Badoer	Ferrari
10-12 Sep 2004	**ITALIAN GRAND PRIX, MONZA**				
14-16 Sep 2004	Silverstone	W,Mc,R,B,T,Jo	1m16.150s	K Räikkönen	McLaren
14-17 Sep 2004	Jerez	F,S	1m16.083s	R Barrichello	Ferrari
14-17 Sep 2004	Mugello	F	1m20.123s	L Badoer	Ferrari
15 Sep 2004	Fiorano	F	58.652s	L Badoer	Ferrari
24-26 Sep 2004	**CHINESE GRAND PRIX, SHANGHAI**				
28-29 Sep 2004	Fiorano	F	57.451s	A Bertolini	Ferrari
28-30 Sep 2004	Jerez	F,W,Mc,R,B,T	1m15.629s	M Schumacher	Ferrari
1 Oct 2004	Fiorano	F	58.890s	L Badoer	Ferrari
8-10 Oct 2004	**JAPANESE GRAND PRIX, SUZUKA**				
12-14 Oct 2004	Jerez	W,Mc,R,B,Ja,T	1m16.298s	F Montagny	Renault
14 Oct 2004	Fiorano	F	58.845s	L Badoer	Ferrari
15 Oct 2004	Vallelunga	F	56.335s	L Badoer	Ferrari
16 Oct 2004	Fiorano	F	1m04.813s	L Badoer	Ferrari
20 Oct 2004	Fiorano	F	n/a	A Bertolini	Ferrari
21 Oct 2004	Fiorano	F	n/a	A Bertolini	Ferrari
22-24 Oct 2004	**BRAZILIAN GRAND PRIX, INTERLAGOS**				

TEAM INITIALS

F	Ferrari	S	Sauber
W	Williams	Ja	Jaguar
Mc	McLaren	T	Toyota
R	Renault	Jo	Jordan
B	BAR	Mi	Minardi

The better **the competition**
The better **the tyre**
The better **for you.**

Nothing pushes technology beyond its limits like racing.
Tyre designers strive for every extra inch of advantage,
for better grip and response in extreme conditions.
The fiercer the fight to develop race winning tyre technology,
the better the tyres we make for you.

Our passion for the very best in technology, quality and service is
at the heart of our commitment to you wherever you are in the world.
Bridgestone wants to inspire and move you.

BRIDGESTONE
PASSION *for EXCELLENCE*

TYRE WARS

Those who analyse every facet of a Grand Prix had a field day in 2004, as the battle for honours between Bridgestone and Michelin was every bit as competitive as the battle between the teams, each tyre manufacturer offering a performance advantage when the conditions suited their tyres. Their Technical Managers explain why.

Pascal Vasselon of Michelin faces up to rival Technical Manager Hisao Suganuma, each accompanied by their respective racing rubber

Competitive tension in Formula One isn't only between drivers or rival teams. Arguably the most intense of all is that between Bridgestone and Michelin in F1's tyre war that's been ongoing since 2001.

Ironically, it's a war that can never be won. Not wholly at any rate. Bridgestone and Ferrari have together won every single world title since Michelin returned to the arena in 2001. But what if, during that time, Michelin flattered its teams, while Bridgestone was made to look better than it was by Ferrari? Who, in that situation, has won the tyre war? The true competitive level of each tyre brand in isolation is rarely apparent.

What is beyond reasonable doubt is that here are the two best competition tyre manufacturers in the world slugging it out and throwing everything they've got into it. It's a fascinating contest.

In 2003, Bridgestone came in for some criticism, especially at Hungary where Michael Schumacher was lapped. One year later, Schumacher's Bridgestone-shod Ferrari annihilated the field at the same Hungaroring track. In between times, Michelin had won just one race. Much of that can be laid at the door of the Ferrari F2004's superiority, but surely not all of it?

Certainly, Bridgestone felt it had made huge strides with its 2004 tyre. All through the off-season, separate development programmes for construction and compounds were being conducted. Only at an Imola test a few days before the first race of the season were the new compounds and constructions brought together in one tyre – and Ferrari's consistently stunning lap times on it made the Japanese company very excited indeed.

The general feeling in 2003 was that Michelin had given its teams a tyre advantage over Ferrari most of the time. With hindsight, that Imola test suggested that Bridgestone was now on a par – at the very least. Furthermore, as if the F2004's downforce wasn't help enough, Bridgestone was definitely favoured by the weather in the first few races. The Australia, Malaysia and Bahrain races were each around 10ºC cooler than forecast, denying Michelin the chance to use its often seen hot-weather advantage.

Although the performance of the tyres may have been similar overall, they still had very different characteristics – even if the new front Bridgestone, with its wider footprint, now looked more like a Michelin than it used to. The Bridgestone still ran hotter than the Michelin, giving it a narrower range of conditions in which it worked well. But when it was in that band it was incredibly consistent, more so than the Michelin, which still suffered initial graining. The other penalty of the Bridgestone's higher running temperature was that it took more running to reach it, and that extracted a big price in qualifying, the early laps or on restarts after the safety car.

At Hockenheim, Bridgestone introduced a new compound that apparently cured another old bugbear of the Japanese tyre: its propensity to blister more readily than the Michelin. At the next race in Hungary, the compound was combined with a new rear construction, and it was with this that Schumacher took his devastating and highly symbolic victory. This tyre, with extra steel in the casing, seemed to have finally nailed the problem of below optimum early-lap temperatures. But there wasn't yet a version of it suitable for high-speed circuits.

Michelin retained its philosophy of having a lighter, more flexible sidewall, and this continued to bring advantages, particularly under braking, traction and over kerbs. It may also have made it more susceptible to failures induced by kerb damage, as we saw in the Belgian GP at Spa-Francorchamps.

The two brands continued to represent two very different technical philosophies, but in their competitive intensity they're remarkably alike. Both the contrasts and similarities are very apparent when you listen to the respective Technical Managers of Bridgestone and Michelin, Hisao Suganuma and Pascal Vasselon. They've known each other for more than a decade, their battles in lower categories now repeated in F1, and they have a healthy mutual respect. We got them together and tried to get them to lower their guard.

Choosing the right tyre for the right conditions was as crucial as ever, especially when track and weather conditions looked set to change

THERE HAVE BEEN SOME BIG LAP-TIME IMPROVEMENTS THIS YEAR. IS IT DOWN TO THE TYRES?

SUGANUMA: No, I don't think so. Of course we try to improve the tyre performance, but 3s in some circuits hasn't come just from tyres. I'd say maybe 30-40% might be possible, but the rest has come from the cars.

VASSELON: We're seeing some very different pictures on different tracks. Sometimes the cars are massively faster – almost 4s at Silverstone, 3.5s at the Nürburgring – while at some other places it was a lot closer to 2003 lap times, such as Indianapolis where the difference was only 1s. Tyres are part of this, cars as well, but I'd add a third parameter, that of track condition. We saw for example at Sepang in the last four years that the pace of the race is going up and down, and there's no logic to it. In the 2002 race it was pretty slow, 2003 was faster. Track conditions explain this. Silverstone this year was really fast.

HAVE THE STRENGTHS OF YOUR RIVAL FORCED YOU TO DISCOVER AND UNDERSTAND THINGS YOU WOULDN'T OTHERWISE HAVE DONE?

SUGANUMA: Of course, when you're sole supplier you don't need to be really on the edge of your performance. Because of the competitive situation, we can improve our tyre. Neither of us wants to be beaten. We're always developing the tyres to keep each other really on the edge.

VASSELON: It's the spirit of competition. Of course you do things you wouldn't do if you weren't forced to by your competitors. Racing is a very strange thing for manufacturers. We are manufacturers and everywhere in industry there's competition, but our rivalry is special because the measure of the competition is very precise. Everywhere else in industry it's a bit more difficult to know exactly where you are. The pressure in motorsport, because of the precision of the measurement, is much higher. Every two weeks something says you've been good or you've been bad, and there's nothing similar in industry. It's a very interesting challenge.

CAN YOU TALK ABOUT SPECIFICALLY WHAT'S DIFFERENT WITH YOUR TYRES AS A RESULT OF THIS COMPETITION?

VASSELON: Everything you can imagine. The regulation concerning tyres isn't very restrictive. We're given a few dimensions, but no restriction in terms of material and design. Because it's so open you can imagine that we push as far as possible in every area. We're interested in fibres of course. We're not very interested in price – not because we love spending money, but simply because the price of the tyre is really nothing compared to the value of the result we achieve. Compounds are difficult to talk about because when you look at the tyre you could imagine you have just one black compound, but there are hundreds of different compounds that all look black. Every single part of the tyre has a different compound, except the tread which has to be uniform. If the regulations allowed it, we'd have five compounds in the tread. We can push really hard in all areas.

SUGANUMA: Yes, the same thing. The tyres consist of the various parts – materials, shapes, constructions – and in this competitive situation we have to think about how we can improve tyre performance in all areas. We study shape, compound, construction and the analysis method of the performance. We're pushing these all the time. It's tough but, as an engineer, it's enjoyable. There's no other kind of tyre engineer who can experience this rapid feedback. Every two weeks we can know, black and white.

PASCAL, WHAT IS THE BIGGEST STRENGTH OF THE BRIDGESTONE?

VASSELON: Oooh, I've got to think hard for this one. Only a joke! What's very interesting in competition is that you can't have a thumbprint of your competitor which is valid. Bridgestone had some strengths in 2001 which are changed now. So at the moment the strength is that their tyres aren't sensitive to conditions. Their performance is very similar and predictable whatever the conditions are.

HISAO, WHAT IS THE BIGGEST STRENGTH OF THE MICHELIN?

SUGANUMA: I think they have a very good tyre in very hot conditions, and several times we have faced a struggle to be competitive with our teams. I met Pascal first in 1994. Since then I have felt that the Michelin way of working is very similar to ours. They're very precise and they work hard and work late. We can feel this similarity, whereas when we fought with Goodyear they were a little bit different. They seemed a bit easy-going. That's not a criticism, it was just a different way of working.

WHAT'S THE ESSENCE OF YOUR TECHNICAL PHILOSOPHY?

SUGANUMA: As I said, the racing tyre consists of various parts. We're working extremely hard in each area. Compared to, say, the 2001 tyre, the tyre we have now I'd say is quite different. Not in a particular area, but in all areas. I'm really happy to see how we can improve.

VASSELON: Our research approach is that we absolutely want to understand, we absolutely want to know what the dominant performance factors have, and then to act. We try to avoid just testing to see what happens. That's an easy way, but there's something frustrating about just trying a few things and then taking the best one. We'd prefer to try to understand the mechanism of what makes an F1 tyre fast, and then you're able to define objective criteria.

HISAO, HOW MUCH OF AN ADVANTAGE IS IT TO DEVELOP THE CAR AND THE TYRES TOGETHER, AS YOU HAVE DONE WITH THE FERRARI?

SUGANUMA: Of course with the collaboration with Ferrari, we could learn a lot and understand how the car is working with the tyre, and Ferrari could understand how the tyre is working with the car. Our working relationship provides us with knowledge to help us to improve the tyre design, and to say, "this area is where we need to work", more than another area. We can know with greater certainty where to put our energy.

ARE THERE ANY DRAWBACKS?

SUGANUMA: The problem with having only one strong team is that if we go in the wrong direction, we get it totally wrong. Also, the testing mileage is limited. So we do laboratory simulation work, but still track testing is the final evaluation. If we had more teams, we'd have more chance to prove whether something was in the right direction or not. With our situation, there's more possibility to go wrong.

PASCAL, WOULD YOU LIKE THE CHANCE TO DEVELOP YOUR TYRE EXCLUSIVELY AROUND THE CAR OF A TOP TEAM?

VASSELON: Not really. It doesn't fit our philosophy of data quality. All research equations require precise measurement. The measurement device we have in F1 is the car. An F1 car is a very bad measurement device because the conditions are variable. Faced with this situation, you have to develop a statistical approach. When you cannot rely on your measurement tool, the only way is to take several measurements – ie, use statistics. When you test with six cars and all six produce the same result, you can be sure. When there are just one or two cars, it's much more difficult.

WHY DO YOU THINK THE MICHELIN COMES UP TO WORKING TEMPERATURE MORE QUICKLY THAN THE BRIDGESTONE, AS WE SAW AT SPA-FRANCORCHAMPS?

VASSELON: It's not something that's easy to answer. It's a combination of all the characteristics of the tyre. It's down to the construction, and then its performance comes from the compound.

SUGANUMA: As Pascal said, it comes from the various areas, and I would say mainly from compound, but the construction needs to help with that characteristic. At the moment we're tuned more to long-distance running, which means we give away something in the initial working range of the tyre. So of course we want to improve in that area, and it's a project.

WHY IN FULL WET CONDITIONS IS THE BRIDGESTONE WET FASTER THAN THE MICHELIN WET, AND WHY IN SEMI-WET CONDITIONS IS THE MICHELIN DRY FASTER THAN THE BRIDGESTONE DRY?

SUGANUMA: Regarding wet tyres, the compounds and the tread pattern design are the two major parts of the performance. In extreme conditions you need to have better aquaplane resistance. Tread pattern design is one issue and also how the compound provides wet grip. Those two things are very important. Our wet tyre, having reasonable wet grip and reasonable resistance to aquaplaning, gives us the competitive situation.

In the case of the dry tyre, it's a question of which range of conditions are we aiming for? To make the working range wider is ideal. The standard tyres need to work in a range of conditions from damp to dry in order to overlap a little with our wet tyre. The wet tyre needs to avoid a performance gap between differing conditions. There needs to be a smooth transition with some overlap. They have to cover each other at the edges.

VASSELON: You have very different wet conditions, and you cannot expect your tyre to cover all of these conditions. We select windows, so it's no surprise that in given conditions you have one tyre better than the others. It's related to the difference of the ranges.

IS IT POSSIBLE TO SCIENTIFICALLY SEPARATE THE PERFORMANCE OF THE TYRE FROM THAT OF THE CAR?

VASSELON: The lateral acceleration is exactly a combination of the grip of the tyre and the downforce the car is able to generate. So looking at acceleration you can't separate what is due to the tyre and what is due to the car. If you really want to separate them, there are two ways: take the same car and test two different tyre types. A rigorous procedure is required, because track testing is never exactly repeatable. So it's not enough. The second way is statistics. You can say that one car may be better than the other, but you can't say that five cars are all worse than five others. From the statistics come the truth, usually. Statistics become more accurate the larger numbers of tests you use. Conversely, reduce the number of events and statistics aren't as precise.

SUGANUMA: I agree. It's difficult to separate. We can measure when the cars are running what force and moment a tyre is producing, but that's also down to the car's aerodynamics and its set-up and the force the tyre has received. So the force generated by the tyre is very much related to the car. To compare the differences in the tyre you need the same car on the same set-up.

FINALLY, WHO HAS THE BETTER TYRE THIS YEAR?

SUGANUMA: I hope you can judge from the results.

VASSELON: It has to be distributed race by race, and to go further we would have to try each tyre on each of the cars at each race.

Pushing a tyre to its limits is a technique used by both manufacturers in their quest to develop their tyres to the maximum

Michelin's dry-weather tyre worked better than Bridgestone's when track conditions were mixed, but it was the other way around in the wet

THE OFFICIAL
Formula 1™
SEASON REVIEW 2004